THOMAS PAINE

THOMAS PAINE
Social and political thought

Gregory Claeys

Associate Professor of History,
Washington University, St Louis

Boston
UNWIN HYMAN
London   Sydney   Wellington

Unwin Hyman Inc.,
8 Winchester Place, Winchester, Mass. 01890, USA

Published by the Academic Division of
Unwin Hyman Ltd
15/17 Broadwick Street, London W1V 1FP, UK

Allen & Unwin (Australia) Ltd,
8 Napier Street, North Sydney, NSW 2060, Australia

Allen & Unwin (New Zealand) Ltd in association with the
Port Nicholson Press Ltd,
Compusales Building, 75 Ghuznee Street, Wellington 1, New Zealand

First published in 1989

Library of Congress Cataloging-in-Publication Data

Claeys, Gregory.
  Thomas Paine : social and political thought / Gregory Claeys
      p.   cm.
  Includes index.
  ISBN 0-04-445089-3. — ISBN 0-04-445090-7 (pbk.)
  1. Paine, Thomas. 1737-1809—Contributions in political science.
I. Title.
JC178.V2C58 1989
320.5′1′092—dc20   89-16531
                                                                          CIP

British Library Cataloguing in Publication Data

Claeys, Gregory
  Thomas Paine : social and political thought
  1. Politics. Theories of Paine, Thomas, 1737–1809
  I. Title
  320.5′1′0924

ISBN 0-04-445089-3
ISBN 0-04-445090-7 pbk

Typeset in 10 on 12 point Palatino and printed in Great Britain by
The University Press, Cambridge

To M.S.G.

CONTENTS

ACKNOWLEDGEMENTS

I am grateful to Geraint Parry for help in the initial stages of writing this book. Gordon Smith of Unwin Hyman has done much to see it through to publication. John Dunn, Gareth Stedman Jones and J. F. C. Harrison remained encouraging as always. Iver Bernstein, Rowland Berthoff, Istvan Hont and David Konig kindly commented on all or parts of the book. My best editor, Christine Lattek, offered many helpful suggestions on the text and, as importantly, remained immensely patient throughout its composition. I have also benefited from discussions with Alan Booth, Iain Hampsher-Monk, John Stevenson, Richard Tuck, and Roger Wells.

Particularly helpful with sources have been the British Library, Bloomsbury, to whose beleaguered employees I am exceptionally grateful for helping to find many of the anonymous works used here; the Cambridge University Library, the Goldsmiths' Library, University of London, and Washington University Library (with particular thanks for their considerable assistance to Anne Barker, Holly Hall, B. J. Johnston, Christine Smith, David Straight, Nada Vaughn and Vicky Witte). I would also like to thank the British Library Newspaper Library, Colindale, the library of the Victoria and Albert Museum, London, the Bibliothèque Nationale, Paris, the Thetford Library, the Edinburgh University Library, the Library of Congress, Rotherham Central Library, the Public Record Office, Chancery Lane and Richmond, and the Library of the American Philosophical Society, Philadelphia. Research for this book was funded in part by grants from the Graduate School of Washington University, St Louis, and the American Philosophical Society, to whom many thanks are due.

Portions of the book have been tested on various audiences. I am especially indebted to the Society for the Study of Labour History and the Thomas Paine Society for their support and helpful comments at their joint Paine conference at Sheffield in April 1987, and to the former society's conference on the French revolution in Britain, held at Nottingham in March 1989. An earlier version of chapter 8 was published in the *Bulletin* of the Labour History Society, to whose editors I am grateful for permission to reprint sections of it here.

Finally, I would like to thank Barbara Fineberg for her most generous gift of a print of Paine in her father's memory; it has scowled at least once during the progress of the manuscript, but has hopefully been propitiated at last.

CHRONOLOGY

29 January 1737	Thomas Paine born at Thetford
1762–74	'Wilkes and Liberty' movement
10 January 1776	*Common Sense* published
4 July 1776	American Declaration of Independence
1779–80	Yorkshire Association meetings
April 1780	formation of the Society for Promoting Constitutional Information
November 1782	end of American War of Independence
1788–90	Dissenting efforts to repeal Test Acts
14 July 1789	storming of the Bastille
4 November 1789	Richard Price's sermon to the Revolution Society
October 1790	United Irishmen formed
November 1790	Burke's *Reflections* published
December 1790	Mary Wollstonecraft's *Vindication of the Rights of Men* published
22 February 1791	The *Rights of Man*, Part One published
19 April 1791	death of Richard Price
7 May 1791	James Mackintosh's *Vindiciae Gallicae* published
July 1791	Church and King Riots
25 January 1792	London Corresponding Society founded
February 1792	The *Rights of Man, Part Second* published
22 May 1792	Royal Proclamation against Sedition, Subversion and Riot
September 1792	cheap edition of the *Rights of Man* (both parts) published
14 September 1792	Paine moves to Paris
21 September 1792	French monarchy abolished
October 1792	first reformers' convention, Edinburgh
late 1792	split in the Whig Party; isolation of Fox
20 November 1792	Association for the Preservation of Liberty and Property formed
18 December 1792	Paine's trial, *in absentia*, for seditious libel
January–February 1793	Aliens Act; Traitorous Correspondence Act
21 January 1793	Louis XVI executed

1 February 1793	France declares war on Britain
February 1793	William Godwin's *Enquiry concerning Political Justice* published
April 1793	second reformers' convention
August 1793	Edinburgh sedition trials
November–December 1793	third 'British Convention' meets at Edinburgh
27 December 1793	Paine arrested in Paris
1794	*The Age of Reason* published
early 1794	further Edinburgh treason trials
May 1794	London treason trials begin; suspension of Habeas Corpus
July 1794	fall of Robespierre
4 November 1794	Paine released
December 1795	the Two Acts (widening the definition of treason and curtailing mass meetings)
1797	*Agrarian Justice* published
1797	Thomas Spence's *The Rights of Infants* published
9 July 1797	death of Edmund Burke
May–October 1798	insurrection in Ireland
July 1799	London Corresponding Society banned
November 1802	Paine returns to the US
February 1804	death of Joseph Priestley
8 June 1809	death of Thomas Paine at New Rochelle, aged 72

INTRODUCTION
THE AGE OF PAINE

I know not whether any Man in the World has had more influence on its inhabitants or affairs for the last thirty years than Tom Paine. There can be no severer Satyr on the Age. For such a mongrel between Pigg and Puppy, begotten by a wild Boar on a Bitch Wolf, never before in any Age of the World was suffered by the Poltroonery of mankind, to run through such a career of mischief. Call it then the Age of Paine. (John Adams to Benjamin Waterhouse)[1]

The problem of Thomas Paine

Two crises at the end of the eighteenth century destroyed the vision of politics which had dominated all previous human history. From the shots fired at Lexington to the storming of the Bastille, a chain of events unfolded which inexorably convinced millions that rule by hereditary monarchies and aristocracies at the expense of the majority was illegitimate in principle. The claim of the majority to political power, though it gained ground slowly in the nineteenth century and is still far from universally granted in practice, is none the less today nearly everywhere conceded in theory, and defines the politics of modernity. Its achievement, not merely industrialization, is commonly said to mark the passage of nations to civility. We nearly all agree that we should be 'democrats', no matter how much we dispute what the term means.

In the first decades of revolution one man more than any other – 'probably the most useful man that ever existed upon the face of the earth', one of his friends said – epitomized the new democratic ideal. Having done much to foment independence in America, Thomas Paine sowed the seeds of revolution in Britain in the early 1790s and went on, though now with a smaller role on a wider political stage, narrowly to escape the guillotine for his efforts in France shortly thereafter. During his life, his writings were read by more men and women than any other political author in history. His interests were wider than the political arena, however. He was among the first to advocate freeing all slaves.

1

He was a pioneer in the field of international arbitration, the inheritor of a solid Quaker tradition in this area. He opposed British colonial policies in India and Africa.

None the less, Paine's reputation rests chiefly upon his great political works, *Common Sense*, which did much to spark the American revolution, and the *Rights of Man*, whose popularity was even greater and set off a much more extensive political debate. Paradoxically, however, Paine's very success also underlies his relative neglect as a thinker today. He was not a trained political philosopher, but a common man with an uncommonly sharp mind who was profoundly angered by the oppression and arrogance of Britain's upper classes as well as by hereditary rule generally. Paine's uncanny ability to give voice to similar resentments in millions of others was an essential component in his popularity on both sides of the Atlantic. But consequently it is often assumed that Paine spoke the unsophisticated thoughts of the multitude, and then moreover as an enthusiast and demagogue pandering to the crowd, 'a mere Hyde Park orator' and vulgarizer of Locke, whose chief work does not constitute 'even a minor' contribution to political theory, and who therefore has no proper place beside the great political thinkers. For decades American historians, as Alfred Young has remarked, thus relegated Paine to the sidelines of their revolution 'as a person of marginal influence' if not dubious moral character. A typical account from the 1930s devotes one paragraph of an 800-page study of the events of 1776 to Paine, dismisses *Common Sense* as 'a useless study of the monarchy' and an 'unpractical attempt at laying down a system of government', and concludes only grudgingly that 'whatever Paine's lack of personal merit, it must be admitted that he did a great service to his times'. In Britain, despite the pioneering work of E. P. Thompson, Albert Goodwin and others, many aspects of Paine's impact remain unstudied, particularly the massive debate which concentrated so singularly upon the *Rights of Man*.[2]

For similar reasons, Paine has achieved little official respectability on either side of the Atlantic. There is no place for him among the pantheon of heroes whose monuments dominate Washington DC, and the American labour movement only distantly recalls his achievements. His birthday is no cause for celebration in Downing Street, though the Thomas Paine Society does much to keep his memory alive. Paris, where he was least successful, has erected a statue of him pleading for the life of Louis XVI. But in Britain (Michael Foot and Tony Benn notwithstanding) and America the few politicians who know any history would rather forget than recall his contribution to modern democracy. Moreover, a surprising proportion of the American public continues to find Painite theology threatening.

Paine has not suffered from complete neglect, of course. He has had many biographers and has been figured in several plays and works of fiction. But in scholarly circles he has only slowly begun to receive his due. His role in the American revolution is now much clearer after recent careful studies by Eric Foner and A. O. Aldridge. But his European writings and their impact remain less well scrutinized and these accordingly receive greater attention here. We recognize the paradigmatic quality of the 'Burke–Paine debate' (we will later see that this is a considerable misnomer when applied to the controversy as a whole). For it was here first established that the battleground of politics would long be dominated by the siege of aristocratic 'tradition' by plebeian 'democracy'. We might even concede Paine's virtually single-handed creation of a mass reading public conscious for the first time of its right to participate in politics. Yet when we study the British debate over the French revolution it is often Edmund Burke who receives greater attention. Paine is merely one of his respondents, albeit the most important. But Paine's brand of popular radicalism is rarely construed as part of the 'great tradition' of political thought upon which we often suppose western civilization is built.

This is curious given the fact that it is Paine's vision, rather than Burke's, which predominates in the modern world. It would be inexplicable except that the revival of Burke has had more to do with the Russian than the French revolution and has consequently resulted in the frequent conservative confusion of the principles of the latter revolution (or indeed any other) with those of Jacobinism. Such an imbalance clearly requires rectification, and by examining Paine's ideas in their context we will find that he was indeed a revolutionary, but not a Bolshevik or a Jacobin. Moreover, there are other weaknesses in the current view of Paine. As Jack Greene has emphasized, it is rare that scholars have been interested in both Paine's American and his European careers, and in both the European sources of his ideas and the bearing of his American experiences on his later thought.[3] This bifurcation in Paine studies, it is hoped, is also partially remedied by this book, by integrating debates about Paine's American and European works.

But reconsidering Paine is necessary not only to temper the political and intellectual preferences of earlier historians and political theorists. A fairer and more detailed treatment of his ideas also affects our assessment of the central arguments of the French revolution debate and their British development during the 1790s. For to take not Paine but Burke as the centre of this controversy is to fail to see how much more this debate centred on the *Rights of Man* than the *Reflections*. Burke's vindication of the *ancien régime* sold some 30,000 copies and generated about fifty responses, ranging from brief pamphlets to William Godwin's three-volume *Enquiry Concerning Political Justice*. Paine sold hundreds of thousands of copies of the *Rights of Man*, and provoked perhaps four to five hundred replies ranging from broadsheets to 700-page tomes. Burke did much to incite the British reaction to the French revolution, but he was much less responsible for its success in eradicating the reform movement, often even going unmentioned in the subsequent pamphlet war. But Paine's name epitomized the principles of the new reformers. The *Rights of Man* redefined the terms in which politics was to be understood and could be countered only by pamphleteers willing to address the people directly. Thousands, too, did not deny the name of 'Painite' when it was thrust upon them, while few termed themselves 'Burkians'. As importantly, Paine's arguments, though often misunderstood, were and remain intellectually as powerful as Burke's. His defence of his own version of modernity is no less reasonable than Burke's championing of its historical predecessor. Nor did Paine marshal his arguments with less care; indeed, contrary to popular assumption, some even of Burke's sympathizers found his account the more hysterical.

This book is not therefore a new biography of Paine. His life is summarized in the next chapter, but those interested in the minutiae of Paineana are directed to several good studies. But no previous account investigates Paine's social and political thought in both its British and American moments, details its eighteenth-century context, examines the ways in which Paine's ideas were actually understood, and further attempts to restore him to the position his contemporaries (at least his supporters) accorded him, that of an important writer on politics and society. Paine's biographers have done great service to his life, but an adventurous career has overshadowed Paine's role in the forging of modern political debate.[4]

This is especially true for the more neglected British side of Paine's thought and thus for the *Rights of Man*, *The Age of Reason* and *Agrarian Justice*. Accordingly, while *Common Sense* and Paine's role in the American revolution are treated in one chapter here and their relation to recent debates in American historiography is summarized, my concentration is upon Paine's most influential as well as intellectually interesting work, the *Rights of Man*, and its British reception and connection to working-class radicalism. This is further narrowed by a focus upon England and Scotland, though detailed work on Ireland and Wales is still needed. While the arguments of all of Paine's major works are assessed here, two chapters detail the reception of the *Rights of Man* and attempt for the first time to scrutinize carefully the enormous pamphlet literature on both the radical and loyalist sides as a means of excavating the contextual meaning of Paine's ideas. Examining the relationship between text and audience, between political debate and popular political movement, alone reveals both the appeal of Paine's ideas and also why efforts to refute them met with some success. For revolution in Britain was not prevented by repression alone. Moreover, we will also see that reading the political thought of this period in terms of this extensive debate, rather than Paine and Burke alone, gives us quite a different view of its contours and relation to both eighteenth- and nineteenth-century political thought. In particular, we will see that much of the controversy did not concentrate solely on natural rights, or the defence or rejection of the new French government, but rather upon the wider question of whether egalitarian republicanism was compatible with a commercial society, or whether, in short, America could be imitated in Europe. Many of the arguments on both sides of this struggle owed something to Burke or Paine, but its centre of gravity, as it will here be termed, was defined by neither, but instead emerged spontaneously as the debate intensified.

With reference to more specific problems which have plagued Paine's previous interpreters, I have attempted to offer a balanced view of the respective weight which should be given to the main sources of Paine's thought: the Whig radical and republican traditions of eighteenth-century Britain, natural law (whose contribution to Paine's thinking has been gravely neglected) and Dissenting Protestantism, particularly deism and Quakerism. Only by understanding the confluence of these streams can we determine Paine's distinctive contribution to political thought. In some instances plausible solutions are proposed to problems where wholly conclusive evidence is lacking. In other areas, new problems are revealed which have been overlooked previously. The existence of a substantial conflict between Paine's religious and political principles, particularly in relation to his later works and his theory of property, is, for example, examined here for the first time.

If one thread runs throughout my interpretation of Paine, it is the attempt to place both his ideas and their reception in the context of the recrafting of republican ideals by political reformers in light of their increasing acceptance of commercial society. During the last twenty years historians of Anglo-American radicalism have divided sharply over whether a neo-classical or 'Harringtonian' republican emphasis upon public virtue and its corruption, or a Lockean and later Smithian liberalism more concerned with rights and their preservation, predominated during the reshaping of late eighteenth-century Whiggism.[5] Like many such debates, the historical truth is far more complex than a thumbnail sketch of seemingly irreconcilable positions may imply. Reformers were not notoriously concerned with paradigmatic purity and freely mixed any arguments which seemed useful. Paine, we will see, contributed much to creating a new ideal of commercial society whose faith in the market (though qualified by Paine's very important welfare proposals) did involve rejecting a republican reliance upon agrarian virtue as the basis of political stability. None the less Paine also sought to retain essential elements of the republican inheritance which have been overlooked in previous interpretations. More than any other political writer, he contested the central Whig preference for a mixed constitution and the political predominance of landed wealth and sought to replace it by a new theory of commercial republicanism based upon popular representative institutions without any hereditary monarchy. But in this 'American' wedding of trade and democracy Paine was also strikingly concerned with maintaining public virtue, and understood this both in terms of classical republican devotion to the common good (applied to a much larger population and thus in many respects intensified) and true Christian brotherhood. To appreciate the novelty of Paine's achievement, however, we must first briefly consider the various strands of eighteenth-century radicalism from which these ideals were to be woven.

British radical traditions, 1688–1789

The parliamentary reform movement began to gather steam only after 1760, and became widely popular only at the French revolution. Beforehand the ruling Whig oligarchy was obliged to pay lip service to the principles of 1688 by which the Protestant succession and a limited monarchy had been secured. But 1688 was construed largely as a conservative defence of 'popular' liberty against an encroaching Catholic monarch, not as a novel effort at revolution seeking greater popular sovereignty or the reform of parliament. Against this oligarchy a few dissident Whig aristocrats and their followers battled, occasionally joined by 'country party' Tories (though their patriarchal model of ideal polity and the cult of Charles the Martyr were anathema to Whigs) advocating some extension of the franchise, a redistribution of Commons' seats to favour the counties and larger boroughs, the enfranchisement of towns, shorter parliaments, reduced governmental expenditures and a diminished influence of the Crown and the government in the Commons.[6]

By mid-century, and among the Nonconformists in particular, the emergence of a new commercial middle order with its own distinctive ideology, social identity and cultural institutions had begun to add momentum to the reformers' cause. Resentful of both the economic dominance of the aristocracy and the Anglican religious monopoly, Dissenting merchants and manufacturers like Josiah Wedgwood tended to be radical in both religion and politics. Moreover, they shared an identity based upon their social and economic position and assumed that the virtues which had brought them success rendered them superior to the uneducated lower as well as the profligate upper classes. Class consciousness and conflict played only a minimal role prior to 1790, however, being strongest among London merchants and tradesmen, but nowhere so narrowly defined that 'the middling orders' did not usually include farmers and gentry as well as merchants and manufacturers. The modern language of class had thus not yet formed.[7] But considering their economic position the middle classes felt their political exclusion keenly. Only 5 per cent of a total population of 8 million in 1790 could vote in England and Wales. In the 1780s 6,000 electors, or a majority of the voters of 129 boroughs, returned 257 MPs, or a majority of the Commons. Fifty MPs were elected by a mere 340 voters. In the early 1790s, 162 people (71 peers and 91 commoners) secured the election of 306 MPs. Moreover, 43,000 electors selected 52 MPs for 23 cities and two universities, while 41,000 chose 369 MPs for 192 towns and boroughs.[8] The boroughs and a few towns were thus grossly overrepresented, and the commercial cities correspondingly neglected. Old Sarum was uninhabited but returned two members, as did the thriving port of Bristol. Cornwall had as many MPs as Scotland. Patronage and corruption were expensive, however: elections could cost upwards of £30,000. But at seven years the life of parliaments gave some opportunity to recoup these expenses.

In arguing against these abuses the reformers relied heavily upon a few key texts which represented divergent but interpenetrating parts of the Whig tradition, notably John Locke's *Second Treatise of Government* (1690), Algernon Sidney's *Discourses Concerning Government* (1698), the writings of the seventeenth century republican James Harrington and his disciples, such as Walter Moyle and Henry Neville, and those of later radicals like John Trenchard and Thomas Gordon. Amongst these writers Locke was the most important, though he did not dominate as absolutely as was once thought. His *Second Treatise* defended the natural equality of mankind and the possession of rights to life, liberty and property as a consequence of God's creation of the world. It argued centrally that political power was limited by the possession of rights to freedom held by all in a pre-political state of nature, which were to be maintained by law in civil society. Natural society had been abandoned only because of the inconvenience of individuals judging the justice of their own claims. The power lodged in a sovereign was accordingly limited by popular consent and a right of rebellion was justified if life, liberty and property were tyrannically infringed upon. Taxation was permitted only by the consent of the majority. These views were popularized widely in both Britain and the colonies by writers like Thomas Pownall and Joseph Towers. For most, the Lockean inheritance was a moderate one. In *A Vindication of the Political Principles*

7

of Mr. Locke (1782), for example, Towers insisted that Locke's followers thought the English constitution was 'so excellently constructed' and its laws 'so well adapted for securing the liberty of the subject' that it was 'preferable to any republic which had yet been constituted'. He also offered an excellent summary of how eighteenth-century reformers read Locke:

> It is the doctrine of Mr. Locke, that all legitimate government is derived from the consent of the people; that men are naturally equal, and that no one has a right to injure another in his life, health, liberty, or possessions; and that no man in civil society, ought to be subject to the arbitrary will of others, but only to known and established laws, made by general consent for the common benefit; that no taxes are to be levied on the people, without the consent of the majority, given by themselves or by their deputies. That the ruling power ought to govern by declared and received laws, and not by extemporary dictates, and undetermined resolutions. That kings and princes, magistrates and rulers of every class, have no just authority but what is delegated to them by the people; and which, when not employed for their benefit, the people have always a right to resume, in whatever hands it may be placed.[9]

Also widely read by Whigs were the writings of Algernon Sidney, a republican martyr executed for his beliefs in 1683. Sidney also rejected the divine right theory of monarchy and saw the sole purpose of government as being the good of the governed. Though liberty alone was the basis of virtue, order and stability in governments and was especially associated with the ancient Roman republic, the best form of government was not purely republican, but a mixture of monarchy, aristocracy and democracy. Its aims, 'to increase the number, strength, and riches of the people', could be met only through conquest, which in turn required both adept commanders and a strong, patriotic people loving liberty and uncorrupted by luxury and private interest. Preserving liberty also required maintaining rights. While man was born naturally free, liberty being 'exemption from the domination of any other', all governments required surrendering some natural liberty. But the right of dominion was based on consent, and kings who exceeded their authority could be resisted, this having been established in Britain prior to the Norman conquest. Such rights were most frequently lost, in turn, as a result of the corruption of manners and a decline in public virtue.[10]

Such themes were echoed in the early eighteenth century by John Trenchard and Thomas Gordon, whose *Independent Whig* and *Cato's Letters* (1720–1) upheld religious liberty and the rights of Dissenters, the right to resist tyranny, the right of freedom of speech and opposition to standing armies, and warned of the dangers of commercial speculation and of the dependency of liberty on public virtue.[11] Trenchard, Gordon and others were especially indebted to the mid-seventeenth century republican, James Harrington, whose own master was Machiavelli. But while the so-called neo-Machiavellian republicans or True Whigs aimed to emulate ancient Greece and Rome, virtually none sought to abolish the monarchy, instead preferring a 'mixed government' where substantial power rested with the Commons, and warning of monarchical and aristocratic encroachments upon it, which upset the balance of the constitution. Far less were they democrats wishing majority rule rather than government by the virtuous, landowning few assumed to represent the genuine interests of all. Some True Whigs, however, were willing to counsel agrarian laws to limit landed estates so that inequality did not threaten liberty. Many also warned of the increasing power of fundholders who held stock in the swiftly growing national debt, and of the economic instability of the movable property of merchants and speculators by comparison with land. And other dangers for public virtue and liberty existed. Standing armies easily became organs of monarchical tyranny. Religious establishments often proved capricious (some Harringtonians were free-thinkers). For the republicans or True Whigs, then, preserving liberty required eternal vigilance, and a Whig oligarchy as much as an arbitrary monarch could upset Britain's delicate constitutional balance.

Despite the varying concerns of Locke and Harrington in particular, too much has been made of the supposed divergences between later 'Lockean' and 'republican' radicals. Reformers held differing views on, for example, the value of increased commerce or wider political participation. But by 1750 such disagreements no longer corresponded with late seventeenth-century Whig positions and most reformers did not see themselves as narrowly 'Lockean' or 'republican'. Thomas Pownall, for example, happily quoted Locke on the origins of the social contract and Harrington on the need to balance property in the commonwealth.[12] None the less as a means of emphasis these labels retain some utility. Broadly speaking, 'republicans' were more alarmed at the spread of luxury and commerce, more often urged the primacy of public virtue, and saw the landed gentry as its best repository. More 'Lockean' reformers concentrated on the right of representation as a means of ensuring consent, sought the extension of the franchise to middle-class merchants and manufacturers (many of whom were also Dissenters) in order to protect 'property' generally, and not only landed wealth, and were more concerned with corruption through arbitrary power than commerce. All agreed that the right to resist tyranny was derived from the 'executive power' all possessed in the state of nature and belonged to 'the people'. These were chiefly understood as men of property, government having been founded to preserve property generally, though the 'people' could also be construed in a wider sense. All defined the English constitution as a limited monarchy whose powers were balanced by both the aristocracy and the commonalty. In practice this meant parliamentary supremacy and the 'independence' of the Commons, with the king naming his own ministers but governing only with parliamentary approval. Rule 'by the consent of the governed' summarized many of these positions.

Natural rights and natural law

Ideas of natural rights were also crucial to the language of reform and merit some further introduction here given their centrality to Paine. Whig reformers did not aim to create a new form of polity, but rather, as the former Cambridge MP Soame Jenyns put it, 'to bring back society to its original state, and to restore mankind to the full enjoyment of their natural rights', an ideal of purification much indebted to Machiavellian republicanism. Three models of rights were particularly important to such arguments: the state of nature ideal often associated with Locke, where political sovereignty derived from a mutual compact between governors and governed which secured rights granted by God and originally defined in the Bible, but inhering in all as psychological properties; the Anglo-Saxon or ancient constitution, which identified annual parliaments and universal male suffrage with pre-Norman Britain and was prominently identified with the Yorkshire True Whig Obadiah Hulme's *Essay on the English Constitution* (1771); and the revolutionary settlement of 1688, a central assumption in the Whig interpretation of which concerned the triumph of popular sovereignty over monarchical tyranny.[13]

These ideal types overlapped to a considerable degree and were accordingly invoked both in isolation and in various mixtures. The scholar and anti-slavery agitator Granville Sharp, for example, alleged that the Saxon leader Alfred's chief inspiration had been Moses. Hulme thought the ancient Greek republics had first properly wielded natural rights, followed by the Saxons, while the great Nottinghamshire reformer Major John Cartwright thought the English constitution perfectly harmonized with that 'great constitution of moral government, called the law of nature'. But there were also tensions between these ideals; Hulme, for example, disparaged the settlement of 1688 as having failed to reinstitute annual parliaments and instead instigated a great neglect of natural rights founded in the ancient constitution. None the less all Whigs agreed that basic or natural rights were divine in origin and unalterable compared to secondary or prescriptive rights, which were historically rooted and mutable. It was widely asserted that the chief end of government (as the Cambridge Constitutional Society, for example, stressed) was securing rather than suppressing natural rights. In particular this meant that the divine, the primitive and later forms of rights were thought of as flowing into and amalgamated in a uniquely British constitution whose restoration was the reformers' chief aim. Rights were 'natural' in that they were ordained by God and inhered in each individual, but also because they were historically part of the British constitution. Thus the Society for Constitutional Information's first address in 1780 took the 'basis and vital principle' of the 'venerable Constitution handed down to us ... from our Saxon and British ancestors' to be that 'LAW, TO BIND ALL, MUST BE ASSENTED TO BY ALL', which required equal representation.[14]

Radical discussions of natural rights were also much indebted to the natural jurisprudence teachings of medieval Christianity which, reformulated in the seventeenth century, remained a dominant intellectual model throughout Europe for another 200 years. Though they attained a degree of independence by the early eighteenth century, natural rights discussions were originally only one segment of the natural law, which systematically addressed the entire range of psychological, moral and political experience in order to determine the meaning of the natural law, or system of rules imposed by God upon man to attain to happiness and knowable through reason. Unfortunately eighteenth-century British natural jurisprudence has been much neglected and its relation to natural rights consequently remains largely unexplored. Usually it is assumed that the central doctrines of natural law were devastated by both the sceptics, led by Hume, who doubted inferences from divine intention or any 'original contract' or state of nature on evidential grounds, and thought the passions predominated over reason in human affairs, and the utilitarians, chiefly Bentham, Paley and Priestley, who provided a new hedonistic foundation for morals. One way around some of these objections had already been suggested by Pufendorf: the necessity for sociable co-operation became the chief source of natural obligation rather than conscious obedience to the demands of virtue.[15] But all that remained in Britain after these assaults, it is usually thought, were the natural law teachings regarding international relations and the regulation of war, which became modern international law, and a few natural rights ideas associated with Locke which, once their systematic context had been removed, limped into the nineteenth century and then expired.

But if the natural law framework of natural rights had in fact been destroyed by 1790 we would have a hard time explaining many aspects of the natural rights debate during the revolution, and certainly the popularity of Paine's political thought and the association of natural rights doctrines with ideas of reason, sociability, reciprocal duties and mutual interdependence. In fact the writings of many jurists circulated widely in late eighteenth-century Britain, among them works by Pufendorf, Burlamaqui, Hutcheson, Vattel and others. Several prominent Whig radicals wrote specifically on natural law, for instance Granville Sharp (*A Tract on the Law of Nature*, 1777). Locke was also deeply indebted to the same tradition, which poses problems for the idea of a separate natural rights discourse and indeed implies that natural rights arguments were only a special branch of natural law teaching. But while the longevity of more systematic natural law teachings is now recognized in relation to the later Scottish Enlightenment, it needs to be stressed for England too, for Paine and others were also much indebted to such views. Texts like Burlamaqui's extremely popular *The Principles of Natural and Politic Law* (1763) examined such questions as the origins of civil society and property, the nature of sociability, the sources of political authority and the definition of rights. To such writers sociability, 'that disposition which inclines us to benevolence towards our fellow creatures', was central to balancing the self-love which ensured self-preservation. From this God-given inclination, right reason derived principles upon which all social laws and moral duties were founded, such as that the public good ought to be the supreme rule and that sociability ought to guide all human affairs, dictating benevolence even towards our enemies.[16]

From such works the radicals derived much, though natural law writers were usually politically more conservative than the natural rights theorists of the 1770s and later. Pufendorf and other opponents of Hobbes emphasized a contractualist and voluntary foundation for political authority. But this was still insufficient for many radicals. Granville Sharp, for example, defended the American colonists by dismissing Pufendorf's argument that it was only a 'notion', not part of the law of nature, that for law to bind all required the consent of all. Instead an 'equitable form of a *reciprocal Covenant*' was the basis for relations between man and God as well as sovereign and subject. The right of all to consent to laws, and therefore to a vote, was thus based in the law of nature.[17]

More acceptable were natural law accounts of the origins of society and of natural rights. To Burlamaqui, for example, God had given the earth to all 'to a common use of whatever the earth produces for their several wants'. Early society was 'a state of equality and liberty' where 'all men enjoy the same prerogatives, and an entire independence on any other power but God. For every man is master of himself, and equally to his fellow-creatures, so long as he does not subject himself to another person's authority by a particular convention.' But a romanticization of this condition was uncommon among British radicals, most of whom believed that natural society was characterized by indigence and want and that the struggles resulting therefrom had led civil government to be founded. None the less the notion of a 'natural' state of man ambiguously meant not only the earliest social state, but also, as Burlamaqui put it, any other 'into which man enters by his own act and agreement ... conformable in the main to his nature' and 'the end for which he was formed'. Correspondingly natural rights were rooted not only in the origins of society, but in man's nature, and 'right' meant 'whatever reason certainly acknowledges as a sure and concise means of attaining happiness'. Consequently this stipulation confined the notion of a right, which was not a simple power to perform an action but one limited by the requirement of seeking the happiness of others. Possessing a right meant anyone could 'make use of his liberty and natural strength in a peculiar manner' as long as this was 'approved by reason'. Thus parents had a right to bring up their own children, but not to harm them, and a sovereign could levy troops for the defence of the state, but not if their families were left unprovided for. A 'right' was thus a moral claim which entailed an obligation, 'a restriction of natural liberty produced by reason', both not to restrict the rights of others, and to assist them in exercising their rights. This emphasis on reason, which was to be central to Paine's definition of rights and his retention of a theory of social obligation, Hume and other critics of natural law found particularly objectionable. But Burlamaqui, for example, was not worried by the problem of weak or deficient reason. Reason approved 'a particular exercise of our strength and liberty' because 'the difference of those judgements arises from the very nature of things and their effects'. Whatever tended 'to the perfection and happiness of man, meets with the approbation of reason, which condemns whatever leads to a contrary end'. If reason did not rule human actions, 'all the rights it grants to man would become useless and of no effect'.[18]

The emergence of the reform movement

So far we have considered only the intellectual bases of eighteenth-century radicalism. Before turning to Paine, however, we need some sense of how the reform movement itself developed. John Brewer has shown that many True Whigs were uninvolved in institutional politics and began to organize only after the accession of George III in 1760. The practical revival of parliamentary reform activities from mid-century onwards was dominated by three movements which will be characterized briefly here: the 'Wilkes and Liberty' agitation of the 1760s, which occasioned an unprecedented popular political participation; support for the American revolution; and the revival of provincial radicalism which followed.[19] These renewed an enthusiasm for parliamentary reform in the early 1780s which retained some momentum even in 1790.

(1) 'Wilkes and Liberty'

John Wilkes, libertine, spendthrift and occasional reformer, provoked one of the most important outbursts of popular radicalism in the middle years of the century.[20] Allied to the elder Pitt, his satirical *North Briton* (which Paine supposedly read) lambasted the policies of Lord Bute's government in 1762–3. When no. 45 of the journal seemingly impugned the king, Wilkes was prosecuted for seditious libel. Since he sat in the Commons, his arrest raised two key issues: the immunity of an MP and, more importantly, the nature of the General Warrant served upon him. Wilkes proclaimed that 'the liberty of the subject at large' was threatened and fervent crowds of supporters took up the slogan, 'Wilkes and Liberty'. Released, Wilkes was re-elected to Parliament in March 1768 with tremendous demonstrations of popular support, his picture appearing in every public house in London, the great symbolic number, '45', on every wall. Having fled a charge of obscene libel for printing a ribald essay, Wilkes surrendered to the King's Bench prison the following month to settle the issue of his outlawry. Eleven were killed in riots on this occasion.

Sentenced to 22 months' imprisonment, Wilkes encouraged the formation of the Society of Supporters of the Bill of Rights in February 1769 to take up the cause of increased representation and annual elections. Expelled from Parliament in April, Wilkes won re-election, but unprecedentedly Parliament chose to seat his defeated opponent. A vast number of petitions from throughout the nation objected, while prominent MPs like Edmund Burke took up the cause. Support came even from the American colonies, whose disillusionment with the Crown can be dated from this point (at least two town names, Wilkesbarre in Pennsylvania and Wilkesboro in Wilkes County, North Carolina, commemorate this enthusiasm).[21] For the first time something like a modern political campaign emerged. Popular meetings of a type never before witnessed drew thousands in protest. Wilkites gained important posts in London elections. Striking weavers in Spitalfields linked Wilkes's cause to their own. After several attempts, Wilkes became Lord Mayor of London in 1774, serving honourably and respectably. Later re-elected to Parliament until 1790, he ended his days as an undistinguished MP with scant interest in reform.

Wilkes was clearly no republican and spoke, for example, of 'rights coeval with the *English* constitution, that perfection of human wisdom, that noblest work of man'. But his cause instigated the involvement in charges of corruption against the government not only of numbers of merchants and tradesmen, but also of the labouring classes. Support for Wilkes has been correlated with rising food prices, and no doubt many artisans and journeymen in the Wilkite 'mob' had known unemployment and hunger. But others, especially Wilkes's supporters among the more middling trades of jewellers, saddlers, ironmongers, brewers and timber merchants, clearly resented their exclusion from politics and identified parliamentary corruption with a restricted franchise. In their eyes 'independence' ought no longer to be associated only with landownership, but should be understood more generally, at least as encompassing all male householders. Wilkes's association with such goals was long-remembered; his last follower died in 1834, having when drunk commonly paraded through the streets of Aylesbury in an overcoat given him by his hero, shouting 'Wilkes and Liberty'.[22]

(2) *The impact of the American revolution*
The American revolution gave an enormous boost to the reform movement. After the colonies assisted Wilkes, his followers in the Society of Supporters of the Bill of Rights in turn sent money as the American conflict worsened, and upheld the right to be represented if taxed, some even venturing the view that 'the fate of Wilkes and America must stand or fall together'. Other Wilkite organizations subscribed funds to the victims of Concord and Lexington in June 1775, as did radicals in debating and convivial clubs like the Robinhood, which comprised mainly tradesmen by the 1770s. Like the Napoleonic threat twenty years later, the coming of war divided the British reformers, bringing upon them what J. H. Plumb has termed 'the stigma of disloyalty'.[23] But parallels were evident from the outset between the colonists' cause and that of domestic radicals. Both rejected the notion of virtual representation, or the view that MPs in the Commons maintained the interests of the entire nation rather than only their constituents. Both insisted that the foundation of government was voluntary consent, that taxation without representation was unjust and that abrogating any contract between governors and governed invoked a right of resistance.

Few connected these issues more successfully than Major John Cartwright, who sacrificed a potential military career by refusing to serve against the colonists. Not only did Cartwright lend much assistance in his *American Independence, the Interest and Glory of Great Britain* (1774), which advocated separate independence for each colony under the Crown, though not a federation of all. His *Take Your Choice!* (1776) established the radical platform of the next several generations in its demands for annual elections, manhood suffrage, equal electoral districts, a secret ballot and payment of MPs. He also insisted that the right of representation could be based only in personality, and not in property. No republican, Cartwright none the less had scant respect for the existing monarchy. Like Hulme and the Dissenting schoolmaster James Burgh, Cartwright also proposed a national convention to begin reforming a Parliament too corrupt to reform itself, a plan suggested at Middlesex in 1769 by the Anglican physician and political writer John Jebb. But while this might involve, as Burgh suggested, acting against existing representatives, its aim was to pressure Parliament, not to replace it.[24]

Though Anglicans like Granville Sharp took up their cause, the American colonists found their main champions in the leading Dissenting radicals. The philosopher and minister Richard Price, for example, wrote extensively on the revolution, seeing its central issue as the equal right of all to share in legislation, legitimate government consisting only in equal laws framed by common consent. Wholeheartedly adopting the demand for independence after 1776, Price cheered the colonists' success as perhaps the most important step ever taken in human improvement. As importantly, he upset conservative Whigs by arguing the colonists' case from a natural rights basis rather than in terms of precedents like 1688 or the ancient constitution.[25]

As John Derry has written, the battle lines which defined the French revolution debate were thus already beginning to form in the mid-1770s. The American conflict revealed increasingly divergent interpretations of the settlement of 1688, and correspondingly of the character of the constitution itself. Everyone knew that this comprised the king, who after 1689 retained considerable powers in his capacity to name ministers, veto legislation and influence foreign policy; the Lords, who shared in legislation and had some judicial functions; and the Commons, who were pre-eminent and held financial power. All conceded that each of these should prevent the others from dominating. But what powers each branch should correspondingly have over the others to accomplish this was more debated. British and colonial radicals agreed that the American cause exemplified the principle of consensual government against the usurpations of an unrepresentative and corrupt parliament as well as the designs of a tyrannical monarch. All Whigs commended the ascendancy of the Commons, but the more radical thought it all too subservient and condemned the government and Crown's corrupt use of patronage and ministerial placemen as a means of extending their powers. Thus the revolution helped to redefine British radical notions of constitutionalism, republicanism and popular sovereignty, making these more popular in imitation of what was thought to be American practice.[26]

(3) *Provincial radicalism: the Yorkshire revival in the 1780s*
The expense of the American wars ensured that radical enthusiasm did not flag at the end of the 1770s. The 'Associated Counties' movement

began in 1779–80 when a number of Yorkshire nobles and gentlemen petitioned Parliament about high taxes and the burgeoning system of sinecures and pensions.[27] Soon delegates from various county organizations met in London to demand annual parliaments, with their chief spokesman, the Anglican clergyman Christopher Wyvill, also seeking to extend the suffrage further into the middle orders. In early 1780, a group of Westminster electors presided over by the Whig leader Charles James Fox more daringly demanded Cartwright's programme of 'universal male suffrage' (meaning men of some property but not the labouring poor), annual elections, equal electoral districts, vote by ballot and the payment of MPs. At this time Cartwright and others also founded the Society for Constitutional Information (SCI), whose members remained active until 1794 and accepted Paine as an honorary member in 1787 on the basis of *Common Sense*. But further reforms were derailed by a week-long, anti-Catholic riot in 1780, which strengthened the government's hand by making any substantial popular political participation suspicious (and which was remembered as proving the dangers of popular enthusiasm in 1792). When the Rockingham Whigs formed a new government in 1782 after the British defeat in America, the reformers' hopes were again raised. But various reform bills were introduced and suffered defeat, the last being Pitt's effort in 1785, which was supported by 174 MPs. Thereafter apathy set in once again, though the SCI continued to be occupied with the anti-slavery cause, prison reform and other issues. Only the coming of the French revolution markedly revived enthusiasm for political change.

By the late 1780s a spectrum of radical opinion had thus developed which exhibited both a common programme and a variety of disagreements. Reformers shared a concern about the inadequacy of the electoral system, the corruption of the Commons by patronage, and the overly long duration of parliaments. They were divided as to how short parliaments should be, usually opting for triennial or annual elections, and who should vote, with most favouring the exclusion of the labouring poor. Some felt universal suffrage and annual elections were, as Jenyns put it, 'totally impracticable'. Wyvill thought universal suffrage acceptable where public safety was not threatened, but proposed a more restricted suffrage anyway. No reformers doubted the need for greater independence of the Commons. But virtually none considered abolishing the monarchy, an independent House of Commons being, as Jenyns put it, 'no part of the English constitution, the excellence of which consists in being composed of three powers, mutually dependent on each other', and the republic established in Britain in the mid-seventeenth century being 'the worst kind of democracy that ever existed'. Finally, reformers were also divided over the growth of cities and luxury. By the 1770s many radicals had forsaken the chief puritan and classical republican objections to commerce and instead saw trade as beneficial and the manners of commercial society as even superior to classical virtue. None the less there remained substantial divisions about the merits of modernity well into the nineteenth century. Prior to the French revolution, for example, the leading Dissenting reformers Joseph Priestley and Richard Price found themselves on opposite sides of this question. Priestley championed commercial development, while Price thought the ideal society lay between savagery and luxury (a point in 1784 he thought best represented by the new state of Connecticut) and warned against the corrupting effects of banks, paper money, the national debt and foreign trade.[28] This debate was to remain important through the 1790s. But long before another powerful voice had also begun to sway public opinion on such issues: that of Thomas Paine.

Notes to Introduction: the age of Paine

1 Quoted in D. Hawke (1961), p. 111.
2 C. Cone (1968), p. 102; R. Fennessy (1963), p. 244; A. Young (1976), p. x; A. French (1934), p. 705.
3 J. Greene (1978), p. 73. A. Ayer (1988) is an important step in redressing these deficiencies, though it is much less concerned with reconstructing political debates than this book.
4 A. Aldridge (1974) reviews the secondary literature on Paine from 1945 to 73. Highly useful on Paineana is R. Gimbel (1959).
5 The republican view is best represented by J. Pocock (most recently, 1985, pp. 215–310), the liberal on the American side by J. Appleby (1976) and the British by I. Kramnick (1977b and 1982). Also essential are C. Robbins (1959) and H. Dickinson (1977). See also J. Reid (1988).
6 L. Colley (1981), p. 15. On convergences between Whig and Tory reformers see Colley (1982), pp. 85–117, H. Dickinson (1977), pp. 14–56, 91–118.
7 On radicalism and the language of class in this period see in particular I. Kramnick (1977b, 1980, 1982).
8 Wyvill's statistics, in E. Black (1963), p. 59.
9 J. Locke (1970), pp. 287–95, 301–5, 343–5, 380–1, 385, 421; J. Towers (1788), pp. 26–7; T. Pownall (1752), pp. 16–17; J. Towers (1782), p. 84, 36–7. On Locke's reception see J. Dunn (1969).
10 A. Sidney (1750), Vol. 1, pp. 102, 186–210, 296–308, 37–9, 441–8, Vol. 2, pp. 38–44, 73, 288, 309–14.
11 D. Jacobson (1965) gives a selection of Trenchard and Gordon's writings.
12 T. Pownall (1752), pp. 16–17, 28–30, 69.
13 [S. Jenyns] (1785) p. 9; [O. Hulme] (1771), pp. 3–33. On the 'Norman yoke' see C. Hill (1954).
14 G. Sharp (1784), p. 3; [O. Hulme] (1771), pp. 2, 127, 149; J. Cartwright (1776), p. 9; T. Northcote (1781), p. 8; C. Wyvill (1794), Vol. 2, p. 465, Vol. 1, pp. 135–6.
15 See especially I. Hont (1987).
16 J. Burlamaqui (1763), Vol. 1, pp. 169–70.

17 G. Sharp (1774), pp. v, xiv.
18 J. Burlamaqui (1763), Vol. 1, p. 41; (1794), Vol. 1, pp. 38, 42–3, 68–75. See my (1989), chapter 1.
19 J. Brewer (1980a), p. 343. On the emergence of radicalism see also Brewer (1976). Surveys of the reform movement include G. Veitch (1913), S. Maccoby (1955a), I. Christie (1962), E. Black (1963), A. Goodwin (1979), pp. 32–98, E. Royle and J. Walvin (1982).
20 On the Wilkites see G. Rudé (1962).
21 See R. Postgate (1956), pp. 162–72 and P. Maier (1963) on Wilkes's impact in America.
22 C. Wyvill (1794), Vol. 1, p. xli; G. Rudé (1962), p. 180; J. Brewer (1980a), p. 345; R. Postgate (1956), pp. 148–9.
23 J. Plumb (1973), p. 86. Recent treatments of this theme include G. Guttridge (1966), J. Derry (1976)(very helpful; see especially chapter 4), C. Bonwick (1977), R. Toohey (1978), J. Bradley (1986). A good unpublished study is A. Sheps (1973).
24 J. Cartwright (1776), p. 89; [O. Hulme] (1771), p. 161; J. Burgh (1764), Vol. 3, pp. 428–60, Vol. 1, p. 6. On Cartwright see F. Cartwright (1826) and J. Osborne (1972) (and on his originality, pp. 22–3). On the development of ideas of a convention or 'anti-parliament' see T. Parsinnen (1973).
25 R. Price (1777), pp. ix, 20–24. On Dissent and the revolution see C. Bonwick (1976).
26 J. Derry (1976), pp. 170, 4; A. Sheps (1975a).
27 See H. Butterfield (1947), E. Black (1963), pp. 31–173, I. Christie (1960) and (1962), pp. 68–120 and J. Dinwiddy (1971). On the origins of the SCI see E. Black (1963), pp. 174–212.
28 [S. Jenyns] (1784), pp. 1–2, 5–6, 21–2; C. Wyvill (1794), Vol. 3, p. 63; R. Price (1785), pp. 66–80.

1

'Apostle of liberty':
the life of Thomas Paine

Like nearly everything else associated with him, the retailing of Paine's life has been contentious. After the *Rights of Man* appeared, the British government for £500 commissioned a slanderous 'biography' of Paine from one 'Francis Oldys', a Tory refugee from Maryland and clerk at the Board of Trade and Plantations named George Chalmers. This reached eleven editions within two years, in the process growing (ever more fictionally) from 25 to over 150 pages, and was abstracted, embellished and widely reprinted.[1] In the late 1790s similarly hostile works appeared by, among others, William Cobbett, then a leading anti-Jacobin but soon to convert to radicalism himself. Early in the new century an apostate radical headed in the opposite direction, James Cheetham ('Cheat 'Em' to Paine's disciples), added another vituperative account. But the Painites retaliated as early as 1793 with brief *Impartial Memoirs* of Paine and after 1815 several more substantial biographies appeared. Since then Paine's character has been assailed and defended many times, his vices greatly exaggerated by his enemies, his virtues trumpeted loudly by his friends. Settling the true facts about several events in Paine's life (his own autobiography having disappeared) remained important until many decades after his death, the last great point of contention being Paine's supposed death-bed reversion to orthodox Christianity.[2]

Thomas Paine was born in the small Suffolk market town of Thetford (which today honours him with a statue and the Rights of Man public house) on 29 January 1737, the son of a small Quaker farmer and stay- (or corset-support) maker. Politically the town was in the pocket of a prominent Whig magnate, the Duke of Grafton, who nominated the two local MPs. The Lent Assizes for the Eastern Circuit were also held there and Paine doubtless witnessed the barbarous penalties meted out to those who defied the law. Raised as a Quaker on his father's side, indeed, Paine was particularly aware of the cruelty of many punishments and frequent use of the death penalty, for the sect was in the forefront of opposition to both and, while later comments reveal that he found the Quaker life dull and colourless, he remained fond of

the 'exceedingly good moral education' it demanded. At his mother's
instructions Paine was confirmed in the Church of England. But he
was puzzled by a sermon on redemption read to him by a relative,
doubting that God would allow his own son to be killed when 'a man
would be hanged who did such a thing' and remaining convinced of
God's greater benevolence.[3]

Despite an aptitude for science and mathematics, Paine was withdrawn from school by his father at the age of 13 to learn the stay-making
business, and remained at this task for some five years. Having already
conceived a desire to see America, however, he doubtless found
the trade constricting. More attractive, too, was the naval life a
schoolmaster had regaled him with, and at 17 Paine slipped away
to join the *Terrible* (its captain's name was Death), a privateer engaged
against French traders.[4] His father rescued him before the vessel sailed,
however, and in its next engagement it lost nearly nine-tenths of its
crew. It was not the first time fortune would smile upon Paine. Though
in 1756 he apparently joined another privateer, the *King of Prussia*,
Paine returned to stay-manufacturing first in London, then Dover,
and finally at Sandwich in Kent, where he married in the autumn
of 1759, and possibly also acted briefly as a Methodist lay preacher.
But his business was unsuccessful and in the following year his wife
died. Soon after Paine decided to become an exciseman. For a time he
examined brewers' casks at Grantham and in mid-1764 was appointed
to observe smugglers at Alford. Ill-paid, and probably also immersed in
his own scientific studies, Paine like many of his colleagues neglected
to examine fully all of the goods brought into local warehouses. For
passing some without inspection he was discharged in August 1765.

Paine now travelled for a time and, though he sued successfully
and was reinstated as an exciseman, no suitable post was available for
him. He taught English briefly in London, again apparently preaching,
and may even have considered becoming an Anglican minister. He
also attended scientific lectures at the Royal Society (later telling a
friend that he had 'seldom passed five minutes of my life, however
circumstanced, in which I did not acquire some knowledge'). Finally
an excise post came open and after a brief period in Cornwall Paine
went to Lewes, Sussex in early 1768, where he boarded with a Quaker
tobacconist. This was an extremely important period in his life. He
seems to have been involved in local charitable work. He began to
be interested in politics, composing an election song for a local Whig
candidate for the respectable sum of three guineas. Soon, too, by one
account, he began to move away from Whiggism, prompted in the
first instance by the none too seditious comment by a friend, over a
glass of punch after a game of bowls, that Frederick, King of Prussia
was 'the right sort of man for a king, for he has a deal of the devil

in him', which led Paine to wonder 'if a system of government did not exist that did not require a devil'. He also began his career as a pamphleteer here. His first work, *The Case of the Officers of the Excise* (1772), detailed the low wages and arduous duties of excisemen, the temptations to dishonesty this incited and the consequent dangers for revenue collection. Paine's talents as a writer were already evident: 'The rich, in ease and affluence, may think I have drawn an unnatural portrait', he proclaimed, adding, 'but could they descend to the cold regions of want, the circle of polar poverty, they would find their opinions changing with the climate.' Paine was also active in a local debating society, the White Hart Evening Club, where he became known as a convivial conversationalist with a taste for oysters and wine. Here, Paine's comrades elected him 'General of the Headstrong War' for his 'perserverance in a good cause and obstinacy in a bad one', as a radical Quaker friend, Thomas 'Clio' Rickman later put it.[5] His only pronounced vice, in fact, seems to have been a predilection towards vanity.

Paine married again in 1771, this time a young Quaker girl, and spent much of the next few years preparing petitions favouring higher excisemen's salaries, a task his colleagues had deputed him for. He also operated a tobacco mill and small grocery shop for a time, but was hard hit when he lost his excise post again in April 1774 (though Chalmers's later accusation that he had been selling smuggled tobacco was groundless). Forced to sell his possessions in order to meet his creditors' claims, Paine separated from his wife (whom he later helped to support) a few months later and never remarried.[6] Returning to London, he followed the 'Wilkes and Liberty' campaign with great interest. He now became acquainted with the writer Oliver Goldsmith and also Benjamin Franklin, whose electrical experiments he admired and to whom he made the famous retort, when Franklin stated, 'Where liberty is, there is my country,' 'Where liberty is not, there is my country.' Franklin saw much promise in Paine and encouraged him to leave for the American colonies, where there was greater scope for his talents.

Soon taking this fateful advice, Paine reached Philadelphia in December 1774 after nine weeks' voyage, having barely survived an outbreak of shipboard typhus. Originally seeking to open a girls' school, he instead with Franklin's assistance became editor of a small paper, the *Pennsylvania Magazine, or American Museum*. To this and other Philadelphia journals he contributed, among other pieces, a defence of modern authors and institutions against the ancient, an important anti-slavery essay at a time (March 1775) when such views were uncommon, and articles condemning duelling, British policy in India, the use of titles and cruelty to animals. He also helped to draft a bill incorporating the American Philosophical Society. As colonial independence neared, he had already begun to establish that vigorous and independent style of radicalism which would become his trademark. But this was not sufficient to earn a living and poor pay soon forced him to leave the paper.[7]

Paine did not initially favour the violent separation of the colonies from Britain. But when the British fired upon a demonstration at Lexington in April 1775, and certainly by late 1775, or barely a year after his arrival, he concluded that independence was inevitable. The cause of separation became soon and long associated with his name and the force of his arguments. The pattern of Paine's political career, as we will see, was already laid: what others hesitantly and often reluctantly felt, he stated unequivocally and in a language all could comprehend.

Much of the autumn of 1775 was devoted to writing *Common Sense*, which 'burst from the press with an effect which has rarely been produced by types and paper in any age or country', as his friend Dr Benjamin Rush put it. None the less Paine's authorship remained unknown at first, partly because he had resided only briefly in the colonies and did not want this to prejudice his readers. Franklin, in fact, was widely believed to have written the piece, though when a loyalist lady denounced him for using the phrase 'the royal brute of Britain' to describe George III, Franklin denied that he would have so dishonoured the animal world. Despite the success of *Common Sense*, Paine gained nothing from it, since he paid the costs of publication (about £40) himself, and further donated the copyright to the colonists' struggle. It was to set a pattern for his entire career, for Paine was usually too proud and too idealistic to accept money for doing what he did best, and was consequently rarely well off.[8]

As the cause of independence gathered steam, Paine assailed vacillating public opinion in Pennsylvania and New York, and warned against accepting prospective English peace proposals. Closely associated with Jefferson for a time, he endeavoured to have an anti-slavery clause inserted into the Declaration of Independence, but it was withdrawn after objections by Georgia, South Carolina and various northern slave suppliers. Meanwhile Paine joined the army. By September he was an aide-de-camp to General Nathaniel Greene with the rank of brigade major and accompanied the Continental Army during its retreat to Newark. Here he began to compose the first of his *Crisis* articles, which did much to raise the colonists' flagging spirits in the face of an apparently hopeless plight.

In early 1777 Paine served as part of a delegation to secure neutrality from some Pennsylvania Indians and in April became secretary to the newly created Committee of Foreign Affairs of the Congress. Philadelphia fell to the British in September and Paine again returned to the field, following Washington to Valley Forge and seeing action on several occasions. He was rarely far from political controversy, however. First he defended at length the Pennsylvania constitution framed by Franklin, which was under assault by opponents of popular government. In late 1778 Paine became involved in a major scandal which made him many political adversaries when he denounced an American envoy to France, Silas Deane, for purportedly defrauding Congress by charging for supplies which Paine felt were a gift. Paine inadvertently undermined his own position, however, by indiscreetly disclosing secret information about France's aid to America at a time of its supposed neutrality. The French envoy was compelled to protest and Paine to defend himself. A fierce debate occupied nearly a week of congressional business in early 1779 and one of Paine's enemies, with whom he would have much to do in the future, Gouverneur Morris, even urged his dismissal on the grounds of his humble social origins alone.[9] Congress refused to discharge him, but Paine resigned his post anyway in the belief that his case would not be fairly heard. Refusing a large bribe from the French ambassador, who hoped to gain the services of his pen for France, he instead became a clerk in the offices of a local lawyer, and in September 1779 complained that he could not even afford to hire, much less to buy, his own horse.

To raise funds Paine now proposed to bring out a collected edition of his writings as well as to commence a history of the revolution which, unlike accounts of ancient wars he knew, would provoke 'moral reflection'. Lacking support for such projects, Paine reminded the government of Pennsylvania of its debts to him. Its assembly accordingly elected him Clerk in November 1779, and in his first day of office Paine probably assisted in introducing an anti-slavery act which passed the following March. But his attention remained focused on the war. The Continental Army was again sinking fast in the winter of 1780 and the new republic was in desperate financial straits. Paine began a subscription fund with $500 of his own money and eventually £300,000 was raised. With two new pamphlets in the spring of 1780, Paine also found his popularity returning, and on 4 July 1780 he was granted the degree of Master of Arts by the newly reconstituted University of Pennsylvania. Later that year he proposed that Congress send him on a secret mission to England to further the American cause by appearing to be an Englishman returning from the colonies certain of American victory.

Resolved to write his history, none the less, and still hoping for congressional support, Paine resigned his clerkship to the Pennsylvania Assembly in November 1780. Before he could commence work, however, one Colonel John Laurens, who had been appointed by Congress to sail for France in search of loans, persuaded Paine to accompany him as his secretary. Paine found himself widely known and respected in France, and their mission was highly successful, 6 million livres being secured with Franklin's help. Returning to Boston in late summer, Paine found he would receive no recompense for the expenses of his trip. In the autumn he appealed to Washington to aid his straitened circumstances. The general, basking in his victory over Cornwallis at Yorktown, agreed that Paine's services to the cause had been essential and arranged for $800 annually to be granted him in return for writing on behalf of the nation, particularly in support of higher state contributions to the national government and an extension of the powers of Congress. A similar sum was to be paid him by the Secretary of Foreign Affairs. By late 1783 Paine had also accepted money from France in gratitude for his militantly anti-British attitude, though these were of course causes which he supported himself. In the coming months Paine wrote warning of overconfidence as negotiations continued and he restrained Washington from hanging a British officer in reprisal for the unwarranted British execution of an American officer. He also tried again to persuade some recalcitrant states to fund the army even as its victory seemed certain. But such efforts had little effect beyond making Paine himself seem a mere agent of the Congress.

Soon after this, Paine moved to Bordentown, New Jersey to be near a Quaker friend, Colonel Joseph Kirkbride. Virtually impoverished after sinking his money into a small house, he continued to hope for congressional relief. Washington recommended that Paine be appointed historiographer to the new nation. But Paine's views favouring a strong national sovereignty over the states evidently deflected congressional sympathy for this proposal. In 1784, however, the State of New York granted him a 277-acre farm with a large house at New Rochelle which had been confiscated from an exiled loyalist. The Virginia legislature attempted a similar grant, but it failed to pass. Pennsylvania granted him £500. Finally Congress, trying to avoid resuscitating the Deane affair again, granted him $3,000, reduced from an original proposal of $6,000. This did not cover Paine's expenses in France, but at least he now enjoyed considerable independence.

During the next several years Paine worked on his favourite scientific project, the construction of the first large single-arch iron bridge.[10] The Pennsylvania Assembly expressed interest in the design, but Paine decided first to visit his mother in England, with a stop in France to seek support for his project as well as for the cause of peace with England. At Paris in the summer of 1787 he was widely fêted, and much attention was bestowed upon his bridge model. At Thetford he found his mother in comfort, stayed with her for several months, perhaps attending a local Quaker meeting house, and settling upon her a respectable allowance. While in Britain he also wrote against the prospect of a new war with Holland and continued his scientific explorations, which included plans for a smokeless candle and for using gunpowder as a motor force.

Paine was now a celebrity here, too, and attracted the attention of engineers and inventors, some of whom set up a workshop for him at Rotherham in Yorkshire. In the summer of 1788 he enjoyed the hospitality of his future nemesis, Edmund Burke, for a week at the country seat of the Duke of Portland, as well as the company of other Whig leaders like Charles James Fox. (Burke was pleased to meet 'the great American' and wrote to the elder Pitt that this was perhaps even better than meeting Washington, since Paine was 'more of a philosopher than his chief'.)[11] In England Paine pressed the cause of friendly relations with France, and carried on a lengthy correspondence with Jefferson and others, partly hoping to convince them of his diplomatic importance in Europe.

But Paine was to become neither diplomat nor inventor. The outbreak of revolution in France proved irresistibly attractive, and when he arrived in Paris in the late autumn of 1789 Paine was welcomed as an American hero, his portrait being seen even in country inns, and Lafayette giving him the key to the Bastille for presentation to Washington. Returning to England in early 1790 to complete his bridge, Paine saw his scientific prospects disappear entirely when his partner, an American merchant, went bankrupt shortly after the model was exhibited in London. But politics loomed ever larger anyway and in the summer of 1790 Paine began writing about the new revolution. He was still engaged at the task when Burke published his *Reflections on the Revolution in France* on 1 November. With many others, Paine was taken aback by the ferocity of Burke's assault, which had commenced with a parliamentary speech on 9 February. He had continued to correspond with Burke until early 1790 on the assumption that any friend of the American revolution must welcome the French, and by agreeing not to discuss France they continued to meet socially later in the year.[12] But Paine could hardly ignore the *Reflections*. His famous defence of the revolution, the *Rights of Man*, appeared in early 1791, just as Paine returned to Paris. It was immediately taken up by the Society for Constitutional Information in London, which Paine had recently joined, and quickly helped to inspire other political organizations.

In Paris Paine followed events closely. He was delighted with Robespierre's efforts to abolish the death penalty and did not lament Louis's flight in June, sure that 'the vices of kings' had been the root of France's misfortunes.[13] He was less happy when the king was arrested and to boot was himself nearly lynched by a mob when he accidentally neglected to decorate his hat with the red, white and blue cockade symbolizing liberty and equality. In July he and Condorcet (whose wife helped to translate Paine's works), Brissot and a few others founded the Republican Society, whose manifesto shortly went up on walls throughout Paris at a time when few revolutionaries were republicans. Its appearance caused a considerable outcry. Assailed by conservative royalists, Paine also found the Jacobins unhappy at such competition. But he pressed home his attack none the less, a day later publishing a refutation of Montesquieu's view that republics suited only small territories. In July he returned to London to celebrate the second anniversary of the fall of the Bastille and to publicize the intimate relationship between French liberty and the cause of freedom and justice in Britain. Staying with Rickman, now a bookseller, Paine spent his time in London writing (including an anonymous anti-slavery tract)[14] and visiting acquaintances like Mary Wollstonecraft, William Godwin, John Horne Tooke, Joel Barlow and Joseph Priestley. In London his activities were closely monitored for a time by a disgruntled customs official and friend of Rickman's named Charles Ross who, unable to support his wife and five children on a meagre salary – the parallel with Paine's own early life is ironic – volunteered to spy on Paine (though calling it a 'disagreeable task') in the hopes of a better post in London. With many of his fellow radicals Paine met at the London Tavern on 4 November 1791 with the Revolution Society, whose focus was now more upon 1789 than 1688. It was here that he proposed the memorable toast, 'The Revolution of the World'.[15]

Amidst growing excitement Paine brought out the second part of the *Rights of Man* in February 1792. When its sales soon vastly surpassed the first part, especially amongst the working classes, the government took the offensive. Paine's publisher was given a summons in mid-May and another arrived at Rickman's house on 21 May, closely followed by a royal edict against seditious publications. Paine immediately addressed an open letter to the Attorney General and appeared in court on 8 June, only to have his trial postponed to December.

Meanwhile events were proceeding quickly in France. Though Paine considered going to Dublin in July after he was elected a member of the radical United Irishmen, French citizenship was conferred upon him in late August 1792 for 'having prepared the enfranchisement of peoples'. Two translations of the *Rights of Man* appeared, and Paine was subsequently elected by no less than four *départements* to the Convention which was to replace the National Assembly. Such acclaim was convenient, for Paine's arrest in London was daily threatened. A warrant reached Dover only twenty minutes after his departure for France on 14 September and only Rickman's quick thinking, by emphasizing that letters of Washington's were among Paine's affairs, prevented him from being further delayed in the Customs House.[16] In his *Letter Addressed to the Addressers*, not published until after his escape, Paine now broke openly from his previous strategy as well as his moderate associates, and argued that a British convention should assemble to abolish the monarchy.

Paine would never return to England. Landing at Calais, the first *département* to nominate him and whose deputyship he accepted, he was greeted with a salute from the harbour cannons and a reception at the town hall. The following evening a box at the theatre was decorated with a banner inscribed to 'the Author of the *Rights of Man*'. At Paris in mid-October Paine joined a committee to form a constitution. Opposing Danton, and indeed much of public opinion, he argued against removing qualifications for judges. Paine applauded the abolition of the monarchy a short time later. But he resisted calls for Louis's life, and a month later found himself virtually alone in his defence of the king.[17]

Meanwhile Paine's reputation in England gathered momentum rapidly. Cheap editions of the *Rights of Man* were soon widely available and Paine's trial for having 'wickedly, falsely, maliciously, scandalously, and seditiously' published his work took place in mid-December. Protesting the 'accumulated mischief' arising from the book, the Attorney General duly secured its proscription; Paine would later frequently offer the toast, 'The best way of advertising good books – by prosecution'. His conviction was a foregone conclusion. None the less Paine's lawyer, Erskine, offered a spirited defence of liberty of the press and had his carriage drawn through the streets by Paine's supporters, though his own advocacy of the cause was motivated as much by ambition as principle.[18]

Now outlawed in England, Paine's defence of Louis in face of fierce opposition made life difficult in Paris. Marat tried to disqualify him from voting on the king's death because of his supposed Quakerism. Paine did agree that the king should be tried, though arguing against his own friends the Girondins that this should be by the Convention rather than direct appeal to the people. But he urged both humanity and prudence: America was now France's sole ally and regarded Louis highly. His execution would only be grist to the mill of counter-revolution. Banishment was preferable, and Paine suggested that the United States might accept Louis.

But the Mountain, the more extreme Jacobins dominated by Robespierre, prevailed, and Louis was guillotined. The Girondins, who represented a more provincial, conservative, federal viewpoint, had failed, but none the less temporarily remained more influential. After war broke out between Britain and France in early 1793, Paine lent his assistance to the Irish revolutionaries gathered in Paris and intrigued with them about the prospects of a French invasion of Ireland. One of their leaders, Lord Edward Fitzgerald, wrote to his mother of Paine: 'I cannot express how kind he is to me; there is a simplicity of manner, a goodness of heart, and a strength of mind in him I never knew a man before possess.' And Paine was generous also to his enemies, even saving the life of a hot-blooded young British captain who assaulted him at a dinner party without knowing that the death penalty had been imposed recently for attacking deputies. Paine's house was frequently host to large numbers of democratic exiles. No doubt, too, he enjoyed life, though there is probably no substance to the report that he had been caught by a fellow deputy 'in the very act of measuring his wife ... *for a pair of stays*' while singing 'ça ira, ça ira, ça ira'.[19] Paine's friends, however, began to lose the upper hand. Amongst the casualties of the assault upon the Girondins which began in April 1793 was the constitution at which Paine, Condorcet and others had long laboured. Its adoption was delayed for several months and, after being accepted in late June, its implementation was quickly suspended. At the same time Marat and Robespierre moved quickly to eliminate their opponents.

Marat in particular saw Paine as threatening the revolutionary dictatorship the Jacobins were anxious to introduce, since he had already condemned the American presidency as concentrating too much power in one individual. Marat suspected Paine's loyalty for other reasons, too. Paine knew some people, like Gouverneur Morris, who thought little of the revolution. He had defended the Spanish-American General Miranda against Jacobin charges of treachery and knew General Dumouriez, who had been accused of seeking a constitutional monarchy and had then defected to the enemy in April 1793. He was friendly with others, like Condorcet, who were themselves increasingly isolated. Marat's opportunity to damage Paine arose in April 1793 when, apparently after hearing rumours of Marat's desire to see his idol executed, a young English devotee of Paine's named Johnson attempted suicide in Paris, leaving a note, which Paine published, accusing Marat of 'assassinating' the cause of liberty. At this time Marat was himself on trial for threatening a dictatorial coup against the Convention. Cleverly exploiting this opportunity, he shifted the focus of the trial to the question of whether his writings had incited Johnson's action and emerged victorious by proving that Johnson was imbalanced. He then accused Johnson of in fact seeking to denounce Paine. The latter survived the charge, but by publicizing Johnson's actions he accidentally paved the way for the Girondins' downfall as well as his own later arrest.

Paine now worried seriously about the course of the revolution, not, as he wrote to Danton in early May, because of France's enemies, but rather 'the tumultuous misconduct with which the internal affairs of the present revolution are conducted'.[20] Warning that too little attention was being paid to moral principles, and that the widespread tendency

29

to denounce political enemies as traitors would undermine public authority, Paine insisted that only establishing a constitution would secure the accomplishments of the revolution. In early June the Convention moved against the Girondins. Paine's position initially remained secure, however, and he was exempted from a law permitting the arrest of foreigners, since both he and the Prussian Anacharsis Clootz were delegates. Condorcet, Brissot and others fled, leaving Paine to represent their views in the Convention. His French, however, was too poor for the cut and thrust of debate and others were now reluctant to translate for him. Even Paine's pen was withdrawn from service, no printer being willing to take his work. But he continued to seek American support for France and helped secure much needed shipments of grain and rice.

Abandoned and depressed, Paine began to drink to console his fears and disappointments, though far less than his later detractors claimed. He found some solace in the company of other exiled radicals like Mary Wollstonecraft, Joel Barlow and Thomas Christie, who often met at Paine's lodgings, three rooms in the rue Faubourg Saint-Denis adjacent to an acre garden of fruit trees, where they played chess and card games, talked politics and offered one another moral and intellectual support.

In mid-July Charlotte Corday assassinated Marat, which raised some hope that the imprisoned and exiled Girondins might be reinstated. Instead Robespierre's rise to power not only doomed many of his erstwhile Convention associates, but nearly resulted in Paine's execution as well. Robespierre had hitherto been friendly with Paine, protecting him from attacks by others and conferring with him occasionally. In August, however, he instigated an address to the Convention from Arras stating that confidence in Paine's abilities was wanting. Paine himself could not understand Robespierre's antagonism and only several years later discovered that Gouverneur Morris, now American ambassador to France and an anti-republican in Washington's cabinet, had accused him of opposing American interests.[21] Since the United States was France's sole ally, such charges were very damaging. Moreover, Morris also suggested that Paine was English rather than American and hence no longer neutral. It was this act, by a fellow American, which would nearly cost Paine his life. In early October he was denounced in the Convention for associating with the imprisoned Girondins, who were executed a month later, and for attempting to defend Louis. Several friends living at Paine's house now fled abroad, warrants for their arrests following a few days later. Watching his own fate unfold, and not knowing whether his own life would be spared, Paine laboured feverishly over his vindication of pure religion, *The Age of Reason*, the first part of which was completed barely hours before his arrest.

Once Paine had been categorized as an Englishman by the Committee of General Security, he was clearly doomed. Two days after Christmas 1793, at three in the morning, he was seized with his landlord and confined in the Luxembourg prison, a former palace which now held British prisoners and some French aristocrats. Though Joel Barlow and others immediately petitioned for his release and offered to take him to America, Paine was to remain in prison for nearly a year, with the Convention blandly justifying itself by arguing that while Paine had been 'the apostle of liberty', none the less 'his genius has not understood that which has regenerated France; he has regarded the system only in accordance with the illusions with which the false friends of our revolution have invested it' (meaning the Girondins), which contradicted 'the principles admired in the justly esteemed works of this republican author'.[22]

Paine was none the less still of value to the Convention. Further action against him was evidently delayed by Robespierre to allow Paine to enlist more sympathy for the French cause from Washington. Morris not only lent Paine no assistance, but may even have conspired to suspend his right of correspondence. Moreover, Morris told Jefferson that Paine was acknowledged as an American in Paris, which hindered further action on his behalf in the United States. In all this Morris colluded with his own agent in the French government, as Moncure Conway discovered in the late nineteenth century, though the Foreign Minister who conspired with him, Deforgues, soon lost his own head after a brief stay in the Luxembourg.[23]

One evening it seemed Paine's own end had also finally come. It was the height of Robespierre's Terror, and some 160 prisoners were due to be executed the following day. The cell doors of the condemned were first indicated with a chalk cross mark. But Paine's door happened to be open when this was applied, 'if happening is the proper word', he later recalled, preferring to assume providential intervention. Consequently the cross was on the inside when the gaolers came, and his life was spared.[24]

The fall of Robespierre paved the way for Paine's release. Fortunately Morris had been succeeded by James Monroe in the summer of 1794. Paine managed to get a letter to him and Monroe agreed that he was an American citizen, assuring him of Washington's continuing friendship as well as that of the American people. None the less Morris had not yet left Paris and Monroe's response took a month to reach Paine, by which time the former minister had safely reached Switzerland. He later argued for the restoration of monarchy in France.

On 4 November 1794, his American citizenship acknowledged, Paine was released. The Convention restored him to its ranks, while a governmental committee proposed to grant him a pension for his literary efforts on behalf of the revolution. Paine refused, deciding instead to return to America to recover from the illnesses he had suffered in prison. Monroe suggested that the Convention send Paine home bearing the treaty of friendship just signed between the two nations. Paine was thankful for such official attention at last, though he was very reproachful towards Washington, even terming him 'treacherous' for having ignored his plight. But the Convention then refused Paine, as one of its members, a passport, arguing curiously that France required his services. Meanwhile the reintroduction of the constitution Paine, Condorcet and others had designed in 1793 was being proposed and Paine wrote his *Dissertation on First Principles of Government* to argue against reviving the monarchy, any property qualification on the suffrage, and an overly powerful central executive where the constitution did not restrain partisan enthusiasm.

After his release Paine returned to the Convention only once, in July 1795. He was weak and a secretary read his speech in French, but Paine's attack on the attempt to restrict citizenship to direct taxpayers and war veterans, or only half the existing population, was vigorous none the less, though it met with 'cold indifference' from the assembly. With the dissolution of the Convention and creation of the Directory in October 1795, his role in the revolution seemingly came to an end. His health threatened to fail him completely in the autumn, when Paine put the finishing touches to part two of *The Age of Reason*. Still angered by America's role in his imprisonment, too, Paine also wrote a strongly worded *Letter to George Washington* in early 1796 attacking the President's competence as both general and politician and insinuating that his proposed commercial treaty with Britain would undermine American independence. This was a sad ending to twenty years' of political association and warm friendship and it cost Paine many friends in America, for Washington was widely respected.[25] None the less Paine continued to aid Franco-American relations at a critical point in their history, for with the passage of Jay's Treaty between Britain and the United States in 1794, important trading rights were extended to Britain, and her differences with America seemed largely reconciled. The French were horrified at what seemed an outright insult given their assistance during the American revolution, if not an abrogation of American neutrality. Paine, however, assailed the British government as if American policy had remained unchanged, and drew up plans for reinforcing commerce with France. Monroe was particularly appreciative of Paine's support of America's reputation.

For some months Paine lived at Monroe's house in Paris, slowly recovering his health but depressed both by the course of the revolution and British criticisms of *The Age of Reason*. In early 1796 he moved to the countryside near Versailles as the guest of a wealthy but radical Paris banker, Sir Robert Smith, whose wife he had befriended (they wrote innocent poems to one another). In April he completed *The Decline and Fall of the English System of Finance*, which predicted the collapse of the funding system under the stress of war and domestic oppression. It met with considerable acclaim in France and Britain, and was soon widely translated. Characteristically, Paine donated the proceeds to relieving debtors imprisoned in Newgate, London.[26]

In 1796, in an effort to combat the danger of atheism he perceived around him, Paine founded the small sect of Theophilanthropists. In an important tract published in England the following year, *Agrarian Justice*, he further refined his views on property and poverty. But he was still anxious to return to America. Monroe was recalled in August 1796, possibly in part because Paine had stayed with him while continuing to write – despite Monroe's remonstrances – against Washington and American policies. Paine travelled with him to Le Havre on his departure, but was deterred from embarking by the presence of so many British warships on the open sea (spies were everywhere: Monroe's ship was in fact stopped and Paine carefully searched for). But Paine's role in France was not yet played out. Returning to Paris, he announced that the war could be successfully ended only if France invaded England, sent George packing to Hanover and established a republic. These sentiments reached important ears and Paine was invited to dinner with Napoleon, who flattered him that he slept with the *Rights of Man* under his pillow, said that every city should have a golden statue of its author erected and consulted Paine on a possible invasion of England. Paine later claimed that he would have accompanied Bonaparte in order 'to give the people of England an opportunity of forming a government for themselves, and thereby bring about peace', and worked for some time on the project, even subscribing 100 livres of his own money. But after Napoleon had built some 250 of a planned 1,000 boats the expedition was abandoned, and Paine later became hostile to Bonaparte, terming him overly bloodthirsty and 'the completest charlatan that ever existed'.[27]

Now residing with Nicolas de Bonneville, the printer of the French edition of *The Age of Reason*, Paine received large numbers of visitors, amongst whom was the inventor Robert Fulton, who later credited him with having been amongst the first to propose steam-powered navigation. Paine's repose was not long-lived, however. Napoleon's *coup d'état* of November 1799 was roundly criticized by Bonneville, who was immediately imprisoned, though Paine himself seems to have preferred Napoleon to the prospect of the return of the monarchy. Bonneville was released, though reduced to severe financial straits, and Paine remained with him, now writing on the necessity for peaceful commercial relations on the high seas. But when his relations with Bonneville incurred further official suspicion he again considered returning to America.

There were further setbacks before Paine's long exile in France came at last to an end, however. Having prospered for a time, the cause of Theophilanthropy met an unsavoury end after Napoleon's concordat with the Vatican in July 1801. In his efforts to expunge republicanism, moreover, the French leader even had Paine's works taken out of the Bibliothèque Nationale. In March, Jefferson, now Vice-President, wrote Paine that an American vessel was available if he required passage to the US. But this invitation was leaked to the American newspapers, and Jefferson was accused by the Federalists of offering to send the ship for the sole purpose of fetching Paine, who thereupon delayed his return once again.

In mid-1802 Paine finally bid farewell to 'restless and wretched Europe'. He was deeply unhappy with the course the revolution had taken, though insisting that its fate had much to do with 'the provocative interference of foreign powers'. He lamented to one of his last visitors, an English radical named Henry Redhead Yorke, 'Republic! do you call this a republic? Why they are worse off than the slaves of Constantinople; for there, they expect to be bashaws in heaven by submitting to be slaves below, but here they believe neither in heaven nor hell, and yet are slaves by choice. I know of no republic in the world except America ... I have done with Europe, and its slavish politics.'[28] He was also extremely unhappy that *The Age of Reason* had proved so unpopular in England. His advice and good intentions seemed everywhere to have been misunderstood, or defied by powers greater than himself. Only in America, with the election of Jefferson in 1800, did the forward march of political progress seem secure.

Paine set sail from Le Havre on 1 September 1802, with Rickman coming from London during the brief Peace of Amiens to see him off. Reaching Baltimore on 1 November, aged 65, he was delighted to find that friends had maintained his property. When invested, the £6,000 it was now worth brought him a sum sufficient to live on. He had been unable to save any money in France, having refused an offer of £3,000 for his two bridge models and given away the proceeds of almost all his writings. But this was to be the best news to await Paine. He expected that at least in republican America, where Jefferson and others had declared his principles to be virtually identical to those of the nation, public approbation for his exertions in Europe and a warm welcome might greet him. But again he was to be sorely disappointed.

Theology was the chief cause of this misfortune. Though deist republicans applauded his return, Paine now found himself not only a pawn in American partisan struggles, but prey, in what Rickman called 'a country abounding in fanatics', to religious enthusiasts of all types. Thousands of republicans turned their backs on him, while his political opponents gleefully seized upon his religious views, with

John Adams's Federalists in particular using Jefferson's friendship with the author of the notorious *Age of Reason* as an excellent pretext for assailing both. Jefferson anxiously avoided religious controversy, even refusing to allow his private letters on the subject to be printed, and consequently was reluctant to meet Paine, though finally inviting him for a visit. But Paine was now everywhere else on the defensive, his political ideals seemingly neglected, the theology he had articulated only as a means of shoring up these ideals condemned. In some places he was jeered by pious mobs egged on by Federalists. At least once he was refused a place on a stagecoach. He was pestered in his private life. One day, during his nap, an elderly woman intruded upon him to warn that Almighty God had sent her to warn him to repent or be damned, to which Paine – his usual sympathy for women deserting him – replied that she obviously could not have been sent 'with any such impertinent message ... He would not send such a foolish, ugly old woman about with His messages.' Someone even shot at his house.[29]

Paine none the less was not to be intimidated and wrote a series of eight public letters defending his views and continuing to support prominent deists like Elihu Palmer. He also vindicated Jefferson on several occasions, particularly where his relations with Paine were concerned. He applauded the purchase of Louisiana and suggested to Jefferson the best means of amalgamating it into the union, later lambasting the Federalists for first urging its seizure by force, then denying its importance after Jefferson's proposed acquisition. He further tried to persuade Congress not to retain slavery there and urged Jefferson to reconsider his views when the United States refused entry to slaves fleeing Santo Domingo in case they incited slave uprisings in America too. Paine's main interest, however, was again building his bridge, and he exerted considerable effort in showing his models to all who were interested. He also planned to reprint his existing works and manuscripts.[30]

Disappointed that no official post was given to him, Paine left Washington in early 1803 and settled in the country near New Rochelle, New York. Besides some 240 acres, his farm consisted of two oxen, a horse, a cow and ten pigs. Here he lived a plain but wholesome life, content to call himself the possessor of six chairs and a table, a straw bed, a feather bed, a tea kettle, an iron pot, a baking and frying pan and a few other implements. His diet was composed primarily of tea, milk, fruit pies, dumplings and an occasional piece of meat. At New Rochelle he continued to receive visitors, and observers noted his kindness to children and animals, his clean appearance and his moderate drinking, if liberality with the snuffbox. But he had not yet retired. In 1803–4 he assisted the Connecticut republicans' effort to secure a constitution to replace the state's royal charter.[31] In 1805 he again defended Jefferson against the Federalist press and involved himself in a debate originating in the New York State legislature on the issuing of charters and, on another concerning Pennsylvania, on several constitutional issues.[32] He also wrote on subjects as diverse as yellow fever, gunboat-building and the origins of Freemasonry.

By 1806 Paine was in financial straits again. For several years he had supported the family of his last French hosts, the Bonnevilles, until this burden forced him to sell his Bordentown property. Though his health troubled him again, Paine was still restless and asked Jefferson if some post could be found for him in Europe if war ended between Britain and France. The poor hospitality America had offered him was now compounded when his right to vote was denied by a few Tories in New Rochelle in 1806, on the grounds that Gouverneur Morris had not recognized him as an American and Washington had not aided him.[33]

In 1807 Paine's powers began to ebb. He continued to ply Jefferson with suggestions and urged mediation between England and France in the interests of peace. In late 1808 he became friendly with a Quaker preacher and watchmaker named Willett Hicks. Early the next year he moved to the house of a niece of Elihu Palmer's and her husband, but here he began to fade rapidly. Even in his last days, however, Paine retained a sense of humour in the face of his opponents. On one occasion an American minister insisted he had recovered the true key to the Scriptures after it had been lost for 4,000 years, and Paine replied only that it must have been very rusty after so long. Nor is there evidence of any death-bed recantation of his religious beliefs, though his enemies whispered that deists plied him with alcohol to stave off a reversion to orthodoxy. Shortly before he died early in the morning of 8 June 1809, two clergymen found a means of entering his room in the hopes of restoring him to the true faith. Paine said only, 'Let me alone; good morning.' His enemies were again disappointed.

Even in death Paine remained a controversial figure. His funeral procession was described as composed of Negroes, drunken Irishmen and an Irish Quaker; in fact two blacks did travel twenty-five miles on foot to offer respects to one who had so often pleaded their cause, while the Quaker was Willett Hicks. To their discredit, however, the local Quakers refused Paine's request to be buried in their cemetery and he was accordingly interred in an orchard on his farm. Ten years later, the English radical William Cobbett reclaimed Paine's bones for England, evidently in the hope of using them as relics to garner support for the reformers' cause. But after he died, Paine's remains disappeared, and no trace of them now exists.[34] No grand tomb will thus ever commemorate Paine's final resting place. But as Andrew

Jackson once remarked, he needed 'no monument built by hands; he has erected a monument in the hearts of all lovers of liberty'. Why his principles came to be so loved, but also so hated, we must now consider.

Notes to Chapter 1: The life of Thomas Paine

1 E.g. H. Mackenzie (1793), J. Gifford (1792).
2 A good review of Paine's early biographers is G. Vale (1841), pp. 4–15. The best modern biography is A. Aldridge (1960), a Basic English version of which has appeared in French, Arabic, Bengali and Urdu. The most detailed early study is M. Conway (1892), though T. Rickman (1908) is valuable for the insights gleaned from personal friendship with Paine. Also helpful are W. Sherwin (1819) and R. Carlile (1819). This chapter is much indebted in particular to the former two of these works. Useful recent treatments include A. Williamson (1973) and D. Powell (1985).
3 Paine (1945), Vol. 1, pp. 496–7. All further references to Paine's writings will be to this nearly complete, standard edition. For works not included in it, see below, n. 14 and p. 61, n. 26. A more accessible collection of Paine's major writings is Paine (1987).
4 See Paine (1945), Vol. 1, p. 405, and A. Barry (1977).
5 T. Rickman (1908), p. 17; *Public Advertiser*, no. 197 (22 August 1808), p. 2; G. Vale (1841), p. 26; Paine (1945), Vol. 2, pp. 3–15, here p. 9. On Paine's charitable activities see A. Williamson (1973), p. 37.
6 Philip Foner claimed that a 1775 essay for a Pennsylvania magazine entitled 'Reflections on unhappy marriages' was Paine's, in which case it was doubtless partly autobiographical (Paine, 1945, Vol. 2, pp. 1,118–20). This ascription, however, is denied by A. Aldridge (1984), p. 287.
7 Paine (1945), Vol. 2, pp. 1130, 16–40, 52–60.
8 Paine (1945), Vol. 2, pp. 182–3.
9 See Paine (1945), Vol. 2, pp. 96–188.
10 For details of Paine's bridge project see W. Armytage (1951).
11 E. Burke (1978), Vol. 5, p. 412; Paine (1908), Vol. 1, p. 329.
12 J. Alger (1889), p. 85; E. Burke (1978), Vol. 6, pp. 67–76.
13 See Paine (1945), Vol. 2, pp. 517–19.
14 Internal evidence suggests that the early nineteenth-century attribution to Paine of *Old Truths and Established Facts* (1792) was probably accurate, though it has not been discussed in any subsequent study of Paine. The 13-page pamphlet repeats Paine's earlier view that Parliament acted contrary to 'all natural rights' (p. 5) in permitting the slave trade and refers to natural law arguments about legitimate and illegitimate enslavement (p. 9).
15 TS11/965/3510A. On the British colony in Paris see D. Erdman (1986), especially pp. 223-43. On Barlow's relations with Paine see J. Woodress (1958), especially pp. 129–41.
16 TS 11/965/3510A. See Paine (1945), Vol. 2, pp. 466–9 for Paine's account of his escape.
17 See Paine (1945), Vol. 2, pp. 551–60.
18 *Trial of Thomas Paine* (1792). A full account of Paine's trial is also in T. Howell (1817), Vol. 22, cols 357–471.

19 M. Conway (1892), Vol. 1, p. 358; Add. MS. 16924 f. 35. On Paine and French politics see Z. Libiszowska (1980).
20 Paine (1945), Vol. 2, p. 1335.
21 Morris also sided privately with Britain against France and was linked to various intrigues to secure Louis's escape. See Morris (1939) for his own account of the revolution.
22 M. Conway (1892), Vol. 2, p. 110.
23 M. Conway (1892), Vol. 2, p. 121. Less convincing is A. Aldridge (1960), p. 212.
24 Paine (1945), Vol. 2, p. 921.
25 Paine (1945), Vol. 2, pp. 691–723. For hostile responses to Paine see *A Letter to Thomas Paine* (1797), [W. Cobbett] (1797), P. Kennedy (1798).
26 Responses to the *Decline and Fall* include S. Pope (1796), who thought it largely repeated Price's objections to the funding system.
27 H. Yorke (1804), Vol. 2, pp. 368–9; Paine (1945), Vol. 2, pp. 680, 1415–16; M. Elliott (1982), pp. 59–61. See Paine (1945), Vol. 2, pp. 675–83 and A. Aldridge (1957) for details.
28 Paine (1945), Vol. 2, p. 683; H. Yorke (1804), Vol. 2, p. 342; M. Elliott (1982), p. 279.
29 T. Rickman (1908), pp. 4, 74. On Paine's reception see J. Knudson (1969).
30 Paine's writings from this period are not all included in Paine (1945). For some omissions see A. Aldridge (1953).
31 See R. Gimbel (1956b) for details.
32 For Paine's anti-Federalist writings see especially (1945), Vol. 2, pp. 1,007–10.
33 Paine (1945), Vol. 2, pp. 1487–8. Cheetham later asserted that Mme Bonneville had been Paine's mistress, but lost the case when she sued him for libel. None the less the judge commended Cheetham's 'useful' biography for helping to curtail Paine's influence (Vale, 1841, p. 153).
34 Paine's bones were last seen in the possession of one B. Tilly, of 13 Bedford Square East, in March 1844 (W. Cobbett, 1847, p. 5). Mysteriously, Romney's famous portrait of Paine also disappeared at some point.

2

'The cause of all mankind': Paine and the American revolution

Colonial radicalism, 1765–76

Common Sense exploded amidst an already volatile debate about colonial rights, imperial arbitrariness, and the possibility of resistance to British rule. American resentment had been instigated primarily by the passage of stamp duties on legal and other documents in 1765, which brought rioting and boycotts of British goods. In the late 1760s protest escalated in reaction to attempts to curtail the powers of colonial assemblies and to increase colonial revenues. The Wilkes case, as we have seen, fuelled unrest. British policy towards Ireland and India also seemed to some to betray the designs of ministerial tyranny. The failure of petitioning increased disappointments and eroded affections. More widely discussed as early as 1770–1 was armed resistance, and the view that colonial government was dissolving and might better be replaced by native rule. Independence was broached, though not widely supported, by 1772, the Dutch model being occasionally suggested. By 1774 the monarch, but a few years earlier the focus of hopes for respite from ministerial intrigue, had himself become a potent symbol of despotism. At Lexington and Concord in mid-1775 revolt finally became war.[1]

Until 1776, however, the colonists' unease produced little support for independence or strong opposition to monarchy among most colonists. As Gordon Wood has emphasized, most Americans believed the mixed British constitution to be the best possible and happily subscribed to the loyalism of John Dickinson's popular *Letters from a Farmer in Pennsylvania* (1768). In this sense the majority were still British and did not yet identify, as Pauline Maier has stressed, with a self-consciously *American* collective entity. Paine himself claimed in early 1775 that 'equality of liberty is the glory of every Briton. He

39

does not forfeit it by crossing the ocean ... A Briton or American ceases to be a British subject when he ceases to be governed by rulers chosen or approved of by himself. This is the essence of liberty and of the British constitution.'[2] But it was the interpretation of precisely what rights this constitution permitted, how far they were 'natural' or bound to precedent, and how far they were owed to all classes, which was to be crucial to the revolutionary debate.

As we have seen, these were also the central issues of eighteenth-century radical Whiggism. The colonists' cause was portrayed primarily in terms of a country or Commonwealthman language of resistance to executive tyranny. British excesses, such as the Stamp Act, were construed as the arbitrary acts of a government whose patronage and corruption demanded further taxation from a population denied the right of representation in Parliament. American liberties were infringed upon both because Parliament was unrepresentative and because colonial policy was dictated more by the monarchy than the Commons.

In the middle and late 1770s, however, this Whiggish protest against tyranny was transformed completely. At independence many colonists – among them Paine – felt that they had inaugurated if not the millennium, then at least a brilliantly innovative polity which offered new hope for other nations. This belief dawned only gradually, however. And even by early 1776, most Americans sought only to reinstate an uncorrupted version of the British constitution. But the sense of uniqueness, and of the creation of a new science of politics, was already afoot. This Paine would contribute to more than virtually any other colonist.[3]

What was distinctive about the new nation was first its republican form. The very strength of the British constitution, Montesquieu, de Lolme and others had insisted, lay in the balance between its three components and the separation of their powers.[4] Republicanism implied not only the absolute predominance of the popular branch of government, but also considerable social equality, a more fervent and widespread devotion to the public good and the willingness to sacrifice private advantage for it, and a reciprocal dedication by the government to public welfare. Policy could reflect only the general will and common good, not that of parties, classes or individuals. The consent of citizens, moreover, was now required to be granted much more frequently, as well as more directly, than earlier Whigs had sought. The first step towards creating this form of republicanism was the argument that parliamentary sovereignty in the colonies had evaporated and that power instead should be wielded wholly in the colonial assemblies, which could more directly represent the colonists' interests and express their active consent to legislation.[5]

The second component in the new idea of government was that this sovereignty was to be asserted by assembling representatives in a constitutional convention rather than through the colonial legislatures. By this means the people would create all parts of government rather than exercising their authority only in the legislature. This view became popular only slowly during the revolutionary period, however. In 1776 most Americans believed only that their colonial assemblies possessed the right to alter fundamental laws, not that they themselves should play an active role in so doing. The 1780 Massachusetts constitution was the first framed by a convention, while that in New Hampshire in 1784 was the first requiring further popular ratification. Gradually, through the 1780s, the states thus conceived that such laws were so much more elemental than ordinary legislation that they required the consent of the people at large outside of their legislative organs. This, as Gordon Wood has emphasized, was 'such a radical innovation in politics that the concept of fundamental law by itself hardly explains it'. 'Conventions' had existed previously in Britain as irregular forms of representation, but without challenging the status and rights of Parliament itself. By the early 1770s, however, the formation of increasingly regular extra-legislative bodies had legitimated the idea that a convention could supplant regular assemblies corrupted by arbitrary power. In 1774–5, and especially after Pennsylvania's moves in 1776, the idea was put widely into practice. When Paine took the idea up in 1776, therefore, his ground was well prepared. Thereafter representative democracy capable of embracing a large territory and based upon the new mechanisms of consent rather than either simple, direct democracy or any form of mixed government came gradually, and especially after the 1780s, to be seen as the great American achievement.[6]

Thirdly, the revolution was correspondingly widely understood to imply a moral reformation whereby the public virtue upon which republics rested was re-created and more widely shared than previously thought possible. Not merely political corruption, moreover, but private moral degeneracy through greed or a senseless immersion in luxury had to be rejected in favour of greater simplicity, self-sufficiency, honesty and moral rigour.[7] These qualities, it was widely recognized, already existed, or at least could be cultivated considerably more easily, in a young agricultural republic than a nation divided by great class distinctions and habits of commercial luxury. American corruptions could be identified with British rule, or with monarchy and aristocracy. Banishing these collectively would leave the nation in a state of pristine moral and political virtue.

Independence sounded: *Common Sense* (1776)

One of the most important contributions to the new political ideal was *Common Sense*, which appeared anonymously in Philadelphia on 10 January 1776. It was immediately perceived as being essentially practical, for it was fortuitously published the same day as reports of George III's hostile speech opening the new session of parliament. The pamphlet owed something to local conditions. Popular demand for greater equality was more widespread in Pennsylvania and consequently here more than elsewhere the revolution was viewed as a struggle between the people (chiefly western settlers and the labouring classes of Philadelphia, the colonies' largest city) and an entrenched Quaker and Presbyterian oligarchy which opposed independence. Paine himself had not favoured independence on arriving in America in late 1774 and recalled that it was then generally regarded as 'a kind of treason' to renounce attachment to Britain. The immediate pretext for declaring independence for Paine was the Battle of Lexington, which took place on 19 April 1775, and which he felt finally proved that the compact between the colonists and Britain had been broken. Moreover, 'during the suspension of the old governments in America, both prior to and at the breaking out of hostilities,' Paine later wrote, 'I was struck with the order and decorum with which everything was conducted, and impressed with the idea, that a little more than what society naturally performed, was all the government that was necessary, and that monarchy and aristocracy were frauds and impositions upon mankind.' This led him to an appreciation of the possibility of independence as well as the wider liberty promised by a new form of government.[8]

After a brief introduction trumpeting the American struggle as 'in great measure the cause of all mankind', *Common Sense* opened by considering the 'Origin and Design of Government in General, With Concise Remarks on the English Constitution'. Government had to be considered as separate from society, Paine began. Society was 'produced by our wants and government by our wickedness; the former promotes our happiness *positively* by uniting our affections, the latter *negatively* by restraining our vices'. Government therefore was merely a 'necessary evil', a 'badge of lost innocence' symbolizing the loss of primitive 'natural liberty'. None the less, since not all heeded the dictates of conscience, government was required to provide order and security. Initially all had legislated and, while representation was later necessary, the *'strength of government, and the happiness of the governed'* always depended upon the common interest of both representatives and represented.[9]

Moving to consider 'the so much boasted Constitution of England', Paine argued that this consisted of three segments, 'the remains of monarchical tyranny in the person of the king', 'the remains of aristocratical tyranny in the persons of the peers' and 'the new Republican materials, in the persons of the Commons'. The freedom of England, Paine insisted, depended solely on the virtue of the latter, for 'in a constitutional sense' neither king nor peers were dedicated to freedom. Denying the central Whig contention that each part balanced the others, Paine argued that the Commons did not, for example, check the king, since this presumed that they were wiser than the monarch and ignored the fact that the king could obstruct bills of the Commons. But the monarchy itself, in any case, was an 'exceedingly ridiculous' institution. Kings were totally ignorant of the world they supposedly governed. Moreover, how could a wise people ever have given a king such powers, while always mistrusting their exercise? In fact the strongest or 'overbearing' part of the constitution simply dominated and at present this was the monarchy. If the king was less oppressive in England than elsewhere, this was only because of the power of parliament, not the system of government itself.[10]

Paine's second section, 'Of Monarchy and Hereditary Succession', pursued this attack by examining the origins of kingship. Created equal, mankind at first had no kings and thus no wars, for it was 'the pride of kings which throws mankind into confusion'. Kingship had originated with 'the heathens', from which it was copied by the Jews, who had survived for some 3,000 years (on the Mosaic account) as 'a kind of Republic'. Quoting at length from the biblical book of Samuel, Paine argued that even God himself had vainly opposed the Jewish request for a king. Eventually the office became hereditary, but for Paine – and this was a vital part of his argument – this was intrinsically unjust, for 'no one by birth could have a right to set up his own family in perpetual preference to all others for ever'. Many kings had originally been mere robbers who imposed their rule by force. Thus had William the Conqueror ascended to the English throne, and consequently 'the antiquity of English monarchy' would 'not bear looking into'. Once they had inherited their positions, moreover, monarchs grew insolent and oblivious to the needs of their subjects. Some perched precariously upon the throne as children; others steadied themselves upon it well into infirmity. Succession crises often provoked bloody civil wars. All that was valuable in the English constitution hence derived from the right of electing the Commons, and even here the king had frequently interfered. The sole duties of the king, in fact, seemed to be waging war and bestowing patronage. With piercing condemnation Paine insisted that one honest man was worth more to society 'than all the crowned ruffians that ever lived'.[11]

Turning to the relations between the American colonies and England, Paine declared the debate over, with only 'arms as the last resource' to 'decide the contest'. The choice lay with the king, but the colonists had accepted the challenge, and therein began 'a new era for politics ... a new method of thinking'. Previously all parties had agreed upon remaining united with Britain, disputing only the means of so doing. But the possibility of reconciliation had now disappeared. It was no longer necessary to stress the natural ties between the colonies and Britain. Britain's enemies, like France and Spain, would befriend America, who was linked to all Europe by emigration, not only to England. American commerce could survive without British 'protection', and indeed would thrive as long as 'eating is the custom of Europe'. Since, as Paine put it, 'our plan is commerce', Britain's opposition to many continental powers in fact diminished American trade and thus its prosperity. "TIS TIME TO PART' was the only conclusion which could be drawn.[12]

Contrary arguments Paine quickly dismissed. Those who opposed independence were untrustworthy, prejudiced, weak and unduly optimistic about European rule. The British had now carried fire and sword to American towns and cities and had severed the loyalties of large numbers of inhabitants. But British strength was also overestimated. Britain no more had the power to conquer the continent than to govern it correctly. It had also shown no tendency to compromise and, even if reconciliation occurred, the king would still be capable of vetoing any colonial legislation, and of exercising his power as arbitrarily. This would discourage emigration and growth and merely provoke further revolt. Only an American and republican government would protect its citizens in peace.[13]

The only grounds to fear independence, then, lay in the colonists' insufficient preparations for liberty. Paine therefore proposed that each colony annually elect an assembly headed by a president and concerned only with domestic policy. These assemblies would be answerable to a Continental Congress composed of at least thirty delegates from each colony, from amongst whom a President would be chosen. To found this government, a 'continental conference' of twenty-six members of Congress plus two members from each provincial convention and five other representatives at large was to be elected. These would frame a 'Continental Charter' establishing the number and authority of the members of congress and assembly and guaranteeing freedom of religion and property, and thereafter dissolve itself.[14]

Paine then turned to consider other implications of independence. For the price of a small but not inconvenient national debt America could build a navy sufficient for its protection. Its need for defence in turn demanded speedy independence, for the growth of commerce diminished 'the spirit both of patriotism and military defense', and indeed had already sapped Britain's strength. Fifty years hence the increase of trade and population would generate many contending interests which did not yet exist. *Common Sense* then concluded with a plea for religious toleration and a summary of some of the main grounds for immediate independence.[15]

Interpreting *Common Sense*

How original was Paine's contribution to the revolutionary debate? Bernard Bailyn has argued convincingly that Paine was most provocative in his rejection of the notion of constitutional balance as a basis of liberty. This broke most sharply from the ideals of 1688 and from Whig republicanism and clearly defined a new *democratic* republicanism.[16] Paine still spoke a republican language of virtue, corruption and decline. But while he understood corruption in much the same way as earlier Whigs, for example, as executive tyranny, his remedy was a representative, democratic rather than mixed republic. Here his argument that hereditary monarchy was wrong because it bound posterity to rule by one family, which considerably extended Locke's notion of consent, was of immense importance.

Defining more precisely this novel form of republicanism is of considerable importance to any classification of early American political thought. The concept of 'modernization' (conceived neutrally) has frequently been applied to American political thinking in this period in an effort to define the novel mental world of the revolution.[17] Jack Greene, for example, argues that the 'modernization of political consciousness' involved 'a wholly new political mentality' which was

> not only receptive but eager for change, oriented toward the present and future rather than toward the past, confident of the efficacy of human reason to shape that present and future, and committed to the revolutionary beliefs that criteria for membership in the political nation should be universalistic rather than prescriptive, and that social and political advancement should be based on achievement rather than ascription.

In Greene's view Paine played 'a central role in the initial phases of this transformation'. Having stripped 'the veil of sanctity from tradition' he convinced thousands that they could survive without Britain and that the patriarchal household, far from being perfection incarnate, was in need of complete reform. If a shared belief in the justice of exchanging deference in return for paternalism was the principal bond holding a monarchical and aristocratic society together, Paine dealt a stunning blow to the system of British paternalism. In part, as Aldridge has justly remarked, much of the great success of *Common Sense* doubtless derived not from its abstract principles, but from its portrayal of the king as a political villain. But Paine showed further that all hereditary monarchy was oppressive, not merely tyranny. Simultaneously, thus, he raised his readers' sense of self-worth and independence and lowered the status of their nominal rulers. Submission and involuntary or merely tacit allegiance now seemed immature. Deference to an illusory superior was foolish. Dependence upon hereditary thieves was insulting. The people had come of age.[18]

A second aspect of Paine's 'modernity' concerns his respect for commerce. Though more classical republicans (like Price) retained fears of the corrupting effects of luxury and selfishness upon the public spirit, most eighteenth-century Whig radicals had reconciled trade and republicanism, and accepted the value of movable as well as landed property to an expanding economy. In America such views were fuelled in particular by the demands of the frontier, the growth of colonial entrepreneurial activity and the absence of a dominant landed oligarchy. But we need to identify Paine's commitment to trade very carefully. *Common Sense* advocated commercial liberty, but none the less assumed a vision of commercial society which even now (much less in 1792) implied far less inequality than did Adam Smith's in the *Wealth of Nations*, published shortly thereafter. In this sense it remained closer to classical republicanism than to the more purely commercial Whiggism of Hume and Smith. And we have seen from Paine's comments on the impact of commerce upon patriotism that he clearly recognized the existence of a fundamental conflict between political virtue and trade. Thus Aldridge is wrong to assume that there was 'absolutely no tension between virtue and commerce' in *Common Sense*, as is Foner to assert that Paine saw no contradiction between 'capitalist enterprise' and virtue. In addition Paine recognized (as we will see) that farmers and landowners had special status economically if not politically, though he broadened the idea of citizenship to encompass possession of all forms of property. Moreover, we will see that despite his views about the simplicity of wants and government in *Common Sense*, Paine was able to shift fairly easily to a greater role for government in the *Rights of Man*, and here too was no dogmatic proponent of *laissez-faire*, but instead urged considerable redistribution of wealth. In this, too, his republicanism was central.[19]

Redefining Paine's commercial republicanism has several consequences for recent debates about late eighteenth-century political thought. Some American historians have associated the unification of democratic republicanism and economic liberalism with the Jeffersonians of the 1790s and have argued against J. G. A. Pocock's insistence, in particular, upon the greater longevity of classical republicanism. Joyce Appleby, for example, sees Paine as among the leading anti-republican apostles of economic liberalism, which is quite correct in so far as Paine clearly assumed that *both* self-interest and virtue could serve as bases for a republican polity and that economic interest was an important component in popular conceptions of the common good. But this was less novel than it may appear. Many late eighteenth-century radicals opposed unrestricted speculation upon the national debt, for example, but not 'honest commerce', and thus sought to reconcile virtue with commerce rather than surrendering any demand for public spiritedness. By such means a republican could favour commerce in 1776. In American terms Paine's commercial republicanism is thus close to the Jeffersonianism analysed by Drew McCoy, who stresses attempts to reconcile republicanism and commerce, and Lance Banning, who views the Jeffersonians less as *opposed* to commerce as a source of corruption than *ambivalent* about it. It is less well described in terms of a 'stunning deflation of classical republicanism' ascribed to him by Appleby, who with Foner and Aldridge wrongly assumes that Paine saw no dangers in commerce, and ignores Paine's republicanism by arguing that in his writings government is conceived only negatively, as a means of restraining vice, rather than positively, as a sphere of citizenship.[20]

In this context it is worth repeating that *Common Sense* did proclaim that 'Trade being the consequence of population, men become too absorbed thereby to attend to anything else. Commerce diminishes the spirit of both patriotism and military defense ... with the increase of commerce England hath lost its spirit.' Not only did trade corrupt public virtue. Paine as we will see also expected that the young republic would be fervently devoted to the public good and that virtue would obviate the need for a bicameral assembly, since the common weal would prevail in all legislative proceedings. This argument was shared by other Pennsylvania radicals, for whom 'virtue' was essential to the creation of unicameral assemblies, though its meaning was narrowed (at least in one interpretation) to only two elements: the independence of the electorate and the integrity of legislators.[21] But this can also be understood as considerably expanding the scope of 'virtue' since there were many more electors than traditional republicans proposed. And legislators were also to be drawn from a much wider population, which assumed that far more would be capable of fulfilling such civic duties. Paine was immensely disappointed when the moral capabilities of Pennsylvania's legislators did not prove up to the task. But though he clearly came to fear the emergence of republican partisanship, his ideal of the undivided republic did not substantially alter even in the 1790s, although Paine later gave greater stress to religion in the hope that it might substitute for any decline in civic virtue.

In another variation on this description of Paine as an advocate of commercial modernity, Isaac Kramnick has seen *Common Sense* as the work of an 'English bourgeois radical' who, after less than a year in America, saw the new world as the means of overthrowing the corrupt aristocracy of the old and replacing it with a 'bourgeois' or 'middle-class' social and political order. Barring minor problems arising from the anachronistic use of 'bourgeois', this interpretation is plausible provided it concedes Paine's republican suspicion of commerce and takes 'middle class' to encompass small farmers, merchants, tradesmen and artisans, which is a somewhat wider definition than that usually given to 'middling orders' in late eighteenth-century Britain.[22] None the less we will see that this is a less accurate description of Paine's views in the 1790s, when a wider suffrage was advocated and Paine had become less suspicious of the politics of the labouring poor.

The commercial ideals of *Common Sense* can also be seen in terms of a rising artisan public courted by Paine, particularly in Philadelphia. In a persuasive account of Paine's American period, Eric Foner strongly defends the view that the distinctive elements in Paine's thought can be explained from this context and that, for example, this urban artisan vantage point drove Paine towards a market economy and away from more suspicious country views of commerce. But this does not require, as Aldridge mistakenly assumes, either that Paine identified himself as an artisan or that he saw the latter as the basis of any polity or economy. Nor does it conflict with Paine's attempt to appeal to a wider audience, or his success in so doing.[23] Indeed Foner also convincingly sees Paine as amongst the first 'intellectuals', a group just beginning to emerge at the end of the eighteenth century. But for this artisan interpretation to be persuasive Paine did have to see himself as representing those whose property was primarily in their labour, and this he clearly did to an important degree. Nor does this inevitably conflict with Kramnick's view, for the essential dividing line for Paine at this time was not between merchants and artisans, but the latter and the labouring poor, who possessed too little property to claim the right to the franchise.

Defining the relationship between republicanism and commerce in the eighteenth century also raises the question of how 'American' *Common Sense* was. Paine had of course only been in the colonies about thirteen months when it was written. In the best brief analysis of the tract, Bernard Bailyn thus concludes that '*Common Sense* was an English pamphlet written on an American theme', and animated by a deep radical and puritan rage and 'an intensity no American could have devised'. Eric Foner agrees that Paine's ideas were formed largely in England. None the less Jack Greene has argued that Paine's political vision was grounded in the rapid social and political change of the American revolutionary period. Aldridge, too, describes Paine's views categorically as an 'American ideology', though without defending this view or considering Paine after 1787.[24] How should we weigh these arguments? It is fair to assume that Paine's irreverence for the British monarchy and aristocracy, his egalitarianism, his Quaker cosmopolitanism and benevolence, his views on commerce and his deism were formed prior to his arrival in America. Afterwards, however, he may well have become a more democratic republican, adopted the view that less 'government' was required and increased his faith in popular representation.

Intellectually, therefore, the primary importance of *Common Sense* lay in its novel republicanism. Paine was not the first to argue for American independence; this had been broadly suggested by Josiah Tucker by 1775 and at the same time detailed by John Cartwright in terms of a league which would retain British naval protection. In America Patrick Henry had begun to broach similar sentiments at about the same time. Moreover, especially given the power of the colonial assemblies, the cause of independence was in some respects far advanced by 1776. But Paine was the first to contend that a constitutional convention was necessary in order for the colonies to establish a new form of government, the final consequence of which was the Federal Convention which founded the United States' constitution. *Common Sense* also called for independence more bluntly than others had done, and moreover appealed to the interests and sentiments of the whole population.

Paine's persuasiveness thus lay both in his definition of the problems to be solved and of the agents to accomplish this. Here his status as a 'free floating' intellectual with scant respect for established authority was central. Unencumbered by local or national political interests, as other popular writers like the Philadelphia-based Benjamin Rush (who read *Common Sense* as it was written) admitted to Paine they were, or by habits implanted by social deference, Paine was able to shake off the mentality of subservience more easily than either native Americans or older emigrants. His very rootlessness was thus a central element in his perspective; he could advocate independence so fervently only because of the strength of his own sense of and desire for independence. Also central was the universalist, humanitarian perspective Paine adopted from Quakerism in particular, and which widened his conception of what people were owed by society. Before *Common Sense*, Gilbert Vale thus argued, the colonists sought to restore 'their old British *privileges*', not to establish their *rights*.[25] Paine taught them a new language of rights which was less historical than universal in scope.

Before turning to examine the impact of *Common Sense* we should briefly consider another pamphlet also written in 1776 and only recently identified by Aldridge as Paine's. *Four Letters on Interesting Subjects* argued that all efforts at reconciliation were exhausted, and charged Britain with inciting rebellion in order to confiscate the colonists' property. The pamphlet is also important because it further details Paine's views on commerce before he read the *Wealth of Nations*. Arguing that future trade between the colonies would be beneficial, at least as long as 'most of their principal articles of commerce differ from each other', Paine asserted that no nation could

> grow rich without communicating a share of that riches to the rest, and in the like manner, no province can grow poor without communicating part of its poverty to others; and on these grounds it is as much our interest, as it is our duty, to promote the happiness of other provinces as of our own. Were Spain, Portugal, and other nations, with whom Britain trades, to grow poor, Britain would grow poor in the same proportion.

This is primarily the natural law notion of commercial interdependence which also underlay the *Wealth of Nations*, but here derived quite independently of Smith, which we will see is of some importance. Finally, the *Four Letters* also revealed crucial developments in Paine's notion of a constitution. He now insisted for the first time that Britain had 'no fixed Constitution' because it lacked written limits to legislative power. England was 'likewise defective in Constitution' on three further grounds: the Crown could increase the number of lords, it could incorporate any town or village it pleased and empower it to elect MPs, while the entire legislature could disincorporate any town and hence abolish its electors. Thus, Paine concluded,

> the English have no constitution, because they have given up everything; their legislative power being unlimited without either condition or controul, except in the single instance of trial by jury. No country can be called *free* which is governed by an absolute power; and it matters not whether it be an absolute royal power or an absolute legislative power, as the consequences will be the same to the people.

Though Paine originally doubted that a republican legislature could be prone to such absolutism, this was the origin of a doctrine prominently displayed in the *Rights of Man*. In the new American usage, a nation possessed a 'constitution' only when the separation and limits of the powers of its various branches were clearly defined in a document accessible to all, not merely a few legal experts, and agreed upon by all acting through special, not legislative, representatives. In its final paragraph *Four Letters* then proposed what colonial historians have described as the first mention of the Council of Censors, whose task was to review Pennsylvania legislation to ensure its constitutionality, and which was to remain the most radical body ensuring popular consent in any state throughout the revolutionary period.[26]

The Tories respond

Common Sense, one observer put it, burst 'forth like a mighty conqueror, bearing down all opposition'. Sales soon vastly surpassed those of any of the other 400 pamphlets of the pre-revolutionary debate: in twenty-five American editions some 120,000 copies were sold in the first three months alone and perhaps half a million in the first year (to a population of some 3 million!). Soon reprinted in Britain, quickly translated into French (its anti-monarchist sentiments expunged), German and Spanish, it played an important role even in the early nineteenth-century independence movements in South America.[27] But its greatest impact was in the British colonies, where, it has often been repeated, 'Paine did more to cause the Declaration of Independence [a document he was once supposed to have written] than any other man'. In March 1776 Washington heard from Virginia that '*Common Sense* is working a powerful change there in the minds of many men' and wrote that its 'sound doctrine and unanswerable reasoning' would 'not leave numbers at a loss to decide upon the propriety of separation'. A New Yorker reported that it was 'eagerly read and much admired'. General Charles Lee called the tract 'a masterly, irresistible performance', while one American officer regarded it as equivalent in morale to 5,000 troops. Individual readers were often overwhelmed; one recorded that 'I could not withhold my assent to the arguments of the victorious author'. *Common Sense* in fact, had 'broken the spell', as Paine later put it, of Britain's hold over the colonies. It convinced Americans, as Gilbert Vale wrote, 'that the British constitution was not *the best that could be*, and that a government of kings, lords, and commons, *might not* be the essence of all that was excellent in each'.[28]

Common Sense effected this 'sudden and virtually complete revolution in attitude' towards British rule (in Cecelia Kenyon's words) by releasing all of the pent-up resentment against the monarch which pervaded colonial America. Loyalty to George III was hard enough by 1776; Paine transformed the king into a tyrant – even 'killed' him metaphorically, it has been suggested – and made attachment nearly impossible thereafter. In this sense the tract was central to defining 'America' in republican terms. Moreover, Paine appealed to an audience hitherto ignored by political writers. As Gordon Wood has written, some of the 'awe and consternation' *Common Sense* aroused 'came from its deliberate elimination of the usual elitist apparatus of persuasion and its acknowledged appeal to a wider reading public'.[29] Paine found particular favour in Philadelphia and other large cities where artisans and tradesmen were as anxious to battle the native aristocracies governing their colonial assemblies as to reject British imperial rule. Part of the appeal of *Common Sense*, then, certainly involved crystallizing and radicalizing their resentments.[30]

In Philadelphia, correspondingly, the Quaker oligarchy was largely opposed to independence, and conservative American Whigs and Tories elsewhere also saw *Common Sense* as 'ruinous and destructive', 'rascally and nonsensical ... a sophisticated attempt to throw all men out of Principles' and 'specious and dangerous'. Some early efforts to counter its effects faltered. When the tract first arrived at Albany, New York, some members of the colonial legislature met to plan a response. Within a few days, however, they were forced to abandon the plan as public opinion surged dramatically in Paine's favour, and tracts opposing Paine were later burned on the common. But several prominent loyalist responses to *Common Sense* did appear. The first was *The True Interest of America Impartially Stated*, published in February 1776 by an Anglican clergyman, Charles Inglis. Standing upon the principles of 1688 and insisting that the British constitution 'approaches the nearest to perfection', Inglis railed against Paine's attempt to redefine the constitution, accusing him of uniting 'the violence and rage of a republican, with all the enthusiasm and folly of a fanatic' and of being motivated by 'some mortifying disappointment' (later critics would frequently accuse Paine of seeking revenge for his loss of employment as an excise official). Only monarchy suited a large territory or empire; a republic fitted neither 'the genius of the people, nor the extent of America'. Rejecting Paine's contrast of society and government, Inglis argued that society was the natural state of mankind instead of being based merely upon human wants (in fact both were essentially agreed on this point). Inglis insisted that society was unimaginable without some form of government and laws, and thus assailed Paine's attempt to legitimate public opinion outside of any legislature, and apart from the wider British society to which he claimed all Americans belonged. Paine's was 'a new, untried romantic scheme' facing 'inevitable ruin', and was 'the last stage of political phrenzy'. America gained many advantages from union with Britain, and ought still to seek reconciliation with the mother country.[31]

Another influential critique of *Common Sense* was John Adams's 'Thoughts on Government', published a few months after Paine's tract. Adams was chiefly concerned to 'depute power from the many to a few of the most wise and good'. He agreed that representative assemblies should 'be in miniature an exact portrait of the people at large', but condemned single assemblies as prone to arbitrariness, greed and ambition. Instead, two houses, the lower electing the upper, with both together choosing a governor, would be superior. Checks over popular power were to be established by granting the governor a veto over the legislature, and the upper house over the lower.[32] Also important was James Chalmers's *Plain Truth*, which argued that independence was 'ruinous, delusive, and impracticable', and accused Paine of being a 'political quack' retailing a 'Quixotic system'. Had he read Montesquieu, Chalmers chastised, Paine would have truly appreciated Britain's form of government. America could not become a republic because of its attachment to the British constitution. In any case pure democracy was impossible and republics were always aggressive. Moreover, America was incapable of winning any conflict with Britain and could expect no foreign assistance. British rule, too, had brought the colonies prosperity and, as in the debate over the *Rights of Man* twenty years later, Paine was accused of opposing commerce. Independence would invite only ruin and was synonymous with slavery. A similar attack on *Common Sense* appeared in a series of letters to the *Pennsylvania Gazette Ledger* by another Anglican clergyman named William Smith. These criticisms Paine answered by denying that reconciliation was desirable or even practicable. Peace commissioners sent by Britain sought only bribery and corruption. The cause of independence, moreover, was now widely supported. But Americans did not seek rule by another European power instead of the British over America, and Paine advised against any future European 'political connections' (and has consequently been acclaimed a founder of American isolationism). Blaming George III for 'all the measures carried on against America', Paine argued that 'all men are republicans by nature, and royalists only by fashion'.[33]

Paine at war: *The American Crisis* (1776–83)

During the revolutionary war Paine wrote a total of sixteen pamphlets on the causes and course of the struggle. These caught the mood of the initially beleaguered revolutionary forces and renewed their faith. Washington, indeed, ordered the first of the *Crisis* series read to his troops before the Battle of Trenton in December 1776. It opened with one of Paine's most memorable lines: 'These are the times that try men's souls. The summer soldier and the sunshine patriot will, in this crisis, shrink from the service of their country; but he that stands it *now*, deserves the love and thanks of man and woman.' Many *Crisis* papers consequently focused upon the vicissitudes of American morale. Initially the Americans seemed outnumbered, undertrained and poorly equipped. Paine told them that God took the side of those who tried to avoid war, and reminded them that the British had been beaten by lesser numbers before (and these led by a woman, Joan of Arc). He praised Washington highly while heaping disgrace upon the slavishly servile American Tories, who told others the cause was lost when they did not actively hinder it themselves. Against those like the Quakers who abjured war altogether on moral grounds, Paine agreed that offensive war was simply 'murder', but justified the right of self-defence.[34]

Subsequent numbers of the *Crisis* touched upon many other issues. The second (January 1777) spurned Lord Howe's offer to pardon all Americans who ceased fighting. Paine detailed the brutality of Britain's campaigns, the wickedness of its cause, and its inability to conquer and garrison large portions of the colonies. On land British officers were about as capable as cowardly dancing masters; Britain's strength lay at sea, and that was no help now. In *Crisis* no. 3 (April 1777) Paine outlined four main arguments for independence: the colonists' natural right to self-rule; their interest therein, principally greater commerce; the necessity for such an act given the colonists' increasing weakness prior to July 1776; and the moral advantages which would result from peace with Europe and among the colonists themselves (which held out the Quaker promise of a general peace besides). The opponents of independence he castigated as fearful, indolent, avaricious and power-hungry, which made it unsurprising that all the prostitutes of New York were Tories. The Philadelphia merchant Quakers he accused of fuelling inflation by raising their prices. But a surplus of currency assisted this, and Paine recommended that all property be taxed at a flat rate to reduce the currency, with all taxpayers swearing an oath renouncing allegiance to Britain to clarify who the Tories really were.[35]

The fourth *Crisis* sought briefly to rally the American forces after their defeat at the Battle of Brandywine in September 1777. In the fifth, published in March 1778, Paine mocked General Howe's new knighthood and abhorred his permitting forged American bills to circulate as a means of undermining the colonists' cause. Despite some British successes, Paine asserted that the British were neither daring fighters nor prudent in their policies towards civilians, which by brutalizing the population had merely fortified the colonists' resolve. To the Americans, Paine denied that classical parallels to their revolution existed. The Greeks and Romans had possessed the spirit of liberty, but while 'they were determined not to be slaves themselves, they employed their power to enslave the rest of mankind'. Since Britain's liberty had been lost through 'a long chain of right reasoning from wrong principles', only the Americans could now preserve freedom. But this required an American victory, and Paine proposed further means of levying troops and furnishing military clothing and equipment. The sixth *Crisis* (October 1778) discussed Britain's offer of complete relief short of independence, while the seventh, written a month later, was a lengthy address to the British people detailing the cruelties of British policy in America and the East Indies. Britons, Paine argued, could expect no commercial gain from a reconquest of the colonies, and should not accept 'national honor' as sufficient cause for continuing the war. Moreover, Britain's national debt was expanding rapidly as a consequence of the war, and the monarch and government would eventually ruin the nation. The interest of the British *people*, therefore, lay in American independence rather than in war.[36]

After a lapse of nearly one and a half years, Paine again addressed the British populace in March 1780 to inform them of the cruelty of their government's war policies, but also of America's fortified resolve to fight to the bitter end. Several months later, as the colonists' struggle reached another low point, Paine wrote another *Crisis* to raise funds for the army. A further *Crisis Extraordinary* addressed the problem of financing the war in greater detail, arguing that American revenues could suffice if they were correctly assessed and collected and sufficient currency for payment was available. Paine then outlined a plan for raising revenue through duties on imports in particular. Similar themes dominated *Crisis* nos 10 and 11 (March–April 1782), which also attacked George III's refusal to acknowledge defeat after Cornwallis's surrender at Yorktown the previous autumn. Two months later Paine reacted to British efforts to sever the alliance between France and the United States, and praised France's unwillingness to conclude a separate peace and the generous French treatment of the Americans. The last several numbers of the *Crisis* argued that Britain would benefit enormously by reduced military expenses by ceding victory to the Americans, and celebrated the final success of 'the greatest and completest revolution the world ever knew'. But Paine warned that national unity was endangered by the weakness of the central government. America anticipated peace and prosperity, but its 'great national character' and ultimately its international security depended upon union. Citing the example of Holland, Paine cautioned that too much decentralized power would endanger the defence of the whole nation. The final *Crisis*, dated 9 December 1783, further warned that perceptions of disunity between the states had occasioned British efforts to prevent American trade with nearby British colonies.[37]

During the revolutionary years Paine wrote a number of other short works which merit brief comment here. His *Letter to the Abbé Raynal*, published in 1782 to correct an inadequate history of the revolution, has been seen as marking a shift from nationalism to internationalism in his thought.[38] But it also extended the implications of Paine's ideas of commercial progress considerably, for Paine now argued that trade could create 'universal civilization'. Mutual wants had 'formed the individuals of each country into a kind of national society', but here civilization had stopped. If the wants of nations could be fulfilled in the same way, however, an international society could be created. This was not a republican view of national self-subsistence and independence, but essentially a natural law view, now probably supported by reading Smith and likely indebted to Hume, which stressed the advantages of interdependence. Barbarians were independent because their wants were few. Modern men depended upon one another because their wants had multiplied. Literature, the arts and science were rapidly uniting the peoples of different nations. Unlike the ancients, they no longer treated one another solely as enemies. Commerce and science in particular could extend civilization by eradicating prejudice and encouraging peace.[39]

Also important in this period was Paine's *Dissertations on Government; the Affairs of the Bank; and Paper Money* (1786), which was principally concerned with the Bank of North America. In 1782 Paine had condoned the issuing of paper money and consequent depreciation of its value during the revolution, arguing that this was done by common consent and had raised money at a time when taxes could not be collected properly.[40] Now, while he was attacked by some as a conservative (though many Philadelphia mechanics supported him), Paine resisted attempts to repeal the bank's charter by describing it as a lawful contract whose preservation guaranteed security of property for all and avoided popular despotism. A public bank's capacity to lend money he defended as a means of assisting commerce and avoiding private usury, though any issuing of paper money not redeemable in specie he rejected as encouraging the exportation of bullion. Later, however, Paine became more critical of bank charters and argued that such legislation might be subjected to time limits. Also interesting for such topics is Paine's *Prospects on the Rubicon* (1787), which condemned the British national debt and warned that it would create two great parties in the state, those paying to service it and those benefiting from it.[41]

American independence as a democratic revolution

America's accomplishments were central to the new political ideal Paine would soon attempt to export to Europe. By the time of the constitution, according to Gordon Wood, the new American science of government could be summed up by five principles: democratic republics, the pervasiveness of representation, the equation of rulers and ruled, the parcelling of power and the end of classical politics. Politically the revolution was inescapably democratic. Well before independence was won, the colonists sought more liberty for themselves, and less for their governors, than any previous mode of rule. Well before the 1787 constitution, the separate states set about transforming habitual modes of government. Relative to the central government they sought a great devolution of power. Internally, no state sought to abolish magistracy, of course. The most radical colony, Pennsylvania, went furthest in the direction of what is sometimes termed an 'internal revolution'. Thus it had the least fear of losing any checks and balances and replaced the governor by an elected council. But all states made their executives more subservient to popular will. Gubernatorial terms were therefore limited, the possibility of re-election curtailed, powers of appointing officials and granting pensions diminished, the spheres of the legislature, judiciary and executive more clearly delineated, and their powers separated. A vast number of judicial, executive and legislative officials who had been appointed under the Crown now became subject to election. The legislatures too were made more representative, though all but three of the early state constitutions (Pennsylvania, Georgia, Vermont) retained two houses with the upper supposedly balancing the lower. Only the most radical (notably the Pennsylvanians, in keeping with their colonial tradition) opposed bicameralism completely until 1790, in part probably owing to Paine's influence. Almost all the early states also introduced annual elections to their legislatures. Numbers of representatives were increased, their accountability to the populace affirmed and electoral districts in many areas equalized. The suffrage was generally extended, but not widely conceded as a universal right, and all of the early states upheld taxpaying or property qualifications for voting (probably 75 per cent of Philadelphia's males could vote in 1776, and 60 per cent of county members in the colony).[42]

Cumulatively, these actions distributed power unprecedentedly away from central government and to the populace. But many of these changes were as much formal as substantive, and did not deprive colonial elites of their political influence. By 1787, moreover, the weakness of the Articles of Confederation was widely evident, and Federalist opinion in favour of greater constitutional checks and balances, a more independent judiciary, bicameralism and increased central power predominated. The Federalists' fear of unchecked democracy, too, was widely shared even by those who rejected its aristocratic implications, including many artisans and labourers. This put an end to the radical demand for more direct and continuous consent, particularly by ensuring the indirect election of both the Senate and President, even though government as a whole was still understood as broadly based upon the consent of the majority.

In part the Federalist reaction occurred because of fears that the demand for democracy masked a social revolution in which artisans, the labouring classes and the poor might connect the cause of independence with their economic lot. Richard Morris has argued that Adams's

'Thoughts on Government' may have been more representative of the opinions of revolutionary leaders than Paine's ideas. But this does not imply that the less articulate and less visible shared such sentiments. Artisans, labourers and small farmers throughout the colonies may not have shared a sense of identical economic interest, but most desired greater independence from colonial elites as well as Britain. In some cases, too, they were willing to resort to violence in order to resist further oppression by local oligarchies. Loyalists (and many American Whigs as well) in turn feared the mob and suspected that the lower classes sought power under the guise of 'independence'. None the less the class dimensions of the revolution and particularly the emergence of a specific 'artisan republicanism' are often difficult to trace. Much of the conflict was fought out in the name of 'the people' and against 'monarchy' and 'aristocracy'. But most colonists none the less agreed that only those with some property should possess the franchise.[43] This limited considerably the possibility of any 'internal revolution', though Paine wanted a very large proportion of the male population to be enfranchised, including many whose 'property' was primarily only in their own labour.

Yet Paine was also both more and less 'radical' than such views might imply. His writings and support for the Pennsylvania constitution show that he sought rule by all classes of freemen. He was directly involved in the radical politics of the Philadelphia artisans and echoed their growing cry for equality and for restrictions on individual wealth, their opposition to the mercantile oligarchy, and their hostility to choosing either wealthy or 'learned' men for their constitutional convention. For this reason his model was not merely 'American', but radical even by American standards. Thus it was no accident that Paine wrote both for and as part of a Pennsylvania readership, the 'Constitutionalist' party, who were considerably more democratic than other groups and had broken most sharply from colonial government in 1776, seizing power at the constitutional convention that year largely because the Whig leadership was unable to stop them. In Pennsylvania mixed governments were rejected in favour of a pure republic, the doctrine of popular sovereignty taken further than elsewhere, and the franchise extended to all freemen aged 21 who paid public taxes, which included most artisans. Here it was also the Constitutionalists, for essentially political reasons linked to their notion of the common good, who supported the movement to fix prices in order to sustain the poor and labouring classes. Price regulation was thus not directly linked to an 'artisan' viewpoint, since not all trades in Philadelphia supported it during the 1779–80 debate about the activities of the price-fixing committees, though merchants tended to be more opposed in principle to such restraints.[44] Here and nowhere else, too, an early draft of the state's Declaration of Rights suggested limiting the concentration of property. Paine's model was therefore less an American than a more narrowly Pennsylvanian or (even more strictly) Constitutionalist model, since here the more elitist 'Republicans' (who came to power in 1789–90) correspondingly sought a second legislative house to balance a single tumultuous assembly, as well as a stronger and more independent judiciary and an executive with a veto power over laws.[45]

But Paine's sense of class loyalty and sympathy did not override his republicanism and his appeal in the late 1770s and 1780s was to the common concerns of all classes, not their separate interests. He sought to destroy oligarchy, but to supplant this by republican rule in the name of the common good by all citizens, not the narrow rule of a single class. The commercial prosperity which would follow the revolution, too, was to benefit all classes, its new wealth spreading like water across an arid landscape. It was expected not to increase economic inequality but to curtail it. In this sense Paine's was neither a 'bourgeois' nor an 'artisan' but a republican vision which encompassed all the middling ranks – including the merchants and artisans often at loggerheads in Philadelphia revolutionary politics – in agriculture, manufactures and commerce. It was also republican in so far as citizens were voluntarily to renounce private advantage in the name of a collective economic good, with public virtue thus restraining self-interest. Paine thus had not slid far down that slippery path from republican civic virtue towards 'free enterpriser' followed by many in late eighteenth-century America.[46]

These achievements, Paine thought, would not long be confined to America alone. Europe groaned under the weight of tyranny and oppression, but millions took heart at America's success. They would discover, and Paine himself would increasingly recognize, that emulating the advantages of a 'new country' where much greater social inequality and poverty existed was not simple. But such complexities were secondary for the moment. First it was necessary to establish that the people possessed the right to greater freedom and equality. Of this, again, one man would persuade them more than any other.

Notes to Chapter 2: The American revolution

1 On colonial radicalism see especially S. Lynd (1968), P. Maier (1972a) and B. Bailyn (1967).
2 G. Wood (1969), p. 11; P. Maier (1972a), p. 246; Paine (1945), Vol. 2, p. 48. The following several pages are much indebted to Wood's interpretation. For a comparison of Paine's and Dickinson's views see A. Aldridge (1976a).
3 G. Wood (1969), p. 44. For the argument that many Americans were already republicans by 1776 see P. Maier (1972a), p. 288. On the notion of America's

millennial role see E. Tuveson (1968), R. Bloch (1985). On millennial allusions in *Common Sense* see S. Newman (1978).

4 J. de Lolme (1853), p. 252; Montesquieu (1949), pp. 149–62; see G. Wood (1969), pp. 46–90, and, on the background to such views, M. Vile (1967).

5 On the debate over sovereignty see G. Wood (1969), pp. 344–89, and E. Morgan (1988), pp. 237–306, and on the early years of the revolution, J. Marston (1987). On shifts in 'republic' and 'republicanism' see W. Adams (1970). On shifting views of consent see D. Lutz (1980).

6 See G. Wood (1969), p. 309, and generally, pp. 306–89.

7 See G. Wood (1969), pp. 91–124.

8 G. Wood (1969), pp. 86–8; E. Douglass (1955), pp. 214–86; Paine (1945), Vol. 1, pp. 25, 143, 406, 496. The most detailed account of *Common Sense* is A. Aldridge (1984), pp. 17–157. See also R. Gimbel (1956a), pp. 15–57, B. Bailyn (1973), D. Wilson (1988), pp. 34–64, A. Aldridge (1976c), and Kramnick's introduction to Paine (1976). Unpublished studies include A. King (1951) and E. Ginsberg (1971). On the Philadelphia artisans in this period see E. Foner (1976), pp. 19–70, 107–44, also C. Olton (1975).

9 Paine (1945), Vol. 1, pp. 3–6.

10 Paine (1945), Vol. 1, pp. 6–9. On the language of 'tyranny' and 'slavery' in this period see J. Reid (1988), pp. 38–59.

11 Paine (1945), Vol. 1, pp. 9–16.

12 Paine (1945), Vol. 1, pp. 17–21.

13 Paine (1945), Vol. 1, pp. 22–7.

14 Paine (1945), Vol. 1, pp. 28–31.

15 Paine (1945), Vol. 1, pp. 31–9.

16 B. Bailyn (1967), p. 285, (1973), p. 40. On the term 'democracy' in this period see R. Lokken (1963) and R. Shoemaker (1966).

17 On the 'modernization' debate in relation to early America see K. Lockridge (1977). Those who use this term refer frequently to the creation of a 'new American type' of individualistic, optimistic, active and self-interested citizen.

18 A. Aldridge (1960), p. 28; J. Greene (1978), pp. 74, 77. In support of the anti-deferential interpretations see also E. Foner (1976), p. 84, R. Bushman (1979), J. Fliegelman (1982), pp. 102–6. On applying the concept of deference to the American revolution see J. Kirby (1970).

19 A. Aldridge (1984), p. 152; E. Foner (1976), p. 190. On the acceptance of commerce in the colonies see G. Nash (1979). For Paine as an economic liberal see J. Appleby (1978). Kramnick also suggests that 'Smith's and Paine's is the basic liberal vision. The social order and the economy are spontaneous and self-regulating mechanisms, peopled by rational, self-seeking individuals ... Government ... merely presides passively over this self-regulating economy and spontaneously harmonious polity' (Paine, 1976, pp. 39–40).

20 J. Appleby (1985), p. 470, and generally (1984), also broadly supported by W. Gavre (1978), especially pp. 309–19; D. McCoy (1980), pp. 89–90, and generally 76–104; L. Banning (1978) and (1986). Appleby acknowledges that Paine elevated 'free association to a new moral plane' but still insists that this entailed a rejection of classical republicanism (1985, p. 470). This debate is also discussed in R. Shalhope (1972, 1982), J. Pocock (1975), pp. 506–52, J. Ashworth (1984) and L. Kerber (1985).

21 Paine (1945), Vol. 1, p. 36; D. Arnold (1976), pp. 50–2, 164. Arnold also argues that the traditional concept of virtue was 'severely abbreviated' in this ideal.

22 I. Kramnick (1977b), pp. 526–30, (1986).

23 E. Foner (1976), pp. 39, 99; A. Aldridge (1978), pp. 131–5. Aldridge mistakenly contends that there was no evidence that one class responded differently to Paine's writings than another (1984, pp. 22–3).

24 B. Bailyn (1973), pp. 92–3; E. Foner (1976), p. xiii; J. Greene (1978), pp. 86–90. The second edition of *Common Sense* described it as by 'an Englishman', but this was not added by Paine himself.

25 J. Tucker (1775), pp. 38–51; J. Cartwright (1774), pp. 8, 13; G. Vale (1841), p. 38.

26 [Paine] (1776), pp. 4–5, 8, 18–20; D. Lutz (1980), p. 133; J. Selsam (1936), pp. 199–210. For identification of *Four Letters* see A. Aldridge (1984), pp. 219–39. The style of the pamphlet is unmistakably Paine's. The Library of Congress copy is bound with *Common Sense* and responses to it. See Bailyn's discussion in (1967), pp. 298–9. The pamphlet is also discussed in J. Selsam (1936), pp. 174–5 and D. Arnold (1976), pp. 29–34, though without ascription to Paine. The Library of Congress catalogue suggests that a further pamphlet important for proposing the Council of Censors, *The People the Best Governors*, may also be Paine's, but as this work urges that no one be allowed to hold public office without affirming the Bible to be divine revelation this is impossible (other Pennsylvania radicals did agree with such an oath: see J. Selsam, 1936, pp. 139–40). On the emergence of the new idea of a constitution see G. Wood (1969), pp. 259–305. On the Council of Censors see L. Meader (1898) and, on more likely authors for *The People the Best Governors*, p. 280.

27 'Rusticus' (1776), p. iii. On the reception of *Common Sense* see A. Aldridge (1984), pp. 158–215 and A. King (1951), pp. 97–117. For the German and German-American impact of Paine see especially M. Kistler (1962). A full bibliography of editions is given in R. Gimbel (1956a). A few British republicans also thought Paine's broadside a fine thing. David Erskine, eleventh Earl of Buchan, said that it treated George III 'as the dog deserves' (C. Robbins, 1959, p. 362).

28 R. Ingersoll in Paine (1908), Vol. 1, p. 290; G. Washington (1931), Vol. 4, pp. 455, 297; G. Vale (1841), p. 50; B. Franklin (1982), Vol. 22, pp. 357 n., 388; G. Vale (1841), pp. 50–1. See also P. Maier (1972b).

29 C. Kenyon (1962), p. 167; J. Marston (1987), pp. 61–3; W. Jordan (1973); G. Wood (1979), pp. 110–11.

30 C. Lincoln (1901), p. 79; E. Douglass (1955), pp. 253–6; P. Foner (1976), pp. 160–3.

31 *The True Merits* (1776), p. 1; *Remarks* (1776), p. 3; E. Douglass (1955), p. 21; H. Rock (1979), p. 41; [C. Inglis] (1776), pp. vi, 10–11, 15, 31, 34, 48–52, 70.

32 J. Adams (1851), pp. 193–200. See J. Porter and R. Farnell (1976) and, on Adams's relation to Burke, R. Ripley (1965).

33 [J. Chalmers] (1776), pp. 2, 5, 7, 10–13, 19–20, 35, 37; Paine (1945), Vol. 2, pp. 61–87, 89.

34 Paine (1945), Vol. 1, pp. 50–7.

35 Paine (1945), Vol. 1, pp. 58–101.

36 Paine (1945), Vol. 1, pp. 102–57; A. Aldridge (1951), pp. 832–3.

37 Paine (1945), Vol. 1, pp. 158–239; A. Aldridge (1951), p. 833.

38 E.g. D. Abel (1942).

39 Paine (1945), Vol. 2, pp. 22, 211–63. On the origins of this view of commerce see my (1988a).

40 Paine (1945), Vol. 2, pp. 228–9. The best account of this episode is E. Foner (1976), pp. 183–209.

41 Paine (1945), Vol. 2, pp. 367–414, 989–92, 642. See A. Aldridge (1949).
42 G. Wood (1969), pp. 197–255, 446–67, 553–64, 593–615; J. Selsam (1936), pp. 173, 186–7; J. Pole (1966), p. 265; D. Lutz (1980), pp. 194, 225–30. On the evolution of the suffrage see E. Douglass (1955) and C. Williamson (1960), pp. 3–116. On the question of increasing democratization in the revolution see E. Douglass (1955), M. Jensen (1957), R. Buel (1964), J. Pole (1966), pp. 169–382, G. Wood (1969), pp. 127–389, P. Maier (1972a), R. Weir (1976), D. Arnold (1976)(a particularly careful study). For the claim that German and Scotch-Irish hostility to Quakers and Anglicans was important here see W. Bockelman and O. Ireland (1974).
43 R. Morris (1962), p. 7; I. Kramnick, in Paine (1976), pp. 46–55; Kramnick (1986). Eric Foner sees no evidence that mechanics identified with the poor beneath them (1976, p. 47). See further P. Foner (1976), especially pp. 123–205. On the 'social' interpretation of the revolution see also R. Berthoff and J. Murrin (1973).
44 See J. Selsam (1936), pp. 94–136, C. Olton (1975), pp. 74–7, E. Foner (1976), p. 123, G. Nash (1979), pp. 381–2 and R. Ryerson (1974). On regulation during the revolution see E. Foner (1976), pp. 145–82, D. Arnold (1976), pp. 127–47, also J. Crowley (1974), especially pp. 76–124.
45 E. Douglass (1955), p. 283. See G. Wood (1969), pp. 226–37, and, on opposition to this constitution in Pennsylvania, pp. 438–46. On the revolution there see C. Lincoln (1901), E. Douglass (1955), pp. 263–86, J. Pole (1966), pp. 250–80.
46 See R. Berthoff (1979).

3

Republicanism contested: Burke's *Reflections* (1790) and the *Rights of Man* (1791–92)

Radicalism and Dissent, 1788–90

For many other reformers besides Paine, the half-dozen years between the ending of the American war and the outbreak of the French revolution were relatively quiet. At the end of the 1780s, however, religious reform again became a heated issue in Britain when the Dissenters renewed their efforts to repeal the Test and Corporation Acts. From the Restoration of 1660, those who dissented from the Thirty-nine Articles of the Church of England (perhaps 6 to 7 per cent of the population in 1790) suffered under restrictive legislation, including being prohibited from election to Parliament or local government posts or receiving a university degree at Oxford or Cambridge. Quiescent though most Dissenters were throughout the eighteenth century, many remained both strongly Whiggish and intensely aware of these disabilities. Encouraged by American independence, Dissenters in London, Manchester, Birmingham and elsewhere surged forward in 1787–90 to petition Parliament to redress their grievances. Concurrently some helped found the Revolution Society, nominally to celebrate the centenary of 1688, but equally to revive reform and repeal the Test and Corporation Acts (which finally occurred only in 1828).[1]

Given these efforts, the extension of religious toleration in France at the revolution inevitably met with the Dissenters' admiration. Many of their leaders quickly distinguished themselves by their enthusiasm for things French, a taste for which they would soon pay a heavy price. What specifically provoked Burke to write the *Reflections on the Revolution in France* (1790) was Richard Price's sermon to the second meeting of the Revolution Society in November 1789, which clearly connected liberty of conscience and the demand for parliamentary reform with the right to resist arbitrary power. With others of the 'New Whigs' sympathetic to the revolution, Price also insisted that the settlement of 1688 had been imperfect, since it had extended neither toleration nor parliamentary representation. The Americans had remedied these deficiencies for themselves. But their revolt had taken place a world away in a young and primitive country. The French revolution correspondingly appeared to most radicals not as merely an extension of American principles, but something much more momentous. To the Whig historian Catherine Macaulay it

> was attended with something so *new* in the history of human affairs; there was something so *singular*, so *unique*, in that perfect *unanimity* in the people; in that *firm* spirit which baffled *every hope* in the *interested*, that they could possibly divide them into parties, and render them the instruments of a resubjection to their old bondage; that it naturally excited the *surprize* and *admiration* of all men. It appeared as a *sudden spread of an enlightened spirit*.

Not a few of the radicals, Macaulay among them, detected the hand of 'benevolent providence' in the advent of the revolution.[2] Joseph Priestley thought it inaugurated the long-awaited millennial state of divine rule. But even moderate reformers hoped that once tyranny was destroyed, a government patterned upon the British constitution would rise from the ashes. For 1789 was to be France's 1688.

Enthusiasm thus quickly revived in several nearly defunct reformers' organizations. The Society for Constitutional Information regained its vigour in 1791 and a new organization, the Society of the Friends of the People, was founded to represent the radical Whiggism of Lauderdale, Cartwright, Sheridan, Whitbread and others. Neither of these groups even vaguely considered reform on the lines of the American model and subscriptions were kept at a guinea and a half annually to ensure a suitably select membership.[3] But pressure for popular participation grew very rapidly. By mid-spring a debate erupted which polarized the reformers and soon left the moderates in a dangerously exposed position.

The 'manifesto of a counter-revolution': Burke's *Reflections on the Revolution in France* (1790)

The first and most crucial blow against the French and anyone who shared their principles was struck by Edmund Burke. Burke had already attacked the revolution in Parliament, but at first was somewhat reluctant to publish his assessment of the virtues of the *ancien régime* and the malevolence of its enemies. When several prominent Whigs attended a dinner at the Crown and Anchor tavern celebrating the first anniversary of the fall of the Bastille on 14 July 1790, however, he hesitated no longer.

The *Reflections* appeared on 1 November 1790. Its arguments, which even Burke admitted were rambling and ill organized, were arranged around three themes: a denunciation of Price's sermon, an attack on the revolutionaries and their principles, and a defence of the British constitution and of prescriptive right. Much of Burke's disagreement with Price stemmed from a different interpretation of 1688, which for Burke exemplified that cautious and deliberate spirit inscribed in the constitution which ensured 'a manly, moral, regulated liberty'. While admitting that the French revolution was 'the most astonishing that has hitherto happened in the world', Burke denied any parallel between 1789 and 1688. French principles, created out of 'the nakedness and solitude of metaphysical abstraction', lay closer to the intolerant puritan spirit of 1649, which Price was accused of reviving. Against Price, too, Burke argued that the king owed his crown to a fixed rule of succession, not the choice of his people. He could not be 'cashiered for misconduct', as Price insisted, because he did not serve the people like other members of government. No 'new government' could be created if constitutional liberties were inherited and defined historically rather than understood as abstract principles.[4]

Burke then returned to the perpetrators of the revolution, whom he described as disenchanted lawyers and 'discontented men of quality' with too little to lose themselves to fear popular fervour, but whose actions would only result in a new nobility of moneylenders and stock speculators. But the main thrust of his argument was directed against their principles. Price had juxtaposed the 'rights of men' to prescriptive right, and Burke conceded that 'real rights of men' did exist (though there are disagreements about what he meant by this), such as the rule of law, the right to justice, to the fruits of one's industry, to non-interference from others generally, and to the inheritance of property. None the less, insisted Burke, these did not include a right to equal *things*, to judge in our own cause, or to defend ourselves exclusively. (Price in fact had not acknowledged such rights either: already the spectre of levelling and the implication that discussing natural rights implied returning to the state of nature hovered threateningly above the debate.) Burke thus conceded that 'rights' were not created only by existing governments, though how such rights were to be used to judge the inadequacies of any government except Britain's was left unclear unless we are to presume the principle of utility served this purpose for Burke. But he then argued that governments existed not to guarantee original rights but 'to provide for human *wants*' (only later to argue, in his *Thoughts and Details on Scarcity*, that 'to provide for us in our necessities is not in the power of government'). Any rights possessed before civil society were greatly altered at its inception and were now 'in a sort of *middle*' incapable of definition. Natural rights might have existed, but only civil rights could be discussed and analysed.[5]

Burke's central argument thus revolved around a theory of human nature and wants, and a notion of history and the fixity of patterns of behaviour and corresponding limits of possible change. Upon this vision, it is now generally agreed, rather than the natural law foundation several postwar historians tried to ascribe to him, Burke's idea of prescriptive right was built. His view of human nature was deeply pessimistic. The passions progressed naturally from frailty to vice, and individual moral failure, not political institutions or their corruption, largely caused social unhappiness. Manners and civilization distinguished modern from barbaric societies and depended upon the spirit of the gentleman and of nobility, owing nothing to the 'swinish multitude'. Nobility was 'the Corinthian capital of polished society', while 'perfect democracy' could generate only the partisan tyranny of the majority over the minority. In this sense the 'age of chivalry', Burke lamented, was already dead in France. Because people were governed by passion rather than reason, moreover, their loyalties were local and limited rather than expansive. Consequently 'just prejudice', especially deference to rank and to the monarchy, bound the British constitution together, aided by the Church of England, the 'body' of true religion being the teaching of obedience to earthly sovereigns. Expediency and utility consequently were central to every political judgement and act. Political obligation, too, derived from the organic and hierarchical nature of society and arose inescapably from each individual's social rank, not from any primordial rights given in the state of nature. The only hope for the revolution in France was to emulate Britain, and to turn away from the 'terrible revolution in property' which its confiscations of church holdings implied, and which left no prescriptive right secure.[6]

Early responses to Burke (1790–92)

The *Reflections* clearly appealed to an unmistakable 'British' tradition shared by many Whigs and Tories alike. George III insisted that every gentleman in the kingdom read it and a large number must have taken his advice, for the book sold about 19,000 copies in the first year and probably 30,000 over the next five. It was quickly translated into French and German and reprinted in Ireland and America. Not one to surrender his profits to the cause, Burke received at least £1,000 for his efforts.

The *Reflections* generated a total of over fifty critical responses. These can be divided into two main categories: works by new Whigs anxious to side with the revolution in the name of 1688 but without going as far as Paine, and those by Painites unwilling to compromise at all with Burke.[7]

The longest and best-known of these rebuttals were mainly of the first type. We will consider several of these in detail here, then Paine's own views, and the Painite reaction in chapter 5.

The first important reply to the *Reflections* was the novelist and historian Mary Wollstonecraft's *Vindication of the Rights of Men*, published in December 1790. Like Burke's work, Wollstonecraft's *Vindication* was not a concise analytical tract, but ranged widely over a number of fronts while concentrating on four main themes. Burke was primarily accused of being the 'champion of property' and of narrowing the defence of liberty to the maintenance of unequal property and, if need be, despotism and tyranny. But not only did the 'demon of property' always encroach upon liberty by creating great inequalities. It also destroyed sociability. 'Among unequals there can be no society', Wollstonecraft asserted, meaning friendship and mutual respect. Secondly, Burke was attacked for championing a 'gothic affability', or condescension and rudeness appropriate to feudalism, but not an advanced commercial society whose manners were defined by politeness and a liberal civility (and this discussion of modernity was to prove central to the entire ensuing debate). Wollstonecraft further defended the idea that rights were inherited by all at birth as rational creatures, especially equal rights to liberty compatible with that of others. Rights derived from God's creation of the world and no prescriptive act could undermine them. Burke was not accused of denying that natural rights existed altogether – which some of his later supporters would assert – but rather of virtually supporting slavery in his defence of prescriptive rights. Finally, Burke was denounced for writing 'sentimental jargon' which appealed only to the sensibility of his readers, instead of guiding their passions by arguing more rationally. (Soon his followers would ascribe precisely this strategy to Paine, and historians have too readily followed them.) Wollstonecraft concluded by praising the unselfish liberty of Greece and Rome, but conceded that the Romans had been only partially civilized compared to the moderns. But of the latter, only the middling orders were fit to rule. A 'fatherly solicitude' for the poor was necessary, but they were also envious 'brutes' corrupted by inequality. The 'vulgar', thus, were *both* the uncultivated poor and the affluent who, as mere creatures of habit, had never developed their own talents and capacities. This was the middle-class philosophy of liberty and civilization *par excellence*.[8]

Probably the best-known of the early replies to Burke was the Scottish philosopher and lawyer James Mackintosh's powerful *Vindiciae Gallicae*, published in early 1791, which more than any other work clarified the moderate Whig position which opposed Burke but also Paine's appeal to the people. Terming the *Reflections* the 'manifesto of a counter-revolution' – and Burke was thereafter often accused of causing the war with France – Mackintosh denied that Burke was a Whig at all. Burke had always abhorred abstract politics, touted aristocracy, and dreaded innovation. If 'Toryism' implied a preference for chivalry, superstition and the landed aristocracy, Burke was clearly more Tory than Whig. This meant that the principles of 1688 were more Mackintosh's than Burke's. That revolution, however, had sanctified the theory, but failed to ensure the practice of free government, because too few were represented in Parliament. The French revolution was justified because France had degenerated into an illegitimate inequality of orders dominated by an exclusive corporate spirit. This violated the natural and laudable tendency of the wealthy to rule everywhere, and revolt there had thus signalled the advancement of freedom by bringing to power that commercial and manufacturing 'middle rank among whom almost all the sense and virtue of society reside', and whose interests were more nearly those of the entire society than were the claims of a small group of unproductive consumers like the landed aristocracy. The natural progress of society was for commerce to overthrow a feudal and chivalric system of manners (while Burke seemed to collapse both stages of development), and for the search for a more perfect system of social and political liberty to follow. This commercial Whiggism dominates Mackintosh's work, though some republican themes were still included, such as a condemnation of standing armies and public debt. Dismissing Burke for first conceding the existence of natural rights, then contradicting himself by denying them, Mackintosh accepted the idea of natural liberty, and argued that the first duty of government was to preserve the natural rights of man, substantiating rights which could not be fulfilled in the state of nature, and thus creating political equality while tolerating a necessary degree of civil inequality.[9]

A close friend of Mackintosh and a fellow Scot was the writer and historian Thomas Christie, whose *Letters on the Revolution in France* were written in January 1791. Christie, too, was surprised that a 'liberal scholar' like Burke who knew 'the patriots of Greece and Rome' should immerse himself in 'gothic feudality', and spurned Burke's 'miserable deformed gothic idol'. Defending Price's right to discuss politics from the pulpit, Christie emphasized that while he respected the British constitution, its authority rested only on *'The Rights of Man'*, which was founded on the great principles of eternal justice and reason. 'The ideas of a Lawyer eternally haunt Burke', he insisted, because Burke saw no other grounds for holding rights than prescription. But natural rights could not be removed by 'the subsequent conventions of civilized society'. Burke was thus no Whig, but had revived the Toryism of 1689 by urging an unchangeable hereditary succession. But though Britain needed a reformation based on 'the opinion of the reflecting and enlightened part of the community' (the opinion of the rest being unprincipled and inherently unstable), Christie thought it lacked 'adequate causes to produce a revolution'. None the less the *Reflections* had angered the unreflecting, most of whom, thought Christie, had not particularly favoured the revolution at first. But to Christie himself the fall of the *ancien régime* was 'the greatest and most glorious event that ever took place in the history of the world' and 'the only revolution that has *completely* respected the rights of mankind ... the only revolution that is likely to change the object of ambition amongst men, and to convert it into an emulation of superior wisdom and virtue, instead of a lust of power and conquest'. The corruption and tyranny of the *ancien régime* rendered its overthrow unavoidable. Burke had greatly exaggerated the accompanying violence. The National Assembly had acted wisely in creating a more rational system of government, and its policies were detailed at great length, with particular praise given to efforts to render the king a constitutional monarch.[10]

A number of replies to Burke were by prominent Dissenters, for whom the *Reflections* was also an irritating defence of the Test and Corporation Acts. Except at the very beginning, the Dissenters were by no means united in applauding the revolution, however.[11] Certainly by mid-1792 many found themselves torn between their hopes that political and religious liberty was being created in France, on the one hand, and the accusation – invoking the spectre of 1649 – of being unpatriotic on the other. Most were reluctant to stick their heads above the parapet and therefore quickly rallied behind the forces of order rather than those of change. The Dissenters had fought hard to achieve respectability during the eighteenth century, and when they were attacked as a group the fear of losing this reputation proved too strong for many.

The most important Dissenting response to Burke was by the Unitarian minister, scientist and philosopher Joseph Priestley, whose fourteen *Letters to the Right Honourable Edmund Burke*, published in Birmingham in 1791, noted that while clergy had universally approved the *Reflections*, it had been reprobated by the Low Church party and Dissenters. Priestley defended the right of revolution and the powers and policies of the National Assembly and in his closing sections heralded the extinction of national prejudices, of the 'bondage of the mind', colonies and war, and the inauguration of a millennium derived from true religion, philosophy, 'good sense and the prevailing spirit of commerce'. He agreed that natural rights were not surrendered in civil society, but he was principally concerned with the established Church, loyalty to which Burke had termed 'the first of our prejudices' or pillars of the constitution. In Priestley's eyes every defence of the French revolution also vindicated the principles of Dissent. The respect paid to any religion or church ought to accord only with its virtue, not its antiquity or proximity to civil power. Conceding that social peace required religion, Priestley none the less argued that electing the clergy on the Dissenting model (as the French sought) would not harm the Church of England. At present Anglicanism was corrupted by the system of preferment by which promotions took place, as well as the wealth of the higher clergy. The state had also 'taken a great deal too much upon it' in attempting to guide religious affairs. The property of the church, moreover, was held in trust for society and could be disposed of by the state as the French had proposed. The Dissenters possessed a right to representation based upon their payment of taxes, benefited the cause of religion in their diversity and would, Priestley promised, continue to assail the alliance between the Crown and the Anglican Church and to press the cause of parliamentary reform.[12]

Joseph Towers was among the other early Dissenting respondents to Burke. Towers insisted that there were 'certainly natural rights, independently of all positive law or appointment', that all legitimate government derived from the people, that men were naturally equal and that taxation required the consent of the majority. His fellow Dissenter Capel Lofft similarly agreed that the only rights surrendered in civil society were those inconsistent with it, vindicated the necessity for revolution in France and devoted much space to defending Rousseau, who was otherwise largely missing from the revolution debate. The consequence of Burke's view of rights, added another critic of the *Reflections*, was that 'the people would, in no case have a right to alter their government'.[13]

Further replies to Burke emphasized various themes. Several accounts mocked Burke as 'the Filmer of the age'. Catherine Macaulay defended republicanism. The radical journalist Charles Pigott attacked Burke for inconsistency considering his views on the American revolution, while an anonymous assailant accused him of defending papism and tyranny. The *Analytical Review* charged that on Burke's principles both the Magna Carta and 1688 would have been considered unacceptable innovations. The poet Sir Brooke Boothby denied that the *ancien régime* was endurable, praised the abolition of religious hierarchies and mocked Burke's idea that the demise of Gothic feudalism entailed an end to learning, the arts, honour and humanity. An SCI member, George Rous, stressed that the location of national sovereignty lay in the people themselves rather than Parliament, but also noted that the House of Lords usefully checked the democratic excesses to which the Commons were occasionally prone. Replying in February 1790 to Burke's speech in the Commons on the revolution, Earl Stanhope chastised him for not condemning the tyranny and cruelty of the *ancien régime* and termed the revolution likely to 'make the world, for centuries, prosperous, free, and happy' as well as conducive to improved relations with Britain. Another Whig response – one of several which defended Price – insisted that the latter merely followed Locke on the question of resistance to unlawful usurpation.[14]

70

By the vehemence of his attack Burke did much to bring the revolution to public attention, forcing many to take sides who had earlier, one Revolution Society member thought, had vague sympathies for the fate of Louis and his queen but equally had resented French interference during the American wars, 'and with these sentiments, they leave them to settle their own government'. A major result of Burke's arguments was to give greater prominence to natural rights ideals than they had enjoyed in radical debates hitherto; as one writer put it, the *Reflections* had the effect of 'producing a general recognition of those inalienable rights, the existence of which it imprudently and weakly questions'. In this respect Burke demanded that Whigs choose between adhering to 'the British constitution' and to natural rights *per se*. Previously no conflict had seemed to exist between these ideals. Whig radicals had always agreed that reform required the restitution of the constitution, which meant safeguarding both natural and civil rights. Now these objects appeared juxtaposed. But to most new Whigs natural rights remained primary, though the British constitution was not far behind. As Christie wrote in 1791, 'there is something that I hold to be greater and dearer than the British or any Constitution: that is, the rights of man, founded on the great principles of eternal justice and reason. It is from these Rights that all particular Constitutions derived their authority, and the British Constitution is respectable only as it is conformable to this unchangeable standard.' Others, too, castigated Burke for describing the British constitution as too complex for most to understand. It rested on only one pivot, the rights of men, and 'On that axis it performs all its revolutions and points to one common centre – the choice of the people'.[15]

Exporting America: the *Rights of Man. Being an Answer to Mr. Burke's Attack on the French Revolution* (February 1791)

Of the responses to Burke, only Paine's succeeded in becoming genuinely popular if not indeed 'one of the most useful and benevolent books ever offered to mankind' (which was Paine's own view).[16] In the first part of the *Rights of Man* Paine addressed one of the central issues of the emerging revolutionary dispute – the nature of rights – at length for the first time in his life. He also argued more strongly for a republican government than contemporary radicals had done. These themes, however, were only systematically articulated in Part Two, published a year later. The first part was less well organized and, like the *Reflections*, was more a series of immediate comments on the revolution rather than a reflective treatise. We will therefore consider the central achievements of the work as a whole in the following chapter, after first examining the arguments of each part here.

The first part of the *Rights of Man* is divisible by subject into eight segments: an introductory section where the question of the right of living generations over earlier ones dominates; Paine's explanation of the origins of the French revolution; a brief account of rights; a lengthy comparison of the existing British government and class system with those intended to be created by the new French constitution; a further analysis of the development of the revolution; the reprinting of the French 'Declaration of the Rights of Man and of Citizens' with Paine's observations thereon; a 'Miscellaneous Chapter' which formed the basis for Part Two; and Paine's brief conclusion.

The *Rights of Man* opened by declaring that the revolution was viewed differently by European peoples compared to their governors. For the former the French cause embraced 'the interests of the entire world', but many of the latter profited from enmity between France and other nations. As a friend to American independence, Burke should have hailed its French counterpart. That he had not, Paine implied, was connected to Burke's rumoured receipt of a secret state pension in return for hiring his pen (in fact Burke was awarded £1,200 annually from mid-1794). The *Reflections*, then, was not a principled treatise, and Burke not an independent writer. For Paine few accusations could be more damning.[17]

Paine's most important initial disagreement with Burke concerned the authority of past legislation over existing generations, for Burke had contended against Price that the settlement of 1688 bound all posterity. Burke thus denied the people's right to choose their own governors, cashier them for misconduct and frame their own government. But the Parliament of 1688 had done just this, Paine thought, but then restricted its own successors. This was inconsistent and unjust: 'every age and generation must be as free to act for itself, *in all cases*, as the ages and generation which preceded it'. 'Governing beyond the grave', or forcing the living to be compelled by the actions of the dead, was tyranny.[18]

Paine's account of the origins and course of events in France was intended chiefly to correct Burke's misperceptions. For Paine 'it was not against Louis XVI, but against the despotic principles of the government, that the nation revolted'. Paine admitted that Louis 'was known to be the friend of the nation' and rarely ruled despotically. But the revolution was for *principles* rather than against *men*, and Louis's moderation did not mitigate his unjust powers. Despotism, moreover, had infiltrated into every corner of France, assuming variously the guises of feudal, ministerial, monarchical, parliamentary, or ecclesiastical tyranny. Burke, concentrating on the personality of the king, lamented the loss of the 'age of chivalry', and did not sympathize with the victims of the Bastille and other prisons, only the few officials killed liberating them. In one of Paine's most memorable phrases, Burke was ridiculed because he 'pities the plumage, but forgets the dying bird'. No great violence had marred the revolution to date, and individual acts of bloody vengeance, such as the affixing of heads to pikes, could be explained by the corruption of public morals through the cruelty of the *ancien régime*.[19]

Paine then turned to rights. Burke appeared to deny that men possessed any rights at all. But this could not be his meaning, Paine assumed. Rights of one kind or another existed, everyone agreed. The chief problem was their origins. But to discover these it was essential to go back 'the whole way', not merely a hundred or a thousand years. The origin of the rights of man was the origin of man himself, at the Creation. All histories thereof, and particularly the Mosaic account, 'whether taken as divine authority or merely historical', agreed 'in establishing one point, *the unity of man*; by which I mean that men are all of *one degree*, and consequently that all men are born equal, and with equal natural rights'. Consequently each generation possessed identical natural rights 'in the same manner as if posterity had been continued by creation'. On these rights were founded civil rights. The former included 'all the rights of the mind' as well as 'all those rights of acting as an individual for his own comfort and happiness, which are not injurious to the natural rights of others'. Civil rights existed because not all natural rights, especially self-protection, could be guaranteed by the individual. Those natural rights 'in which the *power* to execute is as perfect in the individual as the right itself', such as freedom of religion, remained intact in civil society. Others, such as the right to judge in one's own case, were surrendered in exchange for the guarantee of just redress in society, which secured the right more fully, civil power having no mandate to invade any natural right. The divine origin of rights and of the idea of natural liberty was thus central to Paine's account. Civil authority could not defy divine intention, and natural rights always defined the nature and limits of civil rights, with the Bible remaining Paine's principal authority.[20]

None the less two kinds of government in particular did interfere with natural rights: those disguised by superstition and governed through priestcraft; and those based on power and conquest. A third form of government, based on reason, took cognizance of the common rights and interests of mankind and was itself grounded in a mutual compact between a people to form a government, and not between themselves and a ruler, as Locke had assumed. The existing British government was of the second type, having originated in William's invasion of Britain. Moreover, not only was a 'constitution' the sole basis for founding a just government; it could not exist as an ideal alone, but had to assume 'a visible form', by which Paine meant a single document mutually agreed upon. Britain lacked a constitution in this (American) sense and could create one only by calling a national convention to establish a new social compact. But governments had no right to alter themselves, since this 'would be arbitrary', and most previous parliamentary reformers had thus pursued a false path. This view would inspire the chief strategy of the new reform movement of the 1790s.[21]

Paine then turned to expose the wrongs of the existing government and class system. Parliamentary representation was extremely limited and unfairly distributed. Game laws prevented small farmers from taking animals even on their own land. Monopolies inhibited the freedom of commerce. The right to make war lay with kings and ministers, who shouldered few of the subsequent burdens. By contrast, degrading aristocratic titles had been abolished in France. Primogeniture, by which the younger children of the aristocracy were virtually disowned, was to be eradicated there. Paine considered at length why the aristocracy were poor legislators, emphasizing the absurdity of supposing that talent in this field could be hereditary, although the right to exercise it was. The system of taxation and finance merely fuelled the inordinate desires of the aristocracy, moreover, and was a form of 'conquering at home' for the rest of the population. Nor was religion better practised or organized in Britain. The French had raised the salaries of the lower clergy and diminished those of the higher, while abolishing tithes and establishing universal freedom of conscience. Only by separating church and state, Paine insisted, could the naturally 'mild and benign' character of any religion emerge. Finally, while the French constitution left executive power with the king, sovereignty was assigned to the nation and the National Assembly was elected by the people. The House of Commons, however, originated as a boon or grant from the monarchy and did not recognize the principle of popular sovereignty.[22]

After dwelling further on the sources of the revolution and stressing the importance of American inspiration to the French, Paine reprinted the 'Declaration of the Rights of Man and Of Citizens' with a brief explanation of its implications for a notion of the equivalent duties of citizens. In the final segment of the *Rights of Man* Paine offered a series of miscellaneous observations which strengthened his case against hereditary succession, his support of the general will as the basis of political legitimacy, and his growing tendency to equate hereditary succession with despotism, especially for later generations, since the first king in a royal line might have been chosen by all. Paine's conclusion also rejected 'mixed government' as inevitably corrupt and lacking in responsibility either in the king, or the prime minister, who could always hide behind his party. Real government here took place only by the cabinet and through committees. But this was impermissible in 'a well constituted republic' where corrupting compromises between ill-fitting parts were unnecessary. Paine at first denied that he recommended any particular form of government, arguing that

'That which·a whole nation chooses to do, it has a right to do'. None the less he then sided clearly with republicanism, hoping that with a true 'renovation of the natural order of things ... combining moral with political happiness and national prosperity ... the cause of wars would be taken away'. A European Congress similar to plans put forward by Henri IV of France in the early seventeenth century could be convened for the purpose of preventing war. Man was 'not the enemy of man, but through the medium of false government'. The 'age of revolutions' would at last render this clear to all.[23]

Towards Social Justice: the *Rights of Man, Part Second. Combining Principle and Practice* (1792)

The *Rights of Man, Part Second* appeared in February 1792. Wary of Paine's powers, the government tried to prevent its publication. Paine had been recommended by Thomas Christie to a printer named Chapman, who began to set the type, but stopped when he reached a point which 'appeared of a dangerous tendency'. Unmoved by Paine's entreaties, which he later claimed were accompanied by a declamation against all Dissenters as 'a pack of hypocrites', he instead offered to buy the copyright of the text for 1,000 guineas, obviously ministerial funds. Paine of course refused.[24]

'The most impressive of all his writings', a distinguished philosopher has recently termed it, Part Two of the *Rights of Man* is a considerably better organized work, as Paine himself conceded in its preface. Theoretically it is a much more astute attempt to forge a radical philosophy from the suggestive threads left hanging in the brief 'Miscellaneous Chapter' and other sections of its predecessor. Accordingly it was even less a response to Burke, but was instead a tract on social and political thought laid before the public in the hope that monarchy and aristocracy would not 'continue seven years longer in any of the enlightened countries in Europe' once their true rationale unfolded through open debate.[25]

Paine's starting point in Part Two was again the American Revolution and its impact, and indeed the text has been described as considerably more American than French in outlook. America had been 'the only spot in the political world, where the principles of universal reformation could begin'. The diversity of its immigrants and their different religious backgrounds had enforced a spirit of compromise. Conquering the wilderness demanded continuous exertion, which enlarged the mental horizons of the colonists, as well as great co-operation, by which they came to see one another 'not with the inhuman idea of a natural enemy, but as kindred', while old divisions, fomented by the 'quarrels and intrigues of governments', were now superseded. Moreover, America's increasing opulence proved that its government assisted prosperity. By contrast, Europe abounded with 'hordes of miserable poor'. 'The greedy hand of government' could be found 'thrusting itself into every corner and crevice of industry, and grasping the spoil of the multitude', making 'universal civilization and commerce' impossible. Moreover, monarchies were military in nature and aimed at plunder and revenue. Peace, thus, which was to remain as important a goal for Paine as prosperity, required governments to be founded upon a *'moral theory, on a system of universal peace, on the indefeasible, hereditary rights of man'*.[26]

The connection of democratic republicanism and prosperity led Paine, in one of the most famous segments of his work, to elaborate upon the distinction between 'society' and 'government' first tentatively explored in *Common Sense*. Now Paine argued at much greater length that society antedated government and would remain, at least in certain circumstances, 'if the formality of government was abolished'. Society was a 'great chain of connection' based upon 'mutual dependence and reciprocal interest' between landholders, merchants, tradesmen, manufacturers and other occupations whose strong common interest regulated their affairs almost entirely. Thus 'society performs for itself almost every thing which is ascribed to government', while 'a great part' – but not all, we must note – of 'government' was 'mere imposition'. Compelled to co-operate because their wants were greater and more diverse than their individual capacities, people were moreover bound together by 'a system of social affections' which produced a 'love for society'. The more perfect civilization was, thus, 'the less occasion has it for government, because the more does it regulate its own affairs, and govern itself'. Such a stage required 'but few general laws'. Thus uncivilized governments upset rather than reinforced the natural harmony of society. In the Gordon Riots of 1780, for example, government encouragement of anti-Catholic prejudices had fuelled disorder. Excessive and unequal taxation also made the majority poor, desperate and easily provoked into riot. America proved that concord was based upon society, for there different groups intermingled peacefully, 'the poor are not oppressed, the rich are not privileged. Industry is not mortified by the splendid extravagance of a court rioting at its expense ... taxes are few, because government is just.' America hence taught the world that *'government is nothing more than a national association acting on the principles of society'*.[27]

Existing European and indeed all 'old governments' were thus not founded upon 'society' but upon usurpation. In Britain the Norman invasion had established 'a continual system of war and extortion'.

By contrast the 'new system of government' delegated power 'for the common benefit of society', and encouraged 'universal society, as the means of universal commerce' instead of national prejudice. The old form of government Paine now simply termed 'hereditary', the new, 'representative'. *All* hereditary government (and Paine regarded this as his most important argument) was 'in its nature tyranny', because no one could rightfully impose future rulers on later generations. It was also inefficient and truly encouraged 'mental levelling' since any fool might become king, while no one would be stupid enough to propose, for example, that literature become hereditary. Contested hereditary claims also provoked many more wars than popular elections, while kings also encouraged foreign wars.[28]

By contrast the representative system ensured the wisest laws, as evidenced by the best of ancient governments, the Athenian democracy. None the less the ancients had not understood the principle of representation. If they had, monarchy and aristocracy might never have arisen, since they emerged only after society became 'too populous, and too extensive for the simple democratical form'. But 'republic' was not a particular form of government, only one devoted to the common good, which representation best secured. Simple democracies were incapable of governing great populations, but so were monarchies and aristocracies, which were too centralized to know the true state of agriculture, manufactures, commerce and other phenomena in all quarters of society. Representation, however, overcame the difficulties of both form and knowledge, and thus the incapacities of simple democracy, aristocracy and monarchy alike. 'Ingrafting' representation upon democracy permitted both a diversity of interests and an extensive territory and population. Here rulers were never too young or too old, and succeeded one another with peaceful regularity. They governed cheaply and openly, without mystery and intrigue. Who would opt voluntarily for monarchy by comparison?[29]

A representative democracy could not be founded by an existing government, however, but only by a constitution through which a whole people installed a new government. Governing without a constitution was merely exercising 'power without a right', and any people thus possessed the right to form a constitution. In the United States, each state had formed its own government after the Declaration of Independence in July 1776, and Paine used the Pennsylvania example to illustrate how a people could meet in a convention and then govern according to a constitution. Creating the federal government had followed the same pattern, with the people concluding a compact amongst themselves, rather than with government, then writing a constitution which bound the government itself; first the Articles of Confederation, accepted in 1781. The Articles had been found to grant too little power to the federal government, but they had been amended through the same process, each state having elected a convention to consider the new constitution. And after the federal constitution had been accepted, Pennsylvania amended its state constitution according to the same procedure. In all instances the constitution represented a pre-governmental 'society' meeting to compose a particular government.[30]

Britain thus lacked a constitution because its *'controlling* power' lay not in the people but with the government. The Norman tyranny had been amended in various ways. But the Magna Carta 'did not create and give powers to Government' and merely restricted power already usurped. Subsequent shifts of power had similar results: the Bill of Rights established in 1688, for example, reallocated powers, profits and privileges, leaving the people merely the right of petitioning. Coining another oft-quoted phrase, Paine instead called it the 'Bill of Wrongs', perpetrated by some who were never elected, and none elected for the purpose. Nor was there evidence of constitutional control over the oligarchy which arose under Walpole. Its power had been virtually unbounded, the parts of government able only to 'embarrass each other', its capacity to raise taxes seemingly unrestrained. The nation thus was ruled solely by recourse to legal precedents, about which Paine asserted that 'the greater distance of time they are drawn from, the more they are to be suspected'.[31]

Paine then turned to consider the constituent parts of governments. These were usually divided into legislative, executive and judicial branches, but might be reduced to two, legislation and execution or administration, adjudication being merely the latter strictly defined. Considering whether two legislative houses, as in America, or one, as in France, was preferable, Paine reviewed the objections to each without at this point taking sides. But he was certain that no executive should be paid too much, nor entrusted with vast powers which could be exercised without popular consent, such as the British monarch's capacity to form alliances and declare war and peace.[32]

In the final and longest section of the *Rights of Man*, Paine summarized the lessons of America and France. Since all constitutions and governments sought collective happiness, it was legitimate to ask why such 'a great portion of mankind in what are called civilized countries' were 'in a state of poverty and wretchedness, far below the condition of an Indian'. The cause of this, Paine thought, lay not 'in any natural defect in the principles of civilization, but in preventing those principles having an universal operation', which resulted in 'a perpetual system of war and expense, that drains the country, and defeats the general felicity of which civilization is capable'. Though commerce could satisfy the needs of all, governments warred barbarically 'like so many individuals in a state of nature'. Ignoring the more advanced principles of 'civilization', governments extracted from the poor especially 'a great portion of those earnings which should be supplied to their own subsistence and comfort'. Poverty was thus caused by excessive taxation. Only a thirtieth or fortieth of the amount raised was necessary for civil government. The rest was stolen extravagance.[33]

This elaboration of Paine's views on commerce and civilization was central to his broader notions of government and of peace, and accordingly merits closer scrutiny. Vital here was Paine's notion of a system of interdependent needs, which he usually termed 'society', and which was drawn largely from natural law writings. Commerce, Paine thought, was 'a pacific system, operating to unite mankind by rendering nations, as well as individuals, useful to each other. Since each individual was improvable principally 'by means of his interest', if 'commerce were permitted to act to the universal extent it is capable of', it would 'extirpate the system of war, and produce a revolution in the uncivilized state of governments'. Commerce had 'arisen since those governments began' and was 'the greatest approach towards universal civilization, that has yet been made by any means not immediately flowing from moral principles'. Instead of one party (or country) always losing in any exchange, as many earlier economic writers had believed, Paine asserted that needs ideally were mutually fulfilled in trade. The natural course of commerce was 'no other than the traffic of two individuals, multiplied on a scale of numbers; and by the same rule that nature intended the intercourse of two, she intended that of all'. Consequently nature had 'distributed the materials of manufactures and commerce in various and distant parts of a nation and of the world; and as they cannot be procured by war so cheaply or so commodiously as by commerce, she has rendered the latter the means of extirpating the former'. Uncivilized governments had consequently misunderstood commerce completely. By war and taxation they inhibited commercial growth at home as well as abroad. But when nations trading with Britain were harmed, their capacity to buy British goods also lessened. Thus 'the prosperity of any commercial nation is regulated by the prosperity of the rest. If they are poor, she cannot be rich.' Invariably reciprocal, true commerce consisted 'in the balance being a level of benefits among all nations'. Nor should merchants be condemned for profiting on imports and exports, provided nations gained thereby. Paine none the less felt that domestic trade was primary, because its advantages remained at home. Least important was commerce derived from foreign conquest and colonies, since the need to maintain large navies absorbed any trading profits. Mutual interest, not military might, was the best protection commerce could receive.[34]

His general principles established, Paine turned again to condemn flaws in the British system of government. Charters and corporations which gave individuals and associations specified voting and other rights at the expense of the rest of the population were dismissed, as were laws forcing the poor to remain near their birthplace to receive relief. The House of Lords was illegitimate because no other occupation – peers deriving their income primarily from rents – was separately represented, and this monopoly or 'combination' was used in order to deflect taxes from the land to consumption, which further oppressed the middling classes and poor. Paine conceded that agriculture had special status since all were interested in its fruits. But he denied that the aristocracy should be the chief proprietors, since only active farmers did the actual cultivation. The peers, moreover, also had their hands in the public till elsewhere, filling unnecessary offices through patronage and generally burdening the public with their progeny.[35]

The most novel proposals in Part Two were contained in the final segment of chapter 5, where Paine detailed his schemes for the redistribution of wealth. Here he proclaimed for the first time that the aim of government was to provide 'for the instruction of youth, and the support of age, so as to exclude, as much as possible, profligacy from the one, and despair from the other'. These partly republican-inspired goals thus allowed for a more virtuous electorate and greater social equality. But government was thus to be accorded a much more substantial and positive role than Paine had earlier implied and moreover would have to find the money to meet these aims. Since 1688, however, and especially since the Hanoverian succession, taxation had increased considerably with the expansion of both the national debt and current expenses. Though Paine saw some sense in a national debt, since it served 'to keep alive a capital, useful to commerce', vast increases in current expenses were unnecessary. He therefore proposed cutting all unnecessary costs and began by presuming that about £500,000 would suffice for the non-military expenses of the British government, giving 300 representatives a reasonable salary and some 1,773 public servants wages ranging from £75 to £10,000 annually. About £1.5 million would therefore suffice for the peacetime expenses of government, leaving some £6 million remaining to dispense from legitimate existing revenues.[36]

Many of Paine's most intriguing proposals resulted from his efforts to dispose of this surplus. The most important existing problem was the growth of poverty. Rising poor rates, Paine felt, would be largely unnecessary if taxes diminished, since about a quarter of the poor's wages disappeared through taxes upon consumption. He therefore proposed to abolish the poor rates completely, but to remit to the poor double their present support from the rates, or £4 million in total. This they would receive when they were most in need, by instituting a programme which has often been seen as heralding the modern welfare state. To ensure them a minimal education, £4 per year would be allotted to each child under age 14, with parish ministers ascertaining that the funds were so spent. Of the aged, some at 50 (about a third of the total) were already unable to support themselves. These would receive £6 per annum until the age of 60, or about a ninth of a skilled labourer's average wage, and £10 thereafter, and not as a matter of charity, either, but of right, in return for taxes paid over a lifetime of labour. Two-thirds of the society would not require such support, however. Paine then proposed to give ten shillings per year for six years' schooling for children of the near-poor who found this a considerable burden. A further £1 would be given to women on the birth of each child and £20,000 made available to defray the funeral costs of all who died away from home. Next, acknowledging that distress was more extreme in London, Paine proposed that two work-houses be constructed or acquired there in order to provide temporary employment, meals and lodging of a standard at least equivalent to a military barrack, with part of each individual's earnings being returned to them on their departure. Paine estimated that some 24,000 people annually might be helped through this provision. Funds would also be set aside for the maintenance of disbanded soldiers and sailors after a military alliance with France rendered many superfluous. Finally, and most dramatically, Paine proposed a system of progressive taxation on inheritances in order to distribute wealth further. On estates annually worth from £50 to £500, the tax would be only some 3d per pound (1 ¼ per cent) of value, but at £23,000 (equivalent to several million pounds today) it would reach 100 per cent. Estates so large were simply a 'prohibitable luxury' based upon a marginal utility calculation of how far they actually supported any family, though property acquired by honest industry would not be affected, only that received by bequest. By this means the aristocracy would carry its burden of just taxes. But it is important to point out, given the subsequent debate about the *Rights of Man*, that these proposals did not threaten to destroy the existing property system completely. Estates of up to some £13–14,000 a year – a very considerable sum earned by probably only 200 families in Britain – would still produce a profit to their holder, Paine estimated. Larger estates – those owned by approximately the wealthiest 200 families – would have to be divided. Consequently that old republican bugbear, primogeniture, would be abolished, both because it was unjust and 'because the country suffers by its operation'. In addition, Paine urged that all restrictions on workmen's wages be lifted, leaving them 'as free to make their own bargains, as the law-makers are to let their farms and houses'. Doubtless reflecting upon his own experiences many years earlier, he urged increases in salaries for excise officers the lower clergy and common soldiers and sailors. But a further tax upon the profits of holders of stock in the debt (at that time untaxed was to be added to help pay off the national debt.[37]

The *Rights of Man* Part Two concluded with further reflections on a potential military alliance between Britain, France and other countries, since this was essential to Paine's general scheme for reducing taxes, as well as to his commercial ideal. Such an alliance might be begun by confederating the fleets of Holland, Britain and France. No new ships were to be built, and all existing navies could be simultaneously cut back by nine-tenths. With the United States, the alliance might then propose that Spain grant independence to the countries of South America and open them to freedom of commerce. Wishing 'freedom and happiness to all nations', Paine hoped that extending revolution throughout Europe would reduce national animosities and increase religious toleration.[38]

Some of these points were again briefly defended in a pamphlet Paine wrote shortly before his departure for France, the *Letter Addressed to the Addressers* (1792), which remains the best short statement of his republicanism. Here Paine counselled British democrats to convene to form a true national constitution. The notion that Parliament should reform itself he termed 'a worn-out, hackneyed subject', since no government had 'a right to alter itself, either in whole or in part'. He reiterated the right of universal suffrage since all paid taxes on their property or labour. Paine also proposed a general review of laws, to be repeated every 21 years so that obsolete laws no longer crowded the statute books. Finally, he ridiculed the Society of the Friends of the People's demand for 'temperate and moderate' reform, describing them as mere 'place-hunting reformers'. Only two classes existed, those who paid taxes and those who received them, and the Friends of the People merely aspired to join the latter and fatten on the former. Several of these points, particularly the principle of universal suffrage, were later also defended in Paine's *Dissertation on First Principles of Government* (1795), which examined the French constitution of that year.[39]

Notes to Chapter 3: Rights of Man

1   E. Black (1963), pp. 212–18. On Dissent in this period see also J. Creasey (1966), R. Davis (1971), pp. 28–52, G. Ditchfield (1974), A. Goodwin (1979), pp. 65–98. On Dissenting thought see A. Lincoln (1938), H. Dickinson (1977), pp. 197–205, and, in relation to America, S. Lynd (1968).
2   R. Price (1927), p. 466; C. Macaulay (1790), pp. 22, 20.
3   On the impact of the revolution in Britain see P. Brown (1918), C. Cone (1968) and C. Emsley (1979), but especially the modern standard work,

A. Goodwin (1979). The best short survey of the subject is H. Dickinson (1985). For Scotland see H. Meikle (1912). The parliamentary aspects are detailed in S. Maccoby (1955b) and W. Laprade (1970), though the latter is strongly biased against Paine. The best selection of primary sources, though emphasizing conservative and moderate reform opinion, is the 3-volume *A Comparative Display*. Other collections are A. Cobban (1950) and M. Butler (1984). On the Society of the Friends of the People see I. Hampsher-Monk (1978).

4 E. Burke (1987), pp. 7, 10, 14, 24, 33–4. On Burke see F. O'Gorman (1973), C. MacPherson (1980), M. Freeman (1980), I. Kramnick (1977a), F. Lock (1985) and J. Pocock's introduction to E. Burke (1987). A good collection of texts and commentary is I. Hampsher-Monk (1987). Also useful is A. Ayer (1988), pp. 56–71.

5 E. Burke (1987), pp. 35–46, 51–5; Burke (1826), Vol. 4, p. 226. Burke's attack on Price had an important antecedent in Josiah Tucker's *Treatise Concerning Civil Government* (1781; on the text see J. Pocock, 1985, pp. 157–91). For a summary of disagreements about Burke's theory of rights see M. Freeman (1980), pp. 85–93. A longer account is B. Wilkins (1967), pp. 163–246, which argues that Burke continued to believe in natural rights. Burke had earlier argued that 'a conservation and secure enjoyment of our natural rights is the great and ultimate purpose of civil society' (I. Hampsher-Monk, 1987, p. 76).

6 E. Burke (1987), pp. 76, 81, 83–8, 90, 124, 127, 163, 166, 176, 217. For the natural law view of Burke see P. Stanlis (1958) and, for emphases on utility and prescription, P. Lucas (1968), J. Dinwiddy (1974b) and F. Lock (1985), pp. 90–4.

7 On responses to Burke see J. Boulton (1963), pp. 75–96, 151–206, R. Fennessy (1963), pp. 181–212, A. Goodwin (1979), pp. 99–135, and F. Lock (1985), pp. 132–66. Defences of Burke include *A Vindication* (1791), which termed Burke a Whig who none the less upheld divine right (pp. 81, 141).

8 M. Wollstonecraft (1790), pp. 20, 24, 8, 12, 92, 32, 20–2, 78, 66–8, 121, 24, 98, 145, 151, 28. See J. Boulton (1963), pp. 67–76 and M. Myers (1977).

9 J. Mackintosh (1846), Vol. 3, pp. 8, 138, 135, 34–5, 51, 62, 76, 81, 94, 99, 95. On the text see W. Christian (1973b), J. Boulton (1963), pp. 151–84 and L. McKenzie (1980). Pocock contends that the 'Gothic' reading of the *Reflections* was mistaken and that Burke was also defending modern politeness and commerce, which he saw as rooted in older manners (E. Burke, 1987, pp. xxxii–iii, also generally Pocock, 1985, pp. 193–212). But he also argues that Burke in many ways feared the growing influence of the middle classes, and in some respects tried to displace the Scottish vindication of their social, economic and cultural position (1985, pp. 280–1). For the view that Burke caused the war by inciting hatred of the revolution, see the *Morning Chronicle*, 28 January 1796.

10 T. Christie (1791), pp. 5–6, 12–16, 21, 24, 32, 44, 47–8, 58–9, 89–100, 120–1, 149, 207.

11 On Dissenting reactions to the revolution see R. Davis (1971), pp. 53–76 and J. Creasey (1966).

12 J. Priestley (1791b), pp. 22–3, 144–50, 49, 22–33, 86, 55, 73, 52, 131, 139. Other responses to Burke (e.g. *Strictures*, 1791) also concentrated on the issue of religious toleration.

13 J. Towers (1790), pp. 69, 150–1, 155; C. Lofft (1790), pp. 28–9; Lofft (1791); W. White (1792), p. 9.

14 *Wonderful Flights* (1791), p. 21; *Comparative Display* (1970), Vol. 1, pp. 494–519; C. Pigott (1791); *Philo-Theodosius* (1790), p. 6; *Analytical Review*, vol. 8 (1790), p. 303; B. Boothby (1791), pp. 19–22, 42–56, 38; G. Rous (1790), p. 38; *Comparative Display* (1970), Vol. 2, pp. 196–202; E. Stanhope (1790); *An Answer to the Rt. Hon. Edmund Burke* (1791), p. 8.

15 Major Scott (1791), p. 51; *A Letter to a Member* (1791), p. 30; T. Christie (1791), p. 11; B. Bousfield (1790), p. 10.

16 Paine (1945), Vol. 2, p. 444. Useful introductions to the text include Paine (1969a), Paine (1985) and (1987), D. Wilson (1988), pp. 65–95 and A. Ayer (1988), pp. 72–113. A relevant and careful unpublished study is P. Burnell (1972).

17 Paine (1945), Vol. 1, pp. 247–9.

18 Paine (1945), Vol. 1, pp. 250–2.

19 Paine (1945), Vol. 1, pp. 255–61, 265–6.

20 Paine (1945), Vol. 1, pp. 273–6.

21 Paine (1945), Vol. 1, pp. 277–80.

22 Paine (1945), Vol. 1, pp. 281–95.

23 Paine (1945), Vol. 1, pp. 296–344, 251. On Henri's plans for peace see Sully (1909) and, for a general study of such plans, S. Hemleben (1943). Henri's plan was first to destroy the power of the House of Habsburg, then divide Europe into fifteen nations (including four republics) linked by commerce, defended by a single military force (which could be used to conquer parts of Asia and Africa), and governed by a council of sixty-six representatives reappointed every three years. This served as a model for the later plans of William Penn, John Bellers, Rousseau, Saint-Pierre and others. Paine explained a decade later that the best means of setting the plan in motion would be for leading powers like France and Britain to reduce their navies and compel others to do the same (1945, Vol. 2, p. 1476).

24 *The Genuine Trial* (1792), pp. 31–4.

25 A. Ayer (1988), p. 91; Paine (1945), Vol. 1, pp. 348–53.

26 G. Williams (1969), p. 7; Paine (1945), Vol. 1, pp. 353–6.

27 Paine (1945), Vol. 1, pp. 357–61.

28 Paine (1945), Vol. 1, pp. 361–8.

29 Paine (1945), Vol. 1, pp. 368–75.

30 Paine (1945), Vol. 1, pp. 375–81.

31 Paine (1945), Vol. 1, pp. 381–7.

32 Paine (1945), Vol. 1, pp. 387–97.

33 Paine (1945), Vol. 1, pp. 398–400.

34 Paine (1945), Vol. 1, pp. 400–5.

35 Paine (1945), Vol. 1, pp. 406–14.

36 Paine (1945), Vol. 1, pp. 405, 415–21, 32.

37 Paine (1945), Vol. 1, pp. 422–45. My calculations respecting the implications of Paine's proposals are based on G. Mingay (1963), pp. 19–26 and B. Mitchell (1988), p. 153.

38 Paine (1945), Vol. 1, pp. 447–58.

39 Paine (1945), Vol. 2, pp. 469–511, 577–84.

4

Paine's achievement

How we understand Paine depends in part on how we think he constructed his arguments and whom he may have drawn upon in so doing. But the problem of Paine's sources has always proved especially irksome for his interpreters. Though *Common Sense* has been linked inconclusively to Joseph Priestley's *Essay on the First Principles of Government*, the writings of John Milton and a minor seventeenth-century republican, John Hall, it is usually conceded that Paine's early writings responded primarily to specific events. A greater interest in abstract political ideas dates only from the *Rights of Man*, when Paine became a political thinker rather than a pamphleteer arguing a cause.[1] Moreover, Paine's shift of focus to Europe in 1791 altered his thinking on a number of critical issues. Erskine prudently claimed at Paine's trial that the principles of *Common Sense* and the *Rights of Man* were identical, and Paine himself asserted that the only difference was a concern with British instead of American conditions, a view repeated by many historians. None the less this shift was of momentous import for Paine and would underlie his most significant innovations during the 1790s. For the problems of older nations were quite different from those of America and a distinction between the two was to become central to Paine's thought, as well as to the debate which surrounded the *Rights of Man*.[2]

But defining Paine's originality even by the 1790s is not easy. His boastful claims that 'I rarely ever quote; the reason is, I always think' and that he 'neither read books, nor studied other people's opinions' but always 'thought for myself' have frustrated generations of students of his ideas. Clearly this attitude had its uses. As Gwyn Williams has noted, Paine's general insolence was often a far better weapon against deference than carefully marshalled historical argument. His independence seemingly proved that the common man needed no political or intellectual authorities to comprehend and challenge relations of power. With respect to *Common Sense*, for example, Paine argued that he had 'succeeded without any help from anybody', and was not indebted to Locke or anyone else. None the less Paine did read widely; his rooms in Paris, for example, were crowded with pamphlets, journals and other materials, and visitors elsewhere noted similar conditions. But even admirers like Henry Redhead Yorke (who observed this in Paris) asserted that 'The Bible is the only book which he has studied, and there is not a verse in it that is not familiar to him'. However, this was at a time when Paine was especially interested in religious issues. And if he specifically disclaimed ever having had Locke's works in his hands, adding that Horne Tooke had persuaded him Locke was dry, musty and excessively theoretical, Paine mentioned many authorities in his writings. Discussing the immorality of slavery, for example, he alluded to Locke, Carmichael, Hutcheson, Montesquieu, Blackstone and Wallace. Elsewhere he cited, and had clearly read, 'the immortal Montesquieu' on alliances, republicanism and other topics and in a later anti-slavery pamphlet referred to Montesquieu 'and many writers on natural law'. He quoted Rousseau on several occasions in relation to European peace and republicanism. The *English System of Finance* cited Adam Smith extensively and referred to Richard Price. Paine's theological works, which were better annotated, cited Grotius, Whiston and others on the Bible. Moreover, where he did not introduce specific authorities, we must recall another of Paine's strengths: as Yorke and others noticed, he had an astounding memory and remembered 'everything he has written in the course of his life', sometimes reciting lengthy passages from his own works.[3] Thus when Paine had read other authors, too, we may deduce that he could often use their arguments without further reference.

None the less, it is less Paine's precise sources than his interpretation and combination of various ideas which most concern us here. To reassess Paine's intellectual achievements by 1790 we need to examine six aspects of his mature thought in greater detail: the rejection of the inheritance of 1688, and corresponding demand for a constitutional convention; republicanism and the relation of society to government; natural rights and natural law; the theory of civilization and commerce and the social programme of the *Rights of Man*, Part Two; the question of Paine's 'millenarian' or Quaker politics; and Paine's language and appeal.

Constitutionalism, conventions and republicanism

Paine broke from the Whig tradition of the Glorious Revolution more sharply than any other radical. In the first part of the *Rights of Man* he wrote contemptuously that, 'exalted beyond its value', the revolution of 1688 was 'already on the wane, eclipsed by the enlarging orb of reason, and the luminous revolutions of America and France'. It was ridiculous that a free nation 'would send to Holland for a man, and clothe him with power, on purpose to put themselves in fear of him, and give him almost a million sterling a year for leave to submit themselves and their posterity, like bond-men and bond-women, for ever'. There was nothing 'glorious' in 1688 compared to the struggles of America and France. The very rights men and women now sought had not even been debated then (and thus Paine's dismissal of 1688 differed from, for example, Hulme's rejection of the settlement as not restoring ancient Saxon liberties). Nor did modern radicals still retain a slavish obedience towards precedent. Instead they insisted that universal, active consent to the mode of rule was the sole basis of political legitimacy. Fundamental to this view of 1688 was Paine's doctrine of the supremacy of the present generation over its forebears, which asserted (in Gwyn Williams's words) 'the primacy of the present' over 'precedent, organicism and social mysticism'. This owed something to Locke's conception of consent, by which no man was held to have a right to bind his children or posterity in a compact. Cartwright too had argued that corrupt laws were not binding because each House of Commons was responsible to its electors, not bound by its predecessors' acts. But Paine extended this idea to comprise a right to repeal any law, no matter how fundamental. He retained a faith in the role of reason in such judgements, too, which many Whigs, as well as Burke, rejected.[4]

By 1790 Paine also believed that the franchise should be extended much further than most Whigs advised. More importantly, he asserted that Parliament by definition could not reform itself. When trust was forfeited, power devolved once more to the community, who through a constitutional convention ought to form a new compact and issue a written constitution. This definition of 'constitution' was novel in a British context and so was Paine's conception of the rights and duties of a convention. Reformers like Hulme, Wyvill, Burgh, Cartwright and Jebb had suggested imitating the Americans by forming a general radical association to inform Parliament how best to reform itself. But Paine (who urged such a gathering in England as early as March 1789, when George III's insanity was declared) assigned conventions far greater powers, wished them directly to represent a much larger number of citizens, and denied the legitimacy of any government not so formed. This was an 'American' argument because its concept of democratic republicanism went well beyond that of British radicalism, and was both forged in the colonists' revolt as well as rooted in Paine's faith in the greater capacity for independent thought of the Americans compared to their more servile British counterparts.

If Paine's conception of reform was based on the American experience, his recommendation that 'the standard of liberty' be carried to other nations went further still. This he termed 'the peculiar honor of

France' in 1792 and, though Paine abandoned hopes of a French-led European revolution the following year, the later idea of revolutionary internationalism owes much to him. Paine did not always present this ideal consistently, arguing in 1797 that 'one nation has not the right to interfere in the *internal* government of another nation' and that if England chose to keep its king, this was none of France's business.[5] None the less his concern was never with reforming single nations, but with bringing justice to all. 'My country is the world' remains among Paine's most oft-quoted phrases and indicates not only Paine's broad sympathies but a new awareness of an international system of mutually reinforcing tyrannies whose overthrow demanded parallel revolutionary collusion wherever it was possible.

Paine deviated from Whiggism in the goals as well as the means of reform. Most importantly, he was a fully fledged republican, while most radicals before 1791 supported a mixed monarchy with the Commons predominating. In Part One of the *Rights of Man*, Paine conceded the people's right to create or accede to even a hereditary executive, doubtless aware that Lafayette's 'Declaration of Rights' of August 1789 permitted a hereditary monarchy. But he himself clearly believed that representation was always 'debased' when combined with monarchy and in Part Two thus insisted on a pure republic. Pownall, Price, Cartwright and others earlier had suggested that popular sovereignty in America did not require hereditary institutions. But they did not extend such views to Britain or dismiss monarchy entirely. Paine argued that the existence of hereditary monarchy was itself a violation of trust and a proof of arbitrary power. The abrogation of laws was thus not required to prove the existence of tyranny, as Locke had insisted. Hereditary government was always illegitimate because it implied that the consent of each generation to its rulers was not required. Simply put, Paine possessed greater faith in the political capacities of the majority, and was the first to insist that all forms of government not directly based on active popular consent (rather than the passive consent of holding property Locke had permitted) were illegitimate. Locke and others had described hereditary rule as absurd, Paine later wrote, but he alone had condemned it 'on the ground of illegality, which is the strongest of all grounds to attack it upon'. This was Paine's most important innovation in political thought and it took him beyond Whiggism entirely.[6]

Within republicanism, Paine's defence of extensive republics was a consciously modern innovation. The Greeks did not bear imitating, Paine thought, while the Romans 'held the world in slavery, and were themselves the slaves of their emperors'. Moreover, no form of direct democracy should be the republican goal, for this suited only small nations. The representative system alone could amass 'the quantity of knowledge necessary to govern to the best national advantage'. But there remained the question of the best form of democratic republic. Paine originally agreed with Franklin that one legislative house was preferable since further bodies merely bred more parties. By 1786, however, and especially after the controversy over the Bank of North America, Paine conceded that flaws existed in unicameral systems, even arguing that intense partisanship by a majority could render them 'capable of being made a compleat aristocracy for the time it exists ... when the majority of a single house is made up on the ground of party prejudice ... instead of comprehending the good of the whole dispassionately'. This was 'as dangerous to the principles of liberty as that of a despotic monarchy'. In 1791 he thought that some compromise between unicameral and bicameral systems might be possible and in France in 1792 accepted some of the Madisonian argument against faction, agreeing that if a constitution established two legislative chambers 'as a check upon each other ... the result is sure to be advantageous' and now arguing that a single assembly meeting together was 'the worst' form of legislature.[7]

The *Rights of Man* Part Two thus proposed a compromise between single and bicameral assemblies, with a single house dividing for debates to avoid the clashing of passions, and only later voting together. In 1805 Paine suggested that Pennsylvania adopt such a plan, opposing the Federalist cry for an upper house elected only by property-holders and rejecting the premiss that educated men thereby become the political elite. None the less Paine did not believe only in private, or interest-based, virtue, but still hoped for a single legislature where republican virtue prevailed, party prejudices had 'no operation within the walls of the legislature', all would 'unite and agree in the general principles of good government' and 'the public good, or the good of the whole, would be the governing principle of the legislature within it. Party dispute, taken on this ground, would only be, who should have the honor of making the laws; not what the laws should be.' All would be united by the republican goal of seeking equal justice for each citizen, and Paine at one point emphasized that 'I wish with all the devotion of a Christian, that the names of Whig and Tory may never more be mentioned.' A clearer statement of republican idealism could not be asked for, though Paine obviously became increasingly pessimistic about its realization. Correspondingly, this view has been construed as overly optimistic, which by modern standards is doubtless true. But Paine has also been wrongly accused of ignoring the possibility that democracy could degenerate into a tyranny of the majority. He advised, for example, that the American state constitutions 'should be so constructed and secured, as to afford no opportunities for the future abuse of power' when revolutionary enthusiasm had cooled. In the controversy over the Bank of North America, too, he warned that 'despotism may be more effectually acted by many over a few, than by one man over all'.[8]

None the less Paine never anticipated considerable conflict between the executive and legislative branches of a popular government and denied the need for any balancing of them, which implied a republican 'opposition', as he emphasized respecting the French constitutions of both 1791 and 1795. Nor would he concede that any minority 'insurrection' against a majority was ever justified. But while he was much less suspicious of democracy than the Federalists, Paine's views were iconoclastic and non-partisan. Though most anti-Federalists strongly opposed aristocracy, while the Federalists counselled both a strong central government and rule by a 'natural aristocracy', Paine also favoured a strong executive and was amongst the first to argue (in 1780) that the Articles of Confederation were too weak and that the Congress needed strengthening. But the executive in his conception merely implemented laws enacted by the legislature, to which it remained subordinate. Conflict between executive and people was impossible, for American government ought to bear no analogy to the British constitution or the Whig conception of mixed forms of government, which Federalists seemed to think it should. Against the latter Paine thus also argued that a plural rather than a single executive was preferable.[9]

Natural rights and natural law

As its title implies and its readers soon acknowledged, much of the appeal of the *Rights of Man* lay in its focus upon rights. Yet we have seen that rights language had pervaded eighteenth-century politics. Whig writers insisted upon the rights of all to life, liberty and the protection of property, to some participation in government, especially respecting decisions affecting these rights, and to resist arbitrary authority. None the less not all these rights were granted universally, and many were restricted (even the right of resistance) to those of independent means. Much of the great attractiveness of the *Rights of Man* thus was doubtless Paine's invocation of the rights of *all* rather than only narrowly British liberties. By de-emphasizing historically based rights or liberties Paine turned away from the imitation of the ancient or Anglo-Saxon constitution. The state of nature remained as a device for examining and claiming rights, but Paine's was not a backwards-looking, historical argument. This shift consequently radicalized the Whig view while also emphasizing a deeply Christian – especially Quaker – and cosmopolitan view of rights language. Mankind could now be understood as belonging to one universal fraternal community where all possessed equal rights and duties which upheld the fundamental dignity (a word of immense importance to Paine) of each. Some universal implications of rights language had been evident in seventeenth-century debates, for example among the Levellers. The phrase 'the rights of man' had been used before. But only with Paine, it has been emphasized, was the 'fully *universal* character' of rights revealed.[10]

Paine's idea of rights was thus not unchanged from *Common Sense* onwards, as is often assumed, for by the 1790s he agreed that universal male suffrage was a natural right, rejecting his own earlier and more traditional Whig view. In 1778 he had still argued that the franchise could be forfeited by state employees, or by all servants, 'because their interest is in their master' (and thus they lacked sufficient independence), or if someone no longer contributed to taxation or public service.[11] Thereafter he condemned property qualifications for the franchise, and by the 1790s argued for universal male suffrage.

Paine's invocation of natural over historical rights contributed considerably to the longevity of such doctrines at a time when both they and the natural law basis from which they sprang were under increasing attack. But Paine did not defend some form of completely new, abstractly 'metaphysical' rights, like those Burke accused Price and the French of upholding. (Indeed his own conception of rights was no more 'metaphysical' than Burke's idea of the divine right of kings.) Instead he followed most natural law writers in believing that rights derived from the Creation, and the emphasis of most later natural rights authors, that they inhered in each person as psychological properties, both the 'animal right, and the power to act it' being 'supposed, either fully or in part, to be mechanically contained within ourselves as individuals'.[12] Paine's notion that civil rights both derived from but also transmuted some natural rights according to the needs of society (for example losing the right to judge in one's own case) was, as Gierke has emphasized, a prevalent doctrine in natural law. So too was the 'correlativity' idea that possessing rights implied corresponding duties to respect the rights of others, which Paine clearly upheld, and which proves that his theory of rights did not, as Fennessy and others have alleged, simply propose that all individuals had the right to do what they were capable of doing (but Paine's misleading use of 'animal right' is admittedly confusing).[13] By radical Whig standards, then, there was also little novel here, Locke being usually associated with the notion that the social contract fulfilled and protected earlier rights. But Paine's insistence on the inalienability of some natural rights was important given David Hume's powerful and increasingly popular argument that utility was the chief basis of governments, that the state of nature was a fiction and correspondingly that only 'civil' rights existed. This assault on the natural rights ideals, reinforced by William Paley's popular theological utilitarianism and Bentham's dismissal of natural rights as 'pestilential' and 'nonsense upon stilts', prepared the way for much of nineteenth-century British political thought (both Whig and socialist, though not, for example, Chartist) and was in fact one of the chief turning points in the history of political thought in this period.[14]

But historians have wrongly presumed that the rise of a sceptical, historicist utilitarianism simply swept aside natural rights arguments. This teleological interpretation focuses too narrowly on the arguments of a few individuals without reading ideas historically, or in the fullness of their context, and derives from the idea that Burke and Bentham were the next 'great thinkers' to follow Hume in the canon of history of political thought and must therefore have extended his victory over the forces of dark Lockean ignorance. We would have a great deal of trouble accounting for Paine's popularity if this had been the case. Indeed it was far more the diffusion of his natural rights doctrines which forced Whigs finally to reject this inheritance than the arguments of Hume, Burke, Paley and Bentham alone, as we will shortly see. For this reason, too, Paine and not Burke – since the latter largely renounced natural rights in favour of utility – remained far closer to the natural law tradition as it had developed during the eighteenth century, though Paine too touted a vague brand of utilitarianism.[15]

Paine's proximity to the natural law tradition has in fact been virtually ignored in previous interpretations. Largely this is because conservative scholars have wished to claim adherence to natural law doctrines for Burke, even while, for example, defining the core of natural law teaching as the idea of reciprocal rights and duties, a doctrine which we have seen Paine held as well. This view, which aims to portray Paine as a rabid 'individualist', succeeds only by completely neglecting Paine's ideas of sociability, duty and mutual interdependence. More generally, however, this omission is also partly due to the paucity of studies of eighteenth-century natural law, which has contributed to the view that most eighteenth-century British political writers paid little heed to natural law ideals, though Rousseau and others continued the tradition on the continent.[16] Blackstone, for example, notoriously merely touched upon the laws of nature in the introduction to his *Commentaries on the Laws* (1765), and thereafter ignored them. Instead British writers supposedly preferred to discuss the common law and precedent as the basis of political norms and, accepting Hume and Bentham's critique of the rationalist assumptions of the natural law writers, grounded their moral philosophy on the passions rather than conscious obedience to external laws. But while Burke is no longer generally described as a natural law thinker, the jurisprudential debts of eighteenth-century thinkers like Smith, for example, are now increasingly acknowledged.[17] It is also clear that natural law textbooks remained extremely popular in Dissenting academies, at the universities and among the reading public, and that the rationalist aspects of natural law doctrines were not everywhere jettisoned in favour of discussing natural rights alone, or even dispensing with the latter in favour of utility. Though important differences existed in the perspectives of, for example, Grotius, Cumberland, Pufendorf, Wolff, Vattel and Burlamaqui, all of whom were widely read in the eighteenth century, all presumed that a moral law existed which was both prior and superior to governments, was inscribed in the divine order, and was both knowable rationally and operated through the requirement of sociability as well as the restraints of conscience. These assumptions thus continued to be widely popular throughout this period.

What is implied, then, by seeing Paine as part of the natural law tradition? The view that morality operated through the conjunction of conscience and reason and should not be reduced to instinct or the passions Paine clearly accepted; slavery, for example, he condemned as 'contrary to the plain dictates of natural light, and conscience'. In the so-called third part of *The Age of Reason*, not published until 1807, too, he quoted Cicero's view that 'The true law is right reason, conformable to the nature of things, constant, eternal, diffused through all, which calls us to duty by commanding, deters us from sin by forbidding; which never loses its influence with the good, nor ever preserves it with the wicked.'[18] Moreover, unlike many Whigs, Paine also believed that the law of nature was, like the Quaker inner light, comprehensible to all, not merely the most educated. This faith in the common possession of reason clearly underlay his belief that political virtue could be extended more widely than most Whigs thought possible. In addition, Paine also thought the laws of nature were part of the natural, divinely created universal order which was scientifically verifiable in terms of the operations of harmoniously mechanical natural laws, and also demonstrated that harmony between the natural and moral worlds existed. All, too, were capable of understanding these relationships.

A central element of natural law teaching important to Paine concerned the state of nature. The leading seventeenth-century positions on this much-vexed question were those of Hobbes, who described this period as violent and unpleasant, leading mankind to surrender all sovereignty over its rights in a compact with an absolute monarch, and Locke, for whom an era of considerable peace and co-operation ended with a contract by which, in return for obedience, the sovereign protected natural rights on penalty of being overthrown. For Paine the idea of a state of nature was necessary to account for a fundamental constitutional law superior to positive law and formulated outside of government in a convention (and other writers used natural law ideas this way to justify the American revolution, drawing in particular on Pufendorf, Vattel and Burlamaqui).[19] But though one might suspect, given Paine's juxtaposition of 'society' to 'government', that he believed the state of nature to have been relatively idyllic, he did not. Paine portrayed extra-governmental relations as seemingly co-operative. But he also believed that the state of nature had been a period of warfare and conquest. In fact it was only civilized society which functioned harmoniously, and here only within certain limits.

Distinguishing between these views of the state of nature has considerable implications for understanding the single most important natural law contribution to Paine's doctrines. For Paine not only accepted the central jurisprudential juxtaposition of a state of nature to 'society', but also the natural law definition of society as a system designed to ensure survival and satisfy mutual needs, and thus promote sociability. 'Civilization' was based upon an instinctive desire for society or 'system of social affections' as strong as any animal instinct, and reinforced by morality and true religion. But it was also grounded upon the necessity of mutual aid based on the existence of common wants and the deliberate divine distribution of resources unevenly across the world to ensure co-operation.[20]

This form of sociability, reciprocal interest, was intimately bound up with Paine's definition of commerce and was supposed to regulate both domestic and international relations. In their present form the latter were exactly analogous to rule by the strongest in the state of nature. But for Paine this was the consequence of aristocratic and monarchic rule in particular rather than, as most natural jurists believed, human nature as well as the anarchy of the international state system. In one of the *Crisis* pamphlets, thus, Paine wrote: 'In a Christian and philosophical sense, mankind seem to have stood still at individual civilization, and to retain as nations all the original rudeness of nature.' But 'all the great laws of society are laws of nature', and natural sociability, the principle of society rather than the state of nature, could still triumph in government, and could make it more than a merely negative, restraining force. But for Paine this was possible only in a representative republic trading harmoniously with other nations, and only by recognizing the moral duty to support the poor as well as their right to such assistance, not merely the unreciprocal, individualistic right of property to do with its own as it pleased. Hume, Burke and others had also accepted a notion of society as a system of wants. This conception underlay Smith's theory of the division of labour, while for Hume, too, trade lessened international aggression. But Paine identified such benefits only with a commercial republicanism tempered by a humane treatment of the poor and demanded the abolition of monarchy as the price for universal civilization.[21]

That government ought to extend the principles of society was standard in most natural law treatments.[22] But here we encounter an interesting and important anomaly in Paine's political thought. For in *Common Sense* and the *Rights of Man* Part One, Paine had seemingly argued that extending civilization was the goal of *society*, not of government, which evidently inhibited this process. Yet in the *Rights of Man* Part Two, and, as we will see below, *Agrarian Justice*, Paine did not adopt only the 'negative' contractualist view of society often associated with natural law, which narrowed the sphere of government to defence and the enforcement of justice. He also argued from another strand of natural law thinking – which is in fact partly the origin of the modern theory of 'positive liberty' – that it was the government's duty, as the expression of the common good, to promote sociability and a higher level of civilization by maintaining and enhancing the rights of the poor. Such a task could not be entrusted solely to 'society', whose charitable institutions failed to meet these obligations sufficiently. Between 1776 and 1792 Paine thus grappled with the Augustinian argument that government was unnatural and instituted solely to control sin (the view of government usually ascribed to him) and the Aristotelian view that it was natural because merely an extension of society, and ought indeed, in republican form, to extend the virtues of society even further. Between 1791 and 1792 in particular, he decided that trade alone could not assure a subsistence to all and that government would have to promote a more extensive notion of rights than was implied by what we now term a 'negative liberty' conception of commerce and society, where individuals are considered 'free' primarily if the state does not interfere with them. A consistent underlying natural law ideal of social obligation made it possible for his welfare programme to be introduced and maintained by republican governments. But it has confused many subsequent commentators, for whom these administrative burdens of Paine's social programme flatly contradict his demands for minimal government, and who have failed to see that Paine believed republicanism capable of much that other forms of government were not.

There is one central reason why this apparent contradiction was resolved in the *Rights of Man* Part Two. By the 1790s Paine became aware that the ideal of minimal government in fact only applied to 'new countries' with little social inequality. 'Old countries' indeed deserved less burdensome, more evenly distributed taxation and the curtailing of extreme landed wealth. But their greater inequality also meant that more governmental activity was needed to offset its effects, and this was the most important shift in Paine's thinking from *Common Sense* to the *Rights of Man*. This was why he never proposed that his welfare and taxation reforms should apply to America. Paine by 1792 distinguished between the levels of government appropriate to various stages of economic development and realized that there were important parallels between a state of nature and one of advanced civilization. Commerce, he now believed, lacked the capacity to solve the question of poverty once and for all outside of new countries, at least for a very long time to come. This realization culminated in the rights theories of *Agrarian Justice*.

The centrality of Paine's emphasis both on society as a organization for satisfying needs and on individuals as bearers of rights thus does not preclude acknowledging Paine's retention of important republican ideals. The natural jurists did tend to construct persons as individualized bearers of rights and duties who primarily sought the maintenance of order and justice from the state, while republicanism emphasized their civic, military and generally collective responsibilities as citizens. But too sharp a contrast should not be drawn between these perspectives. Paine's theory of society doubtless did construe individuals as utility-maximizing creatures primarily motivated by self-interest in seeking to satisfy their needs. But Paine none the less placed a high value upon citizenship, did not expect public virtue to decline substantially in a commercial republic, and in fact required its maintenance if his political system and his new welfare mechanisms were to succeed. Indeed to Paine it was only in a republic that the demands of natural obligation could be wholly met.

Commerce, wealth and equality

What does this imply for the traditional view of Paine's theory of commerce? The jurisprudential definition of society as a system of wants was clearly central to Paine's commercial ideal, but it is his emphasis on freedom and expansion of trade which has most often been stressed previously, with the implication that Paine had a narrowly 'liberal', restricted definition of property rights.[23] But given Paine's view of social reciprocity such an interpretation is untenable. Paine did indeed often write of government as hindering free commerce, insisting even in the *Rights of Man* Part Two that in England all improvements in agriculture, commerce and the like had been 'made in opposition to the genius of its government'. Every inventor and pioneer hoped that government 'would let him alone'. European poverty, moreover, resulted from 'what in such countries is called government'. But this meant not only taxation, but also failure to maintain the poor, which was the duty of those who possessed property and therefore (given their failure to meet this obligation satisfactorily) of government. And in keeping with his enthusiasm for free trade, Paine was also less fearful than many republicans of the moral corruption which might result from luxury goods introduced by commerce. No puritan in this regard, he thus wrote in 1783 that although new countries should first encourage agriculture, he was 'no enemy to genteel or fashionable dress, or to the moderate enjoyment of those articles of indulgence we are furnished with from abroad' if they were also taxed like agriculture. Eventually, perhaps 'a thousand years hence ... perhaps in less', America might 'be what Europe is now', its liberty sadly declined. But for the present there was no need to worry that commerce would throttle the revolution.[24]

But we have seen that Paine's 'liberalism' requires an entirely different context from that usually assigned it. Paine is often assumed to have been a disciple of Adam Smith on the basis of a few well-worn passages from *Common Sense* and the *Rights of Man*. But since his notion of society as a system of wants and their satisfaction through mutual interdependence obviously preceded the publication of the *Wealth of Nations*, we should be suspicious of such claims. After all, Hume, Priestley and many others also advocated free trade in the late eighteenth century, usually but not exclusively drawing on jurisprudential arguments. None the less such assertions also imply that Paine consequently gave some form of priority to commerce, or thought it advantageous to a nation compared to agriculture. But to complicate matters, Paine has also been identified with a physiocratic emphasis on the primacy of agriculture over commerce. Aldridge, for example, sees Paine as close to Franklin's 'physiocracy' in his view that farmers and cultivators were 'the first useful class of citizens ... because everything comes from the earth' and also describes Paine as 'virtually a mercantilist' because he implied (in *Prospects on the Rubicon*) that gold and silver were alone capital.[25] Other evidence also supports the view that Paine thought agriculture primary. He argued that 'lands are the real riches of the habitable world, and the natural funds of America' in his 1780 defence of the appropriation of western lands by the United States. Discussing farmers in a letter, too, Paine added that after them came manufacturers and mechanics, who contributed 'to the accommodation rather than to the first necessaries of life'. Only merchants and shopkeepers did not produce anything, but lived by exchange and were thus 'convenient but not important'. In 1778, distinguishing sharply between riches in old and new countries, Paine also contended that in old countries wealth only shifted hands, 'without either increasing or diminishing' (implying that commerce did not produce wealth), while in new countries 'there is a real

97

addition of riches by population and cultivation'. Agriculture in a new country was 'the fountainhead' of wealth, trade being only 'the streams which distribute it'. But Paine none the less described both as 'ways of obtaining wealth' and added that neither cultivation nor trade here could be 'too large, too numerous, or too extensive' (he added elliptically that he himself belonged to the first class, being 'a farmer of thoughts, and all the crops I raise I give away').[26]

Commerce thus did not necessarily increase *wealth* narrowly defined as land under cultivation or population, but it augmented wealth and, more importantly, happiness in other ways. Paine did retain some republican prejudices about commerce. Land was 'real riches' in America partly only because the national wealth of many other countries was built on trade and speculation, and thus their 'funds' were 'in general, artificially constructed; the creatures of necessity and contrivance dependent upon credit, and always exposed to hazard and uncertainty'. There was considerable Harringtonian scepticism about the political instability of movable wealth in this view, and Paine obviously did believe that land was a more secure, and commerce a less certain, basis of national wealth. But commerce was far from intrinsically useless and clearly added to the value of the produce it exchanged, while Paine condemned the professions, and especially lawyers (for whom he had a very Quakerish disdain) as frequently unprincipled parasites. As the *Dissertations on Government* emphasized, it had always been 'a maxim in politics, founded on, and drawn from, natural causes and consequences, that the more foreign countries which any nation can interest in the prosperity of its own, so much the better'. Trade therefore created wealth even though it did not fashion physical objects or cultivate food, and within Paine's theory of society as a system of needs-satisfaction there was no contradiction between ascribing some primacy to agriculture and zealously promoting commerce. Smith in fact did the same; it was Ricardo who sought to make Britain the workshop of the world, importing food from others. And although the *Prospects on the Rubicon* argued that a profitable trade brought 'real money', or gold and silver, into a country, Paine did in fact consider paper money (backed by metal) to be capital. *The Decline and Fall of the English System of Finance* (1796) condemned in particular Pitt's issuing of paper money because no metallic security existed, warning that severe currency depreciation would ensue, as had occurred in America.[27]

Like Smith, Paine thus considered commerce and manufacturing as sources of wealth, and was hardly 'physiocratic' despite his occasional terminological imprecision. But by the 1790s Paine was not a 'physiocrat', a 'mercantilist', or a 'disciple' of Smith. His commercial liberalism instead requires different categories of analysis, particularly the jurisprudential theory of needs. But what was distinctive about Paine's views in the 1790s went well beyond any natural law vision. Between the American revolution and the *Rights of Man* his general sympathy for *laissez-faire* did not diminish; he argued in relation to American fishing rights in 1779, for example, that 'wealth like water soon spreads over the surface, let the place of entrance be ever so remote'. The *Rights of Man* again defended the natural laws of trade and hoped reduced taxes would permit their operation. But Paine's scheme for state-enforced pensions, progressive taxation, universal education and assistance to the poor involved a massive redistribution of wealth and restatement of rights wholly alien to the Smithian as well as any jurisprudential vision. Any natural jurist could agree with Paine that 'Humanity dictates a provision for the poor'. But none had ever verged upon his system of poor relief, or stated the right to charity in this manner. Government now had a positive function which 'society' could not perform, which was to alleviate the chief vice of society, the failure of the system of exchange to support the population at all times.[28] Paine's was not a system of natural liberty, but a system of liberty reinforced by newly reconstructed rights to maintenance grounded in the first instance on the social contribution of all. Both republican equality and jurisprudential duties were to be satisfied.

This shift, which was to be even more starkly stated in *Agrarian Justice*, was of enormous importance both to Paine's thought and to the development of rights assumptions generally.[29] By 1792 Paine began to conceive that even though poverty in Britain and its absence in America could in great measure be accounted for by their differing governments and tax burdens, poverty was to some degree, and particularly in old countries, the natural result of commerce rather than of governmental wickedness. Government was still a national association to secure rights and promote 'the greatest quantity of happiness with the *least expense*'.[30] But for advanced countries this did not mean little or no expenditure on the poor. Though his focus was not on the rights of labourers *per se*, which would have required a more Lockean property doctrine focusing on the creation of property by labour than he expressed, Paine contributed to the radicalism of the 1790s a previously unexplored concern for the social consequences of reform. This was a fundamental turning-point in modern radicalism. In 1792 Paine united freedom of trade with a radical theory of social justice and common rights where the poor retained the right to maintenance in all periods of danger, not merely famine. Paine had extended, hardened and institutionalized the duties towards the poor enjoined by the natural jurists and in so doing transformed a soft or imperfect right (or one which could not be compelled) to charity into a hard right to justice enforceable by government. This vision we today identify not with 'negative liberty', but with the welfare state and social democracy, where a regulated economic liberty supposedly predominates, and government substantially mitigates poverty as well as providing some employment for the poor beyond what the market allocates.

As with later visions of the welfare state, however, there were clear limits to Paine's republican egalitarianism. He did not foresee the complete abolition of poverty. Defending the constitution of Pennsylvania in 1777 he pleaded for an equality of rights which would 'Let the rich man enjoy his riches, and the poor man comfort himself in his poverty'. Nearly twenty years later, in 1795, he still maintained 'That property will ever be unequal is certain. Industry, superiority of talents, dexterity of management, extreme frugality, fortunate opportunities, or the opposite, or the means of those things, will ever produce that effect', urging that 'All that is required with respect to property is to obtain it honestly, and not employ it criminally'. What was important, thus, was that property not be made 'a pretense for unequal or exclusive rights' and poverty not become insufferable. But this was still a very radical vision indeed.[31]

Nor was Paine's new social programme more sympathetic to market regulation. He was well aware of the dangers of hoarding, profiteering and the manipulation of food prices in periods of scarcity. During the American revolution he strongly condemned 'monopolizers' (amongst whom he included Silas Deane) as harming the community more than anyone else, even justifying mob action against them. He also warned that abolishing the Bank of North America would allow the market in country produce to be 'monopolized by a few monied men, who would command the price as they pleased' and who thus opposed the Bank 'as standing in the way of their private interest'. Consequently Paine never completely excluded regulation as a temporary measure. At Paris in 1793 he advised Danton that fixing food prices, as the labouring classes in Paris demanded, could be accomplished only by the municipality, not the Convention. Citing his Philadelphia experiences, however, he added pessimistically that regulating the price of salt and flour there had dried up the market. If the Parisians refused to pay more than a certain price for food, thus, 'as they cannot compel the country people to bring provisions to market the consequence will be directly contrary to their expectations, and they will find dearness and famine instead of plenty and cheapness. They may force the price down upon the stock in hand, but after that the market will be empty.'[32]

Paine thus shared certain assumptions about a 'moral economy' but not others. The concept of a 'moral economy' refers primarily to natural law theories of the social obligation to regulate property such that the poor neither starved nor were grossly exploited, and the practice, legislative embodiment and popular awareness of these ideals. The success of this scheme rested upon two assumptions: that in a divinely-ordered world the rich owed the poor a minimal subsistence as a consequence of God's bequeathing the earth to all at the Creation, and that the customary regulation of wages and prices ensured justice as well as social harmony. Paine certainly agreed that the rich as stewards of God's estate owed the poor a subsistence, and recognized (as he wrote in 1791) 'the moral obligation of providing for old age, helpless infancy, and poverty'.[33] For this reason Paine is wrongly categorized as not having challenged 'the property rights of the rich nor the doctrines of *laissez-faire*' because he apparently did not urge the taxation of mercantile capital and profit. For his theory of obligation underlies the social programme of the *Rights of Man* Part Two, as well, as we will see, as *Agrarian Justice*, and this was an enormous barrier to the application of naked *laissez-faire*. But he did not favour any normal regulation of the market, arguing instead that the poor deserved a minimum standard of living, but otherwise assuming that the market could provide normally for all, especially in new countries. Correspondingly the suggestion that Paine saw in the economic world a system of natural harmony similar to a Newtonian conception of the natural world is also of only limited value. That he felt there were important analogies between the natural and commercial world is undoubted, and his plea for governmental simplicity was probably indebted to a mechanical philosophy.[34] But government had to act continuously to ensure the correct balance required by his social programme. This was artificial, not natural harmony.

Again we can see that these views were much closer to a natural law conception of commercial relations than to any vulgar conception of *laissez-faire*. Natural law writers did encourage freedom of trade and believed God had distributed raw materials across the earth to foster human interdependence. But jurists like Vattel (writing in 1758) urged the primacy of agriculture and the creation of public granaries while still supporting free trade. And they strongly upheld the maintenance of the customary standard of living of the poor through charity as well as, when necessary, wage and price controls. Other writers – like Charles Davenant, Dudley North and Henry Martyn – had of course earlier argued for freedom of commerce and were themselves indebted to aspects of the natural law tradition. But Paine's principles are more clearly indebted to mainstream natural law writers than such political economists, though even here he offered the poor a great deal more than the jurists.[35]

Quakerism and the millennium

It has always been assumed that to an important degree religion underlay both Paine's sympathy for the poor and his concern with peace. But the impact of Quakerism on Paine's social programme and his vision of international harmony, once thought powerful, is now given little prominence. Instead the 'millenarian' aspects of his social theory have recently aroused greater interest. None the less each of these questions has a somewhat different bearing on Paine's thought.[36]

Paine's affiliation with the Quakers was not of course theological. Though Quakers were often confounded with deists because of their simple theology and hostility to a professional priesthood, they had long attacked deism themselves, and *The Age of Reason*, as we will see, left little room for Quaker theology. Neither here nor elsewhere did Paine invoke the central Quaker doctrine of the divinely inspired 'Inner Light' as the source of individual religious guidance, though he clearly preferred personal revelation to scriptural authority. Like Franklin, what Paine instead admired were the social virtues and moral steadfastness of the Quakers, their egalitarianism and opposition to war, their plain speech and simplicity (though not their tendency to drabness), and their hostility to aristocracy and a formal clergy.[37]

But did these sympathies make Paine's social theory distinctive? Moncure Conway claimed that Paine's 'whole political system' was 'explicable only by his theocratic Quakerism. His first essay, the plea for negro emancipation, was brought from Thetford Meeting House. His "Common Sense", a new-world scripture, is a "testimony" against the proud who raised their paltry dignities against the divine presence of the lowliest.' We know, too, that Paine was impressed with Quaker philanthropy in founding hospitals, libraries, temperance, abolitionist and other organizations, and their willingness to extend charity into the wider 'holy community'. This accorded with his own aims, and a general debt to the Quakers can certainly be conceded, especially with respect to abolitionism.[38] Interpreting *Common Sense* as a 'testimony' may none the less be pushing this affiliation too far considering the distance of Paine's language from most eighteenth-century Quaker political writing. Paine's conception of *institutionalized* governmental benevolence, too, differed quantitatively as well as qualitatively from Quaker philanthropic policy, for in the *Rights of Man* Part Two the private duty of charity gave way to the notion of a just social reward and the just inheritance of God's world.

More important to Paine were certain aspects of the Quaker attitude towards government. Most Quakers believed that while God's magistracy alone was just, earthly rules were to be obeyed unless they violated the dictates of conscience. William Penn and other Quaker founders were generally Whiggish in their opposition to religious intolerance as well as other matters, but 'quietism' or political non-involvement dominated late seventeenth- and eighteenth-century British as well as American Quakerism. By the early eighteenth century, however, the

Pennsylvania Quakers were divided into factions representing a more radical 'country party' and conservative city merchants. As we have seen, the latter attracted Paine's enmity for their loyalism and pacifism during the revolutionary war, for he thought that Quaker principles should have led them to be the first to support independence.[39] But Paine none the less deeply admired many aspects of Quaker anti-war principles without ever opposing self-defence. In *Common Sense* he advised building an American navy and later aided French preparations for invading England. But like his contemporaries, Kant and Rousseau, who also grappled with the problem of attaining perpetual peace, Paine was deeply attracted by the Quakers' well-known plans for a cosmopolitan and particularly European peace. The leading late seventeenth-century Quaker writer on such topics was William Penn, with whose principles Paine was certainly acquainted, and whose *An Essay Towards the Present and Future State of Europe* (1693) urged the creation of a European assembly to guard against the outbreak of war. This certainly influenced Paine's own proposals for peace in Europe.[40]

How far do such pacific ideals share 'millenarian' characteristics in the sense in which the thought of Price and Priestley (both ministers) has been so described?[41] Many seventeenth-century Quakers, among others, believed Christ would soon return to judge mankind and punish the wicked, though such views were much less in evidence a century later. But Paine even metaphorically avoided such appeals. He did believe that 'Providence' intended peace and plenty. But this did not imply active divine interference to introduce human perfection, only God's good intentions. Paine thus quite happily argued of the French revolution that 'an overruling Providence is regenerating the old world by the principles of the new'. But this assumed neither social or individual perfectibility, which all forms of millenarianism did. Instead Paine insisted that 'we live not in a world of angels. The reign of Satan is not ended; neither are we to expect to be defended by miracles', and elsewhere, referring to constitutions, noted that 'I suppose nothing is perfect, nor ever will [be]', and that 'no constitution could be established in which defects would not appear in the course of time'. He did not deny human weaknesses, merely arguing that 'If all human nature be corrupt, it is needless to strengthen the corruption by establishing a succession of kings'. Nor did he think that poverty would be abolished completely, or that all conflict would cease. He did hope, as he put it in 1792, that it was 'by no means unlikely that ... all the European systems of government will experience a change, and that quarrels among nations will be terminated by pacific methods and not by the ferocious horrors of war'. But practically he recommended only that nations fix treaties of peace for a certain number of years to aid in discussing grievances and preventing future wars.[42] Unlike

Price or Priestley, however, he did not use theological language to describe such prospects. His vision was considerably more secular and republican and less apocalyptic, perfectibilist and Utopian than theirs, and consequently should not be termed 'millenarian'.

Paine's language and appeal

Paine's style was both novel and essential to his popular success. Critics found his wit coarse and language vulgar, but these qualities attracted his readers. However, he is often assumed to have paid a substantial intellectual price for this popularity by simplifying complex doctrines in order to reach the working classes. But Paine did not, as we have seen, merely 'popularize' ideas of natural rights, constitutionalism or the social contract, since much of his social and political thought was his own creation. Moreover, Paine's aim was not only to write for a wide audience, but actually to redefine his readers by pressing a more egalitarian republicanism upon them. Paine's goals were thus emancipatory as well as informative.

Paine sought to re-create his readers in several ways. First, he portrayed them as equal in value as human beings to the landed aristocracy and gentry. 'One honest man', we recall, he thought 'worth all the crowned ruffians' that ever existed. This sense of defiant confidence, coupled with Paine's disdain for established institutions, helped to undermine the deference traditionally paid to the upper classes by artisans and labourers as the price of ostensible paternal care by their betters. This was the first, and in many ways the most important, step in the revolt against the status quo. Typical of the growing distance between Crown and subject was the comment by a group of London mechanics, upon the king's creation of new peers in 1797 at a time of great scarcity of provisions, that 'if his majesty had been invested with a power of creating geese, or pigs, or calves, or oxen, it might, at that juncture, have been much more beneficial to the community at large'. Paine's role in fuelling this growing contempt for authority contributed immensely to the emergence of new forms of class consciousness, though these were expressed primarily in social and political rather than economic terms. In part his appeal, correspondingly, was to the poor, about whom he wrote that 'we have nothing to fear from the poor; for we are pleading their cause'. But elsewhere he stressed that he defended not only 'the cause of the poor, of the manufacturers, of the tradesmen, of the farmers, and of all those on whom the real burden of taxes falls', adding 'but above all, I defend the cause of humanity'.[43]

Direct assault upon the monarchy and aristocracy was also a vital part of Paine's strategy. Humour, sarcasm, exaggeration, paradox, punning and alliteration were some of the principal weapons. The nobility were men of 'no-ability'. Titles marked 'a sort of foppery in the human character which degrades it'. The House of Lords was an association for protecting stolen property. Satan was unforgettably referred to in *The Age of Reason* as 'his sooty highness'. Such descriptions not only struck home; they were sharp and easily remembered. Paine's imagery was also often strongly visual, as when he described Point-No-Point, a shoreline in America which never seemed to end, as similar to Burke's *Reflections*. Apparent absurdities which made his opponents seem laughable were also common. In the *Rights of Man*, for example, Paine compared the English government with a wild beast on the grounds that since Burke disagreed that government was founded on the rights of man, it must be based on other rights. Since only men and beasts roamed the earth, Burke proved government must be a beast.[44]

Paine also used his own authorial position dramatically, rarely retreating into modesty and proclaiming his independence loudly and frequently. Considering the defects of the British government, for example, he portrayed himself as a compassionate man associating with the misfortunate poor: 'In taking up this subject, I seek no recompense – I fear no consequences ... Fortified with that proud integrity that disdains to triumph or to yield, I will advocate the Rights of Man.' Elsewhere Paine insisted that despite humble beginnings he had 'arrived at an eminence in political literature, the most difficult of all lines to succeed and excel in, which aristocracy, with all its aids, has not been able to reach or to rival'. Paine also frequently portrayed his own motives as pure and unbiased. In one of his best-known lines, he announced that 'Independence is my happiness, and I view things as they are, without regard to place or person; my country is the world, and my religion is to do good.' Similarly he wrote that the *Rights of Man* was possessed of 'a spirit of greater benignity, and stronger inculcation of moral principles' than any other political work.[45]

Paine's appeal to a moral code common to all humanity was also central to his style. Often he juxtaposed some corrupt aspect of monarchy or aristocracy to what a pure-hearted man would do or think. 'To read the history of kings', he put it at one point, 'a man would be almost inclined to think that government consisted in stag-hunting, and that every nation paid a million a year to the huntsman', concluding that 'Man ought to have pride or shame enough to blush at being thus imposed upon, and when he feels his proper character, he will'. Such injunctions struck home so well because of Paine's acute awareness of the servility ingrained into and deeply resented by the common people, and correspondingly their widespread desire for independence, which awaited a cathartic moment to erupt into political passion. 'Upon all subjects of this nature', he insisted of the average person, 'there is often passing in the mind a train of ideas he has not yet accustomed himself to encourage and communicate. Restrained by something that puts on the character of prudence, he acts the hypocrite upon himself as well as to others.' Paine was extremely sensitive to the power of the printed word to counteract this reluctance, observing that it was 'curious to observe how soon this spell can be dissolved. A single expression, boldly conceived and uttered, will sometimes put a whole company into their proper feelings, and whole nations are acted upon in the same manner.' Sincerity was thus vital both to Paine's conception of the ideal personality and to his literary style. Monarchy and aristocracy encouraged fawning dissimulation, while republicanism instilled a noble equality of relations, where men saw one another without 'artifice' rather than diffracted through the prismatic language of 'vassalage'. To pass from one to the other, nations needed to be shaken to their senses. To lend this shock was always Paine's foremost aim, and both *Common Sense* and the *Rights of Man* proved indeed capable of provoking extraordinary exercises in mass therapy.[46]

Finally, Paine's sense of the dramatic and apocalyptic also helped to lend his writing a sense of urgency and of removal from cool drawing-rooms into crowded market-places. The question of revolutionizing European governments, he wrote, was more pressing than any other that had ever arisen. It was not 'whether this or that party shall be in or out, or Whig or Tory, or high or low shall prevail; but whether man shall inherit his rights and universal civilization take place? Whether the fruits of his labour shall be enjoyed by himself, or consumed by the profligacy of governments? Whether robbery shall be banished from courts, and wretchedness from countries?'[47] Paine conveyed the sense that a new world was dawning, if only the majority would awaken, throw off the chains of deference and claim the rights which were universally theirs. And hundreds of thousands, as we will now see, were indeed awakened.

Notes to Chapter 4: Paine's achievement

1   A. Aldridge (1960), p. 150.
2   T. Howell (1817), Vol. 22, col. 427. Eric Foner repeats Paine's disclaimer about changes in the *Rights of Man* (1976, p. 87), while Aldridge confusingly claims that the latter is thus not more 'radical' than *Common Sense* (1984, p. 18).
3   Paine (1945), Vol. 1, p. 406, Vol. 2, p. 78; G. Williams (1969), p. 15; [Paine] (1792), p. 9; H. Yorke (1804), Vol. 2, p. 365; Paine (1945), Vol. 2, pp. 16, 79, 91, 598, 652, 862, 869; G. Vale (1841), p. 165. Paine once wrote that neither Locke nor his work was 'ever mentioned during the revolution that I know of. The case America was in was a new one without any former example' (*Public Advertiser*, no. 209, 5 September 1807, p. 2). The best study of Paine's literary references is C. Robbins (1983). See also H. Clark (1932), Aldridge

(1976b), R. Gummere (1965), P. Burnell (1972), pp. 296–304 and D. Wilson (1988), pp. 43–8. Aldridge simply denies that Paine read much (1984, p. 109).

4   Paine (1945), Vol. 1, p. 296; [O. Hulme] (1771), p. 127; G. Williams (1969), p. 14; J. Locke (1970), pp. 364–6; J. Osborne (1972), p. 32.

5   Paine (1945), Vol. 2, pp. 539, 1331, 608.

6   J. Locke (1970), pp. 365–6, 418; *Public Advertiser*, no. 209 (5 September 1807), p. 2. On this article see A. Aldridge (1953). On the emergence of the 'unmixed' theory of democracy in this period see C. Weston (1965), pp. 179–216.

7   Paine (1945), Vol. 2, pp. 54, 584, 598; [Paine] (1776), pp. 19–20; *Pennsylvania Gazette*, no. 2938 (20 September 1786), p. 2; Paine (1945), Vol. 2, pp. 521–34, 585–6.

8   Paine (1945), Vol. 2, pp. 409, 1001–2, 373, Vol. 1, p. 54, Vol. 2, pp. 293, 374; *Pennsylvania Gazette*, no. 2938 (20 September 1786), p. 2; Paine (1969b), p. ix, C. Kenyon (1951); J. Meng (1946).

9   Paine (1945), Vol. 2, pp. 332, 585, 692–3; G. Wood (1969), p. 488.

10 M. Roshwald (1959), p. 378. On rights in this period see also G. Cole (1950), J. Burns (1971) and H. Dickinson (1976). Thomas Spence claimed to have first used the phrase 'the rights of man' in 1780, when, inspired by the independence of a hermit living in a cave by the sea, he inscribed on the cave wall, 'Ye Landlords vile, who man's peace marr/Come levy rents here if you can/Your stewards and lawyers I defy;/And live with all the RIGHTS OF MAN' (Place Papers, set 37, f. 167). He later entitled one of his songs 'The Rights of Man' (1st edn, 1783) as well as one of his lectures.

11 Paine (1945), Vol. 2, p. 287.

12 Paine (1945), Vol. 2, pp. 274–5. A letter to Jefferson in 1789 refined these ideas further, giving virtually the definitions of natural and civil rights offered in the *Rights of Man* (1945, Vol. 2, pp. 1298–9). Paine also clearly believed that no government preserved all natural rights, only those which were consistent with civil society. Any attempt to preserve all would only involve what he once termed an 'Indian Bill of Rights ... fitted to man in a state of nature without any government at all' (1945, Vol. 2, p. 274).

13 O. Gierke (1957), p. 113; R. Fennessy (1963), pp. 169–70. Stanlis asserts that Paine thought each retained the right 'to judge in his own cause' in civil society (1958, p. 147), but Paine clearly argues that this was amended by a corresponding civil right (1945, Vol. 1, p. 276, Vol. 2, p. 274). On the correlativity of rights and duties see R. Tuck (1979), pp. 159–60.

14 J. Bentham (1838), Vol. 2, pp. 489–534 (here, p. 501).

15 P. Gay (1977), p. 18; J. Dinwiddy (1974b).

16 R. Fennessy (1963), pp. 72, 75, makes this error, and thus overly stresses Paine's 'individualism' (pp. 23–8). D. Elder (1951), p. 81, is one of the few studies to touch even briefly on Paine's view of the law of nature. There is no adequate survey of eighteenth-century Anglo-American natural law at all. General reference works include H. Rommen (1949), P. Sigmund (1971) and A. d'Entrèves (1972). Also helpful are K. Haakonssen (1981) and I. Hont (1987). On natural rights in particular see especially R. Tuck (1979) for the seventeenth-century origins, then D. Raphael (1967) and I. Shapiro (1986). On natural law contributions to the American revolutionary debate see B. Wright (1931), E. Barker (1948) and L. Cohen (1978).

17 W. Blackstone (1941), p. 26; E. Barker (1948), p. 311; B. Willey (1957), pp. 14–18; K. Haakonssen (1981).

18 Paine (1945), Vol. 2, pp. 17, 885.
19 E. Barker (1948); L. Cohen (1978).
20 Thus it is ridiculous to suppose, with writers like Stanlis, that Paine sought to return to something like natural society, or that by definition Paine's adherence to natural rights excluded him from adopting natural law doctrines too. Stanlis, for example, argues that in Part Two, Paine thought that all government merely prevented 'men from living according to their original equality in a state of nature' (1958, pp. 146–7). Too similar a line of argument is also taken in P. Nursey-Bray (1968).
21 Paine (1945), Vol. 2, p. 197, Vol. 1, pp. 146, 358, 400. In 1779 Paine discussed America's right to fish its own waters as a 'natural right' because Britain and America lacked any treaty and were therefore 'in a state of nature, not being even within the law of nations'. The anti-statist aspects of Paine's emphasis upon society versus government have been seen as an original contribution to political thought, antedating, for example, Herbert Spencer (R. Adams, 1922, p. 116). There are also interesting comments in J. Keane (1988), pp. 44–50.
22 Thomas Pownall, for example, argued that 'Communion, or the social State, is the real state of the nature of man: And ... Government is a still further Progress of this System, as it arises, by Ways and Means consistent with all the Rights and Liberties of Man, from the Vigor of natural Principles' (Pownall, 1752, pp. 38, 109).
23 E.g. J. Dorfman (1938), H. Collins, in Paine (1969a), p. 27. See E. Foner (1976), pp. 145–82.
24 Paine (1945), Vol. 1, pp. 387, 355, Vol. 2, pp. 350, 358, 1348–9.
25 F. Garrison (1923); A. Aldridge (1960), pp. 121, 291, (1984), p. 52; see Paine (1945), Vol. 2, pp. 637, 1142.
26 Paine (1945), Vol. 2, pp. 283, 329–30, 402, 637–40, 1142, 383.
27 Paine (1945), Vol. 2, pp. 330, 283, 651–74, 685. Paine later claimed that the *Decline and Fall* led to 'so great a run upon the Bank of England' that payments of specie for notes were suspended.
28 Paine (1945), Vol. 2, p. 191, Vol. 1, p. 393. Foner tends to assume that both Paine and Smith sought an egalitarian society of small producers, which places Smith too close to Paine (1976, p. 156). Paine may have been influenced in his discussion of London workhouses by Philadelphia debates (see E. Foner, 1976, p. 46, and G. Nash, 1976, pp. 17–18, who also argues that poverty became increasingly systematic in Philadelphia just prior to the revolution). Foner also sees a stronger commitment to a self-regulating market in the *Rights of Man* than I find (1976, p. 181).
29 See J. Burns (1971), p. 25 and D. Raphael (1967), pp. 62–3 on this point.
30 Paine (1945), Vol. 2, pp. 451, 536.
31 Paine (1945), Vol. 2, pp. 287, 580–1. A. Ayer (1988), p. 109, assumes that Paine sought to abolish poverty entirely.
32 Paine (1945), Vol. 2, pp. 141, 289, 416, 424, 1,337.
33 Paine (1945), Vol. 2, p. 535. Paine also believed that 'education is the right of everyone, and society owes it to all its members equally' (1945, Vol. 2, p. 560). On the application of 'moral economy' to Paine's thought see E. Foner (1976), pp. 145–82 and W. Christian (1973a).
34 E. Thompson (1968), pp. 104–5; H. Clark (1933b), p. 136; P. Burnell (1972), p. 64.
35 E. Vattel (1916), pp. 37–8, 43. On free trade ideas in this period see I. Hont (1989).

36 This trend is already evident in H. Clark (1933a). Aldridge plays down the impact of Quakerism on Paine (1984, p. 88).
37 E.g. Paine (1945), Vol. 2, p. 817. R. Falk (1938) argues for the deist view of Paine.
38 M. Conway (1892), Vol. 1, p. 231. See S. James (1963), pp. 128–40.
39 J. Naylor (1656), pp. 24–7; F. Tolles (1948), p. 15; R. Bauman (1971), pp. 159–83; Paine (1945), Vol. 1, pp. 83, 94. On eighteenth-century Quakerism see F. Tolles (1960) and, for Philadelphia in particular, Tolles (1948). On the influence of Paine's criticisms see A. Mekeel (1979), p. 139, and generally R. Falk (1939). A breakaway group of revolutionary supporters called the 'Free Quakers' was formed in 1781 (R. Bauman, 1971, pp. 166–9). On Quaker attitudes towards social services during the revolution see S. James (1963), pp. 240–67. For a more extended discussion see my (1989), ch. 1.
40 For Paine's view of defensive war see (1945), Vol. 2, pp. 52–60. On the origins of Quaker anti-war beliefs see T. Jones (1972). For Paine's criticism of 'political Quakers' see, e.g., Paine (1945), Vol. 1, p. 83. A good overview of Penn's social theory is C. Robbins (1986). Other Quakers also supported such plans for European peace. A friend and follower of Penn's, John Bellers, for example, urged the ending of war through conciliation in *Some Reasons for an European State* (1711). Penn was no egalitarian, preferring a society of ranks as well as limited monarchy. But he urged the abolition of primogeniture in Pennsylvania and the limitation of landed estates to 1000 acres per family. These views were clearly Harringtonian, and not far removed from the spirit of the *Rights of Man* (F. Tolles, 1948, p. 114).
41 See J. Harrison (1979) and (1988), and J. Fruchtman (1984). For Price and Priestley see Fruchtman (1981) and (1983), pp. 46–80.
42 Paine (1945), Vol. 2, pp. 539, 79, 276, 52, 532–3, 396. Fruchtman (1984) sees Paine as adhering to a 'secular millennialism' which was merely less Christ-centred or prophetic than Priestley's. Harrison (1988) examines the overlapping of popular radicalism and millenarianism, but does not see Paine as a millenarian. Bloch (1985) prefers 'utopian deism' or 'secular utopians' (pp. 190–9), though she also associates Paine with millenarianism. Foner links Paine too closely with perfectibilism (1976, p. 117).
43 *Thoughts on National Insanity* (1797), pp. 27–8; Paine (1945), Vol. 2, pp. 537, 632. On Paine's style see J. Boulton (1963), pp. 134–50 and E. Hinz (1972). The best account of Paine's rhetoric is D. Wilson (1988), pp. 20–9, which plays down claims for its uniqueness. This tends, however, to ignore the Quaker context of Paine's search for 'plainness' of prose and speech. A good study of Paine's metaphors is J. Betka (1975).
44 Paine (1945), Vol. 1, pp. 310, 286, 509, Vol. 2, p. 582, 258, 385.
45 Paine (1945), Vol. 1, pp. 405–6, 413–14.
46 Paine (1945), Vol. 1, pp. 421, 296.
47 Paine (1945), Vol. 1, p. 404.

5

A great awakening:
the birth of the
revolutionary party

I consider a King in England as something which the military keep
to cheat with, in the same manner that wooden gods and conjuror's
wands were kept in time of idolatry and superstition; and in proportion
as knowledge is circulated throughout a country, and the minds of
the people become cleared of ignorance and rubbish, they will find
themselves restless and uneasy under any government so established.
This is exactly the case with the people of England. They are not sufficiently ignorant to be governed superstitiously, nor yet wise enough to
be governed rationally, so that being complete in neither, and equally
defective in both, are for ever discontented and hard to be governed at
all. They live in a useless twilight of political knowledge and ignorance,
in which they have dawn enough to discover the darkness by, and liberty
enough to feel they are not free; constantly slumbering, without an ability
to sleep, without an inclination to rise. (1778)

'Tis a *noble*! 'tis a *virtuous*! 'tis a *Godlike* and an immortal cause in which
we are now mutually embarked. (the Bristol Society for Constitutional
Information, 1792).[1]

'The whiskey of infidelity and treason': the *Rights of Man* and popular politics

In the history of political thought the way in which books are read is
often as important a part of their composite social 'meaning' as what
their authors intended. However we identify the intellectual debts of
particular concepts, or reconstruct the internal relations between
portions of texts, or boldly illuminate thoughts by deducing inten-
tionality, a contextual assessment of 'meaning' demands an analysis
of the reception of ideas. This is nowhere more true, moreover, than
in popular political thought. For here, much more than for more

dispassionate or chiefly analytical treatises on first principles, what constitutes 'reading' is determined less by the structure of ideas than their ability to seize the gist of a particular moment, and to give voice to the inchoate but deeply felt longings of the many. No political tract has ever been published which was more successful in this regard over a similar period of time than the *Rights of Man*. In this and the following chapter, thus, we will consider what Paine's ideas meant to both his followers and their opponents, and how the revolution debate came to be defined by the contest between them.

One of Paine's central aims in the *Rights of Man* was indeed the creation of a popular political movement. Circulating many such works, he correctly surmised in a letter to the leading Manchester radical Thomas Walker, would 'embarrass the Court gentry more than anything else, because it is a ground they are not used to'. It would be wrong, of course, to ascribe the growth of the radical movement of the 1790s to Paine alone. As the prominent London political lecturer and writer John Thelwall pointed out, 'even the popular language of Thomas Paine would not have provoked any very alarming discussion, if the general *condition* of mankind had not pre-disposed them to exclaim – *We are wretched! Let us enquire the cause!*' But the success of his writings surpassed Paine's wildest expectations and was in fact unparalleled in the history of the printed word. The book 'seemed to electrify the nation', one radical later recalled.[2] 'Hey for the New Jerusalem! The millennium! And peace and eternal beatitude be unto the soul of Thomas Paine', blurted one social critic, Thomas Holcroft, to another, William Godwin, on its appearance. No work, echoed Paine's friend Joel Barlow, 'that will be written for ages to come, will surely find a reader who will not have read the *Rights of Man*'. In one London tavern a tailor announced that 'Tom Paine ... was a second Jesus Christ' and 'the only Man to save this Country and the Whole World', while a pamphlet termed him 'a God' compared to princes, bishops, judges and peers. Spies in pubs – much government-subsidized ale was consumed in the name of intelligence-gathering – reported toasts like 'Destruction to the King and Parliament and Success to Tom Paine' and 'Tom Paine's health and success to his proceedings and damn those that are not Tom Paine's'. Soon their children also took up the cry, or at least something like it; at Birmingham in late 1792 some were heard to shout, rather confusedly, 'God save the King and Huzza, Tom Paine for ever' while others mimicked, no more consistently, 'No Presbyterians and Tom Paine for ever' (but so did adult loyalists, as we will see).[3]

Sales of the *Rights of Man* astounded radicals and conservatives alike and cheap editions fuelled demand even more. One printer described by a jealous rival as an 'Adventurer' was alone responsible for producing some 10–12,000 copies per week of the *Rights of Man* and sending 'bales of hundreds of thousands' to Ireland. Entrepreneurs also undertook to sell Paine on their own; two such men 'with large wallets at their backs' were reported to be hawking cheap editions of the *Rights of Man* in villages in the east in late 1792 (though loyalists claimed that some did not know what they were selling), while a Chatham bookseller boasted of selling 1,000 copies. The more philanthropic did not even sell the tract; one person bought 3,000 copies of Part One for free distribution. Part Two went through five editions in a single month and sold at least 10,000 copies a week for a time. Many went for 6*d*, but at least 30,000 copies were sold by political clubs at a groat (4*d*) each, or about a ninth of a skilled labourer's daily wage. A sympathetic 1792 account calculated that 40–50,000 copies of the first part and as many of the second had been bought, while a 1793 pamphlet claimed sales of 'no less than 130,000 copies'.[4] Sherwin thought 100,000 copies of each part of the *Rights of Man* had circulated. But other accounts figure as many were bought between 1791–3 alone and Paine himself thought that 'between four and five hundred thousand' had been sold by 1802. Since Britain had 10 million inhabitants at this time, a modern comparison would require sales of 12 million copies in the USA today. And for every copy circulated, many readers might be found; a Perth cabinet-maker, for example, lent his copy to twelve friends, claiming that he could not 'do a greater service to my country than by making such principles known'.[5] Many who did not read the book itself, moreover, doubtless saw some of the 600 titles[6] generated in the ensuing debate, read excerpts from them in the popular press, or heard them in the form of lectures and sermons.

Most of this enthusiasm was confined to Britain. But in the United States the *Rights of Man* still required nineteen editions between 1791–3 (to Burke's two) to satisfy demand and rendered public opinion more favourable to France, even among the clergy. Initially both Federalists and anti-Federalists collaborated in issuing a complete edition of Paine's works. Radicals in particular read Paine's new work 'with avidity and pleasure', as Jefferson, now Secretary of State, put it, commending the work highly to its first American printer to aid in the fight against Adams, Jay, Hamilton and other 'Tory' anti-Gallicans. These compliments were advertised on the title page of a new edition. In reply a series of letters signed 'Publicola' (often ascribed to John Quincy Adams) lambasted Jefferson and Paine as well as the new French constitution, but without complimenting Burke. 'Publicola' denied that England lacked a constitution and that sovereignty rested outside any representative body except when real oppression was present, which he implied was not the case in Britain. Widely attacked, these letters began a new controversy over political principles in the United States. But by 1793, and especially after the execution of Louis, the Federalists, also fearing popular licentiousness at home, increasingly

112

used the *Rights of Man* to deride the revolution. France's belligerency towards American shipping during the war with Britain together with clerical fears of deism and accusations of the French subversion of American institutions fuelled popular reaction. In 1798 public opinion turned sharply against France, and the Alien and Sedition Acts were passed to suppress the republican opposition. With Jefferson's victory in 1800, however, republican sympathies were again triumphant.[7]

In Britain the *Rights of Man* appeared to many as a political revelation. Millions who had never played any formal role in politics were now jolted to political consciousness by Paine's insistence that as human beings, rather than as members of a social rank, nation or historical epoch, they had rights which could not be abrogated, including representation and the choice of the best form of government for the nation. As the philosopher David Hartley put it, politics were no longer understood as 'limited merely to the arrangement of a balance of powers between the various members of any community, as in a state of contentious society: the doctrine of free compact, founded on the Rights of Man, is now claimed by mankind in a mass, as their indefeasible right'. This appeal to those who (as the Attorney General put it) could not 'from their education or situation in life, be supposed to understand the subject on which he writes', was precisely the argument used to prosecute Paine. But this was what he wanted, and to multitudes the *Rights of Man* was virtually cathartic; as a Sheffield radical put it, the book 'astonishes, while it instructs'. For thousands it inspired an intellectual as well as emotional break which is difficult for us to comprehend. That the common man and woman felt themselves already to be in possession of 'rights' is undoubted. But these were broadly perceived to be limited by custom, tradition and national boundaries. For the disenfranchised to demand the 'Rights of Man' (in print the words were often capitalized or in bold type) was to proclaim a new identity defined by the common right to happiness, political freedom and participation, and to transform the resentment of grievances into a sense of systematic oppression. As a Sheffield radical wrote, 'our views of the Rights of Man are not confined solely to this small island but are extended to the whole human race black or white high or low'. For hundreds of thousands Paine thus illuminated a passage to independence and adulthood after what seemed an eternity of subservience. No work had so challenged the bonds of deference and hierarchy which were the sinews of an aristocratic, agricultural and Anglican nation. The erosion of servility was everywhere; one radical wrote to a loyalist society that 'Men and Angels sing the Eternal immortal Praises' of the *Rights of Man*, and signed himself, 'Not your humble Servant, but the Contrary', which was Paine's concluding line in his *Letter Addressed to the Addressers*.[8]

This process was only partially understood as 'political'. Many of Paine's readers were probably ill acquainted with the intricacies of politics and were in any case contemptuous of existing parties. 'The names of *Pittite* and *Foxite*, with those other blandishments, with which *interest* has contrived to catch the eyes and seduce the attention of the unthinking and the vulgar, are regarded by them as the rattles of childhood', one account put it; 'They aspire to a nobler character; and, instead of consigning their understandings to the custody of others, are determined to take the trouble of thinking for themselves.' Some Painites recalled the Wilkes agitation of the 1760s and many connected Paine's ideas to other issues: anti-slavery, local government reform, food prices, religious toleration. But their sense of higher moral mission, common enterprise and fellowship, and the consciousness of international mission which reached from America to France, were unlike anything seen since the seventeenth-century civil war. For the first time terms like 'citizen' and even 'comrade' were used in a fraternal language of respectful address, beginning a radical tradition unbroken to the present day. Old titles of deference were to be abolished in the new republican spirit. And this was true even in democratic America, where radicals praised the fact that in France 'instead of the ridiculous epithets of Sir, Mr., Esquire, Worshipful, Reverend ... which are all contrary to the principles of a republican government and despicable to every citizen who thinks for himself, we find the social and soul-warming term Citizen applied even to the first servant of that sublime nation'.[9]

Both Paine's reputation and this sense of solidarity were directly linked to the unprecedented growth of popular political organizations, particularly during the peak of the Painite movement, mid–1792 to spring 1793.[10] Many of these associations reprinted cheap editions or synopses of the *Rights of Man*. The Leicester Constitutional Society, for example, produced 10,000 copies of an 'Abstract of the Rights of Man' in late 1792 for distribution to troops and the populace on market day and ensured that every private in the Blues, quartered in the town, was presented with a copy. (Much the same occurred at Dorchester.) In London the Society for Constitutional Information (SCI) praised Paine's 'irresistibly convincing' book, ordered 12,000 copies of the *Letter to Mr. Secretary Dundas* in mid-1792 and sent out nearly 9,000 copies of various of Paine's other works to local distributors.[11] Paine reciprocated such sentiments by offering the very considerable profits (some £1,000 by mid-1792) of the *Rights of Man* Part Two to the SCI on the sixteenth anniversary of American independence, 4 July 1792; the Society refused, saying he deserved some reward himself. The Sheffield SCI reprinted the *Rights of Man* at 6d a copy and offered special thanks to Paine for 'the affectionate concern he has shown in his second work in behalf of the Poor, the Infant, and the Aged'.[12] At Ipswich a dozen clubs each elected a reader who explained 'Paine's pamphlet to those ignorant People who can neither read nor write'. At Hatfield, Yorkshire, a club of a hundred led by a grocer and a dyer had the *Rights of Man* read to them. Everywhere it seemed that a single book might revolutionize an entire society. Some Norwich radicals thus prophesied that 'Mr. Paine's books were to be the medium, through which the prejudices that had grown up under the British constitution were to be got rid of', while other associations hoped 'that in consequence of the effect of this work a complete reform in the present inadequate state of the representation of the people will be accomplished; and that the other great plans of public benefit which Mr. Paine has so powerfully recommended will speedily be carried into effect'.[13]

The most important new political association was the London Corresponding Society (LCS), which, as a later Painite put it, 'first *demonstrated* that the *people* could act for themselves – that they did not want the *assistance* of great men, or popular leaders'. The first working-class or 'popular Radical' organization (in E. P. Thompson's words), the LCS was founded in January 1792 with some assistance from Paine himself and organized into divisions of about thirty members each paying a penny subscription weekly. Delegates from each division met weekly in a General Committee and could be recalled at any time.[14] In their meetings a spirit of equality predominated and efforts to restrict membership were never taken seriously. To the contrary, the society actively resisted attempts at 'leadership' of any type other than directly elected and some adherents boasted that it had 'no leaders and no parties' whatsoever. According to the tailor Francis Place, who knew the society well, its most prominent members were republicans as a consequence of reading Paine, though one prudently denied in 1795 that the LCS circulated the *Rights of Man* on an official basis.[15] The rank and file were artisans, principally shoemakers, tailors and weavers, and tradesmen. Though their goals were also economic – there were a number of strikes in 1791–2 – their chief aim was political organization and education. But such goals could assume many guises, including the threat of imitating France. One LCS branch, for example, circulated an inflammatory handbill advertising a never-performed farce 'for the benefit of John Bull' entitled 'Le Guillotine or George's Head in a Basket', whose leading character was 'Numpy the Third', played by 'Mr Gwelp', which invoked Paine's name for George III (and the LCS was later accused of harbouring such plans on the basis of this farce). Another LCS member entertained his comrades with 'Magic Lanthorn' slides of the Bastille and Louis losing his head, and it was said he carried some unpainted slides which 'were to have on them figures of people in this country whenever the guillotine was introduced'.

Another comrade, a carpenter, made a small wooden model of the offending instrument to show the curious how heads of state fell in France.[16]

The most important provincial radical organizations were the local Societies for Constitutional Information or 'Constitutional Societies'. 'In some parts of England whole towns are reformers', claimed the London radical Maurice Margarot. Sheffield 'and its environs', he thought, counted some 50,000 of the tribe, adding that altogether some *six* or *seven hundred thousand* males, which is a majority of all the adults in the kingdom' (and no doubt an exaggeration) favoured reform. Local associations typically began spontaneously with a few members. At Sheffield, for example, which boasted many literate artisans and tradesmen, the Constitutional Society commenced in late 1791 when 'five or six mechanics', meeting at one of their houses, began

> conversing about the enormous high price of provisions; the gross abuses this nation labours under from the unbounded authority of *Monopolizers* of all ranks, from the KING to the PEASANT; the waste and lavish of the public property by placemen, pensioners, luxury, and debauchery, sources of the grievous burdens under which the nation groans; together with the mock representation of the people.

Soon reprinting an edition of 1,600 copies of the *Rights of Man* for sale at 6*d*, the society claimed that it had 'derived more true knowledge from … Mr Thomas Paine … than from any other author on the subject'. It had 2,000 members within four months, and six months later could amass demonstrations of 5,000 to 6,000. Its petition to Parliament for reform, thrown out as insolent, had some 10,000 signatures.[17] Another provincial hotbed was Norwich, 'the jacobin city', and its surrounding villages. Long a Dissenting stronghold, it was by mid-1792 home to some forty clubs of weavers, shoemakers, manufacturers and shopkeepers combined as the 2,000-strong United Constitutional Societies. Here, on 14 July 1791, the *Rights of Man* was quoted freely against Burke by a Norfolk farmer speaking from the pulpit of St Paul's chapel, immediately provoking the formation of a loyalist society.[18] Manchester was also extremely active under the leadership of the boroughreeve Thomas Walker's Constitutional Society, where Paine's works and others were read aloud and weavers, merchants and manufacturers were Paine's chief adherents (and middle-class involvement in the movement was strong throughout this period). At Birmingham a Society for Constitutional Information was founded in November 1792 and amassed 2,700 signatures for its petition for parliamentary reform in 1793. In the Potteries many journeymen potters read Paine's works, while in the mining districts of the south-west, it was claimed, they were

116

smuggled on the backs of mules and dropped surreptitiously into the pits.[19] In many towns liberals congregated around a newspaper like Benjamin Flower's *Cambridge Intelligencer*. In small villages one or two local craftsmen, often shoemakers, shared radical sentiments and ventured to correspond with a provincial society.

Scotland was also extremely active in the radical cause. Sales of the *Rights of Man* were greater there, many thought, because the lower classes were better educated. Its principles penetrated deeply and were often repeated directly: one radical handbill stated that the nation was the source of sovereignty, the right of altering government lay with the people rather than government, and that government was only a national association acting on the principles of society. By the autumn of 1792 'Paine's pamphlet, or the cream and substance of it' was 'in the hands of almost every countryman' and societies were 'everywhere formed, and clubs instituted for the sole purpose of political debate'. There were 1,200, led by merchants, active at Perth, 6,000 at Stirling and (some claimed) at least 50,000 in the west country, of whom seven-eighths were tradesmen. Everywhere they read the *Rights of Man*, sent privately from Edinburgh, it was alleged, and often distributed for free. At Edinburgh prominent dignitaries like Professor Dugald Stewart welcomed the revolution, joined by students, lawyers, booksellers and merchants. Twenty branches of the Friends of the People represented radical opinion by early 1793; scarcely one met after the treason trials later that year, which also dispersed activities at Dundee, Perth, Stirling and Glasgow, where Professor John Millar led local enthusiasts. Many small towns also possessed plebeian organizations. In the village of Partick in Lanarkshire, for example, radicals indignant 'at the honour of their town having been stained, by the erection of a Burkified society' of loyalists, and 'having attentively perused the whole works of the immortal author of the *Rights of Man*, Thomas Paine', formed in November 1792 an association named 'the Sons of Liberty, and the Friends of Man'. If Paine's principles were adopted everywhere, they hoped, 'tyrants and their satellites would vanish like the morning mist before the rising sun'.[20] At this time the Home Secretary, 'the villan [*sic*] Dundas', was at least once burned in effigy by a crowd of masons and labourers. 'Liberty trees', often laurel branches with gilded leaves and sometimes decorated with candles and apples or signs reading 'liberty and equality', were also erected in many towns and villages. Much of the considerable popular unrest in Scotland throughout 1792 was officially blamed on the influence of Paine's writings. But clearly other causes were at work, since protests were also against enclosures, the ejection of tenants to introduce sheep-farming, high tolls and taxes, the poor harvest that year, and burgh and agricultural reform. Here, as elsewhere, old liberties and new rights joined hands.[21]

Less is known about the radical movement in other parts of the country. A Welsh translation of the *Rights of Man* closely printed on brown paper was distributed for free shortly before Christmas 1792. In Ireland the Dublin Whig Club appointed a committee to decide the best means of disseminating Paine's works, but popular appeal rendered such efforts scarcely necessary. By one account some 20,000 copies of the *Rights of Man* circulated in the city, while Paine himself thought that over 40,000 of Part One had been sold throughout Ireland by November 1791.[22] Artisans were its favoured buyers. At the treason trial of one the gift of a print of Paine was entered as incriminating evidence; at another, at Dublin in 1795, Paine's doctrines were declared to be 'the whiskey of infidelity and treason', which was no mere turn of phrase, since Paine's name was a favourite in radical drinking songs. But Paine's heady doctrines intoxicated other ranks as well. A militia captain was tried for sedition for handing the book to a lieutenant of another regiment with the words, 'read this, it is my creed.' At Wexford, where a short-lived republic blossomed in 1798, Paine's ideas were debated in the streets. The United Irishmen, formed in October 1790 to establish equal rights and parliamentary reform, had contacts with many English organizations as well as with France and were doubtless chiefly responsible for extending Paine's reputation in Ireland. Though it has been claimed that most of them did not follow Paine into republicanism and remained closer to True Whiggism, their plans (revealed under interrogation) 'to form a Republic, independent from England or France; to form a constitution upon the French model' seemingly belies such a view.[23]

The strength of the new movement is everywhere difficult to calculate. The LCS began with some seventy members in April 1792, and by the autumn was enrolling 300 or 400 new members weekly. Meetings commonly attracted many more listeners than members; one division had 112 paying members, but occasionally 700 in attendance. In December 1792 the LCS had perhaps 13,000 members and mustered as many as 150,000 onlookers at some meetings (out of a London population of one million!). Sheffield had another 10,000 and Norwich 2–3,000. The LCS also had connections with (its enemies claimed it was 'actually directing') organizations in Manchester, Bristol, Coventry, Nottingham, Derby and Belper in Derbyshire, Leicester, Cambridge, Royston, Hertford, Norwich, Nottingham, Birmingham, Stockport, Leeds, Sheffield, Bradford, Halifax, Huddersfield, Wakefield, Newcastle upon Tyne, York, Hereford, Edinburgh, Glasgow, Leith, Perth, Stirling, Paisley and other parts of Scotland. One source in April 1792 calculated that the political societies together comprised over 40,000 members.[24] Following a period of decline, the LCS again enjoyed an increase in membership after one of its organizers, the shoemaker Thomas Hardy, was acquitted of high treason in late 1794 (having frequently referred to the *Rights of Man* at his trial). By late 1795 it had 2,000 actually meeting and in 1796 about 1,500 paid-up members.[25]

The government found such numbers and activities threatening for several reasons. By the end of 1792 radical organizations seemed to be growing very rapidly and, moreover, moving ever closer in spirit to events in France. French military victories became the occasion for local celebrations. Sheffield, for example, celebrated the French victory at Valmy in 1792 by 5,000 cutlers carrying pictures portraying Burke astride a pig, the Home Secretary as half-man, half-ass, and an Angel of Peace ministering the *Rights of Man* to suffering Britannia. Fraternal addresses and delegations were also sent to the Convention in Paris. Small wonder, then, that the government began to consider revolution as a real possibility if food prices continued to rise and popular unrest and political organizations proceeded apace. Political polarization increased greatly throughout 1792 and by mid-1793 Britons had begun to divide into what Paine saw as three groups: the 'Revolutionary party', the 'government party', and an 'intermedial party' anxious to end the war primarily on the grounds of its expense.[26]

To the government the radicals were most threatening when they met as a national 'convention', for here they seemed most aware of, and capable of implementing, Paine's theory of sovereignty. A convention was necessary because most people had played no role in electing the present parliament, argued the radical editor Sampson Perry. Reform would come from neither King nor Parliament, but 'by a convention of ourselves and our Societies', asserted another Painite. Preceded by earlier Scottish meetings of Societies of the Friends of the People, the main 'British Convention' occurred in late 1793 when some forty associations from London, Sheffield and parts of Scotland sent 153 delegates to Edinburgh. French terms were used and delegates graced one another with the title of 'Citizen'. The government reacted quickly. Though no force was threatened (there is evidence it was expected), several leaders were arrested at the end of the sittings and sentenced to fourteen years' transportation. In 1794 LCS members none the less pressed for a further convention, rejecting efforts by the SCI to confine their ambitions to a mere 'meeting'. For the language of the former organization was necessary and its import inescapably clear: it was society attempting to reconstitute government.[27]

Paine's presence loomed large over such proceedings long after he had left for France and his principles were celebrated in many other ways. Songs with titles like 'The Triumph of Reason' echoed through radical taverns. Tokens and vases bore Paine's visage or quotes from his works. Slogans adorned walls and placards; for many months a sign hung at the Surrey end of Westminster bridge saying 'Rubbish may be shot by the direction of Thomas Paine' (a Lord of the Bedchamber finally ordered it removed in 1794). Such evidence leaves little doubt of the centrality of Paine's writings to the new political movement. At a dinner marking the anniversary of the LCS in 1795, Paine was the only author honoured with a toast, though after his trial his name was less frequently invoked so openly. None the less the widespread public identification of Paine with the LCS and similar organizations is uncontested. When the publisher Charles Pigott was arrested, thrown into a cell and denied a candle, fire, bed, or chair, his vain protests were answered with the charge 'that we were TOM PAINE's Men, and *rebels*'. In his widely circulated *Pigott's Political Dictionary*, too, a 'Painite' was defined as 'every individual who will not sign his test in Mr. Reeves' [loyalist] Association, will not condescend to kiss the ministerial rod, held out to punish him, or agree to arm for the sake of a constitution senilely adulized, and pompously extolled'.[28]

How Paine was read

Paine's popularity was doubtless aided by Burke's attack on the revolution. The labouring classes, many felt, deeply resented 'their unworthy abuse by Mr. Burke', and 'in their rage, against their detractor ... adopted notions which had never obtained access to their minds before'. Burke's barbs were hurled back at him and his language of declamation became an important ingredient in the new self-identification of the radicals. Thousands took pride in calling themselves members of 'the swinish multitude' and Burke's phrase spawned a host of porcine terms, with the most important radical publisher, Daniel Isaac Eaton, for example, naming characters in his dialogues 'Gregory Grunter' and 'Porculus'. The ensuing controversy thus drove apart and rigidified the views of both contending parties, making it difficult not to take sides.[29]

But most of Paine's partisans did not read Burke but instead reacted directly to the *Rights of Man*. This reading of the text, usually in the small, densely printed cheap edition (it must have weakened many eyes by the fireside), was nothing short of cathartic. Its effect was to create a new political consciousness and the feeling that, as a Scot put it, 'Politics is no longer a Mysterious System but Common Sence (sic)'. This new collective consciousness verged upon being a sense of class identity, but was not based upon narrow economic criteria and obviously cannot be termed 'proletarian' in the nineteenth-century industrial sense. Class and political identity could overlap, for example, at Birmingham in late 1792, when a number of radicals threatened to establish 'a *Rights of Man* club ... which was to consist of the lower classes of people only ... No gentleman to be admitted', so that they could 'instruct the people in

Paine's Principles'. Yet such manifestations of collective identity were broadly derived from a feeling of political exclusion, of shared working, living and cultural conditions, of oppression by the wealthy and of the basic equality of humankind.[30]

How Paine contributed to this new sense of identity can be partly ascertained by examining what parts of the *Rights of Man* were stressed by readers. One recent analysis of the Painite movement in several towns has concluded that Paine's most popular arguments concerned the rights of the living against government by precedent, the doctrine that nations were the only source of sovereignty, the defence of equal natural rights, his attacks upon placemen, pensioners, the aristocracy and higher clergy, and his hope for universal religious toleration. His republicanism was less appealing as was, apparently, any reference to 'levelling' (which Paine hardly made in any case). There are many difficulties, however, in isolating Paine's precise contribution to popular debate. By 1793 his language and arguments had become so pervasive that when Paine was not explicitly cited, evidence of his inspiration is elusive. When the radical United Scotsmen, for example, resolved that mankind were naturally friends, and became enemies only because of corrupt governments, was this principally a Christian homily or a Painite principle? (It was probably more the latter.) What can we assert of Paine's influence in the shift in popular slogans noted by R. B. Rose for Birmingham, for example, where the more vocal in 1790–3 shouted 'Church and King', 'Damn the Jacobins' and 'War and Pitt', and in 1800 'No war', 'Damn Pitt' and 'Large loaves, peace, no taxes, no tithes, free constitution'. Certain themes from the *Rights of Man* do, however, recur more frequently in the popular press and reports of meetings and speeches. Paine's distinction between the benevolence of society and maleficence of government was widely applauded.[31] His notion that 'we have no constitution' was toasted at a Birmingham public house and elsewhere (but also rejected by some radicals). His views on commerce were given extensive circulation. His scheme for progressive taxation also received much praise; for example, from John Thelwall. No doubt the economic calculations of the *Rights of Man* Part Two also impressed many of Paine's readers. At Birmingham, for example, a group of workmen were said to have been drawn to 'the very powerful argument … that they shall have ale at 2*d* a quart', and had indeed gone 'so far in their calculations as to fix that a Man with 3 children will have £50 a year'. The supposition that such views were common, we will see, proved extremely important in the ensuing debate. But otherwise Paine's 'social chapter' was not in fact extensively discussed, at least in print.[32]

Of Paine's political principles, his proposals for adopting an American political model were especially widely praised. Much was made at the Edinburgh convention, for example, of the advantages of American government, though some thought only the suffrage in Pennsylvania and Vermont wide enough.[33] Many felt, as Henry Redhead Yorke stressed in 1794, that America proved a society could flourish without kings, bishops and a nobility. To Charles Pigott, America showed that good government was possible for a tenth or twentieth of what a monarchy cost, and that with 'scarce such a thing known as corruption of rulers'. While Whiggish reformers held such republicanism repugnant, the more plebeian seem to have supported it, though their sentiments were more evident in the taverns and the street and on walls than in print. At his trial for sedition, the London radical John Frost admitted to having responded to a question, in the Percy coffee-house, London, as to what he meant by 'equality', '*Why, I mean* no king.' But other reformers may have agreed with a Norwich radical that 'The jacobins acknowledge kingship, but abominate monarchy. By king, they mean a chief magistrate who rules by law. By monarch, one who is above the law, and rules by his own absolute authority.' Such radicals even suspected the concentration of power in the hands of the American President and welcomed Washington's resignation, despite their admiration for his talents, because of the dangers of 'long-continued power'. The American achievement also implied a distinctively modern notion of democracy which superseded classical ideals. 'Democracy' in Athens, after all, had included more slaves – their presence in America was less often touched upon – than freemen, while the ancient republics had been confined to city-states. Joel Barlow thought Rousseau and others had failed to see that not only was a republic the 'only proper and safe' form of government, but 'its propriety and safety' were 'in proportion to the magnitude of the society and the extent of the territory'. Classical republicanism was thus inverted and modern republicanism legitimated by claiming that their aims could be met only in substantial nations. This was the message of the American revolution. Linked to this sense of the novelty of the 'representative republic', too, was a new concept of revolution which no longer meant returning to an originally uncorrupted foundation. Barlow, for one, insisted in 1792 that 'the change of government in France is, properly speaking, a renovation of society' by which government had been organized 'on principles approved by reason'.[34]

Besides republicanism, Paine's emphasis on rights was enormously important to the reception of the *Rights of Man*. Ideas of rights were now brought far more sharply into focus and invested with a substantially new meaning. Rights now became the moral and political centre of gravity of most radical tracts, and were no longer seen as a privilege to be begged from government, but (as Gilbert Vale later put it) as 'a *power* which could only be exercised by the nation itself'. 'The natural *Rights of*

Man; rights *essential* and *imprescriptable,* because they constitute our very species: Rights undoubtedly inalienable, because no species can cease to be itself, or what it is, without ceasing to exist' was how Sampson Perry defined his political creed. Rights were now widely construed in an anthropological sense, as inhering in each individual regardless of rank, rather than as liberties and privileges dependent on precedent or the fortunes of the English constitution. Some might go back to 1688 or even Alfred, said one Edinburgh convention delegate, but others were for 'disregarding all authorities, and standing up for our rights as *men'.* None the less the foundation document of the LCS stressed that no rights had been lost when society was formed and emphasized that 'men can never barter away the rights of their posterity'. It also sought to *regain* an annually elected parliament, thus introducing an historical argument Paine rarely used, and in fact probably consciously rejected. Members of the LCS never completely relinquished such historical appeals to specific civil and political rights and in claiming 'our natural rights, Universal Suffrage, and Annual Parliaments' simply mixed historical and natural conceptions of rights. The 'Norman Yoke' idea, in particular, in which Saxon liberties were held to have been overthrown by William the Conqueror, was often nearby; at his trial one Scots radical sentenced to transportation, Joseph Gerrald, for example, stated that in Saxon society all had some land and the right to vote. This appeal to a specifically British, historically-rooted constitution, we will see, may indeed have made some loyalist attacks on Paine appear more plausible.[35]

Stress upon the extra-governmental origins of rights rendered some conception of the state of nature central to many Painites. As Paine had realized, the notion that any rights were surrendered in creating government opened the door to the possibility that virtually all rights could have been so bartered. Burke had verged upon this view and often radicals conceded that some rights had been surrendered to secure others more conducive to the common good. But Gerrald among others emphasized that 'It is not true, that when men agree to erect a government they give up any portion of these rights. No: they only adopt a different mode of enjoying them. They give up nothing; but by combining their own *particular* force with the force of others, they adopt a plan, by which they are enabled to possess their rights in greater security.' Henry Redhead Yorke at his trial similarly claimed that it was impossible for rights to liberty or property to be abrogated upon entering society, with each only delegating 'the use of his faculties to the government for the purpose of public convenience'. So, too, the Baptist clergyman William Winterbotham asserted at his sedition trial that there were rights 'SUPERIOR TO SOCIETY, which the individual *cannot cede,* nor the *society accept',* including an absolute right to the necessities of life (which was a gift of God), the right to choose, act and speak according to the rule 'Do unto others', and the right to object to heavy taxation. More Whiggish radicals, despite their disagreements with the Painites, also conceded this point. Mackintosh thought natural sovereignty had been relinquished only in order to avoid abuses resulting from inequalities of strength and skill. Wollstonecraft agreed: government had the duty to destroy any natural inequality by protecting the weak against the strong. None the less the new radicalism gave less stress to the historical existence of a state of nature than the intrinsic possession of rights by all. John Thelwall, for example, defined 'man in his natural state' to mean 'simply as an individual, stripped of all the relations of Society, independent of its Compacts, and uninfluenced by its reciprocations'. Rights hence were defined according to human nature, by wants and their satisfaction, and faculties and their capacity for improvement. Any original right had merely been physical, while society rendered rights moral 'by substituting moral arbitration for physical force'.[36]

Paine's writings thus did not usurp all previous treatments of natural rights. Sidney was not neglected and Thelwall quoted Machiavelli at length on the abrogation of rights through political tyranny. Particularly after the *Rights of Man* was proscribed, Thomas Spence and others continued to quote natural law writers like Pufendorf on the theme of equality, for here they were on safe ground. (Pufendorf indeed was so well known that *Pigott's Political Dictionary*, invoking his sentiments on government, referred readers only to 'his seventh book, chapter five', without any title.)[37] Locke was also widely cited; for example, by Gerrald both at his trial and in the opening sentences of his appeal for a convention, on the right of the people to alter their mode of rule. Passages from the *Second Treatise* on property and money remained especially popular, for they supported the view that all had property in their own person and labour. But many thought that by 1791 Locke had been improved upon. To the Dissenter David Williams, for example, Locke's observations were 'in favour of liberty: but they are general. They state rights which oppressive governments may not dispute: but the mode of asserting, recovering, or preserving them, he does not point out. His mind had not conceived the general and certain remedy of social disorders and the only origin of Political Liberty, in the formation of the whole society into a moral being.'[38]

The natural rights invoked by the Painites did not, however, include equality of property. Thomas Cooper, who also supported political rights for women, cited William Ogilvie's *Essay on the Right of Property in Land* (1781) as 'a very important book too little noticed' which recommended distributing commons and waste lands amongst the poor. Charles Pigott praised republican equality and invoked Rousseau's condemnation of extreme luxury. Otherwise no important radical urged an agrarian law to reduce inequality of property. This point needs stressing given the loyalists' strategy explored in the next chapter. There is no doubt, however, that Paine's egalitarianism constituted an essential part of his appeal; one account asserted that 'nothing ... fascinated the minds of the people so effectually, as the doctrine of the equality of mankind'. In a society where the natural, God-given inequality of men and property was repeatedly taught from pulpit and hustings and probably not hitherto widely doubted anywhere, this is unsurprising. But precisely what 'equality' meant to the radicals is of great importance. What they sought, insisted the *Manchester Herald*, was equality of rights, not levelling. Property derived from industry and good fortune should be allowed to be inherited freely. A 'Visionary Equality of Property' would 'desolate the world, and replunge it into the darkest and wildest barbarism', said a Sheffield reformer. Such a 'ruinous, absurd, foolish and contemptible notion' would never have been heard of, added a Leeds radical, except that it had been 'palmed upon us by wicked or foolish men, for the worst of purposes'. By 'equality', one paper insisted, the reformers meant only equal representation, equal security in the produce of industry, and equal liberty and freedom of religion.[39]

A few radicals did, however, construe the question of equality of property in Christian terms. Eaton praised the Quakers as true levellers, while James Pilkington's *The Doctrine of Equality of Rank and Condition Examined and Supported on the Authority of the New Testament* (1795) insisted that the Scriptures prohibited entry to heaven to the overly wealthy and also applauded the Quakers for having alone made an honest attempt to establish equality amongst themselves.[40] Thelwall, too, noted that the primitive Christians had practised community of goods but added that this was none the less 'a wild and absurd scheme ... not practicable upon any *large scale*'. He also conceded that '*Man has naturally an equal claim to the elements of nature*'. But this meant that because the 'earth has been appropriated, by expediency and compact ... light, air, and water (with some exceptions) still continue to be claimed in common'. Uncultivated land could also still be treated as part of a common inheritance, and was intended, as Sampson Perry emphasized, not for exclusive possession but the general good.[41]

Thelwall thus agreed with Paine that society owed the poor their basic subsistence. But he also shifted from a more general consideration of the rights of man to the rights of labourers. The latter retained a right to receive as much from others as their 'own toil and faculties throw into the common stock', as well as a right to satisfy their 'common appetites' and to enjoy their rational faculties. When 'the territorial monopolist' paid his employees a wage scarcely sufficient for survival,

Thelwall insisted that such an 'unjust agreement, extorted by the power of an oppressor' was 'morally and politically, void'. Instead an 'implied compact ... to promote the accommodation of the whole' derived from the formation of society and the rules of moral justice. Mankind had ceded 'their common interest in the spontaneous produce of the earth' and yielded to 'appropriated culture' because they meant 'to increase the comforts and abundance of all, not the luxury and wantonness of a faction'. All of the advantages of civilized society derived from common labour. The labourer thus retained a right to a portion of social improvement as a consequence of exchanging natural society for civilization. Thus the landed proprietor was 'only a trustee for the community' entitled to 'compensation for the due management of the deposit', but with no right to 'monopolize the advantages'. These views were strikingly similar to Paine's new doctrines in *Agrarian Justice*, published a short time later.[42]

In their views of property the radicals on the whole thus subscribed to the prevalent Scottish enlightenment interpretation of the progress of property through the four stages of hunting and gathering, pastoral, agricultural and commercial societies. One account, for example, noted that the first 'revolution in civil society', the transition from savagery to shepherding, had created an hereditary aristocracy, while the latest led public institutions to be judged 'by the standard of utility'. But few doubted that commercial society was a superior stage and that trade underlay its achievements. Far from disliking commerce, therefore, radicals like the Newark printer Daniel Holt (tried for seditious libel in 1793) warned that 'a country which once loses its liberty, must shortly lose its trade also'. Parliamentary reform thus would restore free trade, curb monopoly and lighten taxation. This was a very common view, though fragmentary (and somewhat suspect) evidence also suggests that Paine's views were sometimes associated with market regulation. A Scot reported in 1793, for example, that 'Paine's book ... has been industriously circulated among the lower classes of our people, and its damnable doctrines eagerly embraced by them. Of liberty and equality they are constantly talking, and of making laws and fixing prices on every necessity of life.' But very few radicals indeed suggested, as Maurice Margarot was later to do, that man had a right to revert to primitive natural purity if need be.[43]

The threat of levelling, we will see, underlay the loyalist reaction to Paine. But Whigs and Whig radicals also felt threatened in particular by Paine's call to the labouring classes to shape their own political destinies. This most sharply demarcated Paine's brand of radicalism and prompted, as we will see, his proscription. It also split the radical movement dramatically.

All change at Hounslow: middle-class radicalism and the Painites

In Parliament the revolution debate drove a substantial wedge between the leading Whig MPs. Fox could not sympathize with Paine and described the *Rights of Man* in 1792 as a libel upon the constitution. None the less he tried to rally the party by proclaiming neutrality towards the revolution. All the same, a split was inevitable between more radical Whigs like Sheridan and Grey and the more aristocratic reformers led by the Duke of Portland, who were spurred on by both Burke and the king. First Fox and Burke themselves broke during an emotional parliamentary sitting, after which Fox cried and was unable to speak for some minutes. Further splits were nearly provoked in late 1792, instigated by disagreements about the Alien Bill and related measures, though about fifty MPs and a few Lords continued to support reform.[44] The government and most of the Whigs soon determined that any call for parliamentary reform merely fuelled the flames of popular protest. Radicalism 'out of doors' had to be eradicated, and it was. Fox and others were alarmed by the attack on British liberties associated with the sedition trials, but they were unable to restrain Pitt. Portland's defection to Pitt's ministry in July 1794, egged on by the Prime Minister, thus effectively ended the Whig opposition.

The Painite phenomenon took many older reformers by surprise. Some of the most influential organizations prior to 1790, such as the Revolution Society, whose members included the Dissenters Richard Price, Andrew Kippis, Abraham Rees, Joseph Towers and Thomas Brand Hollis, played no important role in the subsequent decade. This was not because their principles were unacceptable to the new radicals. The Revolution Society, for example, believed that all authority derived from the people, that the abuse of power justified resistance and that the rights of private judgement, liberty of conscience, trial by jury, freedom of the press and freedom of election 'ought ever to be held sacred and inviolable'. Moreover, the society also corresponded with the French National Assembly, even announcing to them the publication of Part Two of the *Rights of Man* in February 1792. But some programmatic differences between the new and older radicals were important. The Society of the Friends of the People (SFP) (founded in April 1792), which included Lauderdale, Christie, Mackintosh, Andrew Kippis and others who could afford an annual fee of two guineas, did not seek universal suffrage, for example, but a property qualification sufficient to enfranchise 1.5 million heads of households but to exclude 'the lowest and most profligate part of the community'. The most radical Whigs, notably Cartwright, believed universal suffrage a just goal, but were in a minority. Nor were universalized natural rights the core of middle-class radical doctrine. The SFP concentrated in petitions upon warning of the dangers to the balanced constitution of a despotic monarchy or dangerous oligarchy and the corresponding need for shorter parliaments, more equal parliamentary districts and a uniform exercise of the right to the franchise. But it was unwilling to go the whole length of Painism and by 1794 was decidedly reluctant to have anything to do with the LCS.[45]

Once popular upheaval accelerated it was easier for moderate reformers to shy away from further involvement. The Norwich Whig MP William Windham, among others, warned of the perils of reform in the midst of revolution, remonstrating that no sane person would repair his house during a hurricane. But other prominent Whig radicals were sceptical about the French revolution much earlier. Horne Tooke cautioned the Constitutional Society that 'the English nation had only to maintain and improve the constitution which their ancestors transmitted to them' when he felt that Sheridan had too warmly applauded the French. But Tooke did not abjure reform entirely and was himself finally caught up in the reaction. At his own treason trial he protested that while some parts of Paine's works were laudable, he 'highly disapproved of others'. In a phrase that caught the imagination of many, he insisted that while he could travel some distance with Paine in an imaginary stagecoach headed towards reform, 'When I find myself at Hounslow I get out, others may go further.'[46]

Typical of those who were also anxious to alight was Christopher Wyvill, who in 1793 warned those political associations which 'in their rash zeal for liberty' had 'applauded publications [Paine was footnoted] in which the British people are represented to have no Constitution, no political right, but the unavailing right to petition; and the plunder of the rich is held out, as the incentive to the poor, to effect a Revolution in Britain, on the principles of Republican Equality: thus, under the pretext of promoting Personal Liberty, contributing to the ruin of property, the preservation of which was one principal end, for which Society was formed'. Paine himself Wyvill accused of being 'inflamed … by his having been an actor in the Revolution of America' and of failing to see that 'an honest enthusiast may be a dangerous Politician'. He praised Paine's 'strong, though coarse, understanding, with much originality of thought and energy of expression', terming him 'fitted by nature to be a democratic leader; and early prejudice, habit, and a variety of accidental circumstances, confirmed the original tendency of his mind'. But he lamented that Paine had not written 'a more classical composition, in which more attention had been employed to avoid the grossness of indecent language and more solicitude displayed to shun whatever might tend to excite the lower classes of the People to acts of violence and injustice'. By contrast Richard Price, according to Wyvill, had not been such 'an enthusiastic Politician; though active and public spirited, he was cool and rational; though strongly attached to liberty, he was prudent and cautious to avoid unnecessary danger, not to himself, but to the public'. Price had recognized, too, thought Wyvill, that merely emulating America would not introduce prosperity to Britain.[47]

What chiefly irritated the more Whiggish reformers about Paine was thus his appeal to the common people and the implication that they, and not the established opposition, were the legitimate reformers. The *Rights of Man*, Whigs complained, was 'flattering to the feelings of the vulgar' and pandered to the labouring classes by promising them support under a future radical government. Many moderates, at least early on, admired the 'temperate parts' of the *Rights of Man*. Some helped to circulate Paine's works. A liberal gentleman, Thomas Poole, for example, lent the *Rights of Man* to a Bridgwater, Somerset cabinet-maker in December 1792 (who promptly bumped into a local loyalist attorney who tore the pamphlet to pieces). But many moderates were soon driven to deny that Paine was in any sense a Whig. Some cited Locke, for example, on the protection of property as the chief end of government and asserted that if Paine's view of the British 'constitution' were correct, then 'Locke, Montesquieu, and all the great train of statesmen and philosophers, who have extolled the English constitution, were wrong'.[48]

Most Whigs had no desire to embrace Burke either, however. The problem therefore was to define a middle position which, as Catherine Macaulay put it, steered between the parties of 'exultation and rapture' and 'indignation and scorn'. Burke had clearly 'unwhig'd himself' by writing the *Reflections*, as one account put it, but Paine was a simple menace to social order. Each, said the Duke of Norfolk, 'had done infinite mischief' and many other erstwhile reformers felt that both were 'equally dangerous to the public and private tranquillity, and liberty of Great Britain and France. The one served to foster and encourage pride, avarice, ambition, and oppression, among the higher orders of society; the other to create envy, discontent, murmuring, and sedition, among the middle and lower orders.' Some reformers attempted to refute the arguments on both sides. Thomas Green's *The Two Systems of the Social Compact and the Natural Rights of Man Examined and Refuted* (1793), for example, contended that Burke essentially followed Locke in taking 1688 as his model compact, and Paine, Richard Price's concern with natural rights. Both systems erred, the author thought, in grounding the right to govern in a principle distinct from the consequences of such power, which for Green was despotism on Burke's principles and tyranny of the majority on Paine's.[49]

But if Burke's position was contemptible to moderates, the problem of Paine was the more pressing. Whigs therefore sought to place the brakes upon such enthusiasm. One otherwise quite sympathetic 400-page account of radical principles disagreed with Paine on the issue of an hereditary monarchy, squarely accused Paine of being friendly to agrarianism and further criticized him for demanding 'in plain terms ... an instant change of government'. Another pamphlet entitled *Is All We Want Worth a Civil War?* thought Paine was 'too unaware of the delicate line which divides licentiousness from liberty', and warned that his writings had excited 'that dangerous spirit which threatens a total revolution in this country, a measure apparently not to be gained without the horrible disasters of a civil war'.[50]

Moderates were consequently also driven to defend the wisdom of the British constitution. Whigs commonly argued against Paine that the poor could not be politically independent since they were incapable of refusing any assistance from the wealthy.[51] Moreover, Paine had promised too much too fast. In 1792 the SFP censured the Manchester branch of the Society for Constitutional Information, adding that Paine's plans unveiled an 'indefinite language of delusion, which by opening the unbounded prospects of political adventure, tends to destroy that public opinion, which is the support of all Free Governments, and to excite a spirit of innovation, of which no wisdom can forsee the effect, and no skill direct the course'. Reasserting the principles of Whig reform, the Society insisted that

> We view man as he is: the creature of habit as well as of reason. We think it therefore our bounden duty to propose no extreme changes, which ... can never be accomplished without violence to the settled opinions of mankind, nor attempted without endangering some of the most estimable advantages which we confessedly enjoy. We are convinced that the people bear a fixed attachment to the happy form of our Government, and the genuine principles of our Constitution ... We wish to reform the Constitution, because we wish to preserve it.

Although some examinations of the *Rights of Man* attacked Paine's notions of constitution and finance at length, but found his sentiments on rights 'perfectly just', attacks on the Painites by the SFP also frequently insisted that rights were exclusively or at least primarily civil rather than natural and that God did not create men equal but instead gave them unequal powers. The SFP also vigorously denied any parallels between circumstances in France and in Britain. Cartwright, one of Paine's chief opponents in the SFP, was especially hostile to Paine's republicanism, objecting that a republic, while suitable to the new world – Harrington remained his guide – was not appropriate given British institutions and Britain's much greater social inequality. Like some Painite radicals, Cartwright also disagreed strenuously with

Paine's notion of the English constitution and in 1823 finally wrote a work entitled *The English Constitution Produced and Illustrated* to settle the matter. None the less Cartwright too tried to tread his own delicate path between reform and revolution. Observing of 'the stage-coach of reform' that 'a man may travel ... without connecting himself with bad men who may chance to be passengers', he later defended Paine against Arthur Young's hysterically anti-revolutionary *The Commonwealth in Danger* (1795).[52]

Moderates Whigs were thus extremely wary about the class basis of Paine's support, sometimes terming his followers 'Paine's journeymen', as if this alone were sufficient to put them in their place. Most leading Whigs did not collapse into hysteria, as we will see many loyalists were to do. But they too, while willing to agree that 'all mankind start fair in the Race of life', wondered whether Paine's appeal to 'equality' did not invoke the spectre of 1649. Although the SCI circulated the *Rights of Man* and defrayed Paine's expenses during its prosecution, for example, some of its members protested such moves, arguing that the text implied an agrarian law and would in practice probably lead to political tyranny. When the SFP condemned equality of property in late 1792, too, some insisted that this was an attack on Paine. Erring on the side of caution, the society expelled five of its members for corresponding with Jacobins in Paris, prompting members of the SCI to deny that they were republicans or connected to France. But the middle ground disappeared too quickly for such measures to be of much use, the influence of the moderates by 1793 being 'almost entirely annihilated ... from the violence of the tories on the one hand, and that of the republicans on the other', as the *New Annual Register* put it. With the rise of the LCS and the polarization of political debate, the SCI went into steep decline and ceased to meet after its last few members were arrested in early 1794.[53] By pressing the cause of reform at all, the SFP also found itself tarred with a Painite brush. The pronounced defeat of Charles Grey's reform motion in May 1793 nearly finished the Society, though it limped on for another two years, suspending its meetings in May 1795.

But moderate reformers were as alarmed by events in France as the prospect of their imitation in England. Mackintosh wrote to Burke in 1796 that the course of the revolution had led him to reverse his opinions 'on many subjects on which I was then the dupe of my own enthusiasm'. Those who failed to renounce their earlier optimism found that the middling orders could also discipline themselves collectively. Wayward democrats like Henry Erskine, dean of the Faculty of Advocates at Edinburgh, were dismissed from their posts for protesting against the Sedition and Treason Bills. Whig reformers were also relatively easily cowed by the government's onslaught. A meeting of some 200 'Friends of the Liberty of the Press' in late December 1792 at the conclusion of Paine's trial, for example, praised Thomas Erskine's defence, but strongly doubted 'the propriety, at this time, of making the most distant mention of the work called the *Rights of Man*' and accordingly omitted its title and author's name in a resolution.[54]

Moderate Dissenting reformers do not seem to have varied greatly from this pattern. Many were clearly radicalized by the onset of the revolution; Priestley noted in 1791 that 'many of the Dissenters are of late become enemies to all civil establishments of religion'. In some areas they gave initial support to the dissemination of Paine's principles ('small donations' at Sheffield, reported a spy) without becoming over-enthusiastic. Unitarians in various locations voted to praise the *Rights of Man*. Parallels between its views of political liberty and Price's were noted. But other Dissenters were alarmed at any signs of imprudence. Some ransacked works by earlier Nonconformist radicals for use against Paine. 'A British Manufacturer', for example, reprinted a 1759 sermon by Price which was a paean to British laws, government and religion, while a 1794 pamphlet entitled *A Blow at the Root, or Constitutional Liberty Preferable to Jacobinism and Anarchy* consisted predominantly of extracts from Price's works.[55]

Influential Dissenters were thus generally at least cautious about the *Rights of Man*. One of their leading journals, the *Analytical Review*, termed Part One 'one of the most curious, original, and interesting publications which the singular vicissitudes of modern politics have produced' and found 'much originality of thought' in the chapter on civilization in Part Two. Whether or not Britain had a constitution depended on definitions of terms, however, and while Paine's taxation plans were praised as 'in the main judicious and humane', the *Review* doubted that property could ever be accurately assessed. Other Dissenters also played down the political implications of the *Rights of Man* by reading it as primarily a tract on Nonconformity. A letter to one reform journal thus said that 'If we consider the *Rights of Man* as an essay on civil government, Paine has said no more than what many have said before him; if we consider it as a defence of religious liberty, he has said more on a single page on this most interesting subject than other writers have been able to say in a whole volume'. But many Dissenters were clearly sceptical about Paine's attitude to government. Fearing Paine had oversimplified this question, Anna Barbauld, daughter of the leading Dissenter John Aikin, for example, contended that 'the larger and more flourishing any society is, the more occasion it has for Government, because it has more affairs to manage in common, and more cases to determine by particular rules'. It was a lesson Paine himself would only gradually concede.[56]

Many Dissenters were none the less active in the strong middle-class peace movement recently studied by J. E. Cookson. The 'Friends of Peace' were chiefly Whig Dissenters who opposed the war on both religious and political grounds. They included prominent Dissenting reviewers and journalists like Aikin, William Taylor and William Enfield, and their publishers, especially Joseph Johnson and George Robinson. Most of these remained unconnected to artisan radical groups; William Frend and Jeremiah Joyce, who played some part in the LCS, are two exceptions. Most were moderates. The Cambridge Unitarian Frend agreed that imposing the American model on a nation whose 'customs, laws and situation have inured us to habits unknown to the new world ... might be as prejudicial to the happiness of this country, as the imposition of our constitution might be to the inhabitants of America'. Frend also later criticized Paine's taxation schemes as unfair to the middle classes. But another Unitarian, Francis Stone, rector of Cold Norton, Essex, assailed Burke at length and, while touching only briefly on Paine, commended a French scheme for dividing waste lands amongst the members of a universal citizens' militia which was extraordinarily far-reaching in its implications.[57]

Critics from the left

If Paine was too extreme for moderate Whigs, some reformers found him too hesitant. But these few in turn ironically were to play some role in the branding of the Painites as levellers. The eighteenth century had seen few serious defences of much greater equality of property prior to the 1790s; an agrarian law guaranteeing forty acres to all was recommended in Ogilvie's *Essay on the Right of Property in Land*, while Catherine Macaulay urged the equal division of property among all male heirs. But support for agrarian laws in the 1790s was rare. The Manchester radical Thomas Cooper, as we have seen, praised Ogilvie's schemes, as did Paine's friend John Oswald, one Dr William Thomson, and a few others. A general regulation of food prices and wages was also recommended in the London doctor William Hodgson's republican Utopia, *The Commonwealth of Reason*.[58] From 1776 onwards, moreover, a diminutive Newcastle schoolteacher and later London printer named Thomas Spence began to urge the collective ownership of land and by the early 1790s attracted a small but determined band of disciples. Spence himself was to suffer considerably in the reaction; amongst other crimes he was arrested for selling the *Rights of Man* Part Two. But he never lost enthusiasm for his 'Plan' for abolishing private property in land by a meeting of all local parishes, who would thereafter rent the land as small farms, and out of the proceeds pay for government as well as maintaining the poor and unemployed. With the ballot and universal suffrage, political corruption would end. Free schools and libraries, public relief for the ill and granaries for the hungry would be established and a militia substituted for a standing army. Spence thus claimed that Paine 'aimed only at kings', while he went to the root of the problem of inequality, landed property.[59]

Public discussion of community of goods was further provoked by the publication in 1793 of an *Enquiry Concerning Political Justice* by William Godwin, a former Dissenting minister and struggling novelist, historian and playwright. Godwin's audience was clearly very different from Spence's, being mainly young middle-class Dissenters and a few rebellious Anglicans, including Coleridge and Wordsworth. The message of *Political Justice* was also rather different from that of either Paine or Spence. Godwin, for example, initially rejected the use of rights language, preferring to intensify moral duty, and opposed popular political activity or revolution. He did help to promulgate the idea of community of goods, however, and offered an elaborate defence of the stewardship ideal of property as a trust for common use, and especially for the needy. But while Godwin thought a relative equality of property necessary to ensure public virtue and a 'euthanasia' of government (Paine's distinction between society and government being here enthusiastically supported), he urged that such goals could be achieved only by voluntary means. A narrow division of labour and commerce were also generally denigrated by Godwin, who none the less increasingly conceded some of the benefits of affluence in the later 1790s.[60]

Spence and Godwin certainly helped to give currency to the notion of equality of property, though neither even remotely approached Paine's popularity. *The Norwich Cabinet*, for example, defended equality of property at considerable length in 1795 with reference to Godwin, but concluded by proposing that 'a limitation of testamentary donations would be the best mode' for achieving this. But this was of course far closer to Paine's plan than Godwin's, which shows how easily Paine's plans could be associated with much more extreme forms of egalitarianism. As we will now see, this was to prove vital to the cause of counter-revolution.[61]

Notes to Chapter 5: The birth of the revolutionary party

1 Paine (1945), Vol. 2, p. 290; TS11/966/3510B.
2 F. Knight (1957), p. 64; J. Thelwall (1796b), part 1, pp. 82–3; T. Hardy (1832), p. 20. The most detailed accounts of radicalism in this period are E. Thompson (1968), pp. 95–203, J. Walvin (1969)(unfortunately unpublished) and A. Goodwin (1979), pp. 171–450. See also W. Hall (1912), J. Money (1980), E. Royle and J. Walvin (1982), pp. 48–79, H. Dickinson (1977) and

(1985) and G. Gallop (1983), especially pp. 71–112. On the reception of the *Rights of Man* see D. Roper (1978), pp. 190–5, R. Fennessy (1963), pp. 213–43, F. Canavan (1976). A. Ayer (1988), p. 72, inexplicably assumes its political effects were much less powerful than those of *Common Sense*.

3   C. Paul (1876), Vol. 1, p. 69; J. Barlow (1795), p. 6; *The Catechism of Man* (n.d.), p. 24; R. Wells (1983), p. 258; TS11/954/3497; TS11/954/3504; J. Money (1977), p. 263. As A. Aldridge (1960, p. 135) indicates, there is no evidence, as was once assumed, that Godwin assisted Paine in publishing the *Rights of Man*.

4   R. Dozier (1983), p. 100; HO42/23; TS11/965/3510A; *The Life and Adventures of Job Knott* (1798), pp. 18–19; *Analytical Review*, Vol. 12 (1792), p. 303; TS11/966/3510B; J. Cheetham (1817), p. xxii; *An Impartial Sketch* (1792), pp. 8–9; *More Reasons* (1793), p. 9.

5   W. Sherwin (1819), p. 112; Paine (1945), Vol. 2, p. 910; TS11/951/3495.

6   My own estimate, which excludes works solely on the war, economic conditions, or continental developments. At least 200 of these works focus primarily on the *Rights of Man*. The most extensive existing bibliography describes about 350 titles (G. Pendleton, 1982). Related issues are raised in at least 2500 further titles (G. Pendleton, 1976, p. 152).

7   A. Young (1967), p. 349; 'Publicola' (1913), pp. 74–6, 108–9; M. Smelser (1951); G. Nash (1965); C. Hazen (1897), pp. 157–61.

8   D. Hartley (1794), p. 35; T. Howell (1817), Vol. 22, col. 779; B. Damm (1792), p. 4; TS11/952/3496; Add. MS. 16922 f. 143.

9   *An Impartial Sketch* (1792), p. 9; *Report of the Committee* (1799), p. 71; C. Hazen (1897), p. 212.

10   On provincial radicalism see A. Goodwin (1979), pp. 136–70, J. Money (1977), F. Knight (1957) and H. Alves (1981).

11   HO42/22; HO42/23; TS11/961/3507; *The Complete Reports* (1794), p. 22.

12   TS11/962/3508; PC1/44/A155; *The Second Report* (1794), Appendix C.

13   HO42/22; TS11/952/3496; *The Complete Reports* (1794), p. 58.

14   *Black Dwarf*, Vol. 2, no. 35 (2 September 1818), p. 551; E. Thompson (1968), p. 22; Add. MS. 27812 f. 6. A good account of the LCS is given in F. Place (1972), pp. 129–200. Many of its papers have been edited by M. Thale (1983) and are most extensively analysed in J. Walvin (1969), pp. 78–108, 408–604, 792–9. Still useful is H. Collins (1954). Other London societies of the period are also discussed in M. Thale (1989).

15   M. Thale (1983), pp. 160, 307; F. Place (1972), p. 196 n; Add. MS. 27808 f. 113; A. Goodwin (1979), p. 360.

16   TS11/953/3497; *Treason Triumphant* (1795), p. 18; T. Howell (1818), Vol. 24, col. 682; TS11/956/3501–2. The government was especially anxious to find the perpetrators of the 'Gwelp' handbill (PC1/22/A37).

17   *Application of Barruel's Memoirs* (1798), pp. 34, 32; *Chester Chronicle*, no. 885 (25 May 1792), p. 4; *Derby Mercury*, no. 3158 (25 October 1792), p. 4; A. Seaman (1957).

18   G. Williams (1969), p. 64; C. Jewson (1975), pp. 26, 39; Add. MS. 16922 f. 2; M. Wilks (1791), pp. 30, 64. An extensive contemporary account of the Norwich reformers published in 1796 claimed that the authors most favoured there included Locke, Sidney, Marvel, Milton and others. The reformers themselves comprised an atheist and a Jew, an Anglican, Catholics, Quakers and many deists. But all agreed that 'each sect ought to maintain its own clergy, and that the labour of the catholic ought not to be put in requisition for the maintenance of the Church of England man'.

All were 'consequently enemies to the tythe laws [and] to the connection between Church and State' (R. Dinmore Jr, 1796, pp. 10–11). On Dinmore see C. Jewson (1975), pp. 84–5.

19 T. Howell (1817), Vol. 23, col. 1083; A. Booth (1979), pp. 39, 49; J. Money (1977), pp. 223–43; Add. MS. 16920 f. 47. On Walker and Manchester radicalism see P. Handforth (1956) and F. Knight (1957).

20 HO102/5–6; H. Meikle (1912), pp. 91, 145, 82; HO102/4; HO102/60; *Considerations on the French War* (1794), p. 11. See generally J. Brims (1983).

21 HO102/5; T. Howell (1817), Vol. 23, col. 35; K. Logue (1979), pp. 147–54; Add. MS. 16923 f. 10. On radicalism and Scottish nationalism see J. Callender (1792) and J. Brims (1987).

22 *Political Review* (1792), p. 24; Add. MS. 16921 f. 94; *Remarks on Mr. Paine's Pamphlet* (1791), p. iii; S. Cronin (1980), p. 93; Paine (1945), Vol. 2, p. 1322.

23 T. Howell (1819), Vol. 26, cols 427, 343; Vol. 27 (1820), col. 348; W. Kennedy (1976), p. 119; PC1/44/A155. M. Elliott (1982, p. 27) claims that the United Irishmen were less republican. On Paine and popular Irish songs see R. Browne (1964).

24 *An Account of the … British Convention* (1793), p. 40; T. Howell (1817), Vol. 23, col. 1233; *Application of Barruel's Memoirs* (1798), p. 31; G. Veitch (1913), p. 218; *The Complete Reports* (1794), pp. 12–13; F. Oldys (1793), p. 160. See E. Thompson (1968), pp. 167–9.

25 T. Howell (1818), Vol. 24, col. 291; M. Thale (1983), pp. xix, xxiv; F. Place (1972), p. 140. Hardy's trial is one of the best sources for the political views of the LCS (Howell, Vol. 24, cols 199–1407). John Binns claimed that some 12,000 members were paying weekly dues in 1794 (Binns, 1854, p. 45).

26 *Manchester Herald*, no. 37 (8 December 1792), p. 4; Paine (1945), Vol. 2, p. 567.

27 TS11/41/150; TS11/952/3496; M. Thale (1983), p. 132. Minutes of the earlier (December 1792) meetings are printed in H. Meikle (1912), pp. 239–73. See also W. Hall (1912), pp. 182–96 and A. Goodwin (1979), pp. 268–306. For government assessments of the threat of force see TS11/955/3500.

28 *Tom Paine's Jests* (1794), p. 3; *Account of the Proceedings* (1795), p. 3; C. Pigott (1798), p. 5; Pigott (1795), pp. 95–6. On such representations see generally R. Paulson (1983), pp. 57–87.

29 J. M'Phail (1795), p. 21. Eaton is studied in D. McCue Jr (1974).

30 HO102/7; HO42/22.

31 H. Alves (1981), p. 314; *Report of the Committee* (1799), p. 67; R. Rose (1965), p. 11; *The Patriot* (13 April 1792), pp. 23–30.

32 HO42/22; *Manchester Herald*, no. 4 (21 April 1792), p. 4; J. Thelwall (1796a), p. 14; J. Money (1977), p. 231; J. Brims (1983), pp. 228–31.

33 HO102/8. See A. Sheps (1975b) and (1973), pp. 121–262.

34 H. Yorke (1794), pp. 48–9; C. Pigott (1795), p. 116; T. Howell (1817), Vol. 22, col. 476; HO42/22; R. Dinmore Jr (1796), p. 29; *The Cabinet* (1795), Vol. 1, pp. 8, 105; J. Barlow (1792a), pp. 4–5, 1.

35 G. Vale (1841), p. 96; S. Perry (1797), p. 11; HO102/9; *Account of the Proceedings* (1795), p. 3; *The London Corresponding Society's Addresses and Regulations* (1792), pp. 1, 13–14; *The Rights of Citizens* (1791), p. 41; J. Gerrald (1794a), p. 189.

36 *A Narrative* (1797), p. 26; J. Gerrald (1794a), p. 9; *The Trial of Henry Yorke* (1795), pp. 89–90; *The Trial of William Winterbotham* (1794), pp. 78–9; J. Mackintosh (1792), pp. 210–12; M. Wollstonecraft (1794), p. 7.

37 J. Thelwall (1796b), part 2, pp. 37–8, 41–5; *Pigs' Meat*, Vol. 1 (1793), pp. 89–92; C. Pigott (1795), p. 48. The references were to Pufendorf's *The Law of Nature and Nations* (5th edn, 1739).

38 J. Gerrald (1794a), pp. 10–11, (1794c), p. 1; *The Patriot*, no. 8 (10 September 1792), pp. 256–63; *Politics for the People* (1794), p. 151; [D. Williams] (1790), pp. 51–2.

39 T. Cooper (1792), pp. 75, 98–9; C. Pigott (1791), pp. 85–6; *Letters to a Friend* (1792), p. 22.

40 *Politics for the People* (1794), pp. 66–8; J. Pilkington (1795), pp. 13, 41–2. At least one London Quaker sermon mentioned Paine in the context of an end to war (W. Savory, 1796).

41 *Manchester Herald*, no. 37 (8 December 1792), p. 4; TS11/892/3035; TS24/3/30A; *A Picture of the Times*, no. 6 (1795), p. 74; J. Thelwall (1796b), part 1, p. 67; Thelwall (1796b), part 2, pp. 27, 67; S. Perry (1797), p. 23.

42 J. Thelwall (1796b), part 2, pp. 78–82. On the development of Thelwall's views in this period see I. Hampsher-Monk (1989).

43 *The Measures* (1794), p. 28; T. Howell (1817), Vol. 24, col. 1193; S. Bernstein (1945), p. 151; M. Margarot (1812), p. 24.

44 *Parliamentary Register*, 32 (30 April 1792), pp. 469, 478. On the split among the Whigs see F. O'Gorman (1967) and L. Mitchell (1971).

45 *Friends* (1795), pp. 3–4; *Authentic Copy* (1793), pp. 1–2; Add. MS. 27814 f. 70.

46 *The Trial of John Horne Tooke* (1795), p. 92; A. Stephens (1813), Vol. 2, pp. 113, 147, 324.

47 C. Wyvill (1794), Vol. 2, p. 633; (1794), Vol. 5, p. 51; (1794), Vol. 4, p. 75; (1794), Vol. 3, appendix, pp. 70–1; (1792), pp. 59–63, 76. On Wyvill's views in the 1790s see J. Dinwiddy (1971), pp. 3–9.

48 W. Fox (1793), p. 2; W. Belcher (n.d.), p. 7; H. Sandford (1888), Vol. 1, p. 36; *Thoughts upon Liberty* (1793), pp. 4, 13.

49 C. Macaulay (1790), p. 6; J. Wilde (1793), p. 23; E. Burke (1978), Vol. 8, p. 239; [T. Green] (1793), pp. 7–20, 25.

50 *Is All We Want* (1792), p. 10; *Rights and Remedies* (1795), pp. 28–9, 56.

51 *Considerations on the French War* (1794), p. 14; *An Abstract of the History* (1789), pp. 14–15; *The Correspondence of the Revolution Society* (1792), pp. 216–17; *Comparative Display* (1970), Vol. 1, p. 152; C. Wyvill (1794), Vol. 4, pp. 239–40.

52 *Proceedings of the Society* (1792), pp. 30–1; *Remarks* (1792), pp. 73–5; F. Cartwright (1826), Vol. 1, pp. 215, 192, 221; J. Cartwright (1795), pp. xlvi–liii. For radical disagreements with Paine's definition of the British constitution see, e.g., *A Political Dictionary for Guinea-less Pigs*, for which 'constitution' meant 'that form of *government*, which in any country, is established by fundamental laws', including the British form of government (TS11/837/2832). See also *The Patriot* (1792), Vol. 2, pp. 311 ff.

53 T. Walker (1794), p. 46; John Saint John (1791), pp. 32, 124; A. Dalrymple (1793), p. 27; *Considerations on Mr. Paine's Pamphlet* (1791), p. 42; *A Dialogue between an Associator* (1793), p. 12; *Proceedings* (1792), p. 48; *New Annual Register* (1794), p. 6. On the decline of the SCI see J. Walvin (1969), pp. 349–407.

54 J. Cartwright (1795), p. 127; R. Mackintosh (1836), Vol. 1, p. 87; *The Whole of the Proceedings* (1792), p. 8.

55 *Analytical Review*, Vol. 9 (1791), pp. 313, 12, (1792), Vol. 12, pp. 291, 300–3; R. Price (1791), p. 5; H.R.H. (1791), p. 9; *A Blow at the Root* (1794); TS11/966/3510B. On the increasing isolation of the Rational Dissenters in particular, see N. Murray (1975), pp. 125–63.

56 *The Patriot* (11 December 1792), p. 195; A. Barbauld (1792), p. 17.

57 J. Cookson (1982), p. 28; W. Frend (1793), pp. 3–4; Frend (1799), p. iv; F. Stone (1792), pp. 152, 197–8.
58 W. Ogilvie (1781), pp. 73–8; [C. Macaulay] (1767), pp. 36–7; A. Goodwin (1979), pp. 262–3; J. Oswald (1791), p. 59; *Comparative Display* (1970), Vol. 2, p. 631; W. Hodgson (1795), pp. 74–7.
59 T. Spence (1982), pp. 3, 8, 29, 32, 34. On Spence's followers see I. McCalman (1988) and M. Chase (1988).
60 W. Godwin (1976), pp. 701–95.
61 *The Cabinet* (1795), Vol. 3, pp. 281–97.

6

Inequality vindicated: the government party

Come listen, good folks, and a tale I'll relate,
How a Staymaker fain would have made himself great,
And from mending of stays took to mending of State.
Oh, the Reformer of England!

Long may Old England possess good cheer and jollity,
Liberty and property, and no equality.

A Republican's picture is easy to draw,
He can't bear to obey, but will govern the law;
His manners unsocial, his temper unkind,
He's a Rebel in conduct, a Tyrant in mind.[1]

Painophobia unleashed: governmental and loyalist reaction

The Painite movement and the threat of revolution were defeated for three reasons. Most importantly, Britain and France went to war in 1793 and the new principles of reform became 'French' and hostile. This doubtless frightened off thousands of potential reformers. Secondly, the government reacted both quickly and prudently to the upsurge in popular radicalism. Finally, the loyalist movement mushroomed, both spontaneously and under guidance, into a massive and highly successful reactionary force. Heralded by a Royal Proclamation against sedition, subversion and riot published on 22 May 1792 and read aloud to much of the population, loyalism dictated the terms of the revolutionary debate from early 1792 to about the end of 1794. None the less its victory was by no means immediately certain. The king's sentiments prompted an outpouring of loyal addresses (some 32,000 by July, claimed Paine). But the proclamation also had the effect of adding fuel to the flames. As one account put it, 'in remote villages, where hardly two copies of the *Rights of Man* had before been sold,

139

hundreds were now called for, and greedily bought up; the coaches which brought up the addresses, carrying down cargoes of Paine's prohibited works'.[2] Initially this reaction thus probably helped the popular radical movement. Still, prominent Whig leaders like Lord Fitzwilliam soon saw the virtues of the government's anti-sedition legislation. Charles James Fox remained indecisive, defending the revolution but attacking Paine. But most of Parliament backed Pitt, and the basis for an alliance between government and the parliamentary opposition was laid by May 1792.

The battle had scarcely begun, however. As Painite enthusiasm continued to expand, the government became aware that new and more effective countermeasures were required. By late 1792, indeed, it was widely believed both that France intended to export revolution to Britain and that many would welcome the new product. Revolutions have ever bred conspiracy theories and the more paranoid now claimed that while England was his first target, 'an immense number of copies of Mr. Paine's works, in French, Spanish, and Portuguese' were 'about to be placed in a proper train for distribution in Sweden, Denmark, Russia, Germany, Italy, Spain, and Portugal, and their colonies'.[3] Agents and informers, always prone to exaggeration, fanned the embers of paranoia. Strikes and 'riots' were invested with a political significance they lacked in reality. Alehouse verbosity became seditious plotting.

To counter this rising threat two strategies proved most successful: direct prosecutions of the reformers, and the formation of loyalist pressure groups. Prosecutions began with Paine himself, *in absentia*, and then encompassed those who sold the *Rights of Man* and a few other works. In total four pages of the *Rights of Man* (beginning with the statement, 'All hereditary government is in its nature tyranny') were found seditious.[4] Paine's language here, as elsewhere, was strong. But the government was much more concerned with his intended audience, as the Attorney General acknowledged in asserting that 'the first part of the *Rights of Man* being among the judicious classes of the community, he does not fear concerning it; but when it descended and was circulated in the lower order, there the evil begins'. Part One had addressed a limited, refined class of readers. Part Two was offered to all for virtually nothing, men's tobacco, 'even the sweetmeats of children', being wrapped in it.[5]

About a dozen people were prosecuted for selling the *Rights of Man* from December 1792 to August 1793, of whom three were acquitted. The Sheffield radicals, amongst others, consequently felt compelled to cease circulating the *Rights of Man* and by mid-1793 the work was difficult to find elsewhere. Yet gaoling a few booksellers was hardly sufficient to stem the radical tide. The government therefore turned to the political associations. Prominent Scottish reformers like Thomas

Fyshe Palmer and Thomas Muir (tried in part for lending a copy of the *Rights of Man*) were arrested and transported in early 1793, followed by the leaders of the Edinburgh Convention at the end of the year. In 1794 Pitt moved against the London radicals, charging Thomas Hardy, John Thelwall, John Horne Tooke and others. But here, facing an incorruptible jury, the government failed to establish a case and the prisoners were acquitted. Hardy was pulled by the crowd in a carriage through London, pausing briefly in silence before his house, where the violence of his arrest had caused his wife to miscarry and die. But other trials were more successful. The radical doctor William Hodgson, for example, denounced 'George Guelph, a German hog-butcher, a dealer in human flesh by the carcass' somewhat too loudly at the London Coffee-house in late 1793, and spent two years in Newgate for his troubles. These trials terminated only with the 1799 prosecution of the liberal Dissenter Gilbert Wakefield for his reply to a pamphlet by the Bishop of Llandaff, by which time little freedom of criticism survived.[6]

Severe restrictions on oppositional political activity were also an important part of government strategy. In 1794 the Habeas Corpus Act was suspended in order to hold prisoners without trial and, except for the period 1795–7, was not restored until 1802. The Treason Act (1795) widened the definition of treason to encompass writings which incited hatred or contempt of the Crown or government. The Seditious Meetings Act (1795) severely restricted the right to assemble publicly, while the Newspaper Act (1798) tightened controls on various publications. Several organizations were forbidden by the 1797 Unlawful Oaths Act, while the new Combination Acts (1799–1800) crowned the legislation of repression by imposing severe penalties for forming trade unions (these acts were not repealed until 1824). Collectively this legislation created what Francis Place, citing the case of a Lincolnshire blacksmith given twelve months in solitary confinement for damning the king and calling the government a despotism, later called 'years of terror'. A 'disloyal word was enough to bring some punishment upon any man's head', even 'laughing at the awkwardness of a volunteer corps'. As the poet Peter Pindar put it, 'Whoever christens but his *dog*, Tom Paine / (And many an itching tongue can scarce refrain), / The cur and master shall be brought to shame.'[7]

Besides legal repression the government had other means at its disposal. Loyalist morning and evening papers (the *True Briton* and *The Sun*) were founded, with secret service payments helping to ensure their success and free copies being distributed to provincial papers who reprinted annotated material. Altogether the government controlled about nine daily papers in 1790, the opposition, five. Public opinion was also manipulated in other ways. Using an admiral as intermediary, the government paid a Portsmouth printer £175 for 22,000 copies of 'Strictures on Thomas Paine's Works and Character'. 'Oldys's' *Life* became a staple of the growing anti-Painite literature. Some hostile respondents to the *Rights of Man* were also paid by secret service money, like the Rev. Robert Nares in 1792–3.[8]

But anti-Jacobinism was by no means only centrally directed. Once the alarm bell pealed, the gentry, clergymen and substantial property owners formed 'Loyal Associations' which spent large sums distributing cheap or free anti-revolutionary propaganda. Leading these efforts was the Association for the Preservation of Liberty and Property Against Republicans and Levellers of John Reeves, former Chief Justice of Newfoundland, which redefined the revolutionary debate within a matter of months. Formed in November 1792, the association soon prompted the Post Office to survey seditious correspondence and within weeks boasted supporters across the nation. Lincoln College, Oxford, was enrolled in the organization by its rector, while the Society for the Promotion of Christian Knowledge volunteered to distribute association literature. Leading Wyvillites offered their assistance. Branches sprang up in Jamaica and Grenada, and Paine's American enemies venomously decried his role in 1776.[9] In rural Britain a vast number of meetings occurred at the end of the year which, it was claimed, formed 2,000 associations (1,500 is a more likely figure), with 150 in London alone. Letters poured in to Reeves in London reporting local conditions; Worcester, for example, was said to be solidly loyal except for '*ONE* furious Painite'. Some claimed loyalism comprised up to a third of the adult males of Britain. But this is a considerable exaggeration. Local notables, MPs, squires, farmers, the gentry, merchants and manufacturers predominated amongst the committees and their 'popular' character has been overrated. At least four former radical societies changed their names to demonstrate their support for the constitution. But several new associations were also captured by reformers.[10]

Organized loyalism had several objectives. Reeves certainly aimed to encourage heads of families, master-manufacturers and employers to persuade their dependants to avoid reform politics. To this end admonition was useful, but labourers' signatures were also sought deliberately for loyalist petitions. Wider publicity resulted from a vigorous campaign of newspaper advertising, meetings and processions, circulating tracts, placarding broadsides on walls and distributing handbills to loyalist publicans. Many such publications, like the widely dispersed *One Penny-Worth of Truth, From Thomas Bull to His Brother John*, attacked Paine by name.[11] But less subtle forms of persuasion also proved highly successful. Soldiers were disciplined by their officers; a London ensign sent four privates and a corporal to the guardhouse for reading the *Rights of Man*. Innkeepers were threatened with the loss of their licences if they failed to prevent radical meetings and signs quickly went up reading 'NO JACOBINS ADMITTED HERE'. At Leicester, thus, 128 tavern keepers prominently refused to allow subversive gatherings on their premises, while in London, Thomas Hardy lamented, 'the poor publicans were obliged to submit'. Vigilance subsequently ensured that any evidence of alehouse radicalism was censured. Near Wimbledon a local loyalist forced a publican to erase the 'Tom Paine No King Damn the King' chalked on one of his shutters. Some associations rewarded informers. Loyalists also protested weak prosecutions of Painites, objected to defences, such as that offered at Paine's trial, on the basis of liberty of the press and employed legal harassment whenever possible. At Manchester, for example, the prominent radical Thomas Walker was charged with sedition in 1794 and, though his accuser was himself eventually tried for perjury and forced to pay court costs of £3,000, Walker withdrew from politics anyway.[12]

In 1793–4 loyalists turned their attention to the war effort, raising bounties to encourage naval enlistments and collecting for soldiers' uniforms and widows and orphans. They also helped to raise volunteers (eventually some 300,000) to meet the threat of French invasion. Some of these served unwillingly, coerced by their employers, but others needed the pay received for drilling. Enough proved reliable to serve an important domestic purpose, moreover, by threatening reformers, searching their houses and occasionally beating them up.[13]

Intimidation and violence were in fact important elements in both official and popular reaction. Church and King mobs were often given liquor and money to storm the houses of local 'Jacobins', in the Midlands often leading Dissenters whose success and cultural prominence in these strongholds of commerce and manufacturing were doubtless resented.[14] Joseph Priestley saw his house, laboratory and manuscripts destroyed at Birmingham by such a mob after a dinner celebrating the second anniversary of the fall of the Bastille, where 'King and Constitution' had also been toasted. Here rioting, encouraged by an inflammatory handbill blasting ministers as 'hypocrites', lasted five days, with patriotism, anti-Presbyterianism and the cry (curiously reminiscent of Thatcherite Britain) of 'No Philosophers' soon giving way to more plunder and destruction.[15] Similar outrages were perpetrated in Manchester, Nottingham and elsewhere. At Manchester, for example, a Unitarian chapel was stormed by crowds wielding trees as battering rams and Quaker meeting-houses and homes were similarly assailed. Municipal officials stood by and the next day dutifully formed a committee 'for preserving Peace and good order of the Town'. Such connivance, indeed, was widespread, with even the Home Office admitting privately that measures 'not exactly justifiable by law' were necessary if radicalism was to be halted.[16]

Symbolic violence was a more subtle aspect of loyalism and here the focus upon Paine himself was extremely pronounced. His image was portrayed on plates and mugs with the ears of an ass. Tokens showed him hanging from a gibbet. Vases were adorned with verses vilifying him. A favoured display of patriotism was to have the initials T.P. stamped on the underside of boots, the better to trample Paine into the dust. Widely abused in effigy after the beginning of the loyalist onslaught in November 1792, Paine was often represented with a pair of stays beneath his arm, which helped expose his humble origins. After an appropriate display he was nearly always consigned to the flames. Paine burnings in fact soon became the order of the day; the first was in mid-1792, while in the first two months of 1793 there were twenty-six within twenty miles of Manchester alone. In Devon the dreaded figure was drawn in a cart guarded by twelve constables accompanied by 126 horsemen and no less than 4,000 foot soldiers. A volley was fired when the burnt effigy was cut down; it was then hung in chains on a gibbet fifty feet high. At Winchester a Paine was adorned respectably before its immolation (doubtless roasting a gentleman was more amusing) in a black coat provided by the Church, a waistcoat and breeches from the local college, and a hat and wig from the corporation. At Shrewsbury Priestley and Paine were burned together. At Birmingham in the late 1790s a Paine was constructed from a barber-shop wig block and paraded through the streets accompanied by two sweeps, one bearing *The Age of Reason*, the other the *Rights of Man*, both books being burned after their author had dangled on the gallows for a time. Near Dronfield a Paine was hung with such hurried excitement that it fell down and killed an unfortunate bystander; whether he was a loyalist was not recorded.[17]

Some of these incidents were macabre and ferocious. Sometimes a bladder of bullock's blood was attached as a heart, so that passers-by might prick it 'and give the surrounding spectators an idea of a fellow-being bleeding to death beneath the assassinating fury of the multitude', as a disgusted John Thelwall put it. Once a wooden image of Paine was smashed to pieces with a sledgehammer so vigorously that the executioner's hands bled. Even more bizarrely, at Scarborough a Paine manikin cried – doubtless from contrition – when a hidden sponge was squeezed by an attendant after each assault of the vile symbol.[18]

But we must be wary of seeing such enthusiasm as the unrestrained effect of political principle, for self-interest as well as mere excitement were intermixed in such acts. In Suffolk in early 1793, for example, a village rector offered two guineas to a few of his lowly parishioners to burn a Paine, which they duly did. But when a local 'intelligent gentleman' offered them the same amount to burn the rector himself in effigy, they happily performed the act in front of his own house. In 1794, similarly, a Devonshire patriot employed several people for a Paine roasting, and one of them afterwards waited on him 'to know if there was any other *gemman* among his friends, who he would wish to have burned, as they were ready to do it for the same quantity of beer', an offer repeated in Yorkshire. The well-attired Paine consigned to the flames at Shrewsbury was incinerated by a mob who were also paid by the aldermen and mayor to shout 'Church and King' (the local militia refused to join in). But when they had imbibed enough, a loyalist reported, 'some few did cry out – Tom Paine for ever – Tom Paine for ever', adding apologetically in a letter to Reeves, 'but they were very drunk'. Nor should we overestimate the political sophistication of the mob. On one Sheffield account, for example, Paine was burned in one parish 'for being a *Presbyterian* – in another for being a *Jacobite* – in a third for being a *Popish Jesuit* – and in a fourth for being nothing less than the *Devil himself!*' Moreover, like the Royal Proclamation, singling Paine out in this way may often have been counterproductive. A letter from the Tewkesbury Society for Political and Moral Information in July 1793, for example, insisted that 'The burning of Thomas Paine's effigy, together with the *blessed effects* of the present war, has done more good to the cause than the most substantial arguments; 'tis amazing the increase of friends to liberty, and the spirit of enquiry that is gone abroad; scarcely an old woman but is talking politics'.[19]

None the less collectively these measures were fairly successful in stemming the radical tide. At Leicester in late 1792, for example, the radicals were reported to have become '*much* more moderate lately – since the establishment of government societies and the rumour of prosecutions in London'. Loyalism was also boosted tremendously by events in France. Burke's inflamed paranoia seemed prophetic as reports of battlefield atrocities, the arrest and imprisonment of the king in August 1792 and the Parisian massacres in September flowed in. French successes on the battlefield brought radicals swarming back in 1793. But when French armies began to march across Europe, France now seemed the aggressor. Hundreds of reformers, consistent in their loyalties, echoed the thoughts of the radical Norwich literary critic William Taylor, who disliked 'the cause of national ambition and aggrandisement as much as I liked the cause of national representation and liberty'. Most important of all was the outbreak of war between England and France, which made everyone who compared British injustices and French principles a potential traitor.[20]

Painism was not immediately defeated on all fronts, however. Following a period of decline the LCS mushroomed again in 1795 and activities revived in Norwich and elsewhere. Several gatherings in London after 1794 attracted 100,000 spectators (but the Seditious Meetings Act ended these). Food riots also became increasingly common, particularly in 1795. None the less the threat that mass political organization would become mass resistance diminished by 1793 and vanished two years later. Reeves's and many similar associations thus disbanded after 1793. But they had done their job well and, with the State Trials of 1794 and the repressive legislation of 1795 and 1799, played the most substantial role in suppressing radicalism (though there were other threats to order at the end of the decade). Anti-Jacobinism revived in the late 1790s in response to Godwinism in particular. But its character was now primarily literary and its intended audience elite rather than popular.[21]

Scurrilous abuse

How much this impressive victory owed to force and how much to propaganda is difficult to judge. But the public opinion of the literate was probably carried by argument to an important degree. There were many dimensions to this largely unexplored debate. Loyalism sometimes assumed classical forms. In Scotland a government employee published an edition of Aristotle's *Politics* to counter subversive opinion. The Oxford divine Edward Tatham also relied heavily on Aristotle's defence of natural subordination and inequality in his contribution to the defusing of popular discontent, while another anti-Jacobin, James Edward Hamilton, added (with no apparent sense of *double entendre*) that modern mechanics were what 'Aristotle terms slaves'.[22] But while considerable efforts were exerted to convert educated Whigs, many loyalists sought to sway Paine's working-class readers and their success in this regard indeed marked the turning-point in the anti-revolutionary debate.

This, however, required strategies usually deemed unsuitable to gentlemanly discourse. Subterfuge, for example, was thought legitimate for patriotic ends. Works by 'hireling scribblers' (as Paine called them) like 'Oldys's' *Life* were advertised as including 'a Defence of His Writings', while tracts like the *Defence of the Rights of Man* also disguised refutations of Paine. A dialogue between 'Growler' and 'Honestus' entitled *Crowns and Sceptres Useless Baubles* concluded by proving Britons were the happiest people in the world. But more serious efforts at black propaganda were also afoot. At Edinburgh in 1793 appeared *Plain Reasons for Adopting the Plan of the Societies Calling Themselves the Friends of the People ... as Copied from the Works of Mr. Thomas Paine*, by one 'A. Scott, Citizen and Hairdresser'. But the work, with only the barest elements of satire, in fact counselled murdering the king and establishing an equality of ranks, power and wealth. Here and elsewhere Paine's arguments were ridiculously distorted; his advice that past generations not dictate to the present, for example, was twisted into the view that 'It is time, indeed, that a respect for parents and ancestry, and a love for children and descendants, should be laid aside with other prejudices'. In keeping with the idea that Paine had disclaimed 'all ideas of subordination, as contrary to the natural rights and equality of mankind', satires like *A Sketch of the Rights of Boys and Girls* similarly caricatured Paine, Wollstonecraft, Barlow and others as all seeking to abolish parental authority, such that boys need 'no longer servilely endure the galling stripes which, till now, their flesh was heir to'. Another such effort even suggested that, according to Paine, animals, vegetables 'and even the most contemptible clod of earth' were equal to mankind. More serious efforts supposedly advertised the resolution of the 'Society of the Friends of Liberty and Equality' to divide all property equally, with each receiving ten shillings in total. Related pamphlets purported to reveal Paine's employment by the National Convention to gather highwaymen together to storm prisons and the Bank of England. Conservatives then pointed to such tracts as evidence of genuinely revolutionary organizations.[23]

A large proportion of the anti-Painite literature was more abusive of than subversive of radicalism. By June 1792 Paine himself counted some forty attacks on the *Rights of Man* by government agents, Anglican clergymen and landowners in particular. Loyalists competed to heap calumny on Paine, accusing him of virtually every form of personal immorality, religious infidelity and treasonable activity. To William Cobbett, writing as 'Peter Porcupine', Paine was 'the Prince of Demagogues' and worse. For others who insisted on demoting him into the aristocracy, 'prince of villains, that choice spirit of the devil' seemed appropriate. He was not infrequently connected to Robespierre and Marat. The *Rights of Man* was treated no better, one pamphlet noting that 'the chief novelty in it, besides the title, is the mischief'. Nearly every literary form was employed to insult the reformers. Anti-Jacobinism seemed to release a penchant for verse in its adherents and many a poor poet scribbled a few bad rhymes for the cause. Even drama was employed after a fashion, a brief play being written about 'Timothy Factotum, the son of a staymaker ... the corrector of laws, the ruler of kings, the scourge of princes'. A writer for the *Gentleman's Magazine* offered a parody in 1794 based loosely on *Macbeth* and entitled *Confusion's Master-Piece: or, Paine's Labour's Lost*. Loyalists with vocal talents could be marshalled by *The Anti-Gallican Songster* and *The Anti-Levelling Songster*. The latter was entirely filled with anti-Paine songs, one of which, for example, claimed that Paine's doctrine of equality meant that 'An old maid's as handsome as Venus. Each man knows as much as his neighbour, And just the same portion of brains'. Others could hum along to *Tom the Boddice Maker*, which was sung to the doubtless rousing but now apparently defunct tune of 'Bow! Wow! Wow!'[24]

Verse attacks on Paine focused on a handful of themes. Paine's character of course came in for much abuse. Amongst many other failings – his career and second marriage were favoured topics – he was frequently accused of vanity. This, proposed Sir Brooke Boothby, underlay his 'diabolical counsels' and 'certain indications of evil design'. Plagiarism was another favourite charge against Paine, with the works of the Dissenter David Williams and Rousseau's *Social Contract* being amongst the supposed sources of the *Rights of Man*. Paine's flight to France and his association with England's enemies, 'those conceited monkies the French', whose money was purportedly responsible for much of his writings' success, were also frequently condemned. A 1792 pamphlet insisted that a newly minted French citizen and Convention delegate was 'not *your sort*, to tell an Englishman anything for his good'. Hatred of his motherland was accordingly another motive commonly ascribed to Paine. His election to the Convention had been only to 'wound the pride of his country' and once he had been so used, asserted one pamphlet, Paine had been 'condemned to silence and inactivity' (and there was some truth in this). When all else failed, it was simply claimed that Paine had recanted his principles. *The Last Dying Words of Tom Paine, Executed at the Guillotine in France*, for example, gave his final words as being: 'I have lived a dishonest and shameful life, and shall die like a wretch who has been the pest of society.' His advice before being executed at Lincoln was 'Read thy Bible', while another 'confession' recorded Paine's hanging in France for having finally told his hosts ('being a grumbler wherever he goes') 'he thought roast beef and plum pudding better than soup meagre and fried frogs', by virtue of which, at least here, and if only for his gastronomic principles, Tom 'died a patriot'.[25]

Amidst such accusations it was easy to assert that Paine sought trouble for its own sake, and that 'the levelling principles of Paine's productions' had 'infused discontent where satisfaction smiled before'. This quickly became an important conservative theme. A happy and virtuous peasantry had been suddenly rendered miserable merely by reading Paine's exaggerations of 'trifling or imaginary' evils. One tract which accused the English Jacobins of causing high bread prices by sending grain to France was entitled *Britons are Happy, If They Will Think So*, while an 'anti-Gallican song' contained the verses: 'So they tell Tommy Paine / O Pray write a book, / And inform poor John Bull how ill he does look; / For if left to himself, we're afraid he'll not know /

How unhappy he is, and his pulse that its low / That his liberty's gone, and that trade he has none.' The campaign to persuade the labouring classes of their well-being seems to have had some success; in 1793 a Birmingham loyalist, at least, boasted that 'the laudable attempts which have been used to convince the lower orders that they are happy, have already been more successful than we expected'. Correspondingly, a central theme in Reeves's association pamphlets was the unhappiness of the rich, whose 'good living and idleness' brought them 'the gout and many other disorders, which the poor never have, which torment them all day, and won't let them sleep at night' and which made them 'rather objects of pity than envy'. This lament could further be linked to property rights: the rights of the peasantry, one pamphlet claimed, were 'to a comfortable subsistence, and the means of rearing a hardy and laborious family', adding that 'All beyond this does them an injury'.[26]

The motives of Paine's audience were also the target of many a loyalist tract. A Portsmouth naval carpenter said Paine's readers were 'the unprincipled, dissipated, and the extravagant', especially labourers anxious to sate 'new created demands' derived from commerce and unwilling to wait until the price of labour rose naturally. Many accused them of congregating 'merely to drink and swear that they are CLEVER FELLOWS, and expect soon to see one another Parliament Men!' A Scottish account similarly thought radicalism appealed solely 'to *drunkards*, who delight in every occasion that can afford them a pretext for meeting to guzzle and drink; to *schoolboys* and *apprentices*, who are weary of the authority which restrains them from idleness and debauchery; to *journeymen* and other young men, who, having become their own masters, are eager to shew, that it is so, by running headlong into every species of turbulence and licentiousness'. To others the Painites were 'people of desperate fortunes – men who have nothing to lose, have nothing at stake, and who may chance to pick up something in the confusion', such as 'felons, mendicants, pick-pockets and vagrants'. Frequently the reformers were derided as 'Levellers' liable to the same errors, and imbued with the same spirit, as the English revolution 140 years earlier, including a Cromwellian dictatorship, some even saying the French had promised the Presbyterians leadership in a revolutionary government.[27] Some tracts also asserted that Paine was especially popular among northern manufacturers 'restless and eager after change', though the broader question of Painism's relation to a possible 'bourgeois revolution' is too complex to pursue here.

A few loyalist arguments were certainly indebted to Burke. One was that the real 'rights of man' were embodied in the common law and existing privileges of living Englishmen rather than the philosophical fantasies of French dreamers. This is explored in greater detail below. Emphasis was also given to the need to judge existing institutions on the basis of their antiquity alone. Paine's view of the non-binding nature of past contracts was consequently frequently attacked. To one clergyman, for example, Paine's grand error was that he confused 'the idea of national with that of an individual existence'. Individuals could not bind those not yet born, 'and if the nation died as the individual John does, neither could the nation do any thing to bind a future nation which should arise after its decease'. But 'if the nation died which consented to and approved of the national acknowledgement at the revolution, when and where was the movement of its decease?' Correspondingly important, as we will see, was the view that Britain indeed possessed a constitution defined by the Magna Carta, the Bill of Rights and other documents, and that all the great authorities like Locke and Montesquieu conceded this (and many reformers indeed agreed). The *Reflections'* emphasis on a sinful human race requiring religious restraint was important, especially after 1795. Burke's unwillingness to make peace with France was also echoed in the loyalist pamphlet literature. Finally, Burke himself, also briefly responding to Paine in *An Appeal from the Old to the New Whigs*, strenuously insisted that no constitution could be changed without the consent of all parties in the nation and that in any case the multitude 'ought to be the obedient, and not the ruling or presiding part' of the population.[28]

But the form as well as much of the content of most loyalist literature in fact owed little to the *Reflections* and consisted instead of short, simple and often condescending tracts addressed to the labouring classes and concentrating on issues thought to be of importance to them. Some of Paine's opponents had difficulties descending to this level. Archbishop William Paley's well-circulated *Reasons for Contentment* (1792), for example, was a carefully argued tract condemning the envy of the rich because the poor could often more easily attain true happiness by, for example, appreciating fully the value of rest after hard work. But Paley's prose, though clearly designed for their consumption, was too sophisticated for most labourers. Simpler, therefore, was his *Equality as Consistent with the British Constitution* (1792), a dialogue between a master-manufacturer and a workman – the choice of characters is noteworthy – which attacked Paine's supposed doctrine that all were born equal and should remain so, and defended pensions, titles and existing taxes. Paley also insisted that the revolution had merely aggravated poverty in France and condemned the French as Britain's traditional enemy.[29]

None the less even here Paley lacked the common touch and his most important contribution to the debate may indeed have been his popularization of utilitarian ideas, which conservatives adopted to shore up their defence of precedent and expediency without ever wholly embracing a felicific calculus. Far more successful in reaching the people was Hannah More, who earlier had founded schools to inculcate religion and social subordination in poor children. These evangelical concerns were now ripe for expansion and More took up where Reeves had left off. Her first great anti-Jacobin production was *Village Politics* (1793), a smooth dialogue between Jack Anvil the blacksmith and the mason Tom Hod. This the government distributed by the thousands in England and Scotland in the first major effort to strike at what was thought to be the real level of Paine's audience. *Village Politics* extolled poverty and hard work and emphasized the privilege of obeying those who comprehended ideas like 'liberty', which were confusing to the common working man (and other tracts sneered at the tougher Painites' intellectual pretensions, one dialogue attempting to embarrass a simple reformer by warning that 'there is not a Ploughman or Miller in all our parish but holds thy poor weak sophistry in derision'). Taxes and the cost of provisions might be high, More confessed, but French 'liberty' was mere murder. Revolutionary equality would never last, while resistance to civil power entailed disobedience to God. *Village Politics* concluded with Tom Hod burning his copy of the *Rights of Man*. But this was only the beginning of More's efforts. Two million of her later Cheap Repository tracts circulated in their first year of publication alone (1795) and the genre dominated loyalist literature thereafter. Indefatigable, More wrote two or three tracts monthly for about three years, sometimes helped by a few friends, who also corresponded extensively with committees formed throughout the country. The Cheap Repository tracts tended to be moral and religious rather than explicitly political; *The Shepherd of Salisbury Plain* (1795), for example, lauded the virtues of poverty, while other tales praised industry, sobriety, frugality, stoicism and the pleasures of husbandry, most being rural in their setting. More was exceedingly pleased with her success, gloating at Paine that *Village Politics* had 'brought down your huge goliath, the *Rights of Man*, to the ground, and laid him firmly on his back, never to rise again', there being not now a copy of the book 'to be found in any of the book clubs or circulating libraries in our country'.[30]

The veritable flood of conservative literature in 1792–3 responded to the rapid growth of reform organizations and soon began to imitate More's successful techniques. Many of these writings left subtle political argument by the wayside, crudely caricaturing the revolutionary cause, dismissing the English Jacobins as shiftless and lazy and extolling the boundless merits of the British constitution and the natural, modest monarchism of the British people (whereas the French thought themselves capable of anything). Some aimed at a female audience, warning Painite wives that 'if *England* is to become like *France*, they shall lose their husbands, as Marriage goes for nothing there, now'. Their chief form, with titles like *A New Dialogue between Monsieur Francois and John English on the French Revolution*, was the 'dialogue' spoken in 'plain language' and sometimes in dialect; one Edinburgh production by 'Tam Thrum', for example, said that the ideas of the *Rights of Man* 'wou'd never come in ony ordinary man's noddle, if he were na enlightened by that jewel of a book'. They nearly always described a confused labourer about to succumb to 'the poison of discontent' instilled by the *Rights of Man* but finally rescued by superior wisdom, sometimes purveyed by a solid squire, but as often by another labourer.[31]

Let us consider one of these dialogues in greater detail to explore their approach. *Liberty and Equality; Treated of in a Short History Addressed from a Poor Man to His Equals* (1792) begins with an honest young blacksmith named Joe Thomas assaulting one 'Judas MacSerpent' (the Scottish allusion is curious) for terming Englishmen 'slaves' and persuading some, 'who had hitherto lived Happily and Contented, and really wanted for nothing', that they 'were in want of everything, and had no right to be Happy and Contented any longer; no, those privileges were not to be found among the *Rights of Man*'. MacSerpent sends his lawyer with an assault charge, but agrees to compromise if Thomas raises £25 by selling his blacksmith shop, which MacSerpent himself had previously tried to acquire. After much remonstration and terming himself always a friend to the poor, MacSerpent lowers his demand to £10. At this point, however, Squire Compton enters and conveniently produces a treasonous letter ordering MacSerpent to be paid four livres daily to 'serve the cause of France against England' by, for example, not blaming high bread prices on poor harvests and always denying Paine's French citizenship. Confronted, MacSerpent begs forgiveness in return for ignoring Thomas's assault. His former comrades confess to being 'ashamed at our own simplicity that such a Wretch should have talked us so far out of our senses', but also 'frightened at the idea how near we were to having been rebels ... we were conscious, too, we have many of us actually gone so far, as to endeavour to communicate to others, those Maxims MacSerpent had instilled in us'. The squire then lectures on the benefits of different ranks, assuring his listeners that 'the Great have no advantages over You, but what are fully counterbalanced by sufferings you are free from'. As he begins to speak the increasingly contrite artisans and labourers still have their hats on, a habit 'lately imbibed' from MacSerpent's lessons. Gradually, however, all begin to 'think such behaviour was a mark, not of our Liberty, but Impudence', and in succession one after the other 'began to assume a more respectful and becoming deportment, and to bow and thank him for his advice'. The Fat Cooper in particular said that 'he was never so pleased in his life, as he was now, to find he had no occasion to be discontented or envious any longer'. At the end MacSerpent is delivered over to a constable, while his former associates are treated to a bucket of strong beer and drink 'CHURCH, AND KING, AND OLD ENGLAND for ever'.[32]

Religion in fact played no small role in such tracts and Anglican loyalists, while by no means inevitably 'Tory', often spoke of 'Mr Paine's Dissenting associates', as if Dissent itself were synonymous with rebellion. Some linked Paine to Price, while others claimed that Price at least accepted the mandate of 1688, which Paine patently did not (a line John Adams also took). But though the term was primarily directed at 'French' ideals, 'levelling' was also associated with puritan religious enthusiasm. One critic noted 'how similar they all are in their doctrines ... the inalienable rights of the people to form the Government of the Church, taught by Calvin and the Puritans; and the inalienable right of the People to form the Government of the State, taught by the French Democrats'.[33] Another asserted that Paine and the Dissenters sought the destruction of all government, their perfect society consisting 'in every man following his own will in suppressing all magistracy, gentry, clergy, nobility, and monarchy'. The most elaborate forms of this theory uncovered a 'Grand Conspiracy against Social Order' which originated with the London Dissenting intellectuals around the *Analytical*, *Monthly*, *Critical Reviews* and *New Annual Register*, who sought to use religion as 'a mask ... for the worst of purposes'. Such explanations were greatly reinforced by the exiled Abbé Barruel's *Memoirs Illustrating the History of Jacobinism* (1797). Barruel unearthed no less than three separate conspiracies against the old order: one anti-Christian and broadly philosophical; another anti-social and grounded in Illuminism in particular; and a third anti-monarchical. Freemasonry played no small role in these causes, according to Barruel, whose English translator detailed the parallels between the United Irishmen's organization and Masonic ritual, and noted that Paine's works 'were profusely distributed among the Irish'. Barruel was also reinforced by *Proofs of a Conspiracy against All the Religions and Governments of Europe* (1797) by John Robison, the Edinburgh natural philosophy professor, which reached four editions in its first year alone and attacked Priestley in particular and the Masonic peril generally.[34]

Arguments against the *Rights of Man*: property and civilization

Paine's antagonists soon realized that ridicule, threats and crude moralizing alone were insufficient to stem the radical tide. Serious intellectual response was also required. As one of Adam Smith's editors, William Playfair, put it, 'in order to avoid the last excesses of Jacobins, it will be necessary to abandon and disclaim their first principles ... the absurd and dangerous declaration of the rights of man must be exploded'. Fundamental to the more serious responses to Paine was the reassertion of the glory of the British system of checks and balances, truly a constitution because it was a body of fundamental laws, the wisdom of virtual representation, the right of substantial property owners to a preponderant power over legislation, the benefits of limited, historically grounded rights and liberties, and the location of sovereignty in the legislature rather than the whole people.[35] Also important was the defence of a natural social hierarchy bound together by 'duty, affection, and respect', instead of Paine's principles, which in their French practice meant that 'All the ties which formerly bound the individual to the community have been destroyed, and every man has been left free to act from the unrestrained impulse of his own free will'.[36]

These were not new arguments, but neither were they simply 'Tory', though Toryism was now more respectable than at any previous point in the eighteenth century. For the French revolution debate also reshaped Whig discourse, killing off the now dangerously radicalized myths of an older Whiggism, which were struck down not by the single shafts of Hume or Bentham but the massed volleys of the anti-Painites. Against the more abstract vision of a community based upon natural rights enforced by a social contract as well as various historical precedents was now pitted a more deeply, determinately historical, sceptical and utilitarian view which challenged the existence of any contract not enshrined in precedent and rejected natural rights language generally. After 1800 the language of natural rights and the social contract thus became associated primarily with working-class radicalism, not Whiggism. Many loyalists, however, remained loosely Whiggish and, if they admired what they took to be Burke's energetic avowal of the British constitution, they were also unwilling to go to his extreme of 'reviving doctrines superannuated and obsolete even in Spain and Portugal', which indeed were thought by many moderate Whigs to have 'brought Paine's *Rights of Man* upon our backs'. Many objected in particular to the 'erroneous political inference' that the nation had relinquished 'the right of electing their Kings, or any other political right' in 1688. Their concern was not to defend the divine right theory of monarchy, or to increase the king's powers, but to shore up the constitution as a whole. To a degree, as we have seen, this constitutionalist rhetoric was indeed shared by many Painites as well, in so far as they continued to appeal to the virtues of the ancient constitution. In this sense, too, because it defended the status quo, and not some British version of the French *ancien régime*, mainstream loyalism was more Whig than Tory, and less 'a conservative reaction' than 'an attempt to maintain the most liberal constitution in Europe', as one historian has recently argued. But it was a Whiggism transformed, and one whose centre of gravity was indeed much closer in spirit to Mackintosh's, Boothby's and Wollstonecraft's defences of commercial society and manners than to Burke's vindication of the ideals of aristocratic chivalry. Indeed one of the few true Tories active in the debate, John Reeves, was tried for seditious libel in 1796 for writing that the king could govern without the Lords or Commons (whereas Paley, for example, had argued that the king was no master of the common man, and could not interfere with the liberty of any of his subjects). It is for this reason, in particular, that the 'Burke–Paine debate' is a misnomer when applied to the French revolution controversy in Britain. For unlike Burke, most loyalists were not only defending Britain, but believed their country's achievements rested on distinctly modern developments as well as historical compromises, rather than merely 'Gothic' ideals. Thus they sought to defend not only an inequality of ranks generally, but the commercial opulence associated with British inequality in particular.[37]

Property thus loomed large in the new style of conservative Whiggism, but now an historical theory of the evolution of both mobile and landed property supplanted the remnants of the republican theory of the role of landownership in political stability. For Hume, Smith and the other Scottish theorists of commercial society whose accounts aided many loyalist arguments, the attainment of opulence entailed accepting greater inequality than had existed in earlier historical stages. But in absolute terms the poor were now better off than ever they had been under feudalism, much less earlier agricultural or hunting and gathering societies. The republican plea for equality hence seemingly masked a reversion to primitivism from which not even the poor would benefit, and France was to be condemned, as a London doctor put it, for reviving 'these exploded dreams of the golden age, the terrestrial paradise, the millennium'. Inequality of property permitted doctors, lawyers and other trades and professions to thrive and in turn to distribute their largesse to meet the real wants of the poor, the only equality possible between the two being, as one loyalist put it, in the act of charity. From this perspective, the debate about the revolution in France itself was, as Arthur Young put it, not between liberty and tyranny, but 'alone a question of property. It is a trial at arms, whether those who have *nothing* shall not seize and possess the property of those who have *something*.' Property-owners were thus warned that they would soon face beggars with 'the sword in one hand, and *Rights of Man* in the other', demanding 'that which good government tells me is *my own*'.[38]

Two great languages of modernity thus clashed in this debate: the language of natural rights, which proclaimed an equality of citizenship and promised a more virtuous polity; and the language of civilization, especially in the form of commercial society rather than Burkean feudalism, combined with the superior, more pacific manners its habits of trade ostensibly engendered. Republicans continued to argue for both formal political equality and relative economic equality, applying these now to farmers, artisans and merchants, which was the American resolution of this problem, and not only to landowning elites, as classical republicanism demanded. Their opponents offered the usual criticisms of classical republicanism, such as its tendency to become tyrannical and to thrive on war and conquest. But they concentrated on the argument that while 'all levelling notions tend as their ultimate point of perfection' to the savage state, Britain's prosperity and 'all the delicacies of politeness' rested on the country's greater inequality. Paine's tract, as Hannah More put it, was thus only a way of 'making ourselves poor when we are getting rich'. Inequality was not unfair since the rich employed the rest, insisted a Buckinghamshire farmer. One 'Plain Man', probably a shopkeeper, similarly noted that 'I have a set of wealthy customers who put a great deal of money into my pocket in the year, whose expenses, suitable to their rank and situation in life, enable me to enjoy all the solid comforts suitable to mine'. High taxes, too, could be understood as benefiting the working classes because labourers' wages had to be greater to pay them.[39]

Republicanism thus suited only poor, agricultural societies which were incapable of being 'congenial to science, or friendly to commerce' (as a Canterbury printer put it) and implied a return to 'ancient rusticity'. Paine, wrote another loyalist, evidently sought 'to mow down all distinctions of rank and titles, and thereby reduce civilised society to the primitive level of hunters and shepherds' (which explained why the French Jacobins were as ferocious as Indians). Moreover, as one Royal Navy captain put it, not merely opulence but civilization, manners and refinements depended on inequality of property. Other critics similarly insisted that 'Arcadian schemes of polity are only fit for Arcadian manners', that only Spartan simplicity could maintain a government like Paine's, or that the latter was 'calculated for infant society, for shepherds, fishermen, and huntsmen, where the riches of the state is scarce become an object of temptation, or an excitement to plunder'. Since they sought to return to the state of nature, Paine's followers were consequently advised to 'incorporate yourselves with the Indians in the Northern and Western parts of America'. Such comments could be greatly multiplied, for it is clear that the central argument against Paine was not the question of extending political participation, but the problem of reconciling republican ideals with unequal, and especially modern, commercial societies, without destroying their opulence. In essence Paine's critics simply rejected the idea of commercial republicanism by pretending that 'republic' could be understood only in

156

classical terms. And the language of republicanism proved too inelastic to refute this view easily.[40]

Consequently the most powerful charge in the reactionary arsenal was the accusation that the Painites sought to undermine the existing system of property. This became the centre of gravity in the entire revolutionary debate, the logical core around which other arguments swirled. Much more than merely the abusive idea that the 'equality of mankind' could only mean 'that we should all be exactly alike', the vindication of British opulence became the focus of loyalist exertions. Loyalists grew fond of quoting Smith's dictum that the common English labourer enjoyed more luxury than an African king. Inequality was admissible in a high state of civilization because even the poorest were better off than in a predominantly agricultural, more equal republican society; this was indeed the core of Smith's own defence of commercial society. The quickest way of 'refuting' the *Rights of Man* was thus simply to assert that it sought equality of property, even if this 'equality', as we have seen, meant 'levelling' landed estates to an annual value of some £13,000, equivalent to perhaps as much as a million pounds in present terms. But the taxation scheme in the *Rights of Man* Part Two was not read this way, though it was condemned as 'so unprincipled, as to surpass anything that is to be found in the history of the Buccaniers of America. It is an advertisement for general pillage.' Instead Paine was assumed to want to divide all property equally, which, one loyalist calculated, would leave three acres for each to cultivate and, since no one would be left for specialized labour, all would quickly sink into barbarism.[41]

First introduced by Reeves's association in late 1792, this charge soon took a variety of forms. Satirical treatments were common. *A Trip to the Island of Equality* described Paine's principles as operating successfully on an island off Alaska, where all were reduced to wearing fox-skins (there was a small pun here at Whig expense) and living in caves. Parodies of the *Rights of Man*, such as *Buff; or, A Dissertation on Nakedness*, accused Paine of relinquishing religion, literature, the arts, sciences, manufactures and the polite professions. Precise examinations of the economic proposals of the *Rights of Man*, however, were comparatively rare. One Lt Col. Chalmers defended Adam Smith against Paine's criticisms of his treatment of the Bank of England, but also claimed that Smith had been called 'the high priest of democracy' because he seemed to oppose high taxes. A long tract published in Germany accused Paine of corrupting Smith's principles 'by associating them with the temerity of language and inaccuracy of assertion which passion has inspired him with' and of mistakenly defining wealth as specie rather than labour. Another critic invoked the free trade principles of Arthur Young, Hume and Smith, and asserted that Paine intended to prove 'that we have no right to limit the wages of the labourer'.[42]

Various writers accused Paine of offering such encouragements to labour. To the leading anti-Jacobin 'John Gifford' (John Richards Green), Paine thought 'every man ought to resign all he possesses, and put all his property into one common stock-purse, whence it might be distributed in *equal* parts to all the different members of the community: the indolent and the industrious, the lazy and the laborious; the extravagant and the frugal'. Others said the Painites promised labourers three guineas a week without working by dividing property. And if such promises were not explicit, many feared they were understood as tacit. A Durham letter of late 1792 said that local workers 'talk of equality and expect, that all property will be divided in case of a Republic'. An Edinburgh pamphlet insinuated the same, while another report said that the poor had been told each would get ten acres and that 'French equality meant an equal distribution of land which Paine had told them was their natural and original right'. Often it was thus asserted, too, that whatever Paine's followers protested and Paine had written, his system implied equality, even though every sane person knew that inequality based upon differential productivity had been necessary since the state of nature to support an increasing population.[43] If Paine had not urged equality of property in so many words, thus, he had 'insinuated it', and intended others to seek it, or was, at least minimally, read by others as having done so. For many loyalists the issue was hence not what the radicals meant 'or what they now say they mean, but what ... men of plain understandings and common sense would naturally understand them to mean'. One anti-Jacobin thus wrote that Paine's readers 'really did understand' his notion of equality to mean 'an equal right at this moment to equal property'. An equal right to vote, moreover, might be consequently also understood as tending 'to subvert the natural order of things'. In France, after all, universal suffrage had resulted in 'no laws, no government, no order or rule'.[44]

A more accurate charge than that of complete equality was that the radicals sought to transplant American prescriptions to Europe, and here the European implications of Paine's central contention that republicanism and commerce could be reconciled were prominently rejected. America had no indigent poor to support and thus lacked the chief burden of other governments, said the agricultural writer Arthur Young. Its population had 'scarcely become a settled and mercantile people'. Luxury, another observer added, was 'but beginning to be known there', though eventually 'wealth and ease' would 'produce ambition', and ambition, faction. Soon an American commercial and manufacturing aristocracy would overturn the relative equality of the colonial era. Some who rejected Paine's conception of the American model were not ill disposed towards the United States, or at least hastened to insist that its powerful President and senatorial check on popular government did not imply 'like the French, a wild species of republicanism'. John Adams's response to the *Rights of Man* was hence welcomed as proving 'that the American Government is not founded upon the absurd doctrine of the pretended rights of man, and that, if it had been, it could not have stood for a week'. Some thus argued that Paine had used the American model dishonestly, since universal suffrage did not prevail there. Most agreed, however, that if Paine's views applied anywhere, it was only to countries like America, where commerce and manufacturing had made no extensive inroads and much free land existed. Such ideas were 'totally inapplicable to Britain' because it was 'so differently circumstanced in point of wealth and the peculiar dispositions of its inhabitants', especially because they were corrupted by the luxuries and vices of refinement.[45]

This campaign dealt a heavy blow to the reformers' cause, and especially the London Corresponding Society. As Henry Redhead Yorke lamented, the 'wicked manoeuvres' of Reeves's association were very damaging. Though they repeatedly abjured 'the Agrarian position of equalizing property', insisting only on 'equal protection of the law, whereby ... the poorest man [has] an equal chance of obtaining the impartial administration of justice', LCS leaders conceded in 1797 that the campaign had been 'unfortunately too successful'. 'The word equality became the constant theme of abuse, and was construed to mean, not equality of rights, but an equality of property also, in which perverted sense the French had never used it', explained one Painite, warning that while radicals first viewed such doctrines with abhorrence, 'we became familiarized with the name, and ... some of those who do not take the trouble of thinking for themselves, may possibly not detect that absurdity of the doctrine'. Painite pamphlets like *An Explanation of the Word Equality* and *Political Dialogues upon the Subject of Equality* (both *c.* 1792) railed against the 'perverse sense imposed on the word'. Radicals denied that the 'ridiculous idea' of equality of property could be found either in 'the heads of the most violent reformers in France' or anywhere in Paine's writings. But this was all to little avail. Yorke even felt that 'the general terror occasioned by such an insinuation' had brought about war with France.[46]

Natural rights and the state of nature

The loyalist account of British opulence defended modern property rights, but played down or rejected entirely the language of natural rights generally. In dismissing Paine's account of rights, discussions of the state of nature and the rights possessed in it were prominent, for the debate about both equality and rights rested largely upon notions of the origins of society. It was commonly asserted that Paine had misunderstood the relationship between natural and civil society (Price and Priestley had been similarly accused in 1789–90) and that his attempt to replicate natural rights in civil society underlay his misconceptions about rights, natural equality being 'incompatible with the advantages of social life', as one account insisted, deriding the late 'idle and foolish talk about the Rights of Man'. On this question as elsewhere ridiculously extreme views frequently emerged; one cleric, for example, seemed to admit only a natural right to celebrate the blessings of the English constitution. More serious critics usually rejected Paine's distinction between society and government as implying that mankind had once been so good as not to have needed government, or that America had ever lacked such an authority, or that any security of property could exist without one. Many similarly accused Paine of forgetting 'a very essential and operative part of human nature, the passions', and assuming that 'the people will all be regenerated with the government'. The *Rights of Man* thus ascribed 'more virtue and knowledge to mankind than they are really possessed of'. To Paine's claim that the system of commerce mitigated the need for extensive governments, too, one retort was that commerce was only pacific because governments protected its conductors.[47]

But most of Paine's critics were concerned chiefly to deny that rights 'of any kind whatsoever' existed in the state of nature, at least in any sense which might lend Paine support. Everyone was admittedly independent in the state of nature, one wrote, but everyone was also miserable, and the strong preyed continuously on the weak. Yet this 'was a state which modern philosophers have commended'. None the less it was also surely a condition in which no rights existed. Power alone had regulated human relations then, with rights emerging only with society proper, and support for this view was elicited from Grotius, Pufendorf, Burlamaqui and others. 'Natural rights' did not exist for practical men and women: 'all *rights* ... are properly *civil*' (as Edward Tatham put it) or were only 'real' because they were 'secured ... by that form of government under which we live' (said the Duke of York's chaplain).[48] A similar argument, close to Burke's, was that some rights preceded society, but 'no natural rights are retained after entering into society'. Another variation on this theme was to define these original rights as merely 'the rights of a savage, to prey upon the weak and helpless', which had been surrendered for civil rights, 'the rights of society, uniting us for our general happiness, and mutual assistance, and protection'. But this also virtually implied that 'in a natural state, men were possessed of no rights at all. None can be called natural rights which were not possessed in a state of nature; and where the rules of justice are not established, where the strong can enforce obedience, and the weak must yield to oppression, what becomes of the Rights of Man?' Or correspondingly, if such rights were 'natural', they included only the right to eat, drink, sleep, hunt, fish and the like. Some critics further argued that even if an original contract had marked the passage from the state of nature it would not have obliged future generations, who would not have been the real descendants of those who signed such a contract, and who, even if they were, would now be landed proprietors rather than 'the people at large'. If only historical rights were important, too, it was thus legitimate to confine the meaning of terms like 'rights' and 'liberty'. *Village Politics*, for example, began with workman Tom demanding 'I want liberty', and workman Jack responding 'Liberty! what, has any one fetched up a warrant for thee?' 'Liberty' was not admissible as a general concept, thus, but only as a specific right embedded in British law.[49]

Some quite extensive and sophisticated arguments were employed against Paine on this point. In the 620-page jurisprudential account by a conveyancer of the Middle Temple, Francis Plowden, 'state of nature' meant a 'mere theoretical and metaphysical state, pre-existing only in the mind, before the physical existence of any human entity whatever'. Writers like Locke, Plowden asserted, never implied that any historical transition from a state of nature to civil society took place and used the concept only as 'a method of philosophers to discuss the nature of man, before they enter upon peculiar attributes of existing beings'. This meant rights were primarily psychological attributes. A similar argument was that if 'state of nature' meant 'what is independent of society and exists at all times, without any consideration of any thing but itself', as the Edinburgh professor of civil law argued, natural rights were neither created nor abrogated by society but only fully enjoyed there, since they had no security prior to the institution of government. Natural rights could thus signify *jus gentium*, or rights 'co-extensive and coeval with social man', or the 'simple, pure, perpetual, universal dictates of our feelings and our understanding', which increased or diminished anyone's happiness. This could be construed as part of the instinctual law of nature, but also implied an appeal to 'general convenience and utility through experience and history', which was exactly what in 'the *modern rights of men* is not appealed to'. Utility was now to become the new basis of Whig political thought, and 'the great principle on which Government is to be established and maintained'. Because of Paine, clearly, natural rights doctrines became too dangerous to retain, and with them the associated ideas of the original contract and state of nature.[50]

The gist of many of these arguments was thus that Paine's appeal to natural rights implied reinstating natural society. Even before the *Rights of Man* was published, it had been alleged that 'the French have adopted the phantastic theory of mankind existing in a state of nature, and of their having a right to that liberty which such a state would give them'. This theme was now deployed extensively. The fact that Paine thought rights preceded society implied that men could exist individually, outside of society, and that all had 'individual sovereignty to govern' themselves. Paine was thus the 'reducer of civilized society into individual independence'. The counter-argument, of course, was that individuals were secure only where rights were established by laws and sovereignty normally resided with government. And here they were far from wholly independent. Instead of individuals (as opposed to the species) being born free, equal or independent, some of Paine's opponents thus maintained that children were born dependent upon their parents, as well as with different abilities. Many more stressed that while the Adamic patriarchal state might have been idyllic, the Fall had provoked continuous violence as well as the threat of overpopulation, which necessitated the formation of civil society. Pufendorf and Burlamaqui, among others, were enlisted to support the view that while the laws of nature regulating self-preservation and the pursuit of happiness might have governed during natural society, appetites and passions soon led to their relaxation, and to each judging the value of his or her own actions. Consequently all were soon reduced to avarice, envy and mutual oppression. Finally all renounced independence and lodged their rights in the supreme power of the state, which at last permitted 'true liberty' and 'intire independence'. Returning to natural society would thus be reinstating anarchy.[51]

One of the more substantial responses to Paine – some 430 pages long – examined most of these questions, but concentrated on defining the state of nature. Written by one Robert Thomas, minister of Abdie in Scotland, printed at Dundee in 1797, and supported by subscriptions from, among others, Adam Smith's successor at Edinburgh, Dugald Stewart, and the Rev. Hugh Blair, *The Cause of Truth* assumed the state of nature was a fiction in so far as any arrangements made within it could be binding thereafter, and that any early stage of society should be reconstructed through conjectural history rather than philosophical speculation. Here a Christian conception of the state of nature was again important, with the earliest stages of mankind being characterized by sin as well as misery. But Thomas also presumed that society was the natural condition of mankind. All were born within it with 'natural rights', but the state of nature did not define these. Instead natural rights, as part of human nature, were summarized in 'the right which every man has to himself', especially the right to life, and included the rights to liberty and property. Within society, however, men were naturally unequal. Thus, asserted Thomas, 'Mr. Paine's error lies in misrepresenting the original state of man, and in overlooking those variations in the character and situation of men, produced by an original inequality in the formation of their minds and bodies, and by numberless adventitious causes'. A similar view was taken in another lengthy account, William Brown's *An Essay on the Natural Equality of Man*. Professor of moral philosophy and natural law at the University of Utrecht, Brown levelled his entire classical armoury against Paine, citing extensively from Cicero, Seneca, Pliny, Epictetus and Marcus Antonius as well as Bacon, Grotius, Cumberland, Pufendorf, Hutcheson and many others. He also conceded that natural rights existed, being equal rights to life, to the fruits of labour, to the preservation of a fair and honest character and to liberty and private judgement. None the less society rested upon the necessity of subordination and the just demands of authority. Inequalities arose through different talents and dispositions and, though a 'natural equality of man' existed, this meant an equality of obligation and mutual dependence, or the equal duty of all to ensure the preservation and well-being of society.[52]

Several more explicitly theological responses to Paine also addressed these themes. When the Baptist minister William Winterbotham was tried in 1793 for preaching a seditious sermon, his accusers contended that no 'rights of man' existed 'in opposition to the supreme being, while in a state of civil society, man has no rights but what that society which he lives in allows him', any defence of 'absolute' rights thus being 'blasphemy to their Creator, and treason to the constitution'. Other authors agreed that while all rights were derived from God, none existed where no title could be shown. Echoing the same idea, the Rev. John Riland entitled his response to Paine *The Rights of God, Occasioned by Mr. Paine's Rights of Man*. Some critics moreover thought Paine's proposals for relief of the poor, ill and aged would undermine existing rights to charity and eventually degrade the poor further. (This accorded with the clerical explanation that God permitted the existence of rich and poor to ensure the exercise of those virtues necessary to salvation, a theodicy common to natural law texts as well.) Theological critics also objected to any use of the Mosaic account of the Creation to justify modern rights. Some protested that Genesis was Paine's only cited authority for the doctrine of equality but that since only one man was first created, his sons could not have been his equals. No original equality thus existed, and monarchy was a more likely form of original government. Paine's inference that if Genesis was not a divine account it was at least historically accurate was also contested.[53] We will shortly see the relevance of such criticisms to both *The Age of Reason* and *Agrarian Justice*.

Paine's treatment of natural rights and the state of nature was thus widely understood as diverging from the mainstream eighteenth-century position on such questions. Paine, some felt, was 'very anxious … to disclaim the authority of those who have gone before us'. On doctrines like the right of resistance, his views were seen as quite dissimilar from those of natural law writers like Pufendorf, whose definition of a right was also contrasted to Paine's supposed notion of a 'simple power', which might include a right to do wrong (and which we have seen was not Paine's view at all). Jurists like Burlamaqui were also frequently quoted on the disadvantages of popular government, with evidence cited from Greece, Rome, Carthage, Sparta and elsewhere. In fact such writers were more commonly deployed against Paine than was Burke's *Reflections*, for Burke, if he still remained a natural law thinker at all, had indeed only formulated an extreme version of the conservative natural law doctrine, and Paine an extreme rendition of its radical opposite, which again confirms that the Cold War portrayal of Burke as a natural law thinker and Paine as merely a 'radical' is no longer tenable. Many writers also attempted to show that Paine had departed from the Whig canon on these matters. One tract, for example, asserted that 'Those natural rights, whatever they may be, are placed by their new champion above the law; so that he directly contradicts Mr. Locke (whom we are not yet prepared to exchange for him) who says, where there is no law, there is no freedom'. Another thought that for Locke and Sidney natural rights meant that man was 'born with a capacity to acquire that freedom, and all those rights which any other man is capable of enjoying or acquiring' rather than being born with this freedom and these rights himself.[54]

The Painite counterattack

The campaign detailed here was remarkably successful in curtailing the reformers' activities, while efforts to relieve the rural poor facing famine helped to calm discontent for a time. But the cause was by no means defeated after the first wave of reaction in 1792, though Paine's friends had a meagre armoury at their disposal for organized retaliation. At least one Burke was burned in effigy (at Dronfield near Sheffield in early 1793) and hung twenty feet up on a scaffold after being paraded through town with a sign reading 'Edmund Burke the Irish Pensioner. I hate the Swinish Multitude.' But such efforts were rare. Cowed by the enormous efforts marshalled against them, many popular organizations became considerably more cautious, hoping at least to avoid prosecution. The LCS, for example, virtually ceased to refer to Paine after 1793. But in 1794 radical efforts revived, particularly after the London treason trials resulted in acquittals. By the end of the year the LCS claimed some 10,000 members, and Norwich and Sheffield were similarly revivified. Rapidly rising food prices caused widespread rioting in late 1795. New societies were formed and a new campaign to diffuse reform principles was mounted until the passage of the Two Acts in October curtailed activities once again, after it seemed the king had been fired upon on his way to open Parliament (a deed the government tried to lay at the doorstep of the LCS).[55]

While it lasted, however, the anti-loyalist response was sharp and vigorous. Tracts lambasted Reeves's association as 'the Place and Pension Club ... composed of those who actually derive *benefits* from the continuance of present abuses'. Threat begat counter-threat: *A Rod in Brine, or a Tickler for Tom Paine* (1792) was met by *A Rod for the Burkites*. A vast number of satirical tracts played on Burke's reference to the 'Swinish Multitude'. Satirizing the civilization discourse of the loyalists, titles like *The Pernicious Effects of the Art of Printing upon Society Exposed* mockingly decried the 'unparalleled affrontery' of 'the scum of the earth' in 'almost demanding, that political liberty shall be the same to all'. Once it had been proscribed, direct defences of the *Rights of Man* were more difficult. The radicals were thus also driven to subterfuge to disseminate their principles. One strategy was to seemingly assail Paine while quoting extensively from his works, thus emphasizing, for example, as Eaton did, Britain's heavy taxation. Similarly *The Pernicious Principles of Tom Paine, Exposed in an Address to Labourers and Mechanics. By a Gentleman* (c. 1793) purportedly attacked Paine, but only made his case appear more reasonable, while *A Defence of the Political and Parliamentary Conduct of the Right Honourable Edmund Burke* (1794) was nothing of the sort. Paine's name was avoided, but one tract typically noted that 'a late popular writer' described the best form of government, which meant the highest degree of happiness for the people at the least expense, as existing in America. Parts of Erskine's defence of freedom of speech were also commonly reprinted from the legally published account of Paine's trial.[56]

Many responses to loyalist tracts also tried to meet their chief points. Paine thought men were born free and equally possessed of natural rights, it was insisted, but he believed civil distinctions were highly necessary while condemning great inequalities of property. It was not the radicals, insisted John Thelwall, but instead 'Mr B. and his college, who would drive us back into the woods, to learn the arts of civilization and government from the half-naked babarism of the Goths and Germans', adding that 'I would extend civilization: I would encrease refinement'. Respecting the state of nature, it was frequently emphasized that while no 'established maxims or rules' then existed, mankind had none the less been 'actuated by a law antecedent and paramount to all human institutions, REASON, which taught them to pursue their own happiness without encroaching upon the happiness of others'. Civil society existed only to remedy the inconveniences of natural society, the only rights lost being the right to judge in one's own case, to make war, establish treaties and so on. All other rights were preserved, and were founded in antecedent natural rights. There were also several attempts to print natural law tracts sympathetic to Paine's views, of which by far the best known was Volney's *Law of Nature*, though it condemned the state of nature in stronger terms than had Paine, terming man 'the most abject slave' in that condition. Earlier radical and republican authors were also reprinted, and the anti-Painite reaction in fact probably made many more popular. The Sheffield Constitutional Society, for example, published *The Spirit of John Locke on Civil Government*, claiming that since Burke had termed the *Treatise* 'the worst book ever written ... it needs no further recommendation'.[57]

Despite many setbacks, there was some further revival of radicalism again in the later 1790s. The radical editor Sampson Perry noted in early 1796 that political associations seemed to be growing rapidly once more, but by the middle of the year they were again in steep decline, in part because bread prices began to fall. There were a few new attacks on Burke, with some implying that he was a closet Papist as well as a supporter of tyranny. A few Painite tracts appeared near the end of the decade, some condemning large farms and agricultural oppression in particular. Nor was Paine himself forgotten; Thomas Hardy wrote to him even in 1807 that many were 'silently reading ... what you have written'. As we will shortly see, small-scale insurrectionary activities actually increased in importance after 1796, though their numbers were less threatening and they were often apparently leaderless. There was to be no substantial rejuvenation of organized radicalism, thus, until after Waterloo.[58]

Repression, war and the sad course of the revolution in France hence combined to defeat the Painite movement. The Jacobin Terror alone, when its results began to be known, did immeasurable harm to the cause: the 'phoenix of liberty' had become a mere tyranny. Napoleon's conquest of Europe was as important. As Henry Redhead Yorke put it in 1798, the French were no longer 'contending for their liberties and independence, but on the contrary are aiming continuous blows against the liberties and independence of other nations, and especially against England'. Those reformers who visited France during the short peace of 1802–3 returned almost unanimously convinced that freedom had been exterminated there and that Napoleon sought to install himself as monarch. Britain's war against France was thus no longer unjust, but itself contributed to liberty. Given the degeneration of the French republic into despotism, radicals now also denied parallels between the French and American systems and insisted that no matter what had happened across the Channel, America's government was tolerant and free. Another important conclusion commonly drawn from the fate of the revolution was that moral reformation would have to precede political reform. Until this happened, as Yorke put it, 'no real benefit can flow from the extension of the elective franchise, or the limitation of the duration of parliament. It might be appealing only from one set of corrupt men to another set of the same description; not from Philip drunk to Philip sober; but from Philip drunk today to Philip drunk tomorrow.' This perception centrally underlay the anti-political stance of many early socialists.[59]

Religion and revolution

To complete our survey of the Painite movement we need briefly to consider two final questions which have excited considerable interest: how close Britain in fact was to revolution during the 1790s and what role religion may have played in inhibiting greater change. Various views are possible of both the propensity and capacity of the reformers for violent revolt. Some contemporaries or near contemporaries felt revolution had been virtually imminent. The Prime Minister, Pitt, admitted as much in confessing that 'As things are, if I were to encourage Tom Paine's opinions I should have a bloody revolution.' Courts made much of Paine's assertion – it was introduced at Horne Tooke's treason trial, for example – that Parliament was incapable of reforming itself, that reform, therefore, could come only from outside. In 1819, too, the radical *Medusa, or Penny Politician* asserted that if the *Rights of Man* had circulated freely for one year longer, the result would have been just such an upheaval.[60]

Some historians have thought this quite unlikely, however. Malcolm Thomis and Peter Holt, for example, contend that the reformers 'never came close to leading a revolution' because much further education was needed before their societies became sufficiently popular and because most radicals were supposedly bent upon reinstating the ancient British constitution rather than re-enacting the French revolution. Yet this is both an unnecessarily narrow construction of the term 'revolution' and an overly limited interpretation of the radicals' aims. The American revolution was also in many respects 'conservative' in purpose, but it also marked a dramatic severance from the status quo ante, and the foundation of a far more democratic polity. The aim of many British reformers, at least, was little different from this and if successful their reforms certainly would have constituted a 'revolution' in both politics and the system of property (which definition of the term was used at the time and remains acceptable). Obviously the British revolution never occurred. But this was not because it was not intended and could not have developed, but rather because repression, loyalism and war effectively halted the democratic movement. And in face of these forces most middle-class radicals who could have lent further assistance deserted the reformers' standard for the safety of other camps, or fled the battlefield entirely. Nor is it true that the only real popular political consciousness of this period lay in the violently conservative 'sub-political' responses of Church and King mobs, whose numbers were relatively small and whose motives were by no means straightforward.[61] And even if many were bystanders, the hundreds of thousands who appeared in some LCS demonstrations and the thousands active in similar events elsewhere also cannot be dismissed so easily.

The most exhaustive study of insurrection in the late eighteenth century thus concludes that 'in the right circumstances a massive conflagration' was possible. Volunteer militia shirked from being used against food rioters and even deserted and joined in themselves. Deference and obedience faltered even in the regular army and navy; a regiment moved from Canterbury to London was appraised as unsuitable for use against rioters, as its common soldiers were 'Paine's friends' who complained of their pay, while a member of a London-based artillery company claimed in 1794 that half his comrades would join the LCS if they could. Connections between English and Irish conspirators were also well developed. A successful revolt in Ireland would certainly have triggered sympathetic disturbances in England and Scotland, if only because the Irish were so active in British radicalism. Aid from France was available. Propaganda was very widespread, and those who could not afford to buy pamphlets or listen to others read them had merely to open their eyes. A 1793 tract noted that 'Every wall in London has been covered with inflammatory and seditious writings', and broadsides have survived from many other areas. Sufficient numbers were involved: the LCS alone had as many as 10,000 members in the mid-1790s, while Burke perhaps not too inaccurately counted some 80,000 Jacobins (or a total of one-fifth of 400,000 'political citizens ... above menial dependence') in the kingdom. Yet as E. P. Thompson has emphasized, these had very few leaders by 1795 and without leaders they were helpless. The middling orders in particular, who had played so important a part in hoisting the Painite petard in 1792, had mostly deserted the standard a year later. Their role could have been central; Burke greatly feared the resentments of 'monied people' like the East India merchants who supported 'French principles' 'almost to a man' because 'their present importance does not bear a proportion to their wealth'. But it was not.[62]

Evidence of a propensity to violence is as difficult to assess as the chance of its success. The government made much in the early 1790s of the spectre of armed mobs imposing their political will upon the nation. The widespread manufacture of pikes was reported by spies. At Sheffield, for example, one radical claimed under interrogation that his comrades had resolved to learn arms 'that they might be ready to assist their friends the French in case they landed in England'. Here, too, the secretary of the reformers' organization in April 1794 described how pike-blades required hoops for the shafts to fit the top ends, the bottom end of the shafts to be about one inch thick, fir being the recommended wood, and the shafts to be 'selected by persons who are judges of wood'. Blades and hoops together 'properly tempered and polished' were to be sold for a shilling, well within the means of labourers. Enquiries a month later revealed that 4,000 such weapons had been ordered for Perth alone. Some of the wealthier members of the LCS bought muskets and at least planned, even if they never finally organized, the uniformed 'Lambeth Association', whose announced purpose was supposedly to help repel any invasion. The LCS main lecturer, John Thelwall, justified arming in self-defence and himself carried a cane-sword. Prosecutions of the Scottish reformers also led to arming, and one plot, at Edinburgh in early 1794, included plans to capture the castle, the bank and local food supplies, and to petition the king to end the French war, or else. Here and elsewhere in the late 1790s clear connections were also established with Irish rebels which were renewed during the near-famine conditions of 1801-2. A secret organization also existed in the West Riding known as the 'Black Lamp', some of whose members were prosecuted in 1802 for administering secret oaths, though their strength has been disputed. Nor should we isolate the schemes of Colonel Despard, the United Englishman leader executed in 1803 after plans to seize the bank, the Tower and other parts of London were discovered, and whose avowed aim was 'an equalization of civil, political, and religious rights'.[63]

Insurrection may have been closest, a recent account has concluded, in the north-west in particular, where the Two Acts pushed the reformers towards violence in 1796 and later, and the United Englishmen may have had 600 members in 1797-8. They declined in 1799, but were again active in 1801-02 when distress reached new heights. The insurrectionary elements of the native radical movement in the late 1790s seem in fact to have been concentrated in the United Englishmen and a similar group, the United Britons. The former apparently emerged from Manchester reform circles in 1796 and included many soldiers, one of the group's main aims being the subversion of the military.

Some of its adherents evidently contemplated regicide as a means of commencing revolution or if the French landed. They read the *Rights of Man* and *The Age of Reason* and when they drank, toasted 'success to Tom Paine ... wishing his works might prosper'. Most were arrested in 1798. How far these connections constituted a revolutionary 'network' remains a moot point. The United Britons, established in 1797–8, had branches at Spitalfields, Clerkenwell and elsewhere and had amongst their members several Spenceans as well as Despard. Most of these were also apprehended in early 1798. The government claimed that some forty divisions of the United Englishmen existed in London alone, but Francis Place later contended that 'there was not one such division', the society being 'only in an incipient state'. The truth is probably somewhere between these views.[64]

These organizations do not, however, seem to have helped to provoke the most important insurrectionary action of the period, the naval mutiny of some hundred ships at the Nore and Spithead in 1797.[65] Many sailors were doubtless infected with revolutionary principles, particularly on one ship, the *Inflexible*, and one of their principal aims was 'to have the power of dismissing their own officers'. Some recent conscripts, in particular, had read their Paine, some of whose works were in any case sold secretly by boat at the fleet anchorage. A few LCS members, moreover, sought to widen the mutinies to bring about peace. Several sailors later arrested were also connected by the government to a corresponding society at Nottingham. But most do not seem to have been politically disloyal. Nor did French subversion contribute significantly to fomenting rebellion in England and Scotland, though there were rumours of radical workmen suddenly grown flush with French funds. Paine's plans for invasion probably would have found little support in Britain, even had he led a force himself, since for most radicals this passed well beyond what reform justified.[66] At the last debate of the LCS in April 1798, in fact, its secretary condemned the French government and suggested that members enlist in the Volunteers (he was opposed). Ireland, of course, was quite another matter. The United Irishmen were considerably more powerful than their English brethren, quite prepared to counsel force to meet their ends, and happy to secure French military support.[67]

English enthusiasm was muted for many reasons. Traditionally one important cause ascribed to explain a wider propensity to revolt during the 1790s also has a bearing on the next chapter: the spread of Methodism, which according to the French historian Elie Halévy had a powerful conservative influence on the working classes in this period. John Wesley and many Methodist leaders certainly opposed radical political change. Had the nearly 100,000 Methodists in 1795 (versus 30,000 in 1770) thought similarly and acted unanimously, they could have formed the backbone of the loyalist movement. But it is now widely conceded that Halévy's hypothesis must be set aside. Not only did the Methodists make their most substantial inroads into working-class communities only after the main period of repression (1792–5), but they were themselves also deeply divided politically. After the split between the Wesleyan and the Kilhamite Methodists in 1797, in fact, the latter (led by Alexander Kilham and numbering about 5000) were called the 'Tom Paine Methodists' for insisting upon 'democracy' in the form of the popular appointment of new leaders and stewards within the Methodist conference and local control over the exclusion of members.[68] The Kilhamites, of course, were hardly all Painites, as the Wesleyan hierarchy alleged, and Kilham himself wisely claimed not to be a political reformer. But he did invoke the spirit of inquiry generated by the American revolution, insisting with reference to the Methodist organization that 'No government under heaven, except absolute monarchies, or papal hierarchy' was 'as despotic and oppressive as ours is', and hinted that 'a few more revolutions' might be required to purify the sect. Moreover, some Kilhamites, for example, at Sheffield, were certainly members of constitutional societies, while a letter from a village near Wakefield claimed the local Methodists 'read and approved the works of Tom Paine'. At least one itinerant Methodist preacher in North Wales also attacked monarchism and discussed the *Rights of Man* before an audience of 500 miners. Thus there was no substantial correlation, either positive or negative, between loyalism and Methodism. But in one respect and in one area, at least, Methodism did have a stabilizing influence. The split in the LCS over religion in late 1795 was occasioned by the Methodist members' rejection of deism and atheism, and led a large number to withdraw to form a new society, 'The Friends of Religious and Civil Liberty'.[69] But consequently, as we will see, it was less Methodism than Paine himself who undermined the cause of popular reform.

Notes to Chapter 6: The government party

1 *The Reformer of England* (n.d.); *A New Song* (n.d.); *The Republican's Picture* (n.d.).
2 Paine (1945), Vol. 2, p. 480; *Critical Review*, Vol. 5 (1792), p. 583. On loyalism see R. Dozier (1983), to which the following several paragraphs are especially indebted, A. Goodwin (1979), pp. 208–67, H. Butterfield (1949), H. Winkler (1952), G. Newman (1974), H. Dickinson (1977), pp. 270–318, A. Booth (1979), pp. 103–58 and (1983), G. Pendleton (1976), T. Schofield (1984) and (1986) and T. McGovern (1988). The best survey of the war years is C. Emsley (1979). See also Emsley (1985). Some historians see the reaction beginning as early as 1785, in response to pro-American enthusiasm (e.g. G. Williams, 1969, p. 5).

3 *Rights and Remedies* (1795), pt 2, p. 118.
4 T. Howell, Vol. 22 (1817), cols 365–78 (e.g. Paine, 1987, p. 172). On the prosecutions see C. Emsley (1981).
5 *The Genuine Trial* (1792), p. 72; (F. Oldys) (1793), p. 157; T. Howell (1817), Vol. 22, col. 382.
6 W. Sherwin (1819), pp. 137–8; *The Trial of Daniel Isaac Eaton* (1793), p. 38; Add. MS. 27816 f. 331; J. Cookson (1982), p. 102. See A. Goodwin (1979), pp. 307–58.
7 Add. MS. 27808 f. 110; P. Pindar (1809), Vol. 3, pp. 119–20. See A. Goodwin (1979), pp. 451–99.
8 A. Aspinall (1949), pp. 78–9, 153, 166; P. Brown (1918), p. 85; L. Werkmeister (1963), p. 331, and generally pp. 317–80.
9 Add. MS. 16925 f. 159; I. Hunt (1791). On the association see A. Mitchell (1961), E. Black (1963), pp. 233–74, D. Ginter (1966) and J. Walvin (1969), pp. 271–308.
10 R. Dozier (1983), pp. 59–63; E. Black (1963), pp. 249–50; A. Mitchell (1961), pp. 61–7; Add. MS. 16927 f. 3; J. Walvin (1969), p. 327; A. Booth (1979), p. 115; J. Brims (1983), p. 339; D. Ginter (1966). See also M. Quinlan (1943).
11 *Proceedings of the Association* (1792), p. 15; A. Mitchell (1961), pp. 66; R. Webb (1955), pp. 43–4; E. Black (1963), p. 240. 'Thomas Bull' was Sir William Jones.
12 *Manchester Herald*, no. 25 (15 September 1792), p. 2; *The Rights of the Devil* (n.d.), p. 23; A. Patterson (1954), p. 71; Add. MS. 27814 f. 43; 16923 f. 127; *Proceedings of the Friends* (1793), pp. 4–5. On Walker see F. Knight (1957). Gwyn Williams terms him 'the most thorough-going "Painite" in England' (1969, p. 18).
13 A. Young (1898), p. 204. See J. Western (1956).
14 This is stressed in G. Rudé (1964a), p. 140.
15 J. Priestley (1791a); HO33/1; S. Romilly (1840), Vol. 1, p. 449; R. Rose (1960), p. 77. See W. Chaloner (1958).
16 E. Robinson (1955); J. Walvin (1969), pp. 332–3; A. Booth (1983), 298–300; HO42/23. For Manchester see also L. Marshall (1946), pp. 107–20.
17 *The Union*, no. 1 (26 November 1831), p. 14; *Republican*, Vol. 9, no. 4 (21 January 1824), pp. 99–100; J. Walvin (1969), p. 338; HO42/23; *Derby Mercury*, no. 3139 (14 June 1792), p. 4; *Sheffield Register*, no. 294 (18 January 1793), p. 3; no. 299 (22 March 1793), p. 3; Add. MSS. 16928 f. 5; 16924 f. 62.
18 *The Tribune*, Vol. 2 (1794), p. 207; E. Thompson (1968), p. 122; R. Dozier (1983), p. 91.
19 A. Aldridge (1960), p. 182; *Tom Paine's Jests* (1794), p. 35; *Manchester Herald*, no. 4 (26 January 1793), p. 2; *The Complete Reports* (1794), pp. 79–80; Add. MS. 16928 f. 5; *Sheffield Register*, no. 292 (4 January 1793), p. 3; TS11/956/3501. Anti-Jacobite sentiment still had its uses: one old Whig, poring over his newspaper, was heard to exclaim, 'Damn these *Jacobites*! why do they now print 'em *Jacobines*? I thought we had done for 'em all at the battle of Culloden' and wished he was young enough to sally forth once again (*Sheffield Iris*, no. 14, 3 October 1794, p. 3).
20 C. Jewson (1975), p. 91; TS11/954/3504.
21 A. Goodwin (1979), pp. 359–415.
22 H. Meikle (1912), p. 153; E. Tatham (1791), pp. 21–7; J. Hamilton (1791), p. 6.

23 'Signor Pasquinello' (1792), p. 10; A. Scott (1793), pp. 6–7; Mr. Justice Ashurst's Charge (1792); 'Launcelot Light' (1792), p. 6; [T. Taylor] (1792), p. 103; Add. MS. 16923 fols 187–8; A Plot Discovered (1793), p. 3.

24 [W. Cobbett] (1797), p. 5; W. Fancourt (1792), p. 6; J. Brown (1793), p. 53; Principles of Order (1792), p. 8; Principle and Practice (1792), p. 14; Anti-Levelling Songster (1793), p. 5.

25 B. Boothby (1792), p. 107; An Humble Address (1793), p. 9; One Penny-worth of Truth (1792); [A. Young] (1792), p. 3; A Conversation (1793), p. 2; Mr. Miles (1793), pp. 251–3; The Last Dying Words (n.d.), p. 2; A Penitentiary Epistle (n.d.); The End of Pain (n.d.).

26 Thoughts Upon Our Present Situation (1793), p. 4; Britons are Happy (n.d.); The Anti-Gallican Songster, no. 1 (1793), p. 13; G. Croft (1793), p. 28; A Defence (1791), p. 11; [F. Hervey] (1791), p. 18; 'The Plot' (1792), p. 10; A Defence (1791), p. 54.

27 A. Peter (1792), pp. 6, 11–12; Paine and Burke (n.d.), p. 20; Facts (1792), p. 28; Some Remarks (1793), p. 3; A Caution (n.d.); J. King (1793), p. 16; A Few Minutes' Advice (1792), p. 12; The Alarm (n.d.); [W. Sewell] (1791), p. 20.

28 C. Hawtrey (1792), pp. 10–11; J. Young (1794), p. 40; L. Parsons (1793), p. 15; Portrait (1792); E. Burke (1826), Vol. 3, pp. 398, 415. See R. Hole (1983), pp. 66–8, for a summary of several of these points.

29 [W. Paley] (1951), pp. 21–6.

30 H. More (1793); A Few Words (n.d.); W. Roberts (1835), Vol. 1, pp. 413, 456; [H. More] (1794), p. 3. On the Cheap Repository series see S. Pedersen (1986). The most political of the early tracts was Hints to All Ranks of People on the Occasion of the Present Scarcity (1795), which counselled endurance. On the evangelical contribution to the reaction see T. McGovern (1988). On conservative utilitarianism see T. Schofield (1986) and, for an example, A Letter to a Friend (1792), p. 20.

31 John Bull (1792); J. Moser (1796), p. 5; 'Tam Thrum' (1793), p. 11; Dialogue on the Rights of Britons (1792) p. 7; John Bull's Answer (1792).

32 Liberty and Equality (1792), pp. 8, 11, 15–17, 19, 24, 28–9, 32, 35, 39.

33 Letters to a Friend (1792), p. 154; I. Hunt (1791), p. 90; An Address to the Inhabitants (1793), p. 22; [W. Smith] (1791), p. 12; [J. Adams] (1791), pp. 11–12; C. Hawtrey (1792), p. 6; [J. Reeves] (1795), p. 22. One William Lewelyn printed 'Dissenting Minister' prominently on the title page of a response to the Rights of Man, and accused Paine of wanting to make the poor pensioners of the state (Lewelyn, 1793, pt 2, p. 118).

34 Considerations (1792), p. 68; R. Bisset (1796), p. 346; [T. Atkinson] (1798), p. 33; 'Cincinnatus Rigshaw' (1800); Application of Barruel (1798), pp. iii, 2–7; Barruel (1797), p. 38; J. Robison (1797), pp. 360–496. On Robison see J. Morrell (1971). For American parallels see V. Stauffer (1918). Another account thought that revolution was impossible in Ireland because its 40,000 Masons were all opposed to treason (An Important Discovery, 1793, p. 14). Apparently unknown to the translator, Paine himself was intimately acquainted with Masonry, even writing an extended essay on the subject. Whether he was a Mason has never been proved, however.

35 W. Playfair (1795), p. 13; Constitutional Letters (1792), p. 18; A. Dalrymple (1793), p. 13; Fragment of a Prophecy (1791), p. 27; The Interests of Man (1793), pp. 46–8; An Humble Address (1793), p. 15. On these arguments see H. Dickinson (1977), pp. 270–318 and J. Lee (1981).

36 [F. Hervey] (1791), p. 18; J. Jones (1793a), p. 15.

37 *A Letter of Condolence* (1795), pp. 5–6; [W. Sewell] (1791), pp. 51, 55; R. Dozier (1983), pp. 82–3; [J. Reeves] (1795), p. 13; [W. Paley] (1951), p. 24. On the few High Tories of the 1790s see J. Gunn (1983), pp. 164–85. Reeves was aquitted on the basis of the purity of his motives (T. Howell, 1819, vol. 26, col. 596). On him see M. Weinzierl (1985).
38 W. Black (1793), p. 40; *An Exposure* (1793), pp. 59–60; J. Scott (1794), p. 10; A. Young (1792), pp. 4–7.
39 J. Cocks (1793), p. 10; *The Address of a Buckinghamshire Farmer* (1792); *Ten Minutes' Caution* (1792), p. 6; H. More (1793), p. 14; *Free Communing* (1793), p. 30.
40 J. Jones (1793b), pp. 4–5; *Facts* (1792), p. 7; *A Few Minutes' Advice* (1792); J. Courtenay (1790), p. 40; C. Patton (1797); B. Boothby (1792), p. 178; P. White (1792), p. 107; T. Hearn (1793), p. 59; [T. Freeman] (1793), p. 7. On the civilization debate see further my (1987), ch. 1.
41 *A Serious Caution* (1792); W. Black (1793), p. 39; [A. Young] (1792), p. 9; *The Patriot* (1793), pp. 73–5; Add. MS. 16920 f. 17.
42 *A Trip to the Island of Equality* (n.d.); *Buff* (1792), p. 27; Lt Col. Chalmers (1796); R. Dinmore Jr (1796), pp. 20, 32; S. Joersson (1796), pp. 4, 11; *Rights and Remedies* (1795), p 2, p. 161.
43 J. Gifford (1792), p. 32; *A Country Curate's Advice* (n.d.); Add. MS. 16927 f. 47; HO102/6; HO102/60; J. Young (1794), p. 112; W. Fox (1793), p. 12.
44 *The Duties of Man* (1793), p. 25; R. Thomas (1797), p. 37; [T. Atkinson] (1794), p. 14; *A Few Plain Questions* (1793), p. 10.
45 A. Young (1793), pp. 2, 56; *An Appeal to the Common Sense* (1793), p. 21; *A Letter to a Friend* (1792), p. 15; *The Anti-Gallican* (1793), pp. 30–34; J. Cocks (1793), p. 20; W. Miles (1890), Vol. 1, p. 364; 'Martius Modernus' (1793), p. 23. On Young's reaction to the revolution see Young (1898), pp. 198–206. On the use of the American model by Paine's opponents see D. Wilson (1988), pp. 89–95.
46 H. Yorke (1793), p. 34; *Correspondence* (1795), p. 82; *A Narrative* (1797), p. 13; *Newcastle Chronicle*, no. 1484 (8 December 1792), p. 2; *Considerations on the French War* (1794), p. 18.
47 *An Humble Address* (1793), p. 10; *Resolutions of Common Sense* (n.d.), p. 1; *The True Briton's Catechism* (1793), p. 32; W. Keate (1790), p. 53; C. Coetlogon (1792), p. vi ; A. Dalrymple (1793), p. 4; *A Whipper* (1793), p. 24; *Britannia's Address* (n.d.), pp. 6–7; [F. Hervey] (1792), pp. 4–5, 9–10; [W. Drummond] (1793), pp. 1–8.
48 *Six Essays* (1792), p. 2; W. Agutter (1792), pp. 6–7; S. Cooper (1791), p. 63; *A Letter* (1791), pp. 19–20; E. Tatham (1791), p. 39; R. Nares (1792), p. xi.
49 *A New Dialogue* (n.d.), p. 12; *Remarks* (1792), p. 85; *Comparative Display* (1970), vol. 2, pp. 360–1; *Facts* (1792), p. 20; H. More (1793), pp. 3, 12. See also E. Burke (1826), Vol. 3, p. 419.
50 F. Plowden (1792), pp. 14–32; J. Wilde (1793), pp. 575–8. Wilde identified his views with a Roman definition of rights.
51 [C. Hawtrey] (1790), p. 14; *The Interests of Man* (1793), pp. 6, 8–11; *Rights Upon Rights* (1791), p. 5; *Letters to Thomas Paine* (1791), pp. 62, 15–16; T. Molloy (1792), pp. 77–9, 82, 88.
52 R. Thomas (1797), pp. 1, 25–8, 33, 37, 73–5; W. Brown (1794), pp. 14, 50, 108–44, 171–211, 305.
53 T. Howell (1817), Vol. 22, col. 870; *The Origin of Duty* (1796), p. 25; A. Dalrymple (1793), p. 22; *Defence of the Rights of Man* (1791), p. 11; *Remarks on Mr. Paine's Pamphlet* (1791), pp. 16–17.

54 P. Stanlis (1958), p. 16; *Principles of Order* (1792), p. 13; *The Interests of Man* (1793), pp. 13, 16; *A Candid Inquiry* (1792), p. 9; *An Humble Address* (1793), p. 10.

55 J. Cookson (1982), pp. 115–41; *Sheffield Register*, no. 294 (18 January 1793), p. 3; *Derby Mercury*, no. 3192 (31 January 1793), p. 1; *Assassination of the King!* (1795).

56 E. Burke (1978), Vol. 7, p. 340; *The Pernicious Effects* (n.d.), p. 9; *Knave's-Acre Association* (1793), p. 3; *The Pernicious Principles* (n.d.), pp. 2, 8; *The Catechism* (n.d.), p. 20; *Politics for the People*, pt 2, no. 1 (1794), pp. 3–9; *Pig's Meat*, vol. 1 (1793), pp. 168 ff.

57 J. Thelwall (1796b), pt 2, pp. 83–4; *Remarks on the Conduct* (1793), p. 34; *Truth and Reason* (1793), p. 11; *The Political Crisis* (1791), pp. 6, 8, 11–12; C. Volney (1796), p. 4; *The Spirit* (1792), p. viii.

58 *The Argus, or General Observer* (January 1796), p. 248; M. Browne (1796), p. 53; N. Cox (1971), p. 30; T. Marsters, Jr (1798); Add. MS. 27818 fols 72–3. On the revival of radicalism see N. Cox (1971) and J. Hone (1982).

59 *An Appeal to the Common Sense* (1793), p. 10; H. Yorke (1798), pp. 9–10; J. Cookson (1982), pp. 172–3; G. Watson (1799), p. 27; H. Yorke (1798), pp. 85–6. On the horrors of the revolution see, e.g., T. Somerville (1793).

60 J. Ehrman (1983), p. 80 n; *The Trial of John Horne Tooke* (1795), p. 17; *Medusa*, vol. 1, no. 6 (27 March 1819), pp. 40–3.

61 M. Thomis and P. Holt (1977), pp. 5–28; R. Palmer (1959), Vol. 1, p. 188. A good summary of the revolutionary potential of the reformers is H. Dickinson (1985), pp. 43–61. *Pigott's Political Dictionary* defined revolution in 1795 as 'the sudden overturning of an arbitrary government by the people' as well as more generally 'change in the state of a government or a country' and 'a total alteration of the forms of governments, and a reassumption by the People of their long lost rights; a restoration of that equality which ought always to subsist among men' (C. Pigott, 1795, pp. 117–18).

62 HO42/23; R. Wells (1983), p. 255 (supported by R. Dozier, 1972); PC41/A139; TS11/956/3501; *Opinions Delivered* (1793), p. 3; E. Burke (1826), Vol. 4, pp. 338, 14; E. Thompson (1968), p. 196; C. Emsley (1975).

63 *The Decline and Fall* (1796), p. 1; *Assassination of the King!* (1795); *Application of Barruel's Memoirs* (1798), pp. 34–5; TS11/956/3501; TS11/892/3035: HO102/11; *The Trial of Despard* (1803), p. 36. On Despard see M. Elliott (1977), J. Hone (1982), pp. 86–117 and R. Wells (1983), pp. 220–52. On the Black Lamp see J. Dinwiddy (1974a) and F. Donnelly and J. Baxter (1976).

64 A. Booth (1986); PC1/41/A139; PC1/42/A140; R. Wells (1983), pp. 77, 121–8, 167–9, and generally Wells (1978) and (1987) (pp. 120–60 in particular). Add. MS. 27808 f. 92; F. Place (1972), p. 178. See also J. Walvin (1969), pp. 559–604.

65 So argues J. Dugan (1966), p. 63. The government asserted that the United Irishmen were active in the mutinies (ibid., p. 454). On this point see R. Wells (1983), pp. 90–9 and G. Manwaring and B. Dobree (1935), pp. 199–200.

66 PC1/38/A122; *Report of the Committee* (1799), p. 76; HO102/6; T. Howell (1820), Vol. 27, col. 654.

67 See R. Jacob (1937), A. Goodwin (1979), pp. 416–50 and M. Elliott (1983).

68 [A. Kilham] (1796a), p. iii; D. Simpson (1802), p. 334. See E. Thompson (1968), pp. 45–50. On this controversy see E. Halévy (1906), E. Hobsbawm (1957), E. Thompson (1968), pp. 385–440, P. Stignant (1971), J. Walsh (1975),

J. Baxter (1974), E. Itzkin (1975), N. Murray (1975), pp. 216–58, and D. Hempton (1984).

69 [J. Benson] (1796), p. 4; Kilham (1796b), p. 2; Kilham (1795), pp. 12, 60; F. Donnelly and J. Baxter (1976), p. 96; Add. MS. 16925 f. 121; HO42/22; A. Goodwin (1979), p. 371. Kilham later wrote that some Methodists believed 'that I was the same to the Methodists as Tom Paine was to the nation ... that my chief object was to spread anarchy, confusion, and mischief throughout the societies', which is hardly an endorsement of Paine ([Kilham], n.d., p. 144). See B. Semmel (1974), pp. 110–45 and D. Hempton (1984), pp. 66–73.

7

Revolution in heaven:
The Age of Reason (1794–95)

Introduction

Though its title is often appropriated to summarize the aspirations of the eighteenth century, *The Age of Reason* remains Paine's most misunderstood and ill-fated work.[1] Written to combat atheistical tendencies in France, it has itself often been taken as a defence of unbelief. An American president, Theodore Roosevelt, notoriously once termed Paine a 'filthy little atheist' (he meant literally dirty, in light of Paine's later reputation for self-neglect) in his life of Gouverneur Morris. In fact the text, as we will see, is a frank confession of deism, and especially the contention that God's only revelation lay in nature, not the Bible. Largely ignored in France, where unsold stacks of it were reported to be gathering dust, *The Age of Reason* did enormous damage to Paine's political reputation in Britain and America.[2] Eventually it became a foundation text of both the British and American secularist movements, but during the 1790s its impact was primarily negative, and it is difficult not to conclude that its publication, at least in English, was an imprudent move on Paine's part.

But it was also a move which to Paine seemed unavoidable. For the rationale of *The Age of Reason* lay in the course of the French revolution itself, and specifically in the spectacular bloodbaths (by standards less inured than our own) Paine had witnessed. These led him to conclude that the goal of revolution – the improvement of mankind – required the injunction to sociability which he thought belief in a Divinity facilitated. Paine's God, we will discover, is not avenging, punitive and vindictive, but benign, humane and charitable. Faith in such a Deity, he felt, could help others to withstand the temptations which power and corruption amply furnished in the midst of revolution and to remind political actors of the dignity of all mankind. But Paine did not invent this ideal, and before turning to *The Age of Reason* we need first briefly to consider how deism was understood in this period.

177

Deism in the eighteenth century

Earlier deist works had not been directed towards the labouring classes, and correspondingly were not regarded as equally threatening to the established order. Usually taken to have begun with Lord Herbert of Cherbury's *Of Truth* (1624), which attempted to reduce Christianity to a set of simple, reasonable beliefs, deism was confined to select groups of the literate upper classes throughout the eighteenth century. Among others, Hobbes and Shaftesbury in the seventeenth century and Hume and Gibbon in the eighteenth were leading sceptics or 'infidels', while other well-known deists (many were also Freemasons) included radical Whigs like John Toland (*Christianity Not Mysterious*, 1696), Anthony Collins (*Discourse on the Grounds and Reasons of the Christian Religion*, 1733) and Matthew Tindal (*Christianity as Old as the Creation*, 1730). Deism could be radical in its politics, as for Toland, or not; Hume's Whiggism was highly 'sceptical' and verged upon Toryism on occasion. But in no form did it achieve respectability. Hume's opinions, for example, cost him much public approbation.[3]

Eighteenth-century deism relied centrally upon a Newtonian world-view in which the universe was assumed to be governed by fixed and identifiable mechanical laws. Some deists also believed that God suffused nature in a pantheistic manner which verged on the magical (the roots of this view lay in mid-seventeenth-century millenarianism and its adherents included many political radicals). The idea of Providence still had an important role to play, but the notion of direct or miraculous divine interference in human affairs was receding. Locke's argument that knowledge was derived from experience did much to underpin the rationalistic approach to religion. Deists like Shaftesbury correspondingly also argued that the Christian idea of heaven and hell only perverted morals, which should rest upon the pursuit of virtue for its own sake. Consequently deists distinguished centrally between 'natural religion' and 'revealed religion'. While the latter was conceived as traditional Christianity associated with biblical knowledge, 'natural religion' contended that the spectacular complexity and apparent harmony of nature proved the existence of God, though Hume even attacked such arguments from design in his *Dialogues on Natural Religion* (1776). Most deists agreed that whatever could not be reasonably demonstrated as divinely inspired need not be included in Christian belief, but might be regarded as the mythology of a pre-scientific understanding in which the seeds of natural religion were present. What was valuable in the Scriptures, thus, as one deist put it, was only what was 'founded indiscernably in Truth, and apparently supported by Reason' and had 'a natural tendency to promote purity of Heart and Rectitude of Manners'. Deists assumed that all could possess such knowledge (there were important links here to the Quaker notion that all were capable of perceiving the Inner Light). They also asserted that if God's intentions were properly understood, his desire for the happiness of all would be apparent, as well as the human duty to fulfil this mandate by bringing happiness to others.[4]

Not all deists shared exactly the same beliefs, of course. Many positions were taken on the question of revelation. Bolingbroke attempted to offer proofs against the moral character of the Deity and the probability of future rewards and punishments, a trend continued by Hume. But most deists none the less subscribed to a few common principles, and particularly the doctrine, as a 1734 summary of deist principles put it, that nothing could be ascribed to God which was 'not fully manifest to all Mankind by the meer Light of Nature'. Deists also generally agreed that the problem of moral obligation was not insurmountable, since deism taught 'a perfect Rule for all religious Duties, as it proceeds from a Being of infinite Perfection, Wisdom, and Goodness, and needs no Assistance from any external Revelation'.[5]

Deism assumed at least a few popular forms in the eighteenth century. An organization known as the Robin Hood Society, which disappeared around 1773, apparently debated deistic topics, one of its members receiving a year in Newgate for his opinions. The Society of Ancient Deists, based near Hoxton, met for some twenty years between 1770 and 1790. At least one eccentric minister, known as the 'Priest of Nature', preached deist ideas in his chapel in the mid-1770s. It is possible that Paine moved in such circles prior to emigration, particularly when he lived in London. His early religious opinions evidence a deep devotion to what he regarded as the essence of Christianity – benevolence towards all – and a derisory dismissal of all efforts to foist mystical theologies and priestly hierarchies upon the deluded majority. Paine may have preached as a Primitive Methodist at least once in his early years and Arminian Methodism, which stressed that all could attain salvation, may have influenced him in the early 1770s.[6] But his deism, in any case, was certainly settled by the time of the American revolution.

The Age of Reason

The place of Paine in the history of biblical criticism has not generated much scholarly concern and interests few modern readers. Some account of it is necessary here, but two aspects of *The Age of Reason* are more important: its relevance to understanding Paine's religious beliefs generally, and its relation to his social and political ideas and their reception.[7]

The first part of *The Age of Reason* was written to reverse the growing irreligion Paine perceived around him. 'The people of France were running headlong into atheism', Paine later recalled, 'and I had the work translated in their own language, to stop them in that career, and fix them to the first article ... of every man's creed who has any creed at all – *I believe in God.*' The text itself nearly failed to be published at all. Its final sections were written on Christmas Day 1793 and the following two days, shortly before Paine's arrest. Only the kindness of one of his guards in allowing the manuscript to be given to Joel Barlow, in fact, prevented its seizure and possible destruction.[8]

The text opens with Paine's plea for toleration of his religious opinions and with the warning that since France had now abolished the priesthood completely, there was danger that 'in the general wreck of superstition, of false systems of government and false theology, we lose sight of morality, of humanity and of the theology that is true'. Paine then summarized his religion as entailing a belief in only one God, a hope for 'happiness beyond this life', and devotion to 'the equality of man', with religious duties consisting of 'doing justice, loving mercy, and endeavouring to make our fellow-creatures happy'.[9]

Such views seem uncontroversial. The problem was that existing religion did little justice to these beliefs and consisted instead in creeds defined by established churches, be they Jewish, Roman Catholic, Protestant, or any other. Such establishments were not only completely unnecessary, but worse, mere 'human inventions, set up to terrify and enslave mankind, and monopolize power and profit'. 'My own mind is my own church,' declared Paine. No other was required. Indeed the 'adulterous connection of Church and State' and the existence of professional priests selling religion for lucre had made true faith impossible. It was imperative therefore to overthrow 'human inventions and priestcraft' in order to return to a pure belief in one God.[10]

This for Paine principally demanded a massive assault upon the idea that the Bible revealed the will of God. Paine admitted that God was capable of such a communication. The problem was what authority this later carried, since, for example, there was no internal evidence of divinity in the commandments 'revealed' by Moses. If this was true, moreover, there was no reason to believe Christ was the son of God, a view Paine thought mere pagan mythology. He had doubtless been a 'virtuous and amiable man' whose philanthropic morality was still practised by the Quakers. But this lent no credence to the doctrine of the resurrection, or the idea of the need for Christ's sacrifice because Eve had eaten an apple, or the Christian account of Satan.

The Creation itself, and 'the vast machinery of the universe' in all its abundance, were alone necessary to anchor religious belief, not fabulous and superstitious conjectures.[11]

The rest of *The Age of Reason* contrasts false and true religion. Most of the Bible Paine dismissed as mere myth and hearsay. The account of the Creation in Genesis, for example, appeared to be a tradition accepted by the Israelites before they went to Egypt (and Paine's rejection of this account had considerable implications for his theory of property, as we will see in the following chapter). Other parts of the Old Testament were by 'poets and itinerant preachers'; its 'prophecies', for example, were merely ancient poetry. The New Testament, too, commenced with anecdotes about the life of Christ. But there followed a series of letters which transformed Christ's doctrine into 'a religion of pomp and of revenue' whose chief doctrines, like the idea of purgatory, where souls could be released only by prayers bought from the Church, and indeed the whole doctrine of redemption, were constructed merely as 'revenue laws' to fatten the priesthood.[12]

By contrast the 'True Revelation' was the Creation itself. Its immensity revealed the power of God, its order his wisdom, its abundance his generosity. This munificence in turn taught that all should be kind to one another. God could be conceived only as the first cause of the universe, existing because some first cause was necessary, perfect given the structure of the Creation. Natural philosophy, or the study of the Creation, and including mathematics, mechanics and other sciences, was thus the basis of true theology, not Christianity, which concerned only the writings of man. Science, Paine argued, was in fact a progressive form of knowledge which called into question the truth of the Christian faith. Consequently Christianity had long resisted scientific claims. Deism, however, merely required contemplating the wisdom, power and benignity of the Deity. The Quakers had verged upon this religion, but had 'contracted themselves too much by leaving the works of God out of their system', thereby ignoring in their puritan sternness the beauty of a bird's song or of flowers. Science, Paine insisted, also introduced the possibility of a plurality of worlds given the immensity of space. And because God made neither space nor anything else in vain, but organized the universe 'in the most advantageous manner for the benefit of man', the Christian belief that the son of God died for the inhabitants of earth was false. All attempts to base religion on mystery, miracle and prophecy were similarly impositions on mankind, including the idea that mystical withdrawal from the world served God, or that 'degrading the Almighty into the character of a showman' by imputing miracles to him aided true religion. Declaring that all nations and religions at root believed in a God whose attributes were discoverable in nature, Paine closed the first part of his tract.[13]

The second part of *The Age of Reason*, written in late 1795, is a detailed examination of the Old and New Testaments. Again Paine wanted to challenge the idea that many events described in the Bible, including assassinations, rapes, the murder of infants, etc., had been commanded by God. For if this were true, God could not possibly be the foundation of moral justice in the world. Thus it was 'a duty incumbent upon every true Deist, that he vindicate the moral justice of God against the calumnies of the Bible'. But Paine was now concerned less to ridicule the miraculous claims of the Bible than to disprove much of its authenticity and to argue this, moreover, from internal evidence alone. Thus, for example, Paine contended that Genesis, Exodus, Leviticus, Numbers and Deuteronomy, the so-called five books of Moses, were not written by Moses but usually refer to him in the third person. On the basis of his own biblical chronology, Paine argued that these books were actually written some 350 years after Moses' death. This rendered their testimony highly suspect, or at least no more valid than any other ancient tales or fables. Thus the butchery and rapine committed in these books could not have been sanctioned or commanded by God.[14]

Having dismissed Genesis as 'an anonymous book of stories, fables and traditionary or invented absurdities, or of downright lies', Paine applied the same method to the rest of the Bible. Any evidence of immorality he castigated as 'lies, wickedness and blasphemy'. Absurdities like the story of Jonah and the whale he poked fun at. Inconsistencies he exposed mercilessly. How could Samuel have written an account of his own death and burial in the book of Samuel? How could the Psalms be the Psalms of David, when one of them commemorated an event which occurred many centuries after his death? Nor was the New Testament more consistent than the Old. Much of the case for the divinity of Christ Paine again dismissed as mere pagan mythology. Christ's character and morality were inspiring. But this was no reason to presume that the books imputed to the apostles were historical truth and Paine dismissed them all as 'manufactured' long after the fact by persons other than their alleged authors. He went on to ridicule inconsistencies in the various biblical accounts of the crucifixion and resurrection, of the later reappearance of Christ to his disciples and of his supposed ascension into heaven. Throughout Paine disputed the possibility that those who recounted these events had themselves been eyewitnesses to them, and argued that the subsequent Christian Church had adapted the story of Christ to its own purposes, even condoning the forgery of biblical texts when necessary. But Part Two was not entirely destructive. Paine again reaffirmed his concept of deism, defined as 'the belief in one God, and an imitation of His moral character, or the practise of what are called the moral virtues'. He also defended his faith in an afterlife, arguing that this could be inferred from observing the natural world. He again praised the Quakers for caring little about Jesus Christ and calling the Bible 'a dead letter'. For compared to the beauty, the overwhelming magnificence and awesomeness of nature, the Scriptures, he concluded, were 'fit only to excite contempt'.[15]

When we consider how much of *The Age of Reason* was written without the modern tools of biblical scholarship and textual investigation, Paine's exploration of biblical inconsistencies and exposure of illogical assumptions and manifest contradictions is all the more remarkable. For what Paine actually attempted in *The Age of Reason*, without the aid of ancient languages or the comparison of manuscripts, was an *historical* reading of the Bible. His reading was exceptionally careful in the circumstances, and his arguments are often compelling. When we read, for example, that there is mention of 'the kings that ruled in Edom' in Genesis, we agree that this must describe a period after monarchy has been instituted, and cannot therefore refer to the beginning of the world. Except for those disproportionately effectual fundamentalists who persist in believing in the literal truth and divine origin of every word of the Bible and similar sacred works, this is the historical method which modern readers accept as appropriate for approaching the ancient texts of any religion. Paine may have lacked the tools of precise scholarship, but his general approach was impeccably modern. None the less it is easy to see how Paine's readers often took offence at many of his formulations if not his entire enterprise. Paine retained a respectful tone when referring to Christ's own morality and aims. But he was less circumspect about much else. Phrases like 'the monstrous idea of a Son of God begotten by a ghost on the body of a virgin' were not calculated to allay the sensibilities of non-deistical readers. But directness, not diplomacy, was always Paine's strength.[16]

Paine's own theology in *The Age of Reason* was clearly deistic rather than millenarian, and confirms the view that his 'millennium' was explicitly political and economic rather than theological in orientation. Though his concerns here were primarily negative and centred on the destruction of biblical revelation, his positive religious ideal was not future-oriented, and depended upon no direct divine intervention at all. Instead, Paine stated simply that it was possible to lead a moral life while believing that the revelation of God was nature and nothing else. This aim he also sought to put into practice. In early 1797 he founded with a few others the Church of Theophilanthropy in Paris. This institution, devoted to the love of both God and man, flourished for at least a year, during which time its members sang hymns and discussed ethics, theology and philosophy, and established a small library to popularize its principles. It celebrated only four annual festivals, to St Vincent de Paul, Washington (his sins now apparently partially forgiven), Socrates and Rousseau. Paine also planned to introduce the teaching of natural science to artisans and others in conjunction with theology, that all might not only improve their own occupational knowledge, but as well 'be led to see the hand of God in all things', since science was the best proof of God's existence.[17]

Clearly Paine sought to create a civil religion, and the theological principles of *The Age of Reason* certainly corresponded to some degree to the democratic ideals outlined in the *Rights of Man*. But they can also be understood as being even more individualistic in so far as Paine here abandoned any intermediary between man and God and denied virtually any role to a priesthood, while in his politics representation and authority played a more substantial role. A closer parallel is with Paine's internationalism. Paine's deism upheld no narrow church and his conception of the internationally minded republic was deeply indebted to his notion of the Christian brotherhood of mankind, now in the form of a deist brotherhood of observers of nature. To Paine the destruction of revelation did not imply lessening the love of one's neighbour, but a refashioning of the sources of obligation which made such duties necessary. Mutual respect and charity were inscribed in the system of the universe. The priests would answer otherwise. But that was to be expected.

The reception of *The Age of Reason*

Though his critics fulminated that there was 'not one of Paine's objections in his *Age of Reason* that has not been refuted long ago', the work proved to be highly controversial, and aroused more than a few tempers (a fight broke out on the Greenwich-London stage between a gentleman's servant and a recruiting sergeant as to whether Paine was a deist or, as the latter thought, an atheist, which was solved only when the two alighted on the road to settle matters; the sergeant won).[18] In assessing more calmly such reactions we must principally distinguish between the responses of liberal Dissenters, of more deistic radicals and of Paine's opponents. For, far more than with respect to his political writings, the relation between the first two of these groups was to be marred by the publication of *The Age of Reason*. Many Dissenting radicals were simply unable to follow Paine into deism and most felt that their own positions were threatened by his identification of political with religious extremism. A few others, however, argued that this was the only consistent position one could adopt.

The intense reaction to *The Age of Reason* was not simply to its deism. Many of Paine's biblical criticisms were hardly strikingly original, though, for example, he did present the contradictions between the science of astronomy and the Christian scheme more clearly than earlier deists. Instead *The Age of Reason* was 'the most daring and unmasked attack that had ever yet been made on revelation', as one writer put it. None the less its importance often eludes modern readers because it is difficult for us to recapture the mental world of a society where religion remained vital to the daily lives of much of the population. Moreover, Paine's book was probably shocking and provocative even for lapsed Christians who identified themselves only with a few vague doctrines. In addition, much of the hostile reaction to the text also had a secular rationale, as did Paine's original intention in levelling his heavy artillery against the church. For religion, clerics in particular were apt to claim, was amongst the chief pillars of the social order, and an essential element in the loyalty of the labouring classes. 'Church and King' collectively, in fact, were the 'establishment'. Some infidelity no doubt already existed amongst the poor. But *The Age of Reason* gave it a vast new infusion of confidence and consequently seriously threatened the old order. It is thus easy to agree with a Scottish minister, the Rev. G. Bennet, that 'the mischief arising from the spreading of such a pernicious publication was infinitely greater than any that could spring from limited suffrage and septennial parliaments'. In some larger Scottish manufacturing towns, he was horrified to learn, Bibles had actually been burned in reaction to Paine's doctrines. And it circulated in Ireland, where there were a great many Bibles to burn, and not a few citizens who would gladly have added the odd English minister to the pyre.[19]

Contemporaries thus implied that Paine's assault was taken so seriously for two reasons. First, the church was a vital support to the government and the social order, indeed its primary moral underpinning. God sanctioned a 'principle of subordination and dependence ... established through all nature' and frowned upon those who expressed 'a discontent of that state which he has allotted to us'. The established government, some claimed, was 'for the time, of divine authority, by whatever method the power hath been acquired, and whatever the conduct of the rulers may be'. Many opponents of *The Age of Reason* thus conceded with Paine that a deep connection existed between theology and politics by accusing his disciples of aiming to 'first destroy Christianity, and then the British Constitution will fall of course'.[20]

The second rationale went a step further to argue that society would collapse if Paine's doctrines were taken seriously because the basis would have been removed for moral obligation generally, not merely political loyalty. A Liverpool loyalist, for example, accused the readers of *The Age of Reason* of being 'Tired of the galling yoke of moral obligation' and wanting to 'throw off all restraint, and boldly rush into the wilds of eccentricity'. A Baptist minister writing at the turn of the century similarly claimed that

> the sceptical or irreligious system subverts the whole foundation of morals. It may be assumed as a maxim, that no person can be required to act contrary to his greatest good, or his highest interest ... As the present world, upon sceptical principles, is the only place of recompense, whenever the practice of virtue fails to promise the greatest sum of present good ... every motive to virtuous conduct is superseded ... Virtue on these principles, being in numberless instances at war with self-preservation, never can or ought to become a fixed habit of mind ... Rewards and punishments awarded by omnipotent power, afford a palpable and pressing motive, which can never be neglected without renouncing the character of a rational creature.

Another account, rejecting in particular Priestley's denial of any clear connection between church and state, argued that Burke was 'certainly right in asserting that religion is the basis of civil society ... it is asked will religion feed or cloath us? we say it ultimately does both, for without it we cannot have law, and without law we may be deprived of both ... the hinge on which all law turns ... is lent by religion; Property, Safety, Life, depend on that sacred obligation, called an oath: the divine laws form the ground-work and sources of the human, on that solid foundation, the noble edifice is raised; they receive a degree of veneration and awful respect from this connection that no human powers could give them'. Clerics in particular were apt to insist that religion thus played a vital restraining role and required commensurate support from government. A minister at Gray's Inn declared that

> This fatal spirit of independence and pride of intellect, evidently proceeds, and is directly deducible, from ... the spirit of irreligion. For when we have accustomed ourselves to presume entirely upon the sufficiency of our own understanding, to suppose ourselves equal to the comprehension of universal nature, to disdain the submission of our mind to the mysterious calculations of natural, much more revealed religion ... is it surprising, that we should reject all submission to the authority of other men ...?[21]

Yet as we have seen, Paine would not have disagreed with many of these statements, providing they were applied to true and rational religion and not merely a state church. But this was not a point his opponents could concede. Given their depth of feeling, it is not surprising that attacks on Paine's ideas soon poured from the presses. Amongst the approximately fifty (almost entirely hostile) responses to *The Age of Reason* between 1795 and 1799, the most important was Richard Watson, the Bishop of Llandaff's *An Apology for the Bible* (1796), itself written 'in a popular manner' for perusal by Paine's own readers, but conceding so much to Paine's arguments that Watson himself was accused of heterodoxy and passed over for promotion. None the less, the *Apology* provoked Paine to begin a third part of *The Age of Reason*, which was published in 1807, and where, among other things, Paine again emphasized his belief in a future life.[22] Watson acknowledged that what was objectionable about *The Age of Reason* was not Paine's views themselves, but 'the zeal with which you labour to disseminate your opinions, and ... the confidence with which you esteem them true'. But though it was widely distributed as an antidote to Paine, the *Apology* in fact gave greater currency to his ideas, which were extensively quoted in the text. Still, this did not help to turn the tide in Paine's favour. Other critics seized upon the publication of *The Age of Reason* as the ideal pretext for renewing their attacks and launching new pseudo-biographies of Paine, some of which now described him primarily as the 'Author of *The Age of Reason*'. In fact Paine could hardly have offered a more ideal opportunity to pounce upon the radicals just when they had begun to recover. Amongst others, the publication of *The Age of Reason* drew forth the formidable powers of Hannah More once again. Her *A Country Carpenter's Confession of Faith* (1794) delivered forth such jewels of incisive reasoning as the narrator's confession that as a poor man he could not understand how seeds became plants, but since they did, and he could not understand the Bible either, there was no reason to doubt its truth. William Cobbett, too, wrote a vitriolic attack on *The Age of Reason* describing it as 'revolting against God', while the conservative millenarian Joanna Southcott found time to lambast the third part of *The Age of Reason* as late as 1812. Various writers indicated and condemned the apparent connection between republicanism and deism, both of which seemed to be grounded on the idea of the uniformity and perfectibility of the human character. Predictably, perhaps, Paine was abused even more by purely religious writers than by his political opponents, 'Apostle of Beelzebub' and 'Agent of Lucifer' being merely two of the more polite descriptions of his origins and motives.[23]

More exacting critics focused upon several facets of Paine's heterodoxy. Many reviewed the biblical scholarship of the day and attacked Paine's notion of revelation. Some contended that a belief in revelation entailed upholding only the divine missions of Moses and Christ, and their proof by miracles, arguing that only the 'maddest enthusiasts' thought that the entire Bible was revelation. For others the entirety of the Scriptures were clearly the 'word of God', while some thought that 'revelation' meant primarily the means by which God communicated to everyone, not merely what was recorded in print. A number sought to illustrate the intellectual sources of *The Age of Reason*, tracing Paine's views to Hume, Bolingbroke and Hobbes. A few were flabbergasted that Paine refused to recognize sin, or to think that sin deserved any kind of punishment. Some first conceded that he did believe in God, but then affirmed that 'As to his religion, I suspect it to be downright Atheism; because, if God made no revelation to us, and has never discovered himself except by the powers of nature, it is impossible to know that any being, distinct from these powers, and the present system of nature, hath an existence'. But even if nature did demonstrate the wisdom and goodness of the Deity, various critics accounted reading a few verses of the Bible a far easier path to the same conclusion. Some, too, simply accused Paine of insincerity, given his apparently repeated acknowledgement of the divinity of the Scriptures in *Common Sense*, and of inconsistency in his use of the Bible, since he, for example, relied upon it to establish the character of Christ.[24]

Well aware of the limits of mere criticism, the government, supported by the evangelical Society for the Suppression of Vice, decided to prosecute *The Age of Reason* as blasphemous in June 1797, commencing with one Thomas Williams, who received a year's hard labour for selling the work. Williams's trial established that while the circulation of the first part had been quite limited, the second had generated far greater interest. (The Bishop of London later claimed that *The Age of Reason* even circulated among miners in Cornwall.) Its influence was all the greater given the reputation of Paine's political works, admitted the prosecutor, Paine's former defender Thomas Erskine, whose views were soon widely reprinted. Erskine, too, pointed to the centrality of Christianity to the social order generally. 'The religious and moral sense of the people of Great Britain' he saw as 'the great anchor, which alone can hold the vessel of the state amidst the storms which agitate the world'. It was not possible for the common people to be 'set free from all the charities of Christianity' with 'no other sense of God's existence, than was to be collected from Mr. Paine's observation of nature, which the mass of mankind have no leisure to contemplate; which promises no future rewards to animate the good in the glorious pursuit of human happiness, nor punishments to deter the wicked from destroying it even in its birth'. Without the threat of hell and hope of heaven, thus, 'morality' – here synonymous with public order and existing inequalities – would disappear.[25]

Anglican and official reaction of this type was to be expected. It soon became clear, however, that the Dissenters were also embarrassed by *The Age of Reason*, for Paine's theological views now made it still more difficult to support his politics. None the less one of the leading Dissenting periodicals, the *Analytical Review*, acknowledged that Paine's right to challenge revelation could not be contested. 'Truth and good are one', it insisted, and if massive sections of the biblical edifice fell before his guns, the purity of the human spirit would remain unharmed, and would even be enhanced. Nor was Paine's defence of natural religion intrinsically objectionable to Rational Dissenters in particular. None the less the latter included amongst themselves many of the finest biblical scholars of the period. These could not help but judge, as the *Analytical Review* did, that Paine appeared 'ill qualified to do justice to the subject of revelation from his want of erudition'. They warned, too, that while Paine opposed the doctrines of the Fall of Man and of the Trinity, so did other Christians who were still 'desirous of preserving the main trunk' of their religion. More technically, Paine was faulted, for example, for his comparison of the Book of Job and the Psalms with texts composed both before and after each, for his ridiculing the titles of the 'greater' and 'lesser' prophets as if the strength of their prophecy was somehow related to this, rather than the size of their books, and for assailing the term 'New Testament' when, it was asserted, 'New Covenant' was in fact a superior translation of the title.[26]

Paine must have regretted the critical response of several of the most respected radical Dissenters even more. He rarely drew any parallel between his own theology and that of the Unitarians. But he cannot but have been sorry that Joseph Priestley, exiled in Pennsylvania, assailed the 'extraordinary impression that has been made, especially in America' by *The Age of Reason*, and found the book 'full of palpable mistakes with respect to notorious facts, or ... reasoning manifestly inconclusive'. Another liberal Dissenter, Gilbert Wakefield, wrote what the Dissenters generally agreed was the most balanced and successful attempt to refute Paine's work (and was in turn attacked as too heterodox). He condemned Paine's 'superficial and declamatory manner of treating this subject and his egregious deficiency even in the elements of Biblical knowledge', noting that this contemptibly vulgar approach had 'compelled some of his most zealous admirers to admit that he had now stepped over his province'. (Paine replied that Wakefield's talents 'would be best employed in teaching men to preserve their liberties exclusively, – leaving to that God who made their immortal souls the care of their eternal welfare'.) The leading Cambridge Dissenting radical and journalist Benjamin Flower, a former SCI member, also dismissed the work as 'Paine's trash'. Amongst the Irish radicals, too, a similar reaction was evident. The Irish Protestant minister and Jacobin William Jackson even passed the time in solitary confinement awaiting his Dublin sedition trial combating the 'ignorance and misrepresentation' of *The Age of Reason*, and was himself allowed only the Bible with which to do so.[27]

Religion thus served as another wedge driven between the ranks of the more moderate reformers and the Painites. Even those who shared republican beliefs could now battle over theological issues. None the less *The Age of Reason* did find substantial support. The more deistical reformers were of course exceedingly pleased at its publication. Joel Barlow wrote to a friend that he rejoiced 'at the progress of Good Sense over the damnable imposture of Christian mummery'. The Scottish deist George Mackenzie MacAulay applauded Paine's 'plain simple principle' of worshipping 'one Superintending Being, whose powers and existence nothing that is Human can conceive' and his rejection of 'all doctrines resulting from the Imagination of Man'. At Liverpool 'Paine's *Age of Reason* made its appearance: And the spirit of enquiry being once set afloat it met with a welcome reception', as a spy put it, with a group of atheists (predominantly United Englishmen) convening in the Jesus Christ Club to discuss its merits. Some reformers, however, simply ignored the text, or became interested only when it was prosecuted. Major John Cartwright, for example, did not read *The Age of Reason* until 1819, when Paine's disciple Richard Carlile was tried, writing that he had not done so earlier because 'I conceived that he was handling a subject he did not understand', but now acquiring it 'that I may better comprehend the views of our political saints'.[28]

There is thus no doubt of the wide circulation of *The Age of Reason* in the mid- and late 1790s, particularly among the London working classes. As we have seen, religion in late 1795 forced the splitting of the London Corresponding Society, with six entire divisions of Methodists, and as many as several hundred sympathizers, or perhaps a fifth of the membership, seceding when the executive refused to oust deists and atheists from the organization.[29] The conservative William Hamilton Reid, who detected an atheistical conspiracy behind every liberty tree, later claimed that the 'early predilection' of the London Corresponding Society for *The Age of Reason* 'made infidelity as familiar as possible with the lower orders'. Even LCS debates about the book, in which 'as zeal superseded judgement ... the epithets d-m-d fool, and d-m-d Christian, ultimately prevailed', Reid thought had resulted in the publication of 2,000 copies of a cheap edition of *The Age of Reason* (this was in fact initiated by Francis Place, and a much larger edition soon sold which some termed the 'New Holy Bible'). Reid also claimed, however, that 'by adding Deism to its politics' the LCS 'engendered the seeds of its own destruction', with many of its orators 'as if they were aware of going too far, after depreciating the character of the Saviour, in their harangues [God seems to have been christened 'Mr

Humbug'], used frequently to add the ridiculous assertion, that they believed Jesus Christ was a good republican'.[30] Reid's is of course a very biased account. None the less it is surprising how few voices were raised in Paine's defence outside of the radical press. One Thomas Dutton considered that his notion of redemption was just and probably derived from his father's Quaker instruction, and fended off the arguments of Priestley and Wakefield. Some of *The Age of Reason*'s opponents also maintained that despite Paine's errors, the Quakers still exemplified the model of a new form of society. Otherwise Paine found little support indeed. By 1800 a great many recalcitrant Jacobins were being led back into the fold. Repentance became far more commonplace and anti-Jacobins gloried in the claim that some radicals had been converted to Paine's theology, committed various crimes under its influence and then seen the error of their ways (in the case of the Spithead naval mutineers, on the scaffold).[31]

In America *The Age of Reason* became 'the axis about which deist thought' rotated, as one historian has put it. Eight American editions appeared in 1794, seven the following year and two in 1796. In Philadelphia thousands of copies were sold at auctions for a mere cent and a half each, 'whereby children, servants, and the lowest people, had been tempted to purchase'. Here, as in Britain, deism had been confined previously to the upper classes. Now, with Volney's *Ruins* (1791) and the works of the American Elihu Palmer, it reached far larger numbers. 'The strokes of his pen are sufficient to convert many to any falsehood he wishes them to believe', lamented one critic. In Vermont, typically, *The Age of Reason* was 'greedily received'. In fact a deist and French revolutionary vogue seized cottages as well as universities through the late 1790s. At Yale students called one another 'Voltaire', 'd'Alembert' and 'Rousseau', while at Harvard the authorities finally felt compelled in 1796 to issue each student with a copy of Watson's *Apology*. Of the Dartmouth class of 1799 only one student was said to be willing to admit publicly to being a Christian. Earlier rationalist clubs like the Universal Society of Philadelphia were rejuvenated, while new organizations like the Deistical Society, formed in New York in 1796, extended Paine's principles. Baltimore, Philadelphia, Newburgh and other towns had Theophilanthropic Societies, but deistical speculation spread eastwards to the Ohio Valley as well as southwards along the Atlantic seaboard. Freemasonry, which contained a deist element, also grew in popularity throughout this period. This wave of infidelity evidently reached a peak around 1797–1800. At this point, heralded by a series of clerical assaults upon Paine (there were at least fifteen responses during this period), it was met by a fervent movement of religious revivalism which peaked in Kentucky and Tennessee in 1801. The Awakening vigorously set upon Paine's ideas from press and pulpit and deism was virtually eclipsed until its revival after 1820 by Robert Owen and his followers, who were soon linked to Paine's views.[32]

Had Paine lost his head in 1794 he might have kept his reputation, for the latter was ruined by *The Age of Reason*, as well as, in America, his simultaneous attack on Washington. As one historian put it in 1851, 'Had he published or said nothing against that religion which is held sacred by the great mass of our nation he would have remained as he was at first – one of the most popular political men of that time.' (A contemporary put the same sentiment in a premature epitaph: 'Here lies Tom Paine, who wrote in liberty's defense / And in his "Age of Reason" lost his "Common Sense".') American critics were thus more prone to regret that 'one who has written so well on several political points, should not have thought with more justice on religion', and even toasted him proclaiming, 'May his *Rights of Man* be handed down to our latest posterity; but may his *Age of Reason* never live to see the rising generation'. Paine had been of great service during the Revolution, one remarked, but he served now only to disseminate 'VICE and FOLLY, IGNORANCE and IMPERTINENCE'. At least one critic even feared that every syllable of Paine's work evidenced 'the signature of Satan'. The American clergy united in accusing him of inconsistency, poor scholarship and hatred of Christianity. How, for example, asked a Rhode Island Congregationalist minister, could Paine accept the biblical account of the character of Christ and reject most of its particulars concerning his life? Could not 'revelation' be understood as inspiration rather than immediate divine disclosure (which was itself a considerable concession) and the Old and New Testaments in this sense be the word of God? Without such a belief, most contended, morality, prosperity and happiness were impossible. 'Christianity proceeding from God must stand', thundered an Alexandria Presbyterian, prophesying a fate similar to Sodom and Gomorrah if unbelief prevailed in America, and defending the Mosaic account of the Creation as 'so natural and even necessary, that I cannot conceive how it could have been otherwise'. A Newark clergyman mocked Paine's deism as even less sophisticated and compelling than the earlier systems of, for example, Lord Herbert of Cherbury. But he also devoted 650 pages to Paine's arguments and, while willing to concede that 'there is a *possibility* ancient records may be corrupted', he none the less insisted upon the validity of the accounts of revelation given in the Bible and accused Paine of inconsistency for admitting that revelation could exist at all. Other accounts also denied that the Bible defended equality.[33] By 1805, however, Paine's critics were pleased to report that they had now passed through 'a period of no small importance ... ostentatiously indeed denominated the Age of Reason'. Paine had assumed that reason was unlimited, and had failed to see that 'man was *meant to be left in ignorance*' about many aspects of existence.[34] Sobriety had supplanted the delirium of revolutionary intoxication. None the less these controversies continued long into the nineteenth century in America. Abraham Lincoln evidently read *The Age of Reason* and wrote a similar commentary on the Bible which a friend, with an eye to his political future, consigned to the flames for him. The poet Walt Whitman, too, studied *The Age of Reason* as a child and defended Paine publicly in 1877.

Conclusion

Paine's often hostile reception on his return to America in 1802 had, as we have seen, much to do with his religious views, as did his nineteenth-century reputation generally in both Britain and America. If the dissemination of his political principles was the foremost concern in Paine's mind, the publication of *The Age of Reason* was the greatest mistake in his career. But if Paine felt that his political principles could not survive without religious guidance, that atheism, in other words, undermined the rights of man, then Paine's course of action, tragic though it was, was virtually inevitable. Paine himself was surprised by popular revulsion at the principles of *Age of Reason* and later, perhaps with some regret, told a fellow radical that he would not have published it if he had not thought it calculated to 'inspire mankind with a more exalted idea of the Supreme Architect of the Universe, and to put an end to villainous imposture'. Very few, alas, drew such a conclusion.[35] None the less *The Age of Reason* remains one of the few late eighteenth-century tracts on religious controversy still read 200 years later. And while Christian countries no longer rise to theological debate as they once did, Paine's deism probably remains the practical Christianity of many, even if it is still shared by few in theory.

Notes to Chapter 7: *The Age of Reason*

1 Paine used the phrase, 'the age of reason', as early as 1791 (1945, Vol. 2, p. 518).
2 T. Roosevelt (1898), p. 289; *Copies* (1798), p. 25.
3 On religious unbelief see J. Redwood (1976). Its relation to seventeenth century deism and Masonry is best examined in M. Jacob (1981). For America see in particular H. Morais (1934).
4 *Deism Fairly Stated* (1746), p. 95.
5 *Two Letters from a Deist* (1730), p. 24; R. Hall (1800), pp. 3–4; *The Deist Confuted* (1734), pp. 1–2.

6 W. Reid (1800), pp. 87–91. See G. Hindmarsh (1979). Much of the controversy about Paine's early religious practices revolves around the question of the authorship of the so-called 'Forester' articles in the *Sussex Weekly Advertiser* in 1772–3. See G. Spater (1982) for the case against Paine's authorship.

7 On the text see F. Prochaska (1972), M. Williams (1975 and 1976), R. Smith (1977) and A. Ayer (1988), pp. 141–56.

8 Paine (1945), Vol. 2, p. 1436. On the French edition see R. Gimbel (1956b).

9 Paine (1945), Vol. 1, pp. 463–4.

10 Paine (1945), Vol. 1, pp. 464–5.

11 Paine (1945), Vol. 1, pp. 465–72.

12 Paine (1945), Vol. 1, pp. 472–82.

13 Paine (1945), Vol. 1, pp. 482–512.

14 Paine (1945), Vol. 1, pp. 514–24.

15 Paine (1945), Vol. 1, pp. 515–602.

16 Paine (1945), Vol. 1, p. 553.

17 Paine (1945), Vol. 2, pp. 744–56.

18 E. Nares (1805), p. 85; *Sheffield Iris*, no. 14 (3 October 1794), p. 3.

19 G. Bennet (1796), pp. 88–90; R. Jacob (1937), pp. 189–90. For a typical defence of the worth of church to state see the Buckingham JP and Rev. D. Scurlock's tract (1792). On popular infidelity see M. Williams (1976), but also F. Prochaska (1972), who argues its strength has been exaggerated. On the reception of *The Age of Reason* see also D. Roper (1978), pp. 203–9.

20 J. Scott (1793), p. 9; T. Broughton (1820), p. 20; T. Scott (1792), p. 5. See generally W. Stafford (1982).

21 R. Hall (1800), pp. 10–11; [W. Odell] (1792), p. 9; A. Binns (1796), p. 19; W. King (1793), pp. 26–7.

22 See Paine (1945), Vol. 2, pp. 848–93.

23 R. Watson (1796), p. 2; *Extracts* (n.d.); [H. More] (1794), p. 11; W. Cobbett (n.d.), p. 1; J. Southcott (1812); *Christianity the Only True Theology* (n.d.), p. 7; J. Coward (1796), p. 16; T. Scott (1796), p. 113.

24 T. Scott (1796), pp. 104–11; T. Hincks (1796), p. 111; V. Knox (1795), Vol. 1, p. 51; J. Estlin (1796), p. 12; S. Drew (1820), p. 67; *The Age of Infidelity* (1796), p. 138; J. Tytler (1797), p. 54 (which plagiarizes from J. Auchincloss, 1796, p. 35); M. Nash (1794), p. 60.

25 W. Reid (1800), p. 29; F. Place (1972), pp. 159–60; Add. MS. 35143 f. 34; T. Howell (1819), Vol. 26, cols 653, 668 and generally 653–720. Erskine was accused of hypocrisy by Williams's counsel (J. Martin, 1797, pp. 28–9). Paine also responded to Erskine (1945, Vol. 2, pp. 728–48).

26 *Analytical Review*, Vol. 19 (1794), pp. 159–70.

27 J. Priestley (1796), pp. 65–6; G. Wakefield (1795), p. 11; *Memoirs of Wakefield* (1804), Vol. 2, p. 19; Paine (1945), Vol. 2, pp. 1382–3; J. Priestley (1794), p. 28; M. Nash (1794), p. 2; M. Smith (1979), p. 91; W. Jackson (1795), pp. 1, 92.

28 J. Woodress (1958), p. 218; W. Mackenzie (1916), p. 170; PC1/44/A161; F. Cartwright (1826), Vol. 2, p. 156.

29 PC1/23/A38.

30 D. Miles (1988), pp. 32–4; W. Reid (1800), pp. 3, 5–9, 31; Add. MS. 35143 fols 34–52; PC1/23/A38. Reid also noted that the LCS often proposed the Quakers 'as a model to other Christian denominations' (p. 35).

31 T. Dutton (1795), pp. 8, 123; J. Bonsell (1798), pp. 12–13; D. Simpson (1802), p. vi; W. Grisenthwaite (1822).

32 H. Morais (1934), p. 120 and, generally, pp. 120–78; E. Boudinot (1801), p. xx; G. Nash (1965), pp. 402–3; G. Koch (1933), pp. 130–46, and J. Turner (1985), pp. 1–113; *Divine Oracles* (1797), p. 4; T. Broughton (1820), p. 247. Bibliographical details of American responses to *The Age of Reason* are given in A. Morse (1909), pp. 217–19. Also useful is J. Fowles (1797). The reaction of Virginia clerics to the text is discussed in J. Smylie (1973). Two British responses are analysed in R. Popkin (1987).
33 L. Judson (1851), p. 461; D. Nelson (1800), p. 61; F. Sheldon (1859), p. 14; U. Ogden (1795), Vol. 1, p. 14; W. Patten (1795), pp. vii, 22, 46, 105; J. Muir (1795), pp. v, 22–3, 143–64; U. Ogden (1795), Vol. 1, pp. 57, 319–21; S. Stilwell (1794), pp. 5–6.
34 E. Nares (1805), pp. 17, 23.
35 H. Yorke (1804), Vol. 2, p. 360.

8

Revolution in civilization: *Agrarian Justice* (1797)

While *The Age of Reason* caused a great public outcry, *Agrarian Justice* is the most neglected of Paine's chief works. Even major studies of Paine have usually paid it little heed; Aldridge, for example, cursorily dismisses the pamphlet as 'a proposal for an inheritance tax'. Closer examinations have seen its significance as lying in Paine's inclination towards communal ownership in his later years, a view which this chapter shows to be false, and as indicating Paine's growing interest in religion in the mid-1790s, which is more plausible. It has also been claimed that *Agrarian Justice* opened the way to considerable state intervention in its defence of the poor, though this tends to ignore a similar trend in the *Rights of Man*, Part Two.[1] A more careful study of the work, however, shows that its significance lies primarily in Paine's articulation of several new arguments for restricting private property, which thereby refined considerably his theories of both progress and property rights and linked the two together. For Paine by 1796 had lost much of his earlier bland commercial optimism and had come to believe that 'old countries' like Britain endemically created a class of poor who required and had a right to public support. This was to be met by redistributing existing tax revenues and taxing landed estates. But *Agrarian Justice* made far more sweeping claims on behalf of the poor to what Paine now argued was common wealth, particularly all improvements on landed property, than had the *Rights of Man*. Moreover, Paine now saw poverty as originating partly in inadequate wages and economic oppression, and not merely in taxation. This was an extremely important shift in his ideas of commerce, though some of his supporting arguments also exposed inconsistencies in Paine's thinking, particularly in his use of the natural law tradition.

Central to *Agrarian Justice*, in fact, was Paine's attempt to revive natural law teaching about the original community of property ordained by God. Here a crucial distinction, never before discussed by Paine, was between 'natural property', or that given us by the maker of the universe, 'such as the earth, air, water', and 'artificial property' created by mankind. Paine now maintained that man had a 'natural birthright' in the former which was still recognized among primitive societies like the North American Indian tribes. But since no one could return to this state from civilization – despite the accusations of many opponents of the *Rights of Man* – Paine proposed that landowners should pay both a lump sum and an annuity to all deprived of their birthright. A large portion of his new plan to tax landed property now appeared to hinge upon conceding this right.

This argument was more traditional, but less innocent, than it appears. Why did a confirmed, proselytizing deist like Paine introduce divine intention into a statement about property rights? Paine had considerable faith in the providential governance of the natural and social worlds. But did he contradict or subvert his own theological beliefs, especially those expressed in *The Age of Reason*, by exploiting popular preconceptions about more specific mandates of God's will because more compelling arguments were unavailable?[2] It is suggested here that Paine recognized the weaknesses of a recourse of this type and introduced two further pillars to shore up his case: his 'principle of progress' (as it will be termed here) and a theory of 'social debt' by which the rich as stewards of God's bequest always owed part of their wealth to society. These addenda, however, were both secular, one referring to a historical state of nature where divine intentions were not at issue, the other to any advanced state of civilization. They help to establish Paine as an important transition figure in radical debates about property in this period in so far as the secularization of natural law discussions about God and the state of nature were central to the evolution of property theory in this period.

Agrarian Justice: natural jurisprudence secularized

The measures for alleviating poverty proposed in *Agrarian Justice* are often seen as an improved version of the scheme offered in the *Rights of Man*, which was to be paid for out of the redistribution of existing, excessive taxation and the institution of a plan of progressive taxation on land. No lengthy justification for these measures was offered in the *Rights of Man*, a general right to relief in old age being defended on the basis of taxes already paid. These reforms were aimed at undermining the aristocratic system and making the overall tax burden fairer. To this end, condemning large estates as 'a luxury at all times', Paine also distinguished between property justly earned and that for which little or no effort was exerted in order to justify new types of taxes, claiming that 'It would be impolitic to set bounds to property acquired by industry, and therefore it is right to place the prohibition [on maximum incomes from land] beyond the probable acquisition to which industry can extend; but there ought to be a limit to property, or the accumulation of it by bequest. It should pass in some other line. The rich in every nation have poor relations, and those very often near in consanguinity.' But the arguments urged for redistributing property in *Agrarian Justice* were quite unlike anything Paine had previously formulated, and can be interpreted as considerably more radical than the plans of the *Rights of Man*. Philip Foner even contended that in *Agrarian Justice* 'Paine supported the communistic aspects of Babeuf's theories' because these were 'correctly aimed at the removal of social inequalities in property'.[3] But it will be suggested here that this view mistakes Paine's arguments for his programme. Only by considering how each relates to his theory of commerce and the tradition of natural jurisprudence which underlay this, however, and finally how Paine's theology limited his ability to use this tradition, can the proposals in *Agrarian Justice* be fully illuminated.

Written in the winter of 1795–6, *Agrarian Justice* was published when Paine was provoked by the Bishop of Llandaff's sermon on 'The Wisdom and Goodness of God, in having made both Rich and Poor', which drove Paine to retort that 'It is wrong to say God made *rich* and *poor*; He made only male and female; and He gave them the earth for their inheritance.' Paine commenced by distinguishing between natural and artificial forms of property. Equality in the latter was 'impossible; for to distribute it equally it would be necessary that all should have contributed in the same proportion, which can never be the case; and this being the case, every individual would hold on to his own property, as his right share'. But of 'equality of natural property ... the subject of this little essay', Paine insisted that 'Every individual in the world is born therein with legitimate claims on a certain kind of property, or its equivalent'.[4]

In his initial justification of this right Paine's starting point differed clearly from the *Rights of Man*. Gone was what still remained of the simplistic confidence in the development of commerce of *Common Sense*. Instead, Paine asked

> whether that state that is proudly, perhaps erroneously, called civilization, has most promoted or most injured the general happiness of man ... On one side, he is dazzled by splendid appearances; on the other, he is shocked by extremes of wretchedness; both of which it has erected. The most affluent and the most miserable of the human race are to be found in the countries that are called civilized.

The great novel claim of *Agrarian Justice*, then, was that poverty not only resulted from but also increased with civilization. To condemn the existence of poverty amidst plenty Paine needed to adopt some critical perspective and could now have moved easily in the direction of Rousseau's defence of simplicity. He did in fact advert to 'the natural and primitive state of man'. The North American Indians, for example, lacked 'any of those spectacles of human misery which poverty and want present to our eyes in all the towns and streets of Europe'. But if poverty only blighted civilized nations, 'the natural state' lacked 'those advantages which flow from agriculture, arts, science and manufactures'. An Indian's life might be 'a continual holiday, compared with the poor of Europe', but it was 'abject' compared to that of the rich in modern societies. Moreover, it was 'never possible to go from the natural to the civilized state', if only because hunting, the principal occupation of the natural state, required ten times more land to support any population than did agriculture. What could be done, however, was 'to remedy the evils and preserve the benefits that have arisen to society by passing from the natural to that which is called the civilized state', by acknowledging 'the first principle of civilization … that the condition of every person born into the world, after a state of civilization commences, ought not to be worse than if he had been born before that period'. We will later see what consequences this principle, undeveloped at this point by Paine, would have for the argument of *Agrarian Justice*.[5]

Paine next introduced a new proposition which, it will be suggested, was highly contentious given his sceptical deism, though he clearly believed it served a vital function here. This was the view that 'the earth, in its natural, uncultivated state was, and ever would have continued to be, *the common property of the human race*. In that state every man would have been born to property. He would have been a joint life proprietor with the rest in the property of the soil, and in all its natural productions, vegetable and animal.' The purpose of invoking this mainstream natural law supposition was to create a new notion of property rights. Although, in a cultivated state, it was 'impossible to separate the improvement made by cultivation from the earth itself, upon which that improvement is made', it was 'the value of the improvement, only, and not the earth itself, that is individual property'. But how could the improvement but not more remain with the improver? Paine did not arbitrarily decide that at some point not industry but inheritance was the source of wealth, which was where the *Rights of Man* had left the matter hanging, or simply define 'a limit to property, or the accumulation of it by bequest'. Instead he introduced a new principle which justified a tax upon all landed wealth without having to solve the sticky issue of what portion of landed produce derived from effort and what from the land itself. By virtue of this new claim of rights, every landed proprietor owed the community a '*ground-rent*'.

Upon this, rather than the mere condemnation of excessive 'luxury', Paine's new taxation plan was to be based.[6]

But it was not merely the contention that the earth historically *had* once been common property that was central to Paine's case. Instead the original bequest of the whole earth to all by God at the Creation was crucial here. Not only did this argument seem far more securely rooted than Paine's attack upon primogeniture. It also allowed for the provision of rights claims which merely recognizing the existence of a state of nature did not permit (and in any case as we have seen there were considerable disagreements about what rights had existed then). Moreover, it lent Paine's case an important pedigree. As is well known, this argument was in fact central in natural jurisprudence theories of property. Its origins lay in the biblical account of the Creation, by which dominion over the earth was vested in the first man and woman and all their descendants. Most Christians, however, as well as the leading natural jurists Paine might have read, Grotius and Pufendorf, had concluded that God gave the earth to all in common only *negatively* (in the jurists' term), that is, to develop individually as the need arose (principally from the pressure of population). From this interpretation of the origins of mankind there emerged in the eighteenth century the four stages theory of the progress of property to which many Scottish theorists adhered. The latter agreed at the same time that God had not intended a *positive* community of property in which goods were to remain in common in perpetuity.[7] Only a few late eighteenth-century writers contested this conclusion, namely William Ogilvie, to some extent Robert Wallace, and Thomas Spence.[8]

Agrarian Justice also sought to invoke the authority of the biblical and jurisprudential accounts without reaching a communistical conclusion. By rejecting a more purely historical interpretation of common property and insisting that God meant all to share the earth, Paine promoted a *contemporary* right to property which a strictly stadial theory – in so far as it also historicized the possession of rights as well, leaving any original rights only in the first stages of society – had necessarily to reject, at least in this form. Natural law writers usually acknowledged the recurrent importance of those common property rights granted to all at the Creation in one important respect, arguing that the needy could invoke the right of charity from the rich when their survival was threatened, and could (some added) even steal in cases of dire necessity. Moreover, they also derived from this original inheritance the right in famine to have grain sold to them at the normal market price, again because God had ordained the subsistence of all. But Paine's conception of the application of original rights to the modern world was much wider than this. His distinction between agricultural improvements and landed property in fact relied upon

200

reconceptualizing divine intention. For if God's intentions had been other than Paine assumed, a labour theory of property might, for example, minimally be conceded which justified a right to some agricultural produce (at least to that possessed by slothful or absentee landlords), and other bases for such rights could also be offered, such as utility. But no *collective* right to any fixed portion of the proceeds of landed property, especially by the poor, could be *as firmly* grounded without a divine mandate. If it could not be proved that divine intention favoured a wide, later application of an original community of goods, the right of the poor to any of this inheritance would accordingly be gravely weakened, as it indeed was when Malthus dismissed any right to charity in his *Essay on Population* (1798). Paine's argument thus succeeded only because of a theologically based workmanship model. Man had not made the earth, and 'though he had a natural right to *occupy* it, he had no right to *locate as his property* in perpetuity any part of it; neither did the Creator of the earth open a land-office, from whence the first title-deeds should issue.'[9]

From this argument Paine now declared that since cultivation first began, a landed monopoly had dispossessed at least half the population from the soil. These should therefore be compensated by receiving £15 at age 21 (or about half a year's wage for an agricultural labourer), and £10 annually from the age of 50 onwards. This would bring about a 'revolution in the state of civilization' analogous to a republican revolution in government. None the less this was not an argument against private appropriation, but an attempt to ensure that as social wealth increased the rich would pay more into the fund supporting the poor, such that all would benefit by affluence. Yet Paine was apparently not satisfied with his case. For *Agrarian Justice* also put forward two further claims on behalf of the dispossessed, which to my mind indicate Paine's unease about enlisting theological support for his property doctrines (of which more below), and his sense that God's will failed to provide a sufficiently compelling ground for his taxation scheme.[10]

The first of these was what I will call Paine's 'principle of progress'. This alleged that 'no person ought to be in a worse condition when born under what is called a state of civilization, than he would have been had he been born in a state of nature', and consequently that in the case of a worse civilized condition, provision had to be made 'by subtracting from property a portion equal in value to the natural inheritance it has absorbed'. Why was this argument, again common to the jurists, required? Paine had already established, and repeated a few pages later even more bluntly, that land was 'the free gift of the Creator in common to the human race.'[11] If this ensured a natural right to some proportion of improvements to land, why introduce a further principle, for which no grounding was offered, and which is not clearly connected to the rest of Paine's argument? Was Paine insecurely aware that only divine intention, and not the natural jurisprudential account from which he had drawn these ideas (Grotius was a probable source), could support the kind of indisputable and extensive rights argument he was making here? Or did he consider no heavenly mandate precise enough to encompass the rising standard of living since the state of nature and think some supplementary revelation, so to speak, was necessary to establish that God intended not only that all were entitled to a subsistence appropriate to the state of nature, but also to standard-of-living increments?

Evidence of Paine's insecurity about his interpretation of divine intention can also be deduced from the fact that he proceeded to offer a second rationale for divided improvements on land. Now he suggested that while land was given by God to all,

> Personal property is the *effect of society*; and it is as impossible for an individual to acquire personal property without the aid of society, as it is for him to make the land originally. Separate an individual from society, and give him an island or continent to possess, and he cannot acquire personal property. He cannot be rich ... All accumulation, therefore, of personal property, beyond what a man's own hands produce, is derived to him by living in society; and he owes on every principle of justice, of gratitude, and of civilization, a part of that accumulation back again to society from whence the whole came.

As with Paine's principle of progress, this was a secular argument intended to augment the inadequacies of the theological account. But the notion of such a social debt also permitted *all* property, and not only the land, to be taxed or otherwise distributed for the common good. The funds by which the national debt was serviced, for example – which Paine wished to tax – here faced a burden of social responsibility, while they would be omitted from the scope of divine intention, which referred only to landed property (Genesis not having foreseen the development of financial speculation). So did wealth derived from manufacturing. The third of Paine's arguments in favour of redistribution in *Agrarian Justice* thus particularly permitted a claim of justice for wage-labour, which was impossible under the divine intention argument, which referred only to the landless, and difficult (because of the vagueness of the precept) under the principle of progress. This concern with wage-labour was indeed another dramatic development in Paine's theory of justice and proceeded from the realization that 'the accumulation of personal property is, in many instances, the effect of paying too little for the labor that produced it;

the consequence of which is that the working hand perishes in old age, and the employer abounds in affluence'.[12]

So far it has been suggested that Paine developed three arguments for redistributing property in *Agrarian Justice*. He began by accepting a broader interpretation of the consequences of God's grant of property to all than most jurists conceded. A contemporary right was extended to *all* without land, and not merely the needy, of a portion of any improvements on land in perpetuity, and not merely subsistence goods for a short period. To this were added two further arguments, one based on Paine's principle of progress, the other upon a general duty owed by the wealthy to society generally. These arguments gave Paine's claims a much greater scope than his deductions from divine intention allowed; indeed he might now have retitled the work 'Agrarian, Commercial and Manufacturing Justice'. Yet we have also indicated that Paine may have felt uncomfortable about using the divine argument to begin with and that this at least partly underlay his reinforced argument. Let us now examine more closely why there were good reasons, grounded in Paine's religious beliefs, for such unease.

Deism and the Creation

We have seen that Paine is better classified as a deist than a Quaker, despite his many affinities with the latter sect. But even within deism there was a fairly wide spectrum of belief, and the implications of seemingly minor shifts of theological doctrine for the social, political and economic theory of particular thinkers remains a difficult and largely unexplored topic. We must concentrate here, therefore, on the single question of whether Paine's deism contradicted his appeal to divine intention to bolster his account of property rights and duties.

As we saw in the last chapter, Paine's deism included a belief in one God and the hope 'for happiness beyond this life'. *The Age of Reason*, however, argued that Christianity was deeply corrupted by priestcraft and superstition. Hence claiming that the Bible was 'revelation' and the work of God was patently ridiculous. The account of Creation in Genesis, in particular, was merely 'an anonymous book of stories, fables and traditionary or invented absurdities, or of downright lies'. Paine again rejected its veracity in his response to Erskine's prosecution of *The Age of Reason* and Richard Watson's attack upon the book. Revelation lay in nature; only here was the universal message of God apparent. God was the 'first cause' of the Creation, but otherwise was knowable only through the scientific exploration of the natural world. And even here there were doubts, for Paine conceded at one point, somewhat inconsistently, that 'the power and wisdom He has manifested in the structure of the Creation that I behold is to me incomprehensible'.[13]

But the revelation of nature was hardly devoid of moral implications for mankind, for divine intention suffused nature in the form of Providence. Though he derided 'the God Providence' as one of the five Gods of Christian mythology, Paine as we have seen was deeply convinced that the Creator had 'organised the structure of the universe in the most advantageous manner for the benefit of man' and that there existed 'an Almighty Power that governs and regulates the whole'. Deism in fact consisted in 'contemplating the power, wisdom and benignity of the Deity in his works, and in endeavouring to imitate Him in everything moral, scientifical and mechanical'. Were the benevolent designs of the Deity not included in Paine's religion he would have been a mere worshipper of nature. As it was, his social theory owed much to his belief in Providence, which underpinned, for example, the optimistic elements of his theory of commerce. Elsewhere we find him praising 'the hand of Providence', describing God as 'an infinite protecting power' and implying that Providence intended America as an asylum for persecuted Europeans and had even helped to save Paine himself from the guillotine. He also paid homage to the 'unerring order and universal harmony reigning throughout the whole' of the works of creation, particularly as evidenced by the operations of the planetary system (and he remained a Newtonian, in 1797 invoking the rotation of the planets as proof of an external cause of the world).[14]

Given these views, several disturbing questions arise about Paine's use of divine intention to bolster the rights claims in *Agrarian Justice*. First, having so often discounted the biblical account of Creation, which stated that God bequeathed the earth to all in common, how could Paine have supposed that this occurred? It is unlikely that he altered his views on the Bible during this period, even if he became more 'religious' in some general sense as a consequence of the Terror in France. Defending *The Age of Reason* in 1797, in fact, Paine specifically mocked Genesis again, arguing that it inconsistently asserted that the first man and woman were given dominion over the whole earth, and then over only a single garden. How then could land be 'the free gift of the Creator in common to the human race', if no certain account of the will of the Creator remained? No matter how much faith Paine placed in Providence, and in the intention of the Deity to provide for mankind, we cannot reason specifically from this that 'Providence' offered mankind the earth in common at the Creation and, more importantly, in perpetuity.[15] Such rights could not be deduced from the motion of the planets. Nor did Paine's claims exactly coincide with jurisprudential accounts of property, though he followed their discussions of original communal property – which did not challenge the veracity of Genesis – in accepting an account of its dissolution which was broadly historical. Paine thus agreed that landed property arose with cultivation and existed neither 'in the first state of man, that of hunters', nor 'in the second state, that of shepherds', where property was only in flocks and herds. But as was suggested above, the four stages theory of the evolution of modes of subsistence did not *necessarily* entail the notion that any *common property rights* were given to all in a state of nature which could be invoked in later stages of society. Such rights were asserted by the jurists because they followed the Christian account of God's gift of the world to all in common. This formed the basis for soft or imperfect rights to charity and the most compelling claim to subsistence. What *Agrarian Justice* thus proposed was a variation upon this conception, substituting a general right to subsistence for the specific right of the necessitous, or, if we like, transmuting an imperfect right to charity into a perfect right to assistance. This paralleled his efforts in the *Rights of Man* and represents, as we have seen, a step of immense importance in the history of ideas of public welfare.[16] But embracing the theological assumptions and rights conclusions of natural jurisprudence was inadmissible in a purely secular and historical account, or one where no biblical account of Creation could be admitted (which for these purposes was but a step removed from secularity). An historical account or one which rejected Genesis might well acknowledge that community of property had once existed, but could not argue logically from this a case for contemporary rights to assistance.

One other way out of this problem would have been to claim that common property rights belonged to individuals as psychological properties, and not as the result of original divine behest. As we saw, Paine defined rights generally as 'contained within ourselves as individuals', and pertaining 'to man in right of his existence'. Rights inhered in individuals and were not derived from any conjectural state of nature or specifically granted by divine injunction, though this was their original source. But Paine's earlier definitions made no mention of property rights, either individual or collective, positive or negative. Nor is there reason to assume Paine altered this aspect of his definition of rights by arguing, for example, that all mankind were equally God's children and *as such* invested with this right.[17] Such rights, indeed, can hardly be construed as inhering in individuals, even if God intended the general well-being of all. And a more specific interpretation of God's intentions was not possible given Paine's view of the Bible.

Thus Paine either adopted the account in Genesis, by way of extending natural law arguments, and here violated his own principles of biblical interpretation, or he extended his notion of Providence unreasonably far. His theory of natural rights did not include such a conception of an original community of goods, nor did historical theories of the evolution of property derive these subsequent rights from this condition even where their initial existence was conceded. It is also unlikely that Paine, in reaction to the atheism or immorality around him, became increasingly Christian and therefore legitimately reintroduced a Christian account of the disposition of property at the Creation, for he continued to reject Genesis after 1796.

But while Paine lapsed into an inconsistent natural law defence of an original community of goods in order to strengthen his argument in favour of a limited redistribution of landed property, he did not believe that a positive community of goods was possible or accept the communistic implications of Babeuf's theories. Paine opposed Watson's blatantly apologetic defence of inequality, arguing that this tended only 'to encourage one part of mankind in insolence'. Between the existing system and complete equality of property were a vast number of possible social systems, however. Paine's new formulation of the question of property did not retreat as dramatically as might appear from his notions of free commerce as they were expressed between 1776 and 1791. But he had become more pessimistic about the natural tendency or even ability of 'civilization' to extinguish poverty on its own accord, at least in the short run. Put another way, he again reformulated his theory of property to account for the progress of commerce in 'old countries', where inequality of wealth posed a far greater problem than in America. *Agrarian Justice* thus strengthened Paine's argument in favour of redistribution without leaning towards a Spencean, Godwinian, or Babeuvian scheme for community of goods. A deduction from divine intention, as we saw above, was, however, merely one of three arguments for a more favourable distribution of property. The other arguments – deduced from Paine's theories of progress and of the social nature of accumulation – were considerably more secular and did not involve Paine in the kind of contradictions delineated above. Instead they demarcated a vital shift in thinking about rights of the poor. To this extent Paine's efforts represent an important transitional stage in the radical secularization of natural law arguments. For Paine's was a middle position between the Spenceans and others who unabashedly appealed to divine intention in support of positive community of goods, and the Owenite socialists of the early 1820s and later, who, both more historicist and more consistent in their deism, rejected completely appeals to the state of nature and founded property rights entirely upon labour, and community of goods upon its economic and moral advantages rather than its divine origins.[18]

The reception of *Agrarian Justice*

The complex implications of these positions were not of course recognized by most of Paine's readers. Very little in fact is known about popular reactions to *Agrarian Justice*, though the revival of radical activity in 1796–7 clearly aided its circulation. Several cheap editions appeared in Manchester and elsewhere, at any rate, and the LCS founder Thomas Hardy wrote to Paine that it was 'one of the best little things you ever wrote'. Segments of *Agrarian Justice* were reprinted by exiled radicals in America like Richard Lee, with a full edition appearing in Albany and another at Philadelphia in 1797. Ironically, it is possible that Paine unintentionally helped to guide some radicals towards the principle of community of goods. A letter found among the papers of the London reformer John Bone, later to become one of the first radicals to ally himself with the founder of British socialism, Robert Owen, praised *Agrarian Justice* and asked for fifty copies to be sent to Maidstone. Most reformers, however, probably accepted the view that Paine mainly sought to articulate or strengthen a right rather than to establish a new ideal of property. One radical, for example, argued that 'THE LAWS OF NATURE allow a community of interest in the fruits of the earth ... THE LAWS OF THE LAND, on the contrary say, every man shall be secured in the possession of that which he has *honestly* acquired', adding that 'Paine's *Agrarian Justice* best reconciles the difficulty arising from the extremes of natural and acquired right to the soil' by most clearly promoting the public good.[19]

Intellectually the most important response to *Agrarian Justice* (though its circulation was negligible) was Thomas Spence's *The Rights of Infants* (1797). Spence congratulated Paine on having finally 'thought fit to own, with the Psalmist, and with Mr. Locke, that "God hath given the earth to the children of men, given it to mankind in common" '. But having acknowledged the principle, Spence thought Paine had succumbed to expediency in refusing to confront its full implications. Instead of returning all land to communal ownership, Paine insisted only on the provision of 'poor, beggarly stipends' based upon 10 per cent of land values. But Spence saw no reason why the other 90 per cent should be retained by landowners, since all improvements of such property after the state of nature were owed principally to 'the labouring classes', who not only worked the land, but also constituted the major part of demand for food and hence also paid the costs of cultivation. Consequently reclaiming all land as common property was justifiable in Spence's view and Paine's efforts at compromise were dismissed.[20] This ideal remained an important undercurrent in British radicalism until at least the mid-nineteenth century, though it never surpassed Paine's ideas in influence.

Notes to Chapter 8: *Agrarian Justice*

1 A. Aldridge (1960), p. 241; M. Conway (1892), Vol. 2, p. 257; J. Eayrs (1952), p. 300.
2 Paine has been accused of inconsistently using biblical quotations while disbelieving they were inspired by God as early as *Common Sense* (A. Aldridge, 1984, p. 105).
3 Paine (1945), Vol. 1, pp. 434, 607.
4 Paine (1945), Vol. 1, pp. 606–7.
5 Paine (1945), Vol. 1, pp. 609–10, 619.
6 Paine (1945), Vol. 1, pp. 610–11. This has also been acknowledged by, e.g., G. Gallop (1983), pp. 229–30.
7 See, e.g., H. Grotius (1925), Vol. 2, p. 186, S. Pufendorf (1934), p. 537. On the development of the four stages theory of property see I. Hont (1987). See also my (1987), pp. 1–33.
8 W. Ogilvie (1781), p. 11 ('the earth having been given to mankind in common occupancy, each individual seems to have by nature a right to possess and cultivate an equal share'); R. Wallace (1761), pp. 38–40, 66; T. Spence (1793), pp. 21–2; Spence (1797).
9 Paine (1945), Vol. 1, p. 611. Compare J. Barlow (1792a), p. 88.
10 Paine (1945), Vol. 1, pp. 612–13, 621.
11 Paine (1945), Vol. 1, pp. 613–20. For an earlier treatment of this theme see V. Gibbens (1942), pp. 191–204.
12 Paine (1945), Vol. 1, p. 442.
13 Paine (1945), Vol. 1, pp. 464, 474, 493, 520, 529, 729–31, 765–71, 482–4, 486. See further pp. 794–6, 799–800.
14 Paine (1945), Vol. 1, pp. 498, 503, 599, 498, Vol. 2, pp. 90, 920, 305, 752, 816, 748–56, Vol. 1, p. 164.
15 Paine (1945), Vol. 2, p. 731. See J. Viner (1972), especially pp. 27–85, where Providence is never connected with such a right.
16 Paine (1945), Vol. 1, p. 611. See, e.g., H. Grotius (1925), pp. 188–9 for the origins of this view. No natural law thinkers prior to the eighteenth century were in this sense wholly secular. For Pufendorf, for example, the obligation inherent in the natural law could not be derived from human association, but required God (1934, pp. 216–17). Such assumptions were also clearly important to republicans: Sidney, for example, wrote of natural liberty that 'God only confers this right upon us, can deprive us of it' (1750, Vol. 2, p. 288).
17 Paine (1945), Vol. 1, p. 611, Vol. 2, p. 274, Vol. 1, pp. 275–6.
18 See my (1987), pp. 30–32.
19 Add. MS. 27808 fols 72–3; R. Twomey (1974), p. 97; *Report of the Committee* (1799), p. 53; *The British Crisis* (1797), p. 39. An important radical text which probably took Paine's discussion as its point of departure was by the London doctor Charles Hall (1805).
20 T. Spence (1982), pp. 46–53. There is no evidence that Spence's works circulated much outside of London and even in the LCS they do not seem to have been widely read.

Conclusion
Political Saint:
The Legend of
Thomas Paine

Paine's reputation

The dawn of the new century found British radicalism in virtual eclipse. But though repression in the 1790s forced hundreds of reformers to emigrate, Britain's loss was America's gain, for the Painites remained politically active in the new world, assisting in the defeat of Federalism and victory of the more republican views of Jefferson (whom they supported to a man) in 1800. Over the next decades they also helped to popularize that ideal of commercial republicanism in which considerable social egalitarianism coexisted harmoniously with commerce and industry.[1] The early American labour movement thus did not soon forget Paine and radical artisan organizations like Tammany Hall in New York celebrated his birthday well into the nineteenth century. But for the wider public, Paine became a pariah because of his religious principles. When a new edition of Joel Barlow's great poem *The Columbiad* omitted any mention of Paine, T. J. Wooler explained that *'Thomas Paine* was so unpopular in *America*, on account of his theological writings, that the mention of him would have hindered the sale of the book'. Paine thus already had two distinct reputations, and when in 1803 he was reported to be about to visit New England one observer hence wrote that 'The name is enough. Every person has ideas of him. Some respect his genius and dread the man. Some reverence his political, while they hate his religious, opinions. Some love the man, but not his private manners. Indeed he has done nothing which has not extremes in it. He never appears but we love and hate him. He is as great a paradox as ever appeared in human nature.'[2]

In Britain Paine cast a long shadow over the radical movement. His doctrines clearly suffered by the decline of France under Napoleon into what the *Cambridge Intelligencer*, welcoming the new century, termed 'complete DESPOTISM'. For one conclusion many drew from this development was that 'the principles of the last revolution must be renounced, the rights of the people must not be at the mercy of every villain, who, if he possesses abilities, may watch his opportunity, and by the sword overturn one Constitution, to place himself at the head of another'. When the revival of the reform movement began in the early years of the new century, many Painites were no longer active, or had grown more cautious, and the ideology and strategy of the 1790s were less in evidence. The central figures now, as before 1792, were Whiggish reformers like Sir Francis Burdett, to whom Paine's appeal and tactics were anathema. Burdett thus did not emphasize natural rights, but historic liberties and the costs of government and inadequate state of the representation. To Burdett the reformers wanted *no speculative plans, no new systems or novelties of any kind; we only want to be put back again in the situation that the country was formerly placed with respect to its rights*. The only danger in reform, one of his followers added, was 'in its being the work of a party, the Jacobins ... if it is espoused by the middle and higher ranks, it can be injurious to none; a limited monarchy is the best practical form of government, and this we should take care to preserve; a republic will never thrive in Britain'. Another moderate reflected that Paine had been 'a man of strong sense, but of no reading, not even on political subjects' because he thought an original contract was necessary to grant rights and had asserted that Britain had no constitution. The radical leader Henry Hunt also deprecated the republication of Paine's works. But respectable reformers could not entirely ignore Paine, and indeed still used his name when it was of value. Burdett himself, referring to his own imprisonment, dismissed 'the BILL OF RIGHTS', noting that 'Well might Paine call it the Bill of Wrongs'.[3]

After Waterloo the reform movement expanded rapidly, and soon the 'old Jacks', as the Painites came to be called, had followers of their own. The new movement mainly comprised 'the lowest orders of the people, that is to say, operative tradesmen and labourers', who had been Paine's main readers. By 1817 Paine's name was once again on the lips of every working class radical and his enemies sought to blacken leading reformers like W. T. Sherwin and Richard Carlile by describing them as the 'avowed and genuine followers of Thomas Paine' and associating them with his theology. Radical journalists like Sherwin reprinted the *Rights of Man* in instalments and insisted that Paine was 'the greatest political reasoner that ever existed'. Other of Paine's works, notably *The Decline and Fall of the English System of Finance*, were also republished by his followers, with the Spencean Thomas Evans arguing in 1819 that all its prophecies had come true.[4] Again radicals began to point insistently at the United States, arguing that its success wholly vindicated Paine's opposition to monarchy and, as the journalist T. J. Wooler put it, both 'the fallacy of the European system of policy' and the inadequacies of classical republicanism. Most influential of all was Paine's great new champion, the apostate loyalist William Cobbett.

Though his own critics lost little time in reprinting his earlier views as *Cobbett's Opinion of Tom Paine*, Cobbett by 1815 had become an immensely popular critic of pensions, placemen, 'Old Corruption' and 'The Thing' generally. But he also had considerable differences with Paine, seeking more to restore an idyllic agricultural past than to create a commercial republic and opposing both republicanism and cosmopolitanism in favour of a limited monarchy governing a fervently patriotic population. The pattern was thus set for Paine's post-war disciples, who took from the master what they deemed useful and set aside the rest.[5]

This process of adaptation was integral to the creation of the mythical Paine, for Paine the symbol had many uses a precise reading of his works might fail to furnish. Constructing the Paine legend had several stages. Highly important amongst these was the celebration of Paine's birthday, 29 January, which first became important in the early 1820s. Though this festival appears to have been initiated by Wooler early in 1818, it may also have been celebrated continuously since Paine's death in 1809, at least in London, where its fourteenth anniversary was proclaimed in 1823. At that meeting some 500 attended and many more went away disappointed, while similar celebrations took place at Hyde, Bath, Huddersfield, Bolton, Edinburgh, Aberdeen, Dundee, Leeds, Birmingham, Oldham, Manchester, Hull, Norwich, Stockport, Stokesley, Ashton-under-Lyme and Newgate. Paine now took his place among many other radical icons. At Edinburgh in 1822, for example, about fifty 'freethinkers' assembled in a High Street tavern from six until midnight to toast Paine, the People, the republicans of Haiti, relief from an oppressive clergy, the ending of slavery, freedom of the press, and other causes, and to sing, recite poetry and collect funds for imprisoned martyrs. At Boston some inhabitants substituted a toast to 'the immortal memory of Thomas Paine' for the usual acknowledgement of the anniversary of George IV's accession, since both fell on the same day. Birmingham boasted a Paine Club. At Stockport those assembled described themselves as 'republicans', while at Stokesley they were 'lovers of Civil and Religious Freedom'.[6]

At such events the problem of Paine's religion occasionally emerged. Rare was the occasion when, as at Leeds in 1823, a speaker reflected that Paine's deism was unacceptable, but only because he was himself a complete materialist. Most reformers would have nothing to do with Paine's theology. The radical journalist John Wade bluntly dismissed Paine's 'horrid piece of blasphemy'. Cobbett wisely evaded the entire issue, insisting that matters of religion be left to private conscience, and indeed remained an Anglican throughout his life, defending his radicalism in traditional theological terms. At his trial in 1820 Henry Hunt, too, both denied seeing any reformer read Paine's religious works

211

and begged not to have his own views identified with those of Paine's main theological disciple, Richard Carlile.[7]

Carlile in fact did much to fuel the postwar Painite revival. Having in his own youth been 'ignorant and silly enough' to help burn the great radical in effigy, Carlile now saw Paine as 'our great and only prototype ... the father of every Representative Republic and all sound Republican principles' and the only person to have seen the true connections between politics and theology. Carlile's devotion to Paine was nearly complete. He named his son Thomas Paine Carlile, and when this boy died, named the next the same, much offending the cleric who registered the fact. He served several terms in prison for selling Paine's theological works at his 'Temple of Reason' and endured a lifetime of insults like that delivered by a man who stopped in front of his shop one day and exclaimed, 'Ah, Paine is now in hell, and Carlile will soon follow him.'[8] But Carlile, too, did not share all of Paine's views, conceding one God or first cause who was wise, powerful and good, the equality of nature, and the duty of man to 'do as he would be done by', but castigating Paine for having been unwilling to 'give up that sensual and childish ideal of a paradisical future state'. By 1822, moreover, he rejected Paine's theological views entirely by becoming an atheist and materialist. Like Paine he did, however, oppose equality of property, defending only equality of rights and arguing that necessary inequalities arose naturally from differences in labour, enterprise and inheritance. But though Carlile helped to found organizations like the Birmingham Paine Club in the early 1820s, he felt that 'no club can give force to the political principles of Thomas Paine'. 'I saw that at starting in politics', he proclaimed, 'and that is one reason why I have never joined a political club of any kind.' Carlile's failure to form more lasting political organizations in fact probably helped to dissipate Paine's influence by the late 1820s. But in any case he also diverged fundamentally from Paine by insisting (quite wrongly) that in his theory of rights Paine always intended an historical description of existing wrongs rather than any abstract, metaphysical account. In fact this was precisely how Carlile avoided the problems of divine intention and the state of nature pointed to in the last chapter. Paine, Carlile insisted, had 'used the phrase, "Rights of Man"; but he used it in the clear relation to monarchical despotism. It was always so understood from him, and unless the phrase has some such relation, it is meaningless. There can be no *rights of man*, without pre-existing wrongs.'[9]

The great debate over the first Reform Act renewed Paine's reputation once again, and his views were associated with freedom of trade, democracy, and cultivating waste lands to employ the poor. Several new editions of the *Rights of Man* appeared and Carlile claimed that Paine had 'risen like a phoenix from the embers, and is becoming, as he ought to be, the universal political preceptor'. In probably the last important attack on the *Rights of Man*, the Reverend Francis Thackeray, 'repeatedly shocked and disgusted by the glaring parade with which the works of Thomas Paine are offered for public sale' in some of the main streets of London, blasted their author at length, warning that 'Time has not destroyed the name or opinions of Thomas Paine – both are still producing considerable effects upon society'. Paine's theological critics responded once again, too, assailing *The Age of Reason* and its disciples (particularly Robert Owen) at great length for creating a 'modern Babel' of religious confusion. In 1833 Paine's birthday was still celebrated at Glasgow, Paisley, Greenock, several places in London and many other towns. During the Chartist movement, too, Paine's works were again widely read and quoted, with William Carpenter, for example, invoking his views on paper money in 1837 and George Jacob Holyoake bringing out a new life of Paine in 1840. As late as 1852, the Sheffield Chartist and Owenite Isaac Ironside noted that only three birthdays were publicly celebrated by the Sheffield working classes: those of Paine, the poet Robert Burns and Christ.[10] Even in 1880, in fact, the ex-Chartist W. J. Linton claimed that Paine's principles remained 'the political Gospel of our English working classes'. Paine's continental reputation was also long-lived, while in America his birthday was still celebrated, particularly by the German forty-eighters, until at least the 1890s, when some of the nationalist followers of Edward Bellamy were also among his admirers.[11]

The emergence of social radicalism

By 1850, however, Paine's thought had been widely challenged by other approaches to society and politics. That the substance of his social and political analysis receded much more quickly than Paine's general popularity was partly the result of innovations by 'followers' like Carlile, and partly caused by the emergence in the 1820s and 1830s of new and highly influential forms of radical social analysis more concerned with industrialization, the division of labour and the rapid expansion of market and class relationships. Older forms of radicalism and republicanism now came to be seen as wanting in economic sophistication. Moreover, these new approaches incorporated two forms of assault upon the language of natural rights. The first of these came from the socialism of Robert Owen and his followers, many of whom, though sympathetic to radicalism, were reluctant to discuss rights other than the right of the labourer to the produce of labour. The second was derived chiefly from Benthamism and political economy. Together these criticisms – both of which had a considerable impact

213

on popular radicalism – helped to create what I have elsewhere termed 'social radicalism', where greater emphasis was now given to economic than political relations. The struggle for political rights, particularly in the Chartist movement, ensured that Paine's ideals remained important to working-class radicalism. But these now had to contend with other, sometimes incompatible, goals as well as alternative explanations of working-class distress. This conflict between newer and more traditional forms of radicalism thus enlarged the spectrum of radical debate continuously throughout the nineteenth century and in fact still haunts many important political disputes today.[12]

The Owenite disagreement with Paine, whose essence would be taken up by later forms of socialism, concentrated upon the argument that taxation did not chiefly cause distress and consequently that parliamentary reform would not end poverty.[13] Instead the socialists contended taxation was 'but as a feather in the scale, when weighed against the wealth that is absorbed by the monopolies practised in the present competitive system'. Thus Owenism sought to abolish economic competition and to move the unemployed (and later the entire nation) to mixed agricultural and manufacturing communities where goods would be held in common. But such solutions were much less compelling for radicals than the Owenite analysis of economic distress. The main cause of poverty, the socialists claimed, was an economic system where 'buying cheap and selling dear' overproduced some goods while ignoring the need for others. If the working classes were remunerated sufficiently to consume in proportion to their needs, overproduction would not occur. If goods were moreover exchanged on the basis of their labour value, profit would be eliminated and a fair system of exchange would ensure a just reward for labour. Such arguments appeared increasingly plausible given the exceptionally rapid growth of the manufacturing system after 1815 and the onset of increasingly severe commercial crises. As America began to industrialize, moreover, it too began to exhibit serious poverty and inequality. Several leading Chartists, notably Bronterre O'Brien, who had a following of many thousands, were converted to such a socialist analysis, though without conceding that political reform was fruitless.[14]

But the socialist economic analysis alone did not weaken Paine's appeal. Much more important to radicals like the woolcomber and journalist John Wade was the new language of political economy, particularly in conjunction with Bentham's critique of natural rights. Wade thought Paine 'an excellent man' of many talents whose none the less terrible 'ignorance of what constitutes *right*' had been shared by the leaders of the French revolution, which had failed largely through promulgating 'impracticable nonsense on the natural freedom and equality of man'. For Wade neither savages with their different degrees of strength nor civilized men divided by social institutions were 'born equal'. Powers alone were derived from nature; rights were possessed only in society and only utility defined their limits. Men, for example, held no natural right to exercise the franchise at age 21. But since some maturity of judgement and a degree of independence had been attained by that age, it was regarded as suitable.[15] Political economy and its emphasis upon the rights of labour assisted in partly displacing a Painite discourse on the rights of man by redefining the sources of working-class oppression. The categories of productive and unproductive labour, drawn initially from Smith's *Wealth of Nations*, helped in particular to categorize the labouring classes as actively 'productive' because they generated wealth, rather than as merely passively impoverished, disenfranchised, oppressed and overtaxed. Instead of seeing only the beneficiaries and victims of taxation, radicals increasingly divided society into only two groups, *'the unproductive classes'*, who included lawyers, parsons and aristocrats, and who were 'idle consumers, because they waste the product of the country without giving anything in return', and the productive classes, 'who by their labours increase the funds of the community, as husbandmen, mechanics, labourers, etc'. Such language did not necessarily imply seeing working master-manufacturers as exploiters of the lower orders. But it could be used to condemn 'capitalists' who lived from interest on the national debt or any other funds without working themselves.[16] These were the roots of much of the radical and socialist language of mid- and late Victorian Britain.

By mid-century, and particularly after the failure of Chartism, few radicals thus believed that the 'corruption' of pensioners and placemen explained unemployment, a blighted industrial landscape, glutted markets, widespread misery in the factory districts, long hours of labour and low wages, and the steadily increasing gap between rich and poor. Paine's ideas, none the less, remained extremely popular well into the late nineteenth century. But the 'social' analysis of polity and economy begun chiefly by Owen, together with the growing popularity of liberal political economy, did displace to a considerable degree older radical views, while the capacity of the state to reform itself and respond to working-class distress also undermined the older view that it was too deeply corrupted to perform such acts.[17] By 1850, from an analytical rather than merely symbolic viewpoint, the age of Paine was at an end.

The modernity of Thomas Paine

Yet it is precisely those doctrines which Paine did come to symbolize which have grown steadily more popular and are once again in the late twentieth century at the centre of political debate. Today we rarely advert to an original social contract or the divine origins of rights to support our claims for equality or justice. But the call for 'human rights' and the demand for universal recognition of certain inviolable principles of freedom of thought, speech and association, gain increasingly in importance and have become one of the defining characteristics of modern politics. Burke remains of considerable historical interest, but who today takes his prescriptions seriously? It is Paine's message instead which remains relevant to those substantial parts of the globe which do not yet enjoy those rights which he insisted were inscribed in the fact of being human. Few monarchies now require a Painite assault, but there is no shortage of tyrannies awaiting overthrow, or of oppressed peoples seeking self-determination. Democracy with Paine came to mean the right of the majority to supersede the political monopolies of a powerful and wealthy minority. Humanity meant the right of all to a dignified level of subsistence, and the duty of the affluent to help provide it, which we today associate with the welfare state.

The two themes of rights and democracy, then, are the chief legacy of Thomas Paine. More than anyone else, it was he who transformed the narrow vision of the 'liberties of Englishmen', which implied no corresponding rights for Frenchmen, and the natural rights of Christians, not shared by infidels, into a cosmopolitan vision which afforded protection and sustenance to all. He insisted on an ideal of the equality of rights and mutual respect which was stunningly radical in his own time, but is now central to modern civility. Through him millions came to see that humiliating subservience was degrading and that the average man and woman could achieve greater dignity. 'He makes the blind to see / What slaves and dupes they be', his followers thus sang to the tune of 'God Save the King' in the 1790s. Perhaps only an apostate Quaker, exiled Englishman and adopted American with French sympathies could have been so insistently rebellious. But Paine's belief in democracy remained part of the principles of 1848, 1871 and 1917, and is as surely invoked today, from Soweto to Moscow and Beijing to Harlem. In this sense, then, the age of Paine has barely begun.

Notes to Conclusion: the legend of Thomas Paine

1   Thus it has been argued that Paine helped 'to modernize' the exiled radicals by persuading them of the viability of a commercial republic (M. Durey, 1987, and R. Twomey, 1974, pp. 138–70). See also Durey (1985). See A. Sheps (1973) for the early period of exile and Twomey (1974) and (1984) for the later.
2   E. Foner (1976), pp. 264–8; S. Wilentz (1984), pp. 153–5; E. Link (1942), pp. 109, 202, 209; *Black Dwarf*, Vol. 1, no. 16 (22 April 1818), p. 255; V. Stauffer (1918), p. 77.

3   *Cambridge Intelligencer*, no. 338 (4 January 1800), p. 2; *Flower's Political Review*
    (May 1808), p. 331; ibid. (April 1800), p. 256; ibid. (January 1810), p. 59;
    ibid. (Suppl. 1807), p. 555; ibid. (October 1811), pp. 150–8 *et seq.*; *Republican*,
    Vol. 6, no. 11 (9 August 1822), p. 322. On Hunt see J. Belchem (1985). On
    Paine's British reputation see E. Royle (1988) and George Spater (1988). On
    the longevity of his political ideals see J. Belchem (1981).
4   *Hints* (1819), p. 21; J. Harford (1819), pp. 18–19; *Sherwin's Political Register*,
    vol. 1, no. 7 (17 May 1817), p. 111; T. Evans (1816), p. 1.
5   *Black Dwarf*, vol. 1, no. 34 (17 September 1817), p. 567; *The People*, no. 3 (3
    May 1817), p. 79. On Cobbett and Paine see C. Young (1977), I. Dyck (1988)
    and D. Wilson (1988).
6   *Black Dwarf*, vol. 2, no. 3 (21 January 1818), p. 39; *Republican*, vol. 6, no. 6
    (7 February 1823), pp. 177, 181; vol. 5, no. 4 (22 February 1822), pp. 234–5;
    Lion, vol. 2, no. 19 (7 November 1829), p. 577; *Black Dwarf*, vol. 10, no. 9
    (26 February 1823), p. 321; *Republican*, vol. 5, no. 10 (8 March 1822), p. 4.
    On the emergence of these radical festivals see J. Epstein (1988).
7   *Republican*, vol. 6, no. 10 (7 March 1823), p. 302; *Gorgon*, vol. 1, no. 29 (5
    December 1818), p. 229; *Black Dwarf*, vol. 3, no. 49 (8 December 1819), pp.
    802–3; S. Bamford (1984), p. 260.
8   *Republican*, vol. 1, no. 1 (27 August 1819), p. 1, vol. 5, no. 1 (4 January 1822),
    pp. 5, 9–10, no. 2 (11 January 1822), p. 34; vol. 3, no. 8 (16 June 1820), p.
    266; vol. 1, no. 10 (29 October 1819), p. 147; J. Jones (1819); *The Report of
    the ... Mock Trials of Richard Carlile* (1822), p. iv. On Carlile's view of Paine
    see J. Wiener (1988), and generally Wiener (1983). On early secularism see
    E. Royle (1974).
9   *The Deist* (1819), vol. 1, p. 15; *Republican*, vol. 4, no. 2 (8 September 1820), p.
    42; *Gauntlet*, no. 26 (13 October 1833), p. 401; J. Wiener (1988), pp. 115–20;
    E. Royle (1988), p. 17; *Republican*, vol. 6, no. 17 (20 September 1822), p. 520;
    Prompter, no. 30 (4 June 1831), p. 485.
10 *The Rights of Nations* (1832), pp. 388–90; *Prompter*, no. 3 (27 November 1830),
    p. 38; F. Thackeray (1831), p. iv; *Gauntlet*, no. 2 (17 February 1833), p. 20;
    London Journal, no. 39 (7 June 1837), p. 220; *Sheffield Free Press*, no. 58 (7
    February 1852), p. 7.
11 W. Linton (1880), p. 88; G. Spater (1988), pp. 138–45; E. MacNair (1957),
    p. 119.
12 For further discussion see my (1989), ch. 1.
13 This is not to argue that radicals in the 1790s were not conscious of eco-
    nomic grievances. High bread prices, for example, were sometimes blamed
    on an artificial scarcity created by a 'cabal of speculators'. Organizations
    like the Stockport Friends of Universal Peace and the Rights of Man,
    composed of yeomen, farmers, manufacturers and labourers, also believed
    that 'it is our labour that is the support of every state', and specifically the
    monarchy, priesthood and aristocracy (*Manchester Herald*, no. 9, 26 May
    1792, p. 4; ibid., no. 23, 1 September 1792, p. 1). See my (1989), chs. 3 and 4.
14 *Prompter*, no. 19 (19 March 1831), pp. 311, 314.
15 *Gorgon*, Vol. 1, no. 14 (22 August 1818), pp. 105–10. Wade later noted that
    he had managed 'to offend a great number of our readers' in his articles
    on Paine and reiterated that his only disagreement with Paine concerned
    natural rights (vol. 1, no. 31, 19 December 1818, p. 248).
16 *Gorgon*, vol. 1, no. 12 (8 August 1818), pp. 90–1. See generally my (1987).
17 On the latter argument see G. Stedman Jones (1983), pp. 90–178.

Bibliography

(The place of publication of books and pamphlets is London unless otherwise noted.)

(a) Manuscript sources

Additional Manuscripts, British Library
Home Office Papers (HO), Public Record Office
Place Papers, British Library
Privy Council Papers (PC), Public Record Office
Treasury Solicitor's Papers (TS), Public Record Office

(b) Works by Paine

[Paine, Thomas] (1776), *Four Letters on Interesting Subjects* (Philadelphia, Pa).
[Paine, Thomas] (1792), *Old Truths and Established Facts. Being an Answer to A Very New Pamphlet Indeed.*
Paine, Thomas (1908), *Life and Writings of Thomas Paine*, ed. Daniel Edwin Wheeler (New York: Parke).
Paine, Thomas (1945), *The Complete Writings of Thomas Paine*, ed. Philip Foner (New York: Citadel Press).
Paine, Thomas (1969a), *The Rights of Man*, ed. Henry Collins (Harmondsworth: Penguin).
Paine, Thomas (1969b), *The Rights of Man*, ed. Arthur Seldon (Dent).
Paine, Thomas (1976), *Common Sense*, ed. Isaac Kramnick (Harmondsworth: Penguin).
Paine, Thomas (1985), *The Rights of Man*, ed. Eric Foner (Harmondsworth: Penguin).
Paine, Thomas (1987), *The Thomas Paine Reader*, ed. Isaac Kramnick and Michael Foot (Harmondsworth: Penguin).

(c) Bibliographies

Aldridge, A. O. (1974), 'Thomas Paine: a survey of research and criticism since 1945', *British Studies Monitor*, vol. 5, pp. 3–29.
Gimbel, Richard (1956a), *Thomas Paine. A Bibliographical Checklist of 'Common Sense'* (New Haven, Conn.: Yale University Press).

218

Gimbel, Richard (1959), 'Thomas Paine fights for freedom in three worlds. The new, the old, the next. Catalogue of an Exhibition Commemorating the One Hundredth Anniversary of His Death', *Proceedings of the American Antiquarian Society*, vol. 70, pp. 397–492.
Gimbel, Richard (1976), *The Thomas Paine Collection of Richard Gimbel in the Library of the American Philosophical Society* (Wilmington, Delaware, Scholarly Resources Inc.).
Pendleton, Gayle Trusdel (1979), 'Three score identifications of anonymous British pamphlets of the 1790s', *Notes and Queries*, n.s. 26, pp. 208–17.
Pendleton, Gayle Trusdel (1982), 'Towards a bibliography of the *Reflections* and *Rights of Man* controversy', *Bulletin of Research in the Humanities*, vol. 85, pp. 65–103.
The Thomas Paine Collection at Thetford. An Analytical Catalogue (Norwich: Norfolk County Library, 1979).
Wilson, Jerome (1974), 'Thomas Paine in America: an annotated bibliography 1900–1973', *Bulletin of Bibliography*, vol. 31, pp. 133–51, 180.

(d)   Dissertations

Alves, Helio Osvaldo (1981), 'The Paineites. The influence of Thomas Paine in four provincial towns 1791–1799', University of London PhD.
Arnold, Douglas M. (1976), 'Political ideology and the internal revolution in Pennsylvania, 1776–1790', Princeton University PhD.
Betka, James A. (1975), 'The ideology and rhetoric of Thomas Paine: political justification through metaphor', Rutgers University PhD.
Booth, Alan (1979), 'Reform, repression and revolution: radicalism and loyalism in the north-west of England, 1789–1803', University of Lancaster PhD.
Brims, John (1983), 'The Scottish democratic movement in the age of the French revolution', University of Edinburgh PhD.
Burnell, Peter J. (1972), 'The political and social thought of Thomas Paine 1737–1809', University of Warwick PhD.
Cox, Nicholas (1971), 'Aspects of English radicalism: the suppression and re-emergence of the constitutional democratic tradition, 1795–1809', University of Cambridge PhD.
Elder, Dominic (1951), 'The common man philosophy of Thomas Paine', Notre Dame University PhD.
Gallop, Geoffrey (1983), 'Politics, property and progress: British radical thought, 1760–1815', Oxford DPhil.
Gavre, William (1978), 'Republicanism and the American revolution: the collapse of the classical ideal', University of California, Los Angeles PhD.
Ginsberg, Elaine K. (1971), 'The rhetoric of revolution: an analysis of Thomas Paine's *Common Sense*', University of Oklahoma PhD.
King, Arnold K. (1951), 'Thomas Paine in America, 1774–1787', University of Chicago PhD.
McCue, Daniel L., Jr (1974), 'Daniel Isaac Eaton and *Politics for the People*', Columbia University PhD.
Murray, Nancy U. (1975), 'The influence of the French revolution on the Church of England and its rivals, 1789–1802', Oxford University DPhil.
Pendleton, Gayle T. (1976), 'English conservative propaganda during the French Revolution, 1789–1802', Emory University PhD.
Schofield, Thomas (1984), 'English conservative thought 1789–1796', University of London PhD.

Seaman, W. A. L. (1954), 'British democratic societies in the period of the French revolution', University of London PhD.
Sheps, Arthur Neal (1973), 'English radicalism and revolutionary America', University of Toronto PhD.
Smith, Martin John (1979), 'English radical newspapers in the French revolutionary era, 1790–1803', University of London PhD.
Smith, Robert Francis (1977), 'Thomas Paine and the American political tradition', University of Notre Dame PhD.
Twomey, Richard J. (1974), 'Jacobins and Jeffersonians: Anglo-American radicalism in the United States 1790–1820', Northern Illinois University PhD.
Walvin, James (1969), 'English democratic societies and popular radicalism, 1791–1800', University of York PhD.
Wells, Roger (1978), 'The grain crises in England, 1794–6, 1799–1801', York University DPhil.

(e) Primary sources: periodicals

Analytical Review (1790–3).
The Argus, or General Observer (1796).
Black Dwarf (1817–19).
The Cabinet (3 vols, Norwich, 1795).
Cambridge Intelligencer (1793–1803).
Chester Chronicle (1791–2).
Critical Review (1790–5).
Derby Mercury (1791–3).
Flower's Political Review and Monthly Register (1808–11).
The Gauntlet (1833).
The Gorgon (1818).
The Lion (1828–9).
The London Journal (1837).
Manchester Herald (1792–3).
The Medusa; or Penny Politician (1819).
The New Annual Register (1790–9).
Newcastle Chronicle (1792–3).
The Parliamentary Register (1792).
The Patriot (Edinburgh: 1793).
The Patriot: or, Political, Moral and Philosophical Repository (3 vols, 1792–3).
Pennsylvania Gazette (1786).
The People (1817).
A Picture of the Times (1795).
Pig's Meat (3 vols, 1793–5).
Politics for the People (1794).
The Prompter (1830–1).
Public Advertiser (New York), 1807.
The Republican (1819–26).
Sheffield Free Press (1852).
Sheffield Iris (1794).
Sheffield Register (1793–4).
Sherwin's Political Register (1817).
The Tribune (3 vols, 1793–6).
The Union (1831).

(f) Primary sources: books and pamphlets

An Abstract of the History and Proceedings of the Revolution Society (1789).

Account of the Proceedings at a General Meeting of the London Corresponding Society ... 29th of June, 1795 (1795).

An Account of the Proceedings of the British Convention (1793).

[Adams, John] (1791), *Observations on Paine's Rights of Man* (3rd edn, Edinburgh).

Adams, John (1851), 'Thoughts on government' (1776), in *The Works of John Adams*, Vol. 4 (Boston, Mass.).

The Address of a Buckinghamshire Farmer (1792).

An Address to the Inhabitants of Great Britain and Ireland, in Reply to the ... Rights of Man (1793).

The Age of Infidelity, Part Two (1796).

Agutter, William (1792), *Christian Politics; or, The Origin of Power and the Grounds of Subordination.*

The Alarm; Being Britannia's Address to the People (n.d.).

Anketell, Rev. John (1796), *Strictures upon Thomas Paine's Age of Reason* (Dublin).

An Answer to the Right Honourable Edmund Burke's Reflections on the Revolution in France (Dublin: 1791).

The Antigallican (1793).

The Anti-Gallican Songster, No. 1 (1793).

The Anti-Levelling Songster, No. 1 (1793).

An Appeal to the Common Sense of the British People on the Subjects of Sedition and Revolution (1793).

Application of Barruel's Memoirs of Jacobinism to the Secret Societies of Ireland and Great Britain (1798).

Assassination of the King! The Conspirators Exposed (1795).

[Atkinson, Thomas] (1794), *A Concise Sketch of the Intended Revolution in England.*

[Atkinson, Thomas] (1798), *An Oblique View of the Grand Conspiracy against Social Order.*

Auchincloss, J. (1796), *The Sophistry of ... Mr. Paine's Age of Reason* (Edinburgh).

Authentic Copy of a Petition ... by the Members of the Society of the Friends of the People (1793).

Bamford, Samuel (1984), *Passages in the Life of a Radical* (1884) (Oxford: Oxford University Press).

[Barbauld, Anna] (1792), *Civic Sermons for the People, No. 2.*

Barlow, Joel (1792a), *Advice to the Privileged Orders, Part One.*

Barlow, Joel (1792b), *A Letter to the National Convention of France.*

Barlow, Joel (1795), *Advice to the Privileged Orders, Part Two.*

Barruel, Abbé (1797), *Memoirs Illustrating the History of Jacobinism* (4 vols).

Belcher, William (n.d.), *Holcroft's Folly.*

Bennet, Rev. G. (1796), *A Display of the Spirit and Designs of those Who, Under Pretext of a Reform, Aim at the Subversion of the Constitution and Government* (Carlisle).

[Benson, Joseph] (1796), *The Discipline of the Methodists Defended.*

Bentham, Jeremy (1838), *The Works of Jeremy Bentham*, Vol. 2.

Binns, Abraham (1796), *Remarks on a Publication, Entitled, A Serious Admonition to the Disciples of Thomas Paine* (Stockport).

Binns, John (1854), *Recollections of the Life of John Binns* (Philadelphia, Pa).

Bisset, Robert (1796), *Sketch of Democracy*.

Black, William (1793), *Reasons for Preventing the French, Under the Mask of Liberty, From Trampling Upon Europe*.

Blackstone, William (1941), *Blackstone's Commentaries on the Law* (1765–9) (Washington DC: Washington Law Book Co.).

A Blow at the Root (1794).

Bonsell, John (1798), *The Ram's Horn Sounded Seven Times* (Norwich).

Boothby, Sir Brooke (1791), *A Letter to the Right Honourable Edmund Burke*.

Boothby, Sir Brooke (1792), *Observations on the Appeal from the New to the Old Whigs*.

Boudinot, Elias (1801), *The Age of Revelation. Or the Age of Reason Shewn to Be An Age of Infidelity* (Philadelphia, Pa).

Bousfield, Benjamin (1790), *Observations on the Right Honourable Edmund Burke's Pamphlet, on the Subject of the French Revolution* (Dublin).

Britannia's Address to the People (n.d.).

The British Crisis; or, the Disorder of the State at Its Height (1797).

Britons are Happy, If They Will Think So (n.d.).

Broughton, Thomas (1820), *The Age of Christian Reason*.

Brown, Rev. James (1793), *The Importance of Preserving Unviolated the System of Civil Government in Every State*.

Brown, William (1794), *An Essay on the Natural Equality of Man*.

Browne, M. C. (1796), *A Leaf Out of Burke's Book ... In Reply to His Letter to a Noble Lord*.

Buff; or, A Dissertation on Nakedness: A Parody on Paine's Rights of Man (1792).

Burgh, James (1764), *Political Disquisitions* (3 vols).

Burke, Edmund (1826), *The Works of the Right Honourable Edmund Burke* (7 vols, Boston, Mass.).

Burke, Edmund (1978), *The Correspondence of Edmund Burke* (Cambridge: Cambridge University Press).

Burke, Edmund (1987), *Reflections on the Revolution in France*, ed. J. G. A. Pocock (Indianapolis, Ind.: Hackett).

Burlamaqui, J. (1763, 1794), *The Principles of Natural and Politic Law* (2 vols, 1st and 3rd edns).

Butler, Marilyn (ed.) (1984), *Burke, Paine, Godwin and the Revolution Controversy* (Cambridge: Cambridge University Press).

Callender, James (1792), *The Political Progress of Britain* (Edinburgh).

A Candid Inquiry into the Nature of Government, and the Right of Representation (1792).

Carlile, Richard (1819), *Life of Thomas Paine*.

Cartwright, F. W. (1826), *The Life and Correspondence of Major Cartwright* (2 vols).

Cartwright, Major John (1774), *American Independence the Interest and Glory of Great Britain*.

Cartwright, Major John (1776), *Take Your Choice!*

Cartwright, Major John (1792), *A Letter to the Duke of Newcastle*.

Cartwright, Major John (1795), *The Commonwealth in Danger*.

The Catechism of Man (n.d.).

A Caution Against the Levellers (n.d.).

[Chalmers, James] (1776), *Plain Truth: Addressed to the Inhabitants of America. Containing Remarks on a Late Pamphlet, Intitled Common Sense* (Philadelphia, Pa).

Chalmers, Lt Col. (1796), *Strictures on a Pamphlet Written by Thomas Paine on the English System of Finance*.

Cheap Repository Tracts (2 vols, 1795–6).

Cheetham, James (1809), *The Life of Thomas Paine* (New York).

Christianity the Only True Theology; or, An Answer to Mr. Paine's Age of Reason (n.d.).

Christie, Thomas (1791), *Letters on the Revolution in France*.

'Cincinnatus Rigshaw' [Professor of Theophilanthropy, member of the Corresponding and Revolutionary Societies, Brother of the Rosy Cross, Knight Philosopher of the Illuminati, and Citizen of the French and Hibernian Republics] (1800), *Sans Culotides*.

Civil Prudence, Recommended to the Thirteen United Colonies of North America (Norwich, Conn.: 1776).

Cobban, Alfred (ed). (1950), *The Debate on the French Revolution 1789–1799* (Nicholas Kaye).

Cobbett's Opinion of Tom Paine (1817).

Cobbett, William (n.d.), *Observations on the Character and Motives of Paine in the Publication of His Age of Reason*.

Cobbett, William (1796?), *Life of Thomas Paine*.

[Cobbett, William] (1797), *A Letter to the Infamous Tom Paine* (Glasgow).

Cobbett, William (1847), *A Brief History of the Remains of the Late Thomas Paine*.

Cocks, John Somers (1793), *A Short Treatise on the Dreadful Tendency of Levelling Principles*.

Coetlogon, Rev. C. E. de (1792), *The Peculiar Advantages of the English Nation*.

A Comparative Display of the Different Opinions of the Most Distinguished British Writers on the Subject of the French Revolution (1970) (2 vols, 1793; 3 vols, 1811) (reprint edn, New York: AMS Press).

The Complete Reports of the Committee of Secrecy of the Houses of Lords and Commons (1794).

Confusion's Master-Piece: or, Paine's Labour's Lost (1794).

Considerations on Mr. Paine's Pamphlet on the Rights of Man (Edinburgh: 1791; London: 1792).

Considerations on the French War (1794).

Constitutional Letters in Answer to Mr. Paine's Rights of Man (1792).

A Conversation ... Between Thomas Paine, Marat, Petion, Dumourier and Roland (1793).

Cooper, Samuel (1791), *The First Principles of Civil and Ecclesiastical Government Delineated* (Yarmouth).

Cooper, Thomas (1792), *A Reply to Mr. Burke's Invective against Mr. Cooper and Mr. Watt* (2nd edn).

Copies of Original Letters Recently Written by Persons in Paris to Dr. Priestley in America. Taken on Board of a Neutral Vessel (3rd edn, 1798).

The Correspondence of the London Corresponding Society (1795).

The Correspondence of the Revolution Society in London, with the National Assembly, and with Various Societies of the Friends of Liberty in France and England (1792).

A Country Curate's Advice to Manufacturers (n.d.).

Courtenay, J. (1790), *Philosophical Reflections on the Late Revolution in France*.

Coward, J. (1796), *Deism Traced to One of Its Principal Sources*.

Croft, George (1793), *Plans of Parliamentary Reform, Proved to Be Visionary* (Birmingham).

Dalrymple, Alexander (1793), *The Poor Man's Friend: An Address to the Industrious and Manufacturing Part of Great Britain* (Edinburgh).

Damm, Benjamin (n.d.), *An Address to the Public, on True Representation and the Unity of Man*.

The Decline and Fall, Death, Dissection and Funeral Procession of His Most Contemptible Lowness the London Corresponding Society (1796).

A Defence of the Constitution of England (1791).

A Defence of the Political and Parliamentary Conduct of the Right Honourable Edmund Burke (1794).

Defence of the Rights of Man (1791).

Deism Fairly Stated and Fully Vindicated (2nd edn, 1746).

The Deist Confuted (1734).

The Deist, or Moral Philosopher (2 vols, 1819).

De Lolme, J. L. (1853), *The Constitution of England (1784)*.

A Dialogue between an Associator and a Well-Informed Englishman, on the Grounds of the Late Associations (1793).

Dialogues on the Rights of Britons, between a Farmer, a Sailor, and a Manufacturer (1792).

Dinmore, R., Jr (1796), *An Exposition of the Principles of the English Jacobins* (Norwich).

Divine Oracles the True Antidote Against Deism (Providence, Rhode Island 1797).

Drew, S. (1820), *Remarks on the First Part of a Book Entitled 'The Age of Reason'* (2nd edn).

[Drummond, William] (1793), *Philosophical Sketches of the Principles of Society and Government*.

The Duties of Man in Connexion With His Rights (1793).

Dutton, Thomas (1795), *A Vindication of the Age of Reason*.

The End of Pain. The Last Speech, Dying Words and Confession of Tom Paine (n.d.).

Equality No Liberty; or, Subordination the Order of God (Edinburgh: 1793).

Estlin, John Prior (1796), *Evidence of Revealed Religion ... with Reference to ... the Age of Reason* (Bristol).

Evans, Thomas (1816), *Christian Policy the Salvation of the Empire*.

An Explanation of the Word Equality (c. 1792).

An Exposure of the Domestic and Foreign Attempts to Destroy the British Constitution (1793).

Extracts from the Life of Thomas Paine (Author of 'The Age of Reason') (n.p., n.d.).

Facts, Reflections, and Queries, Submitted to ... the Associated Friends of the People (Edinburgh: 1792).

Fancourt, William (1792), *Britons and Fellow Countrymen* (Wellingborough).

A Few Minutes' Advice to the People of Great Britain on Republics (Bristol: 1792).

A Few Plain Questions to the Working People of Scotland (3rd edn, 1793).

A Few Words, But No Lies; From Roger Bull to His Brother Thomas (n.d.).

Fowles, John (1797), *The Truth of the Bible Fairly Put to the Test* (Alexandria).

Fox, William (1793), *An Examination of Mr. Paine's Writings*.

Fragment of a Prophecy Lately Discovered in the Cell of a French Hermit. By a Convert from the 'Society for Revolutions' (1791).

Franklin, Benjamin (1982), *The Papers of Benjamin Franklin* (New Haven, Conn.: Yale University Press).

Free Communing; or a Last Attempt to Cure the Lunatics, Now Labouring Under That Dreadful Malady, Commonly Called the French Disease (Edinburgh: 1793).

[Freeman, Thomas] (1793), *An Address to the Disaffected Subjects of George the Third*.

Frend, William (1793), *Peace and Union Recommended to the Associated Bodies of Republicans and Anti-Republicans* (St Ives).

Frend, William (1799), *Principles of Taxation*.

Friends of the People (1795).

The Genuine Trial of Thomas Paine for a Libel (1792).

Gerrald, Joseph (1794a), *The Defence of Joseph Gerrald on a Charge of Sedition* (Edinburgh).

Gerrald, Joseph (1794b), *The Trial of Joseph Gerrald* (Edinburgh).

Gerrald, Joseph (1794c), *A Convention the Only Means of Saving Us From Ruin* (3rd edn).

Gifford, John (i.e. John Green) (1792), *A Plain Address to the Common Sense of the People of England, Containing an Interesting Abstract of Pain's Life and Writings.*

Godwin, William (1976), *An Enquiry Concerning Political Justice* (1793), ed. I. Kramnick (Harmondsworth: Penguin).

[Green, Thomas] (1793), *The Two Systems of the Social Compact and the Natural Rights of Man Examined and Refuted.*

Grisenthwaite, W. (1822), *A Refutation of Every Argument Brought Against the Truth of Christianity and Revealed Religion by Thomas Paine* (Wells).

Grotius, Hugo (1925), *De Jure Belli ac Pacis* (1625) (Oxford: Clarendon Press).

Hall, Charles (1805), *The Effects of Civilization upon the People in European States.*

Hall, Robert (1800), *Modern Infidelity Considered With Respect to Its Influence on Society* (Cambridge).

Hamilton, James Edward (1791), *Reflections on the Revolution in France, By the Rt. Hon Edmund Burke, Considered; Also, Observations on Mr. Paine's Pamphlet, Intitled the Rights of Man.*

Hardy, Thomas (1832), *Memoir of Thomas Hardy.*

Harford, John S. (1819), *Some Account of the Life, Death, and Principles of Thomas Paine* (Bristol).

Hartley, David (1794), *Argument on the French Revolution* (Bath).

[Hawtrey, Charles] (1790), *Free Thoughts on Liberty and the Revolution in France.*

Hawtrey, Charles (1792), *Various Opinions of the Philosophical Reformers Considered, Particularly Pain's Rights of Man.*

Hearn, Thomas (1793), *A Short View of the Rise and Progress of Freedom in Modern Europe.*

[Hervey, Frederick] (1791), *A New Friend on an Old Subject.*

[Hervey, Frederick] (1792), *An Answer to the Second Part of the Rights of Man.*

Hincks, T. (1796), *Letters Originally Addressed to the Inhabitants of Cork, in Defence of Revealed Religion, Occasioned by the Circulation of Mr. Paine's Age of Reason in That City* (Cork).

Hints Addressed to the Radical Reformers (Glasgow, 1819).

Hodgson, William (1795), *The Commonwealth of Reason.*

Holyoake, George Jacob (1840), *The Life of Paine.*

Howell, T. B. (ed.) (1817–20), *A Complete Collection of State Trials* Vols 22–7.

H.R.H., *Dr. Price and the Rights of Man* (1791).

[Hulme, Obadiah] (1771), *An Historical Essay on the English Constitution.*

An Humble Address to the Most High, Most Mighty, and Most Puissant the Sovereign People (1793).

Hume, David (1903), *Essays Moral, Political and Literary* (1741–2) (Grant Richards).

Hunt, Isaac (1791), *Rights of Englishmen. An Antidote to the Poison Now Vending by the Transatlantic Republican Thomas Paine.*

An Important Discovery; or, Revolution in Great Britain and Ireland Impossible (1793).

[Inglis, Charles] (1776), *The True Interest of America Impartially Stated* (2nd edn, Philadelphia, Pa).

The Interests of Man in Opposition to the Rights of Man (Edinburgh: 1793).

Is All We Want Worth A Civil War? (1792).

Jackson, William (1795), *Observations in Answer to Mr. Thomas Paine's 'Age of Reason'* (Dublin).

225

Jacobson, David L. (ed.) (1965), *The English Libertarian Heritage. From the Writings of John Trenchard and Thomas Gordon in The Independent Whig and Cato's Letters* (New York: Bobbs-Merrill).

[Jenyns, Soame] (1784), *Thoughts on a Parliamentary Reform*.

[Jenyns, Soame] (1785), *Every Man His Own Law-Maker; or, The Englishman's Guide to a Parliamentary Reform*.

Joersson, S. A. (1796), *Adam Smith, Author of an Inquiry into the Wealth of Nations and Thomas Paine, Author of the Decline and Fall of the English System of Finance* ('Germany').

John Bull, In Answer to His Brother Thomas (1792).

John Bull's Answer to His Brother Thomas's Second Letter (1792).

[John Saint John] (1791), *A Letter from a Magistrate to Mr. William Rose, of Whitehall, on Mr. Paine's The Rights of Man*.

Jones, John (1793a), *The Reason of Man: With Strictures on Paine's Rights of Man* (Canterbury).

Jones, John (1793b), *The Reason of Man: Part Second. Containing Strictures on Rights of Man* (Canterbury).

Jones, John Gale (1819), *The Speech of John Gale Jones Delivered at the British Forum*.

Judson, L. Carroll (1851), *The Sages and Heroes of the American Revolution* (Philadelphia).

Keate, William (1790), *A Free Examination of Dr. Price's and Dr. Priestley's Sermons*.

Kennedy, P. (1798), *An Answer to Paine's Letter to General Washington* (Philadelphia, Pa).

Kilham, Alexander (1795), *The Progress of Liberty Amongst the People Called Methodists* (Alnwick).

[Kilham, Alexander] (1796a), *An Appeal to the Methodist Societies of the Alnwick Circuit*.

Kilham, Alexander (1796b), *A Candid Examination of the London Methodistical Bulletin* (Alnwick).

[Kilham, Alexander] (n.d.), *The Life of Alexander Kilham* (Nottingham).

King, John (1793), *Mr. King's Speech at Egham, with Thomas Paine's Letter to Him* (Egham).

King, Walter (1793), *Two Sermons Preached at Gray's Inn Chapel*.

Knave's-Acre Association Resolutions ... of the Place and Pension Club (1793).

Knox, Vicesimus (1795), *Christian Philosophy* (2 vols).

The Last Dying Words of Tom Paine, Executed at the Guillotine in France on the First of September 1794 (n.p., n.d.).

'Launcelot Light' (1792), *A Sketch of the Rights of Boys and Girls*.

A Letter from a Magistrate to Mr. William Rose (1791).

A Letter of Condolence and Congratulation from Antichrist to John Bull (1795).

A Letter to a Friend in the Country: Wherein Mr. Paine's Letter to Mr. Dundas is Particularly Considered (1792).

Letter to a Friend on the Test Laws (1791).

A Letter to a Member of the National Assembly (1791).

A Letter to Thomas Paine, in Answer to His Scurrilous Epistle Addressed to Our Late Worthy President Washington (New York: 1797).

Letters to a Friend, on the Late Revolution in France (1792).

Letters to Thomas Paine; in Answer to His Late Publication on the Rights of Man (1791).

Lewelyn, William (1793), *An Appeal to Men against Paine's Rights of Men* (Leominster).

Liberty and Equality; Treated of in a Short History Addressed from a Poor Man to His Equals (1792).

The Life and Adventures of Job Knott, Buckle-Maker (11th edn, Birmingham, 1798).

Linton, W. J. (1880), *James Watson. A Memoir.*

Locke, John (1970), *Two Treatises of Government* (1690), ed. Peter Laslett (Cambridge: Cambridge University Press).

Lofft, Capel (1790), *Remarks on the Letter of the Right Honourable Edmund Burke Concerning the Revolution in France* (Dublin).

Lofft, Capel (1791), *Remarks on the Letter of Mr. Burke to a Member of the National Assembly.*

The London Corresponding Society's Addresses and Regulations (1792).

[Macaulay, Catherine] (1767), *Loose Remarks on Certain Positions to Be Found in Mr. Hobbes' Philosophical Rudiments of Government and Society. With a Short Sketch of a Democratical Form of Government.*

[Macaulay, Catherine] (1790), *Observations on the Reflections of the Right Honourable Edmund Burke on the Revolution in France.*

Mackenzie, Henry (1793), *The Life of Thomas Paine.*

Mackenzie, W. C. (ed.) (1916), *The War Diary of a London Scot (Alderman G. M. Macaulay) 1796–7* (Paisley: Alexander Gardner).

Mackintosh, James (1846), *Vindiciae Gallicae, Defence of the French Revolution and Its English Admirers* (1792), in *Miscellaneous Works*, Vol. 3.

Mackintosh, Robert J. (1836), *Memoirs of the Life of the Right Honourable Sir James Mackintosh* (2 vols).

Margarot, Maurice (1812), *Proposal for a Grand National Jubilee* (Sheffield).

Marsters, Thomas, Jr (1798), *A View of Agricultural Oppressions: And of Their Effects Upon Society* (2nd edn, Lynn).

'Martius Modernus' (1793), *Political Essays ... Interspersed with Constitutional Disquisitions on the Wild Prospect of Imprescriptible Rights.*

The Measures of Ministry to Prevent a Revolution, Are the Certain Means of Bringing It On (1794).

Memoirs of the Life of Gilbert Wakefield (2 vols, 1804).

Miles, W. (1890), *The Correspondence of William Augustus Miles on the French Revolution 1789–1817* (2 vols, Longmans, Green).

Molloy, Tobias (1792), *An Appeal from Man in a State of Civil Society to Man in a State of Nature* (Dublin).

Montesquieu, Baron de (1949), *The Spirit of the Laws* (1748) (New York: Hafner Press).

More Reasons for a Reform in Parliament (1793).

More, Hannah (1793), *Village Politics. Addressed to All Mechanics, Journeymen, and Day Labourers* (Durham).

[More, Hannah] (1794), *A Country Carpenter's Confession of Faith.*

Morris, Gouverneur (1939), *A Diary of the French Revolution* (2 vols, Boston, Mass.: Houghton Mifflin).

Moser, Joseph (1796), *An Examination of the Pamphlet Entitled Thoughts on the English Government.*

M'Phail, James (1795), *Remarks on the Present Times.*

Mr. Justice Ashurst's Charge to the Grand Jury of the County of Middlesex (1792).

'Mr. Miles' (1793), *The Conduct of France towards Great Britain Examined.*

Muir, James (1795), *An Examination of the Principles Contained in the Age of Reason* (Baltimore, Md).

Nares, Edward (1805), *A View of the Evidences of Christianity at the Close of the Pretended Age of Reason* (Oxford).

Nares, Rev. R. (1792), *Principles of Government Deduced From Reason*.

A Narrative of the Proceedings at the General Meeting of the London Corresponding Society Held on Monday, July 31, 1797 (1797).

Nash, Michael (1794), *Paine's Age of Reason Measured by the Standard of Truth*.

[Naylor, James] (1656), *Love to the Lost: and a Hand Held Forth to the Helpless*.

Nelson, David (1800), *An Investigation of That False, Fabulous and Blasphemous Misrepresentation of Truth … the Age of Reason* (Lancaster).

A New Dialogue between Monsieur Francois and John English on the French Revolution (n.d.).

A New Song (n.d.).

Northcote, Thomas (1781), *Observations on the Natural and Civil Rights of Mankind*.

[Odell, William] (1792), *An Impartial Defense of the Established Church*.

Ogden, Uzal (1795), *Antidote to Deism. The Deist Unmasked; or an Ample Refutation of All the Objections of Thomas Paine to the Christian Religion* (2 vols, Newark).

Ogilvie, William (1781), *An Essay on the Right of Property in Land*.

'Oldys, Francis' [George Chalmers] (1791, 1793), *The Life of Thomas Paine*.

One Penny-Worth of Truth, from Thomas Bull, to His Brother John (1792).

Opinions Delivered at a Numerous and Respectable Meeting in the Country (1793).

The Origin of Duty and Right in Man, Considered (1796).

Oswald, John (1791), *Review of the Constitution of Great Britain* (3rd edn).

Paine and Burke Contrasted (n.d.).

Paley, William (1792), *Reasons for Contentment, Addressed to the Labouring Part of the British Public*.

[Paley, William] (1951), *Equality as Consistent with the British Constitution* (1792) in Reginald Reynolds (ed.), *British Pamphleteers* (Allan Wingate).

Parsons, Sir Lawrence (1793), *Thoughts on Liberty and Equality*.

Patten, William (1795), *Christianity the True Theology, and Only Perfect Moral System; in Answer to 'The Age of Reason'* (Warren).

Patton, Charles (1797), *The Effects of Property upon Society and Government Investigated*.

A Penitentiary Epistle, Found in Tom Paine's Portfolio, the Morning after His Execution at Lincoln (n.d.).

The Pernicious Effects of the Art of Printing upon Society Exposed (n.d.).

The Pernicious Principles of Tom Paine, Exposed in an Address to Labourers and Mechanics (n.d.).

Perry, Sampson (1797), *The Origin of Government, Compatible With, and Founded on the Rights of Man, with a Few Words on the Constitutional Object of the Corresponding Society*.

Peter, Alexander (1792), *Strictures on the Character and Principles of Thomas Paine* (Portsmouth).

Philo-Theodosius; or, a New Edition of Theodosius, with a New Character of Mr. Burke (1790).

Pigott, Charles (1791), *Strictures on the New Political Tenets of the Rt. Hon. Edmund Burke*.

Pigott, Charles (1795), *Pigott's Political Dictionary*.

Pigott, Charles (1798), *The Case of Charles Pigott*.

Pilkington, James (1795), *The Doctrine of Equality of Rank and Condition Examined and Supported on the Authority of the New Testament*.

'Pindar, Peter' [i.e. John Wolcott] (1809), *The Works of Peter Pindar* (4 vols).

Place, Francis (1972), *The Autobiography of Francis Place (1771–1854)*, ed. Mary Thale (Cambridge: Cambridge University Press).

Playfair, William (1795), *The History of Jacobinism. Its Crimes, Cruelties and Perfidies.*

A Plot Discovered, or an Intercepted Letter to Thomas Paine, Member of the National Convention of France, From His Friend in London (1793).

'The plot found out', in *Publications Recommended to the Perusal of the Public* (1792).

Plowden, Francis (1792), *Jura Anglorum. The Rights of Englishmen.*

The Political Crisis: or, A Discussion of the Rights of Man (1791).

Political Dialogues upon the Subject of Equality (2nd edn, Edinburgh: 1792).

Political Review of Edinburgh Periodical Publications (Edinburgh: 1792).

Pope, Simeon (1796), *A Letter to the Rt. Hon. William Curtis ... on the National Debt ... and In Reply to Paine's 'Decline and Fall of the English System of Finance'.*

Portrait of the Constitution (1792).

Pownall, Thomas (1752), *Principles of Polity, Being the Grounds and Reasons of Civil Empire.*

Price, Richard (1777), *Additional Observations on the Nature and Value of Civil Liberty and the War with America.*

Price, Richard (1785), *Observations on the Importance of the American Revolution* (Dublin).

Price, Richard (1927), *A Discourse on the Love of Our Country* (1789), in A. C. Ward (ed.), *A Miscellany of Tracts and Pamphlets* (Oxford: Oxford University Press).

Price, Richard (1791), *Britain's Happiness, and Its Full Possession of Civil and Religious Liberty, Briefly Stated and Proved.*

Priestley, Joseph (1791a), *An Appeal to the Public, on the Subject of the Riots in Birmingham* (Birmingham).

Priestley, Joseph (1791b), *Letters to the Right Honourable Edmund Burke* (Birmingham).

Priestley, Joseph (1794), *An Answer to Mr. Paine's Age of Reason* (Northumberland Town).

Priestley, Joseph (1796), *Observations on the Increase of Infidelity.*

Principle and Practice Combined: or, The Wrongs of Man. An Oration (1792).

Principles of Order and Happiness Under the British Constitution (1792).

Proceedings of the Association for Preserving Liberty and Property Against Republicans and Levellers (1792).

Proceedings of the Friends to the Abuse of the Liberty of the Press (1793).

Proceedings of the Society of the Friends of the People (1792).

'Publicola' (1913), 'Letters of Publicola' (1791), in *Writings of John Quincy Adams*, ed. W. C. Ford (New York: Macmillan), pp. 65–110.

Pufendorf, Samuel (1934), *The Law of Nature and Nations* (1672) (Oxford: Clarendon Press).

[Reeves, John] (1795), *Thoughts on the English Government.*

The Reformers of England. A New Song (n.d.).

Reid, William Hamilton (1800), *The Rise and Dissolution of the Infidel Societies in this Metropolis.*

Remarks on the Conduct, Principles, and Publications, of the Association ... for Preserving Liberty and Property against Republicans and Levellers (1793).

Remarks on a Late Pamphlet Entitled Plain Truth (Philadelphia: 1776).

Remarks on Mr. Paine's Pamphlet, Called the Rights of Man (Dublin: 1791).

Remarks on the Proceedings of the Society of the 'Friends of the People' (1792).

Report of the Committee of Secrecy of the House of Commons (1799).

The Report of the Proceedings of the ... Mock Trial of Richard Carlile (1822).

The Republican's Picture. To Be Sung by Every Honest Englishman (n.d.).

Resolutions of Common Sense, for the Preventing of Popular Delusion from Political Orators (n.d.).

Rickman, Thomas (1908), 'The life of Thomas Paine' (1819), in Daniel Edwin Wheeler (ed.), *Life and Writings of Thomas Paine*, Vol. 1 (New York: V. Parke).

Rights and Remedies, or the Theory and Practice of True Politics (1795).

The Rights of Nations. A Treatise on Representative Government, Despotism and Reform (1832).

The Rights of the Devil; or Consolation for the Democrats (n.d.).

Rights Upon Rights with Observations Upon Observations (1791).

Riland, Rev. John (1792), *The Rights of God, Occasioned by Mr. Paine's Rights of Man*.

Roberts, William (1835), *Memoirs of the Life and Correspondence of Mrs. Hannah More* (2 vols, New York).

Robison, John (1797), *Proof of a Conspiracy against All the Religions and Governments of Europe* (Edinburgh).

Romilly, Samuel (1840), *Memoirs of the Life of Sir Samuel Romilly* (3 vols).

Roosevelt, Theodore (1898), *Gouverneur Morris* (New York: Houghton Mifflin).

Rous, George (1790), *Thoughts on Government: Occasioned by Mr. Burke's Reflections*.

Russell, Lord John (1844), *Memorials and Correspondence of Charles James Fox* (4 vols).

'Rusticus' (1776), *Remarks on a Late Pamphlet Entitled Plain Truth* (Philadelphia, Pa).

Sandford, Mrs. Henry (1888), *Thomas Poole and His Friends* (2 vols).

Savory, William (1796), *An Alarm: or Three Sermons Preached in Houndsditch*.

'Scott, A.' (1793), *Plain Reasons for Adopting the Plan of the Societies Calling Themselves the Friends of the People, and Their Convention of Delegates, as Copied from the Works of Mr. Thomas Paine* (Edinburgh).

Scott, James (1793), *A Sermon Preached at Park-Street Chapel*.

Scott, James (1794), *Equality Considered and Recommended, in a Sermon*.

Scott, Major (1791), *A Letter to the Rt. Hon. Edmund Burke* (Dublin).

Scott, Thomas (1792), *An Impartial Statement of the Scriptural Doctrine, in Respect of Civil Society*.

Scott, Thomas (1796), *A Vindication of the Divine Inspiration of the Holy Scriptures*.

Scurlock, Rev. David (1792), *Thoughts on the Influence of Religion in Civil Government*.

The Second Report from the Committee of Secrecy of the House of Commons (1794).

A Serious Caution to the Poor (1792).

[Sewell, William] (1791), *A Rejoinder to Mr. Paine's Pamphlet, Entitled The Rights of Man*.

Sharp, Granville (1774), *A Declaration of the People's Natural Right to a Share in the Legislature*.

Sharp, Granville (1777), *A Tract on the Law of Nature*.

Sharp, Granville (1784), *An Account of the Ancient Division of the English Nation into Hundreds and Tythings*.

Sherwin, W. T. (1819), *Memoirs of the Life of Thomas Paine*.

Sidney, Algernon (1750), *Discourses Concerning Government* (1698) (2 vols, Edinburgh).

'Signor Pasquinello' (1792), *Crowns and Sceptres Useless Baubles*.

Simpson, Rev. David (1802), *A Plea for Religion and the Sacred Writings.*

Six Essays On Natural Rights, Liberty and Slavery, Consent of the People, Equality, Religious Establishments and the French Revolution (1792).

Smith, Joseph (1796), *An Examination of Mr. Paine's Decline and Fall of the English System of Finance.*

[Smith, William Cusac] (1791), *Rights of Citizens; Being an Inquiry into Some of the Consequences of Social Union, and an Examination of Mr. Paine's Principles Touching Social Government.*

Some Remarks on the British Constitution (Salford: 1793).

Somerville, Thomas (1793), *The Effects of the French Revolution* (Edinburgh).

Southcott, Joanna (1812), *An Answer to Thomas Paine's Third Part of the Age of Reason.*

Spence, Thomas (1793), *The Rights of Man* (4th edn).

Spence, Thomas (1797), *The Rights of Infants.*

Spence, Thomas (1982), *The Political Works of Thomas Spence*, ed. H. T. Dickinson (Newcastle upon Tyne: Avero).

The Spirit of John Locke on Civil Government Revived by the Constitutional Society of Sheffield (1792).

Stanhope, Earl (1790), *A Letter from Earl Stanhope to the Right Honourable Edmund Burke: Containing a Short Answer to His Late Speech on the French Revolution.*

Stephens, Alexander (1813), *Memoirs of John Horne Tooke* (2 vols).

Stilwell, Samuel (1794), *A Guide to Reason or an Examination of Thomas Paine's Age of Reason* (New York).

Stone, Francis (1792), *An Examination of the Rt. Hon. Edmund Burke's Reflections on the Revolution in France.*

Strictures on the Letter of the Right Hon. Edmund Burke, on the Revolution in France (1791).

Sully, Duc de (1909), *The Great Design of Henry IV from the Memoirs of the Duc de Sully* (Boston, Mass.: Ginn).

'Tam Thrum' (1793), *Look Before Ye Loup; or, A Healin' Sa' for the Crackit Crowns of Country Politicians* (Edinburgh).

Tatham, Edward (1791), *Letters to the Rt. Hon. Edmund Burke on Politics.*

[Taylor, Thomas] (1792), *A Vindication of the Rights of Brutes.*

Ten Minutes' Caution from a Plain Man to His Fellow Citizens (1792).

Thackeray, Rev. Francis (1831), *Order against Anarchy, Being a Reply to Thomas Paine's Attack upon the British Constitution, Entitled 'The Rights of Man'.*

Thale, Mary (ed.) (1983), *Selections from the Papers of the London Corresponding Society 1792–1799* (Cambridge: Cambridge University Press).

Thelwall, John (1795), *The Speech of John Thelwall at the Second Meeting of the London Corresponding Society.*

Thelwall, John (1796a), *Sober Reflections on the Seditious and Inflammatory Letter of the Right Honourable Edmund Burke.*

Thelwall, John (1796b), *The Rights of Nature against the Usurpations of Establishments.*

Thomas, John (1831), *The Challenge of a Deist Accepted.*

Thomas, Rev. Robert (1797), *The Cause of Truth, Containing ... A Refutation of Errors in the Political Works of Thomas Paine* (Dundee).

Thoughts on National Insanity (1797).

Thoughts upon Liberty and Equality (Dublin, 1793).

Thoughts Upon Our Present Situation (1793).

Tom the Boddice Maker: To the Tune of Bow! Wow! Wow! (1793).

Tom Paine's Jests (1794).

Towers, Joseph (1782), *A Vindication of the Political Principles of Mr. Locke.*

Towers, Joseph (1788), *An Oration Delivered at the London Tavern.*

Towers, Joseph (1790), *Thoughts on the Commencement of a New Parliament.*

Treason Triumphant Over Law and Constitution (1795).

The Trial of Daniel Isaac Eaton ... For Selling a Supposed Libel, A Letter, Addressed to the Addressers, by Thomas Paine (1793).

The Trial of Edward Marcus Despard, Esquire, for High Treason (1803).

The Trial of Henry Yorke (1795).

The Trial of John Horne Tooke, On a Charge of High Treason (Newcastle: 1795).

Trial of Thomas Paine (1792).

The Trial of William Winterbotham ... for Seditious Words (2nd edn, 1794).

A Trip to the Island of Equality; or, an Extract from Russian Voyages (n.d.).

The True Briton's Catechism (1793).

The True Merits of a Later Treatise ... Intitled Common Sense (1776).

Truth and Reason against Place and Pension (1793).

Tucker, Josiah (1775), *The Respective Pleas and Arguments of the Mother Country and Of the Colonies* (Gloucester).

Tucker, Josiah (1781), *A Treatise Concerning Civil Government.*

Two Letters from a Deist to His Friend, Concerning the Truth and Propagation of Deism, in Opposition to Christianity (1730).

Tytler, James (1797), *An Answer to the Second Part of Paine's Age of Reason* (Edinburgh).

Vale, Gilbert (1841), *The Life of Thomas Paine* (New York).

Vattel, Emmerich de (1916), *The Law of Nations or the Principles of Natural Law* (1758) (Washington DC: Carnegie Institute).

A Vindication of the Rt. Hon. Edmund Burke's Reflections on the Revolution in France (1791).

Volney, C. F. (1796), *An Abridgement of the Law of Nature.*

Wakefield, Gilbert (1795), *A Reply to Thomas Paine's Second Part of the Age of Reason.*

Walker, Thomas (1794), *A Review of Some of the Political Events Which Have Occurred in Manchester during the Last Five Years.*

Wallace, Robert (1761), *Various Prospects of Mankind, Nature, and Providence.*

Washington, George (1931), *The Writings of George Washington* (Washington DC: Government Printing Office).

Watson, George (1799), *Thoughts on Government.*

Watson, Richard (1796), *An Apology for the Bible in a Series of Letters Addressed to Thomas Paine* (3rd edn).

A Whipper for Levelling Tommy (1793).

White, Peter (1792), *Rational Freedom: Being a Defence of the National Character of Britons, and of Their Form of Government* (Edinburgh).

White, William (1792), *A Dissertation on Government.*

The Whole of the Proceedings at the Meeting of the Friends of the Liberty of the Press (1792).

Wilde, John (1793), *An Address to the Lately Formed Society of the Friends of the People.*

Wilks, Mark (1791), *The Origins and Stability of the French Revolution.*

[Williams, David] (1790), *Lessons to a Young Prince* (4th edn).

Wollstonecraft, Mary (1790), *A Vindication of the Rights of Men* (2nd edn).

Wollstonecraft, Mary (1794), *An Historical and Moral View of the Origin and Progress of the French Revolution.*

The Wonderful Flights of Edmund the Rhapsodist (1791).

Wyvill, Christopher (1792), *A Defence of Dr. Price and the Reformers of England.*

Wyvill, Christopher (ed.) (1794–1802), *Political Papers* (6 vols, York).

Yorke, Henry Redhead (1793), *These are the Times That Try Men's Souls!*

Yorke, Henry Redhead (1794), *Thoughts on Civil Government.*

Yorke, Henry Redhead (1798), *A Letter to the Reformers.*

Yorke, Henry Redhead (1804), *Letters from France in 1803* (2 vols).

[Young, Arthur] (1792), *A Plain and Earnest Address to Britons* (Ipswich).

Young, Arthur (1793), *The Example of France a Warning to Britain* (Bury St Edmunds).

Young, Arthur (1898), *The Autobiography of Arthur Young*, ed. M. Betham-Edwards (Smith, Elder).

Young, John (1794), *Essays on the Following Interesting Subjects* (Edinburgh).

(g) Secondary sources I: books

Adams, Randolph G. (1922), *Political Ideas of the American Revolution* (Durham: Trinity College Press).

Aldridge, A. O. (1960), *Man of Reason. The Life of Thomas Paine* (Cresset Press).

Aldridge, A. O. (1984), *Thomas Paine's American Ideology* (Associated University Presses).

Alger, John G. (1889), *Englishmen in the French Revolution* (Sampson, Low, Marston, Searle & Rivington).

Appleby, Joyce (1984), *Capitalism and a New Social Order. The Republican Vision of the 1790s* (New York: New York University Press).

Aspinall, A. (1949), *Politics and the Press c. 1780–1850* (Home & Van Thal).

Ayer, A. J. (1988), *Thomas Paine* (Secker & Warburg).

Bailyn, Bernard (1967), *The Ideological Origins of the American Revolution* (Cambridge, Mass.: Harvard University Press).

Banning, Lance (1978), *The Jeffersonian Persuasion: Evolution of a Party Ideology* (Ithaca, NY: Cornell University Press).

Barker, Ernest (1948), *Traditions of Civility* (Cambridge: Cambridge University Press).

Bauman, Richard (1971), *For the Reputation of Truth, Politics, Religion and Conflict among the Pennsylvania Quakers 1750–1800* (Baltimore, Md: Johns Hopkins University Press).

Belchem, John (1985), *'Orator' Hunt and English Working-Class Radicalism* (Oxford: Clarendon Press).

Black, Eugene C. (1963), *The Association. British Extraparliamentary Political Organization 1769–1793* (Cambridge, Mass.: Harvard University Press).

Bloch, Ruth H. (1985), *Visionary Republic. Millennial Themes in American Thought, 1756–1800* (Cambridge: Cambridge University Press).

Bonwick, Colin (1977), *English Radicals and the American Revolution* (Chapel Hill, NC: University of North Carolina).

Boulton, James (1963), *The Language of Politics in the Age of Wilkes and Burke* (Routledge & Kegan Paul).

Bradley, James E. (1986), *Popular Politics and the American Revolution in England. Petitions, the Crown, and Public Opinion* (Macon, Georgia: Mercer University Press).

Brewer, John (1976), *Party Ideology and Popular Politics at the Accession of George III* (Cambridge: Cambridge University Press).

Brown, P. A. (1918), *The French Revolution in English History* (Frank Cass).

Cannon, John (1973), *Parliamentary Reform 1640–1832* (Cambridge: Cambridge University Press).

Chase, Malcolm (1988), *The People's Farm. English Agrarian Radicalism 1775–1840* (Oxford: Oxford University Press).

Christie, Ian (1962), *Wilkes, Wyvill and Reform. The Parliamentary Reform Movement in British Politics 1760–1785* (Macmillan).

Claeys, Gregory (1987), *Machinery, Money and the Millennium. From Moral Economy to Socialism, 1815–1860* (Princeton, NJ: Princeton University Press).

Claeys, Gregory (1989), *Citizens and Saints. Politics and Anti-Politics in Early British Socialism* (Cambridge: Cambridge University Press).

Colley, Linda (1982), *In Defiance of Oligarchy. The Tory Party 1714–60* (Cambridge: Cambridge University Press).

Cole, G. D. H. (1950), *Essays in Social Theory* (Macmillan).

Cone, Carl B. (1968), *The English Jacobins. Reformers in Late 18th Century England* (New York: Scribner).

Conway, Moncure (1892), *The Life of Thomas Paine* (2 vols, Knickerbocker Press).

Cookson, J. E. (1982), *The Friends of Peace. Anti-war Liberalism in England, 1793–1815* (Cambridge: Cambridge University Press).

Crowley, J. E. (1974), *This Sheba, Self. The Conceptualization of Economic Life in Eighteenth-Century America* (Baltimore, Md: Johns Hopkins University Press).

Davis, Richard W. (1971), *Dissent in Politics 1780–1830. The Political Life of William Smith, MP* (Epworth Press).

D'Entrèves, A. P. (1972), *Natural Law* (Hutchinson).

Derry, John (1976), *English Politics and the American Revolution* (Dent).

Dickinson, H. T. (1977), *Liberty and Property. Political Ideology in Eighteenth-Century Britain* (Weidenfeld & Nicolson).

Dickinson, H. T. (1985), *British Radicalism and the French Revolution 1789–1815* (Oxford: Blackwell).

Douglass, Elisha (1955), *Rebels and Democrats. The Struggle for Equal Political Rights and Majority Rule during the American Revolution* (Chapel Hill, NC: University of North Carolina Press).

Dozier, Robert R. (1983), *For King, Constitution and Country. The English Loyalists and the French Revolution* (Lexington, Ky: University Press of Kentucky).

Dugan, James (1966), *The Great Mutiny* (Deutsch).

Ehrman, John (1983), *The Younger Pitt. The Reluctant Transition* (Stanford, NJ: Stanford University Press).

Elliott, Marianne (1982), *Partners in Revolution. The United Irishmen and France* (New Haven, Conn.: Yale University Press).

Emsley, Clive (1979), *British Society and the French Wars 1793–1815* (Macmillan).

Erdman, David V. (1986), *Commerce des Lumières. John Oswald and the British in Paris, 1790–1793* (Columbia, Mo.: University of Missouri Press).

Fennessy, R. R. (1963), *Burke, Paine and the Rights of Man* (The Hague: Martinus Nijhoff).

Fliegelman, Jay (1982), *Prodigals and Pilgrims. The American Revolution against Patriarchal Authority, 1750–1800* (Cambridge: Cambridge University Press).

Foner, Eric (1976), *Tom Paine and Revolutionary America* (Oxford: Oxford University Press).

Foner, Philip S. (1976), *Labor and the American Revolution* (Westport, Conn.: Greenwood Press).

Freeman, Michael (1980), *Edmund Burke and the Critique of Political Radicalism* (Oxford: Blackwell).

French, Allen (1934), *The First Year of the American Revolution* (Boston, Mass.: Houghton Mifflin).

Fruchtman, Jack, Jr (1983), *The Apocalyptic Politics of Richard Price and Joseph Priestley* (Philadelphia, Pa: American Philosophical Society).

Gay, Peter (1977), *The Enlightenment. An Interpretation* (New York: Norton).

Gierke, Otto (1957), *Natural Law and the Theory of Society 1500 to 1800* (Boston, Mass.: Beacon Press).

Goodwin, Albert (1979), *The Friends of Liberty. The English Democratic Movement in the Age of the French Revolution* (Hutchinson).

Gunn, J. A. W. (1983), *Beyond Liberty and Property. The Process of Self-Recognition in Eighteenth-Century Political Thought* (Montreal: McGill-Queen's University Press).

Guttridge, G. H. (1966), *English Whiggism and the American Revolution* (Berkeley, Calif.: University of California Press).

Haakonssen, Knud (1981), *The Science of a Legislator. The Natural Jurisprudence of David Hume and Adam Smith* (Cambridge: Cambridge University Press).

Hall, Walter P. (1912), *British Radicalism 1791–1797* (New York: Columbia University Press).

Hampsher-Monk, Iain (ed.) (1987), *The Political Philosophy of Edmund Burke* (Longman).

Harrison, J. F. C. (1979), *The Second Coming. Popular Millenarianism 1780–1850* (Routledge & Kegan Paul).

Hawke, David (1961), *In the Midst of a Revolution* (Philadelphia: University of Pennsylvania Press).

Hazen, Charles (1897), *Contemporary American Opinion on the French Revolution* (Baltimore, Md: Johns Hopkins University Press).

Hemleben, Sylvester John (1943), *Plans for World Peace through Six Centuries* (Chicago: University of Chicago Press).

Hempton, David (1984), *Methodism and Politics in British Society 1750–1850* (Hutchinson).

Hone, J. Ann (1982), *For the Cause of Truth. Radicalism in London 1796–1821* (Oxford: Clarendon Press).

Jacob, Margaret C. (1981), *The Radical Enlightenment: Pantheists, Freemasons and Republicans* (Allen & Unwin).

Jacob, Rosamond (1937), *The Rise of the United Irishmen, 1791–94* (Harrap).

James, Sydney V. (1963), *A People Among Peoples. Quaker Benevolence in Eighteenth-Century America* (Cambridge, Mass.: Harvard University Press).

Jewson, C. B. (1975), *The Jacobin City. A Portrait of Norwich in Its Reaction to the French Revolution 1788–1802* (Blackie).

Jones, T. Canby (1972), *George Fox's Attitude Toward War* (Annapolis, Md.: Academic Fellowship).

Knight, Frida (1957), *The Strange Case of Thomas Walker* (Lawrence & Wishart).

Koch, G. Adolf (1933), *Republican Religion. The American Revolution and the Cult of Reason* (New York: Henry Holt).

Kramnick, Isaac (1977a), *The Rage of Edmund Burke: Portrait of an Ambivalent Conservative* (New York: Basic Books).

Laprade, William (1970), *England and the French Revolution 1789–1797* (1909) (New York: AMS Press).

Lincoln, Anthony (1938), *Some Political and Social Ideas of English Dissent 1763–1800* (Cambridge: Cambridge University Press).

Lincoln, Charles (1901), *The Revolutionary Movement in Pennsylvania 1760–1776* (Philadelphia, Pa: University of Pennsylvania).

Link, Eugene P. (1942), *Democratic-Republican Societies, 1790–1800* (New York: Columbia University Press).

Lock, F. P. (1985), *Burke's Reflections on the Revolution in France* (Allen & Unwin).

Logue, Kenneth J. (1979), *Popular Disturbances in Scotland 1780–1815* (Edinburgh: John Donald).

Lutz, Donald S. (1980), *Popular Consent and Popular Control. Whig Political Theory in the Early State Constitutions* (Baton Rouge, La: Louisiana State University Press).

Lynd, Staughton (1968), *Intellectual Origins of American Radicalism* (New York: Vintage Books).

Maccoby, S. (1955a), *English Radicalism 1762–1785* (Allen & Unwin).

Maccoby, S. (1955b), *English Radicalism 1786–1832* (Allen & Unwin).

MacNair, Everett (1957), *Edward Bellamy and the Nationalist Movement, 1889–1894* (Milwaukee, Wisc.; Fitzgerald).

MacPherson, C. B. (1980), *Burke* (Oxford: Oxford University Press).

Maier, Pauline (1972a), *From Resistance to Revolution. Colonial Radicals and the Development of American Opposition to Britain, 1765–1776* (New York: Knopf).

Manwaring, G. E. and Dobree, Bonamy (1935), *The Floating Republic. An Account of the Mutinies at Spithead and the Nore in 1797* (New York: Harcourt, Brace).

Marshall, Leon S. (1946), *The Development of Public Opinion in Manchester, 1780–1820* (Syracuse, New York: University of Syracuse Press).

Marston, Jerrilyn (1987), *King and Congress. The Transfer of Political Legitimacy* (Princeton, NJ: Princeton University Press).

McCalman, Iain (1988), *Radical Underworld. Prophets, Revolutionaries and Pornographers in London, 1795–1840* (Cambridge: Cambridge University Press).

McCoy, Drew (1980), *The Elusive Republic. Political Economy in Jeffersonian America* (Chapel Hill, NC: University of North Carolina Press).

Meikle, H. W. (1912), *Scotland and the French Revolution* (Glasgow: Maclehose).

Mekeel, Arthur J. (1979), *The Relation of the Quakers to the American Revolution* (Washington DC: University Press of America).

Miles, Dudley (1988), *Francis Place 1771–1854* (Brighton: Harvester Press).

Mingay, G. E. (1963), *English Landed Society in the Eighteenth Century* (Routledge & Kegan Paul).

Mitchell, B. R. (1988), *British Historical Statistics* (Cambridge: Cambridge University Press).

Mitchell, L. G. (1971), *Charles James Fox and the Disintegration of the Whig Party* (Oxford: Oxford University Press).

Money, John (1977), *Experience and Identity. Birmingham and the West Midlands 1760–1800* (Montreal: McGill-Queen's University Press).

Morais, Herbert M. (1934), *Deism in Eighteenth-Century America* (New York: Columbia University Press).

Morgan, Edmund S. (1988), *Inventing the People. The Rise of Popular Sovereignty in England and America* (New York: Norton).

Morse, Anson (1909), *The Federalist Party in Massachusetts to the Year 1800* (Princeton, NJ: University Library).

Nash, Gary B. (1979), *The Urban Crucible. Social Change, Political Consciousness, and the Origins of the American Revolution* (Cambridge, Mass.: Harvard University Press).

O'Gorman, Frank (1967), *The Whig Party and the French Revolution* (Macmillan).

O'Gorman, Frank (1973), *Edmund Burke: His Political Philosophy* (Allen & Unwin).

Olton, Charles S. (1975), *Artisans for Independence. Philadelphia Mechanics and the American Revolution* (Syracuse, New York: University of Syracuse Press).

Osbourne, John (1972), *John Cartwright* (Cambridge: Cambridge University Press).

Palmer, R. R. (1959), *The Age of the Democratic Revolution. A Political History of Europe and America, 1760–1800* (2 vols, Princeton, NJ: Princeton University Press).

Patterson, A. Temple (1954), *Radical Leicester. A History of Leicester 1780–1850* (Leicester: University College).

Paul, Charles Kegan (1876), *William Godwin: His Friends and Contemporaries* (2 vols, Henry S. King).

Paulson, Ronald (1983), *Representations of Revolution (1789–1820)* (New Haven, Conn.: Yale University Press).

Plumb, J. H. (1973), *In the Light of History* (Allen Lane).

Pocock, J. G. A. (1975), *The Machiavellian Moment. Florentine Political Thought and the Atlantic Republican Tradition* (Princeton, NJ: Princeton University Press).

Pocock, J. G. A. (1985), *Virtue, Commerce and History* (Cambridge: Cambridge University Press).

Pole, J. R. (1966), *Political Representation in England and the Origins of the American Republic* (Berkeley, Calif.: University of California Press).

Postgate, Raymond (1956), *That Devil Wilkes* (Dobson).

Powell, David (1985), *Tom Paine. The Greatest Exile* (New York: St Martin's Press).

Raphael, D. D. (ed.) (1967), *Political Theory and the Rights of Man* (Bloomington, Ind.: Indiana University Press).

Redwood, John (1976), *Reason, Ridicule and Religion. The Age of Enlightenment in England 1660–1750* (Thames & Hudson).

Reid, John Phillip (1988), *The Concept of Liberty in the Age of the American Revolution* (Chicago: University of Chicago Press).

Robbins, Caroline (1959), *The Eighteenth-Century Commonwealthman* (Cambridge, Mass.: Harvard University Press).

Rock, Howard B. (1979), *Artisans of the New Republic. The Tradesmen of New York City in the Age of Jefferson* (New York: New York University Press).

Rommen, Heinrich (1949), *The Natural Law. A Study in Legal and Social History and Philosophy* (Herder).

Roper, Derek (1978), *Reviewing Before the Edinburgh 1788–1802* (Methuen).

Royle, Edward (1974), *Victorian Infidels: The Origins of the British Secularist Movement, 1791–1866* (Manchester: Manchester University Press).

Royle, Edward, and James Walvin (1982), *English Radicals and Reformers 1760–1848* (Lexington, Ky: University Press of Kentucky).

Rudé, George (1962), *Wilkes and Liberty* (Oxford: Clarendon Press).

Rudé, George (1964a), *The Crowd in History, 1730–1848* (New York: John Wiley).

Rudé, George (1964b), *Revolutionary Europe 1783–1815* (Fontana).

Rudé, George (1980), *Ideology and Popular Protest* (Lawrence & Wishart).

Selsam, J. Paul (1936), *The Pennsylvania Constitution of 1776* (Philadelphia, Pa: University of Pennsylvania Press).

Semmel, Bernard (1974), *The Methodist Revolution* (Heinemann).

Shapiro, Ian (1986), *The Evolution of Rights in Liberal Theory* (Cambridge: Cambridge University Press).

Sigmund, Paul E. (1971), *Natural Law in Political Thought* (Cambridge, Mass.: Winthrop).

Stanlis, Peter (1958), *Edmund Burke and the Natural Law* (Ann Arbor, Mich.: University of Michigan Press).

Stauffer, Vernon (1918), *New England and the Bavarian Illuminati* (New York: Russell & Russell).

Stedman Jones, Gareth (1983), *Languages of Class. Studies in English Working-Class History 1832–1982* (Cambridge: Cambridge University Press).

Thomis, Malcolm I. and Peter Holt (1977), *Threats of Revolution in Britain 1789–1848* (Macmillan).

Thompson, E. P. (1968), *The Making of the English Working Class* (Harmondsworth: Penguin).

Tolles, Frederick B. (1948), *Meeting House and Counting House. The Quaker Merchants of Colonial Philadelphia 1682–1763* (Chapel Hill, NC: University of North Carolina).

Tolles, Frederick B. (1960), *Quakers and the Atlantic Culture* (Macmillan).

Toohey, Robert E. (1978), *Liberty and Empire. British Radical Solutions to the American Problem 1774–1776* (Lexington, Ky: University Press of Kentucky).

Tuck, Richard (1979), *Natural Rights Theories. Their Origin and Development* (Cambridge: Cambridge University Press).

Turner, James (1985), *Without God, Without Creed. The Origins of Unbelief in America* (Baltimore, Md: Johns Hopkins University Press).

Tuveson, Ernest (1968), *Redeemer Nation. The Idea of America's Millennial Role* (Chicago: University of Chicago Press).

Veitch, George (1913), *The Genesis of Parliamentary Reform* (Constable).

Vile, M. J. C. (1967), *Constitutionalism and the Separation of Powers* (Oxford: Clarendon Press).

Viner, Jacob (1972), *The Role of Providence in the Social Order* (Philadelphia, Pa: American Philosophical Society).

Webb, R. K. (1955), *The British Working-Class Reader 1790–1848* (Allen & Unwin).

Wells, Roger (1983), *Insurrection. The British Experience 1795–1803* (Gloucester: Alan Sutton).

Wells, Roger (1987), *Wretched Faces: Famine in Wartime England* (New York: St Martin's Press).

Werkmeister, Lucyle (1963), *The London Daily Press 1772–1792* (Lincoln, Nebr: University of Nebraska Press).

Weston, Corinne (1965), *English Constitutional Theory and the House of Lords 1556–1832* (Routledge & Kegan Paul).

Wiener, Joel (1983), *Radicalism and Freethought in Nineteenth-Century Britain: The Life of Richard Carlile* (Westport, Conn.: Greenwood Press).

Wilentz, Sean (1984), *Chants Democratic. New York City and the Rise of the American Working Class, 1788–1850* (Oxford: Oxford University Press).

Wilkins, Burleigh (1967), *The Problem of Burke's Political Philosophy* (Oxford: Clarendon Press).

Willey, Basil (1957), *The Eighteenth-Century Background* (Chatto & Windus).

Williams, Gwyn A. (1969), *Artisans and Sans-Culottes. Popular Movements in France and Britain during the French Revolution* (New York: Norton).

Williamson, Audrey (1973), *Thomas Paine. His Life, Work and Times* (Allen & Unwin).

Williamson, Chilton (1960), *American Suffrage. From Property to Democracy 1760–1860* (Princeton, NJ: Princeton University Press).

Wilson, David A. (1988), *Paine and Cobbett. The Transatlantic Connection* (Montreal: McGill-Queen's University Press).

Wood, Gordon (1969), *The Creation of the American Republic 1776–1787* (Chapel Hill, NC: University of North Carolina Press).

Woodress, James (1958), *A Yankee's Odyssey. The Life of Joel Barlow* (New York: Lippincott).

Wright, Benjamin F. (1931), *American Interpretations of Natural Law* (Cambridge, Mass.: Harvard University Press).

Young, Alfred (1967), *The Democratic Republicans of New York 1763–1797* (Chapel Hill, NC: University of North Carolina Press).

Young, Alfred (ed.) (1976), *The American Revolution. Explorations in the History of American Radicalism* (DeKalb, Ill: Northern Illinois University Press).

(h)   Secondary sources II: articles

Abel, Darrel (1942), 'The significance of the letter to the Abbé Raynal in the progress of Thomas Paine's thought', *Pennsylvania Magazine of History and Biography*, vol. 66, pp. 176–90.

Adams, W. P. (1970), 'Republicanism in political rhetoric before 1776', *Political Science Quarterly*, vol. 85, pp. 397–421.

Aldridge, A. O. (1949), 'Why did Thomas Paine write on the bank?', *Proceedings of the American Philosophical Society*, vol. 93, pp. 309–15.

Aldridge, A. O. (1951), 'Some writings of Thomas Paine in Pennsylvania newspapers', *American Historical Review*, vol. 56, pp. 832–8.

Aldridge, A. O. (1953), 'Thomas Paine and the New York *Public Advertiser*', *New York Historical Society Quarterly*, vol. 37, pp. 361–82.

Aldridge, A. O. (1957), 'Thomas Paine's plan for a descent on England', *William and Mary Quarterly*, vol. 14, pp. 74–84.

Aldridge, A. O. (1968), 'Thomas Paine and the classics', *Eighteenth-Century Studies*, vol. 1, pp. 370–80.

Aldridge, A. O. (1976a), 'Paine and Dickinson', *Early American Literature*, vol. 11, pp. 125–38.

Aldridge, A. O. (1976b), 'Thomas Paine and the *idéologues*', *Studies on Voltaire and the Eighteenth Century*, vol. 151, pp. 109–17.

Aldridge, A. O. (1976c), 'The influence of New York newspapers on *Common Sense*', *New York Historical Society Quarterly*, vol. 60, pp. 53–60.

Aldridge, A. O. (1978), 'The problem of Thomas Paine', *Studies in Burke and His Time*, Vol. 19, pp. 127–43.

Andrews, Stuart (1983), 'Tom Paine in France', *History Today*, vol. 33, pp. 5–11.

Appleby, Joyce (1976), 'Liberalism and the American revolution', *New England Quarterly*, vol. 49, pp. 3–26.

Appleby, Joyce (1978), 'Modernization theory and the formation of modern social theories in England and America', *Comparative Studies in Society and History*, vol. 20, pp. 259–85.

Appleby, Joyce (1985), 'Republicanism and ideology', *American Quarterly*, vol. 37, pp. 461–73.

Armytage, W. H. G. (1951), 'Thomas Paine and the Walkers: an early episode in Anglo-American co-operation', *Pennsylvania History*, vol. 18, pp. 16–30.

Ashworth, John (1984), 'The Jeffersonians: classical republicans or liberal capitalists?', *Journal of American Studies*, vol. 18, pp. 425–35.

Bailyn, Bernard (1973), 'The most uncommon pamphlet of the revolution. *Common Sense*', *American Heritage*, vol. 25, pp. 36–41, 91–3.

Banning, Lance (1976), 'Jeffersonian ideology and the French revolution: a question of liberticide at home', *Studies on Burke and His Time*, vol. 17, pp. 5–26.

Banning, Lance (1986), 'Jeffersonian ideology revisited: liberal and classical ideals in the new American republic', *William and Mary Quarterly*, vol. 43, pp. 3–19.

Barry, Alyce (1977), 'Thomas Paine, privateersman', *Pennsylvania Magazine of History and Biography*, vol. 101, pp. 451–61.

Baxter, John (1974), 'The great Yorkshire Revival 1792–6: a study of mass revival among the Methodists', *Sociological Yearbook of Religion in Britain*, vol. 7, pp. 46–76.

Belchem, John (1981), 'Republicanism, popular constitutionalism and the radical platform in early nineteenth-century England', *Social History*, vol. 6, pp. 1–32.

Bernstein, Samuel (1945), 'English reactions to the French revolution', *Science and Society*, vol. 9, pp. 147–71.

Berthoff, Rowland (1979), 'Independence and attachment, virtue and interest: from republican citizen to free enterpriser, 1787–1837', in Richard Bushman *et al.* (eds), *Uprooted Americans* (Boston, Mass.: Little, Brown, 1979), pp. 97–124.

Berthoff, Rowland and John Murrin (1973), 'Feudalism, communalism and the yeoman freeholder: the American revolution considered as a social accident', in S. Kurtz and J. Hutson (eds), *Essays on the American Revolution* (Chapel Hill, NC: University of North Carolina Press), pp. 256–88.

Bockelman, Wayne and Owen Ireland (1974), 'The internal revolution in Pennsylvania: an ethnic-religious interpretation', *Pennsylvania History*, vol. 41, pp. 125–59.

Bonwick, Colin (1976), 'English Dissenters and the American revolution', in H. C. Allen and Roger Thompson (eds), *Contrast and Connection: Bicentennial Essays in Anglo-American History* (Athens, Ohio: Ohio University Press), pp. 88–112.

Booth, Alan (1983), 'Popular loyalism and public violence in the north-west of England, 1790–1800', *Social History*, vol. 8, pp. 295–313.

Booth, Alan (1986), 'The United Englishmen and radical politics in the industrial north-west of England, 1795–1803', *International Review of Social History*, vol. 31, pp. 371–97.

Brewer, John (1980a), 'English radicalism in the Age of George III', in J. G. A. Pocock (ed.), *Three British Revolutions: 1641, 1688, 1776* (Princeton, NJ: Princeton University Press), pp. 323–67.

Brewer, John (1980b), 'The Wilkites and the law, 1763–74: a study of radical notions of governance', in John Brewer and John Styles (eds), *An Ungovernable People. The English and Their Law in the Seventeenth and Eighteenth Centuries* (Hutchinson), pp. 128–71.

Brims, John (1987), 'The Scottish "Jacobins", Scottish nationalism and the British union', in R. A. Mason (ed.), *Scotland and England 1286–1815* (Edinburgh: John Donald), pp. 247–65.

Browne, Ray (1964), 'The Paine–Burke controversy in eighteenth-century Irish popular songs', in Ray Browne, W. Roscelli, A. Loftus (eds), *The Celtic Cross: Studies in Irish Culture and Literature* (West Lafayette, Ind.: Purdue University Press), pp. 80–97.

Buel, Richard (1964), 'Democracy and the American revolution: a frame of reference', *William and Mary Quarterly*, vol. 21, pp. 165–90.

Burns, J. H. (1971), 'The rights of man since the reformation: an historical survey', in Francis Vallat (ed.), *An Introduction to the Study of Human Rights* (Europa), pp. 16–30.

Bushman, Richard (1979), '"This new man": dependence and independence, 1776', in R. L. Bushman *et al.* (eds), *Uprooted Americans* (Boston, Mass.: Little, Brown), pp. 77–96.

Butterfield, Herbert (1947), 'The Yorkshire Association and the crisis of 1779–80', *Transactions of the Royal Historical Society*, vol. 29, pp. 69–92.

Butterfield, Herbert (1949), 'Charles James Fox and the Whig opposition in 1792', *Cambridge Historical Journal*, vol. 9, pp. 293–330.

Canavan, Francis (1976), 'The Burke-Paine controversy', *Political Science Reviewer*, vol. 6, pp. 389–420.

Chaloner, W. H. (1958), 'Dr. Joseph Priestley, John Wilkinson and the French revolution, 1789–1802', *Transactions of the Royal Historical Society*, vol. 8, pp. 21–40.

Christian, William (1973a), 'The moral economics of Tom Paine', *Journal of the History of Ideas*, vol. 34, pp. 367–80.

Christian, William (1973b), 'James Mackintosh, Burke, and the cause of reform', *Eighteenth-Century Studies*, vol. 7, pp. 194–206.

Christie, Ian (1960), 'The Yorkshire Association, 1780–4: a study in political organization', *Historical Journal*, vol. 3, pp. 144–61.

Claeys, Gregory (1988a), 'Reciprocal dependence, virtue and commerce: some sources of early socialist cosmopolitanism and internationalism in Britain, 1790–1860', in F. L. van Holthoon and Marcel van der Linden (eds), *Internationalism in the Labour Movement to 1940* (Leiden: Brill), Vol. 1, pp. 234–58.

Claeys, Gregory (1988b), 'Thomas Paine's *Agrarian Justice* (1796) and the secularization of natural jurisprudence', *Bulletin of the Society for the Study of Labour History*, vol. 52, part 3, pp. 21–31.

Clark, Harry Hayden (1932), 'Thomas Paine's relation to Voltaire and Rousseau', *Revue Anglo-Américaine*, vol. 9, pp. 305–18, 393–405.

Clark, Harry Hayden (1933a), 'An historical interpretation of Thomas Paine's religion', *University of California Chronicle*, vol. 35, pp. 56–87.

Clark, Harry Hayden (1933b), 'Toward a reinterpretation of Thomas Paine', *American Literature*, vol. 5, pp. 133–45.

Cohen, Lester (1978), 'The American revolution and natural law theory', *Journal of the History of Ideas*, vol. 59, pp. 491–502.

Colley, Linda (1981), 'Eighteenth-century English radicalism before Wilkes', *Transactions of the Royal Historical Society*, vol. 31, pp. 1–19.

Collins, Henry (1954), 'The London Corresponding Society', in John Saville (ed.), *Democracy and the Labour Movement* (Lawrence & Wishart), pp. 103–34.

Creasey, John (1966), 'Some Dissenting attitudes towards the French revolution', *Transactions of the Unitarian Historical Society*, vol. 13, pp. 155–67.

Cronin, Sean (1980), 'Thomas Paine and the United Irishmen', *Bulletin of the Thomas Paine Society*, vol. 6, pp. 93–6.

Dickinson, H. T. (1976), 'The rights of man from John Locke to Tom Paine', in O. D. Edwards and G. A. Shepperson (eds), *Scotland, Europe and the American Revolution* (Edinburgh: EUSP), pp. 38–48.

Dinwiddy, J. R. (1971), 'Christopher Wyvill and reform 1790–1820', *Borthwick Papers*, no. 39, pp. 1–32.

Dinwiddy, J. R. (1974a), 'The "Black Lamp" in Yorkshire 1801–1802', *Past and Present*, no. 64, pp. 113–23.

Dinwiddy, J. R. (1974b), 'Utility and natural law in Burke's thought: a reconsideration', *Studies in Burke and His Time*, vol. 16, pp. 105–28.

Ditchfield, G. M. (1974), 'The parliamentary struggle over the repeal of the Test and Corporation Acts, 1787–1790', *English Historical Review*, vol. 89, pp. 551–77.

Donelly, F. K. and John Baxter (1976), 'Sheffield and the English revolutionary tradition, 1791–1820', in Sidney Pollard and Colin Holmes (eds), *Essays in the*

Economic and Social History of South Yorkshire (Sheffield: South Yorkshire County Council), pp. 90–117.

Dorfman, J. (1938), 'The economic philosophy of Thomas Paine', *Political Science Quarterly*, vol. 53, pp. 372–86.

Dozier, Robert (1972), 'Democratic revolution in England: a possibility?', *Albion*, vol. 4, pp. 183–92.

Dunn, John (1969), 'The politics of Locke in England and America in the eighteenth century', in John Yolton (ed.), *Problems from Locke* (Cambridge: Cambridge University Press), pp. 45–80.

Durey, Michael (1985), 'Transatlantic patriotism: political exiles and America in the age of revolutions', in Clive Emsley and James Walvin (eds), *Artisans, Peasants and Proletarians 1760–1860* (Croom Helm), pp. 7–31.

Durey, Michael (1987), 'Thomas Paine's apostles: radical emigrés and the triumph of Jeffersonian republicanism' *William and Mary Quarterly*, vol. 44, pp. 661–88.

Dyck, Ian (1988), 'Debts and liabilities: William Cobbett and Thomas Paine', in Ian Dyck (ed.), *Citizen of the World. Essays on Thomas Paine* (New York: St Martin's Press), pp. 86–103.

Eayrs, James (1952), 'The political ideas of the English agrarians, 1775–1815', *Canadian Journal of Economics and Political Science*, vol. 18, pp. 287–302.

Elliott, Marianne (1977), 'The "Despard Conspiracy" reconsidered', *Past and Present*, no. 75, pp. 46–61.

Elliott, Marianne (1983), 'French subversion in Britain in the French revolution', in Colin Jones (ed.), *Britain and Revolutionary France: Conflict, Subversion and Propaganda* (Exeter: University of Exeter Studies in History, No. 5), pp. 40–52.

Emsley, Clive (1975), 'Political disaffection and the British Army in 1792', *Bulletin of the Institute of Historical Research*, vol. 48, pp. 230–45.

Emsley, Clive (1981), 'An aspect of Pitt's "Terror" prosecutions for sedition during the 1790s', *Social History*, vol. 6, pp. 155–84.

Emsley, Clive (1985), 'Repression, "Terror" and the rule of law in England during the decade of the French revolution', *English Historical Review*, vol. 100, pp. 801–25.

Epstein, James (1988), 'Radical dining, toasting and symbolic expression in early nineteenth-century Lancashire: rituals of solidarity', *Albion*, vol. 20, pp. 271–91.

Falk, Robert (1938), 'Thomas Paine: deist or Quaker?', *Pennsylvania Magazine of History and Biography*, vol. 62, pp. 52–63.

Falk, Robert (1939), 'Thomas Paine and the attitude of the Quakers to the American revolution', *Pennsylvania Magazine of History and Biography*, vol. 63, pp. 302–10.

Forbes, Duncan (1982), 'Natural law and the Scottish Enlightenment', in R. H. Campbell and A. S. Skinner (eds), *Origin and Nature of the Scottish Enlightenment* (Edinburgh: John Donald), pp. 186–204.

Fruchtman, Jack (1981), 'Politics and the apocalypse: The republic and the millennium in late-eighteenth century English political thought', *Studies in Eighteenth-Century Culture*, vol. 10, pp. 153–64.

Fruchtman, Jack (1984), 'The revolutionary millennialism of Thomas Paine', *Studies in Eighteenth-Century Culture*, vol. 13, pp. 65–77.

Garrison, Frank (1923), 'Paine and the physiocrats', *The Freeman*, vol. 8 (November), pp. 205–6.

Gibbens, V. E. (1942), 'Tom Paine and the idea of progress', *Pennsylvania Magazine of History and Biography*, vol. 66, pp. 191–204.

Gimbel, Richard (1956b), 'The first appearance of Thomas Paine's *The Age of Reason*', *Yale University Library Gazette*, vol. 31, pp. 87–9.

Gimbel, Richard (1956c), 'New political writings by Thomas Paine', *Yale University Library Gazette*, vol. 30, pp. 94–107.

Gimbel, Richard (1959), 'The resurgence of Thomas Paine', *Proceedings of the American Antiquarian Society*, vol. 69, pp. 97–111.

Gimbel, Richard (1960), 'Thomas Paine fights for freedom in three worlds. The new, the old, the next', *Proceedings of the American Antiquarian Society*, vol. 70, pp. 397–492.

Ginter, Donald (1966), 'The loyalist association movement of 1792–93 and British public opinion', *Historical Journal*, vol. 9, pp. 179–90.

Greene, Jack P. (1978), 'Paine, America, and the "modernization" of political consciousness', *Political Science Quarterly*, vol. 93, pp. 73–92.

Gummere, Richard (1965), 'Thomas Paine: was he really anticlassical?', *Proceedings of the American Antiquarian Society*, vol. 75, pp. 253–69.

Halévy, E. (1906), 'La Naissance du Méthodisme en Angleterre', *La Revue de Paris*, pp. 518–39.

Hampsher-Monk, Iain (1978), 'Civic humanism and parliamentary reform: the case of the Society of the Friends of the People', *Journal of British Studies*, vol. 18, pp. 70–89.

Hampsher-Monk, Iain (1989), 'John Thelwall and the eighteenth-century radical response to political economy', *Historical Journal*, vol. 32 (forthcoming).

Handforth, Pauline (1956), 'Manchester radical politics, 1789–1794', *Transactions of the Lancashire and Cheshire Antiquarian Society*, vol. 66, pp. 87–106.

Harrison, J. F. C. (1988), 'Thomas Paine and millenarian radicalism', in Ian Dyck (ed.), *Citizen of the World. Essays on Thomas Paine* (New York: St Martin's Press), pp. 73–85.

Hill, Christopher (1954), 'The Norman yoke', in John Saville (ed.), *Democracy and the Labour Movement* (Lawrence & Wishart), pp. 11–66.

Hindmarsh, G. (1979), 'Thomas Paine and the Methodist influence', *Bulletin of the Thomas Paine Society*, vol. 6, pp. 59–78.

Hinz, Evelyn J. (1972), 'The "reasonable" style of Tom Paine', *Queen's Quarterly*, vol. 79, pp. 231–41.

Hobsbawm, Eric (1957), 'Methodism and the threat of revolution in Britain', *History Today*, vol. 7, pp. 115–24.

Hole, Robert (1983), 'British counter-revolutionary popular propaganda in the 1790s', in Colin Jones (ed.), *Britain and Revolutionary France: Conflict, Subversion and Propaganda* (Exeter: University of Exeter Studies in History, No. 5), pp. 153–69.

Hont, Istvan (1987), 'The language of sociability and commerce: Samuel Pufendorf and the theoretical foundations of the "Four-Stages Theory"', in Anthony Pagden (ed.), *The Languages of Political Theory in Early-Modern Europe* (Cambridge: Cambridge University Press), pp. 253-76.

Hont, Istvan (1989), 'Economic limits to national politics: a reconsideration of neo-Machiavellian political economy', in John Dunn (ed.), *Economic Limits to Modern Politics* (Cambridge: Cambridge University Press) (forthcoming).

Itzkin, Elissa (1975), 'The Halévy thesis–a working hypothesis? English revivalism: antidote for revolution and radicalism 1789–1815', *Church History*, vol. 44, pp. 47-56.

Jensen, Merrill (1957), 'Democracy and the American revolution', *William and Mary Quarterly*, vol. 20, pp. 321–41.

Jordan, Winthrop (1973), 'Familial politics: Thomas Paine and the killing of the king', *Journal of American History*, vol. 60, pp. 294–308.

Keane, John (1988), 'Despotism and democracy. The origins and development of the distinction between civil society and the state 1750–1850', in John Keane (ed.), *Civil Society and the State. New European Perspectives* (Verso), pp. 35–71.

Kennedy, W. Benjamin (1976), 'The Irish Jacobins', *Studia Hibernica*, vol. 16, pp. 109–21.

Kenyon, Cecilia (1951), 'Where Paine went wrong', *American Political Science Review*, vol. 45, pp. 1086–99.

Kenyon, Cecilia (1962), 'Republicanism and radicalism in the American revolution: an old-fashioned interpretation', *William and Mary Quarterly*, vol. 19, pp. 153–82.

Kerber, Linda (1985), 'The republican ideology of the revolutionary generation', *American Quarterly*, vol. 37, pp. 474–95.

Kirby, John (1970), 'Early American politics – the search for ideology: an historiographical analysis and critique of the concept of "deference"', *Journal of Politics*, vol. 32, pp. 808–38.

Kistler, Mark (1962), 'German-American liberalism and Thomas Paine', *American Quarterly*, vol. 14, pp. 81–91.

Knudson, Jerry W. (1969), 'The rage around Tom Paine. Newspaper reaction to his homecoming in 1802', *New York Historical Society Quarterly*, vol. 53, pp. 34–63.

Kramnick, Isaac (1977b), 'Religion and radicalism. English political theory in the Age of Revolution', *Political Theory*, vol. 5, pp. 505–34.

Kramnick, Isaac (1980), 'English middle-class radicalism in the eighteenth century', *Literature of Liberty*, vol. 3, pp. 5–48.

Kramnick, Isaac (1982), 'Republican revisionism revisited', *American Political Science Review*, vol. 87, pp. 629–64.

Kramnick, Isaac (1986), 'Tommy Paine and the idea of America', in Paul J. Korshin (ed.), *The American Revolution and Eighteenth-Century Culture* (New York: AMS Press), pp. 75–91.

Lee, Janice (1981), 'Political antiquarianism unmasked: the Conservative attack on the myth of the ancient constitution', *Bulletin of the Institute of Historical Research*, vol. 54, pp. 166–79.

Libiszowska, Zofia (1980), 'Thomas Paine et la Gironde', *Acta Universitatis Lodziensis*, s. 1, no. 71, pp. 87–105.

Lockridge, Kenneth (1977), 'The American revolution, modernization, and man: a critique', in Richard Maxwell Brown and Don E. Fehrenbacher (eds), *Tradition, Conflict, and Modernization. Perspectives on the American Revolution* (New York: Academic Press), pp. 103–19.

Lokken, Roy (1963), 'The concept of democracy in colonial political thought', *William and Mary Quarterly*, vol. 16, pp. 568-80.

Lucas, Paul (1968), 'On Edmund Burke's doctrine of prescription; or, an appeal from the new to the old lawyers', *Historical Journal*, vol. 11, pp. 35–63.

Maier, Pauline (1963), 'John Wilkes and American disillusionment with Britain', *William and Mary Quarterly*, vol. 20, pp. 373–95.

Maier, Pauline (1972b), 'The beginnings of American republicanism', in *The Development of a Revolutionary Mentality* (Washington DC: Library of Congress).

McGovern, Trevor (1988), 'Conservative ideology in Britain in the 1790s', *History*, vol. 73, pp. 238–47.

McKenzie, Lionel (1980), 'The French revolution and English parliamentary reform: James Mackintosh and the *Vindiciae Gallicae*', *Eighteenth-Century Studies*, vol. 15, pp. 264–82.

Meader, Lewis (1898), 'The Council of Censors', *Pennsylvania Magazine of History and Biography*, vol. 22, pp. 265–300.

Meng, John J. (1946), 'The constitutional theories of Thomas Paine', *Review of Politics*, vol. 8, 283–306.

Mitchell, Austin (1961), 'The Association Movement of 1792–3', *Historical Journal*, vol. 4, pp. 56–77.

Money, John (1980), 'British history and the French revolution', *Canadian Journal of History*, vol. 15, pp. 416–30.

Morrell, J. B. (1971), 'Professors Robison and Playfair, and the Theophobia Gallica: natural philosophy, religion and politics in Edinburgh, 1789–1815', *Notes and Records of the Royal Society of London*, vol. 26, pp. 43–63.

Morris, Richard B. (1962), 'Class struggle and the American revolution', *William and Mary Quarterly*, vol. 19, pp. 3–29.

Muzzey, David S. (1926), 'Thomas Paine and American independence', *American Review*, vol. 4, pp. 278–88.

Myers, Mitzi (1977), 'Politics from the outside: Mary Wollstonecraft's first vindication', *Studies in Eighteenth-Century Culture*, vol. 6, pp. 113–32.

Nash, Gary (1965), 'The American clergy and the French revolution', *William and Mary Quarterly*, vol. 22, pp. 392–412.

Nash, Gary (1976), 'Poverty and poor relief in pre-revolutionary Philadelphia', *William and Mary Quarterly*, vol. 33, pp. 3–30.

Newman, Gerald (1974), 'Anti-French propaganda and British liberal nationalism in the early nineteenth century', *Victorian Studies*, vol. 18, pp. 385–418.

Newman, Stephen (1978), 'A note on *Common Sense* and Christian eschatology', *Political Theory*, vol. 6, pp. 101–8.

Nursey-Bray, P. F. (1968), 'Thomas Paine and the concept of alienation', *Political Studies*, vol. 16, pp. 223–42.

Palmer, R. R. (1942), 'Tom Paine. Victim of the Rights of Man', *Pennsylvania Magazine of History and Biography*, vol. 61, pp. 161–75.

Parsinnen, T. M. (1973), 'Association, convention and anti-parliament in British radical politics, 1771–1848', *English Historical Review*, vol. 88, pp. 504–33.

Pedersen, Susan (1986), 'Hannah More meets Simple Simon: Tracts, Chapbooks, and Popular Culture in late eighteenth-century England', *Journal of British Studies*, vol. 25, pp. 84–113.

Penniman, Howard (1943), 'Thomas Paine – Democrat', *American Political Science Review*, vol. 37, pp. 244–62.

Popkin, Richard (1987), 'The *Age of Reason* versus *The Age of Revelation*: two critics of Tom Paine: David Levi and Elias Boudinot', in J. A. Lemay (ed.), *Deism, Masonry and the Enlightenment* (Newark, Del: University of Delaware Press), pp. 158–70.

Porter, J. and R. Farnell (1976), 'John Adams and American constitutionalism', *American Journal of Jurisprudence*, vol. 21, pp. 20–33.

Prochaska, Franklyn K. (1972), 'Thomas Paine's *The Age of Reason* revisited', *Journal of the History of Ideas*, vol. 33, pp. 561–76.

Quinlan, Maurice (1943), 'Anti-Jacobin propaganda in England, 1792–1794', *Journalism Quarterly*, vol. 16, pp. 9–15.

Raphael, D. D. (1967), 'Human rights, old and new', in D. D. Raphael (ed.), *Political Theory and the Rights of Man* (Bloomington, Ind.: Indiana University Press), pp. 54–67.

Ripley, R. (1965), 'Adams, Burke, and eighteenth-century conservatism', *Political Science Quarterly*, vol. 80, pp. 216–35.

Robbins, Caroline (1983), 'The lifelong education of Thomas Paine (1737–1809)' *Proceedings of the American Philosophical Society*, vol. 127, pp. 135–42.

Robbins, Caroline (1986), 'William Penn, 1689–1702: eclipse, frustration, and achievement', in Richard S. Dunn and Mary Maples Dunn (eds), *The World of William Penn* (Philadelphia, Pa: University of Pennsylvania Press), pp. 71–84.

Robinson, Eric (1955), 'An English Jacobin: James Watt, Junior, 1769–1848', *Cambridge Historical Journal*, vol. 11, pp. 349–55.

Roper, Ralph (1944), 'Thomas Paine: Scientist-Religionist', *Scientific Monthly*, vol. 58, pp. 101–11.

Rose, R. B. (1960), 'The Priestley riots of 1791', *Past and Present*, vol. 18, pp. 68–88.

Rose, R. B. (1965), 'The origins of working-class radicalism in Birmingham', *Labour History*, vol. 9, pp. 6–14.

Roshwald, Mordecai (1959), 'The concept of human rights', *Philosophy and Phenomenological Research*, vol. 19, pp. 354–79.

Royle, Edward (1988), 'The reception of Paine', *Bulletin of the Society for the Study of Labour History*, vol. 52, no. 3 (November), pp. 14–20.

Ryerson, R. A. (1974), 'Political mobilization and the American revolution: the resistance movement in Philadelphia, 1765 to 1776', *William and Mary Quarterly*, vol. 31, pp. 565–88.

Schofield, Thomas (1986), 'Conservative political thought in Britain in response to the French revolution', *Historical Journal*, vol. 29, pp. 601–22.

Seaman, Allan (1957), 'Reform Politics at Sheffield, 1791–97', *Transactions of the Hunter Archaeological Society*, vol. 7, pp. 215–28.

Shalhope, Robert (1972), 'Toward a republican synthesis: the emergence of an understanding of republicanism in American historiography', *William and Mary Quarterly*, vol. 19, pp. 49–80.

Shalhope, Robert (1982), 'Republicanism and early American historiography', *William and Mary Quarterly*, vol. 39, pp. 334–56.

Sheldon, Frederick (1859), 'Thomas Paine's second Appearance in the United States' *Atlantic Monthly*, vol. 4, pp. 1–17.

Sheps, Arthur (1973), 'Ideological immigrants in revolutionary America', in Paul Fritz and David Williams (eds), *City and Society in the Eighteenth Century* (Toronto: Hakkert), pp. 231–47.

Sheps, Arthur (1975a), 'The American revolution and the transformation of English radicalism', *Historical Reflexions*, vol. 2, pp. 3–28.

Sheps, Arthur (1975b), 'The Edinburgh Reform Convention of 1793 and the American revolution', *Scottish Tradition*, vol. 5, pp. 23–37.

Shoemaker, Robert (1966), '"Democracy" and "republic" as understood in late eighteenth-century America', *American Speech*, vol. 41, pp. 83–95.

Smelser, Marshall (1951), 'The Jacobin phrenzy: federalism and the menace of liberty, equality, and fraternity', *Review of Politics*, vol. 13, pp. 457–82.

Smylie, James (1973), 'Clerical perspectives on deism: Paine's *The Age of Reason* in Virginia', *Eighteenth-Century Studies*, vol. 6, pp. 203–20.

Spater, George (1982), 'The author of "A Forester" Article', *Bulletin of the Thomas Paine Society*, vol. 7, pp. 53–6.

Spater, George (1988), 'The legacy of Thomas Paine', in Ian Dyck (ed.), *Citizen of the World. Essays on Thomas Paine* (New York: St Martin's Press), pp. 129–48.

Stafford, William (1982), 'Religion and the doctrine of nationalism in England at the time of the French revolution and Napoleonic wars', in S. Mews (ed.), *Religion and National Identity* (Oxford: Blackwell), pp. 381–95.

Stignant, P., 'Wesleyan Methodism and working-class radicalism in the north, 1792–1821', *Northern History*, vol. 6, pp. 98–116.

Thale, Mary (1989), 'London debating societies in the 1790s', *Historical Journal*, vol. 32, pp. 57–86.

Twomey, Richard (1984), 'Jacobins and Jeffersonians: Anglo-American radical ideology, 1790–1810 ', in Margaret Jacob and James Jacob (eds), *The Origins of Anglo-American Radicalism* (Allen & Unwin), pp. 284–99.

Walsh, J. D. (1975), 'Elie Halévy and the birth of Methodism', *Transactions of the Royal Historical Society*, vol. 25, pp. 1–20.

Walvin, James (1977), 'The English Jacobins, 1789–1799', *Historical Reflections*, vol. 4, pp. 91–110.

Wecter, Dixon (1942), 'Hero in reverse', *Virginia Quarterly Review*, vol. 18, pp. 243–59.

Weir, Robert (1976), 'Who shall rule at home: the American revolution as a crisis of legitimacy for the colonial elite', *Journal of Interdisciplinary History*, vol. 6, pp. 679–700.

Western, J. R. (1956), 'The Volunteer Movement as an anti-revolutionary force', *English Historical Review*, vol. 71, pp. 603–14.

Wiener, Joel (1988), 'Collaborators of a sort: Thomas Paine and Richard Carlile', in Ian Dyck (ed.), *Citizen of the World. Essays on Thomas Paine* (New York: St Martin's Press), pp. 104–28.

Weinzierl, Michael (1985), 'John Reeves and the controversy over the constitutional role of parliament in England during the French revolution', *Parliaments, Estates and Representation*, vol. 5, pp. 71–7.

Williams, Michael J. (1975), 'The 1790s: Paine and the Age of Reason', *Bulletin of the Thomas Paine Society*, vol. 5, pp. 13–27.

Williams, Michael J. (1976), 'The 1790s: the impact of infidelity', *Bulletin of the Thomas Paine Society*, vol. 6, pp. 21–30.

Winkler, Henry R. (1952), 'The pamphlet campaign against political reform in Great Britain, 1790–5', *Historian*, vol. 15, pp. 23–40.

Wood, Gordon (1979), 'The democratization of mind in the American revolution', in Robert Horwitz (ed.), *The Moral Foundations of the American Republic* (Charlottesville, Va: Virginia University Press), pp. 102–28.

Young, Claribel (1977), 'A reexamination of William Cobbett's opinions of Thomas Paine', *Journal of the Rutgers University Library*, vol. 39, pp. 7–28.

INDEX